Index to the 1800 Massachusetts Federal Census
for the Counties of
Norfolk & Suffolk

Rebecca M. Sullivan
Deborah Lee Larsson

Index to the 1800 Massachusetts Federal Census
for the Counties of
Norfolk & Suffolk

October 2014

ISBN: 978-1502766274

FOREWARD:

This is the fourth volume of several containing the heads of household that were enumerated in the 1800 United States Federal Census in Massachusetts. Our fourth volume is comprised of those towns in Norfolk & Suffolk County. Most of the census records for Suffolk County were destroyed. Hingham & Hull are the only remaining records. In order to make it easy for the researcher, towns are alphabetized, followed by an alphabetical index of Norfolk & Suffolf county.

We have made every attempt at correctly transcribing each town. However, many of these documents are torn, covered with ink, tape marks, rips and poor handwriting. Spelling errors have been left as they were originally written. Any names & enumerations illegible are denoted with an asterisk.

This book should be used as a guide and research aid. When possible the actual image should be obtained for proper verification and citation. Visit the National Archives website to find out more on how to obtain census images. www.archives.gov/research/census.

In order to get all of the information on one page to make for easy reading we had to reduce the size of the font.

Drop us a line, we'd love to hear what you're researching:
rsulli1219@aol.com

Becky & Deb
October 2014

Check out our other books:

INDEX

Norfolk County Stats

Microfilm Reel Number: M32-18

Town:	Page Numbers:	Enumerated By:
Bellingham	158-162	Unknown
Braintree	66-73	Ebenezer Thayer
Brookline	114-115	Unknown
Canton	129-134	Unknown
Cohasset	152-155	Unknown
Dedham	136-144	Unknown
Dorchester	51-63	Unknown
Dover	149-151	Unknwon
Foxborough	22-26	Unknown
Franklin	163-169	Unknown
Medfield	85-90	Unknown
Medway East Parish	91-94	Unknown
Medway West Parish	95-97	Unknown
Milton	44-50	Unknown
Needham	145-149	Unknown
Quincy	39-43	Stephen Badham
Randolph	123-128	Unknown
Roxbury	99-115	John Parker
Sharon	31-36	Unknown
Stoughton	117-122	Elijah Dunbar
Walpole	26-31	Unknown
Weymouth	74-82	Unknown
Wrentham	170-182	Unknown

INDEX

Suffolk County

Suffolk County Stats

Microfilm Reel Number: M32-16

Town:	Page Numbers:	Enumerated By:
Hingham	137-146	Samuel Norton
Hull	147	Unknown

Norfolk County

TOWN	PG#	LN#	LAST NAME	FIRST NAME	FREE WHITE MALES under 10	10 to 16	16 to 26	26 to 45	45 and over	FREE WHITE FEMALES under 10	10 to 16	16 to 26	26 to 45	45 and over	TOTAL ALL OTHER	TOTAL SLAVES	TOTALS	DISTRICT/ TOWNSHIP	NOTES
Bellingham	158	1	Fairbanks	Joseph	2	1	1		1	1		1	1	1			9		
Bellingham	158	2	Partridge	Job		1	1	1	1	1	2	2		1			10		
Bellingham	158	3	Partridge	Joseph	1	2	1		2	1		2		2			11		
Bellingham	158	4	Combs	John	1			1				1	1	1			5		
Bellingham	158	5	Wiswell	David	4			1		1			1				7		
Bellingham	158	6	Holbrook	Seth		2	1		1	1		4	1				10		
Bellingham	158	7	Hill	David	1	1		1					1	1			5		
Bellingham	158	8	Schamels	John	1	1	1	2	1	1	1	3	2	1	1		15		
Bellingham	158	9	Heath	Daniel	1			1					1	1			4		
Bellingham	158	10	Holbrook	Stephen			1	1					1				3		
Bellingham	158	11	Holbrook	Darius	1		1						1	1			4		
Bellingham	158	12	Holbrook	Abigail										1			1		
Bellingham	158	13	Holbrook	Nathan	1			1					1				3		
Bellingham	158	14	Holbrook	Aaron			1	1				1	1	1			5		
Bellingham	158	15	Holbrook	Amzi	1			1		3		1	1				7		
Bellingham	158	16	Thompson	Joseph		2	3	1	1			1	1				9		
Bellingham	158	17	Howard	Elisha				1					1				2		
Bellingham	159	1	Forrester	Ezra			1	1	1	1	1	1	1	2			9		
Bellingham	159	2	Potter	Olney	2			1		1			1				5		
Bellingham	159	3	Spears	Benjamin		1		1		4			1				7		
Bellingham	159	4	Alden	Elijah			1			1		1					3		
Bellingham	159	5	Dewing	Elijah	2			1		3	1		1				8		
Bellingham	159	6	Butterworth	Otis	1	1		1		1			1				5		
Bellingham	159	7	Bass	Benjamin		1		1	1				1	1			5		
Bellingham	159	8	Penniman	Daniel			1		1	1	1		1				5		
Bellingham	159	9	Penniman	Nathan			1			1			1				3		
Bellingham	159	10	Smith	Pelatiah	1		3		1	2		2					9		
Bellingham	159	11	Bates	John			1			2		1					4		
Bellingham	159	12	Combs	Jesse	2			1		1			1				5		
Bellingham	159	13	Force	Amariah	2			1		2			1	1			7		
Bellingham	159	14	Hill	Sarah	1	1				2			1				5		
Bellingham	159	15	Kilburne	Henry			1			1		1					3		
Bellingham	159	16	Hill	Jonathan				1					1				2		
Bellingham	159	17	Adams	Samuel	3	1	3	1			1	1	1				11		
Bellingham	159	18	Adams	Amos	3	1		1			1	1	1				8		
Bellingham	159	19	Adams	Obadiah				1					1				2		
Bellingham	159	20	Adams	Levi			2			1			1				4		
Bellingham	159	21	Darling	Simon	2			1					1				4		
Bellingham	159	22	Cobb	Samuel				1					1				2		
Bellingham	159	23	Adams	Caleb		1	1			2			1	1			6		
Bellingham	159	24	Burr	Elisha		1	2	1	1		1			1			7		
Bellingham	159	25	Holbrook	Jesse				1						2			3		
Bellingham	159	26	Holbrook	Molly	3	1	1						2	1			8		
Bellingham	159	27	Thayer	Alpheus	4	1		3				1	1				10		
Bellingham	159	28	Wight	Eliab	2		2	1		1	2		1	1			10		
Bellingham	159	29	Wight	Abram		1		1		1			2	1			6		
Bellingham	160	1	Holbrook	Henry		1	1	1		1		2					6		
Bellingham	160	2	Cook	Elias	2			1				1	1				5		
Bellingham	160	3	Cook	Abner	1			1					1				3		
Bellingham	160	4	Ellis	Amos		1		1				2		1			5		
Bellingham	160	5	Holbrook	Amasa	2		1	1		2			1				7		
Bellingham	160	6	Cook	David	1	2		1						1			5		
Bellingham	160	7	Cook	Daniel	2			1		1		2	1				7		
Bellingham	160	8	Cook	John			1		1	1			1				4		
Bellingham	160	9	Bates	Ezekiel		1		1	1	2		1	1				7		
Bellingham	160	10	Bates	Ezekiel Jun			2						1				3		
Bellingham	160	11	Twichell	Morris	1			1					1				3		
Bellingham	160	12	Thompson	Amos	2			1		1			1	1			6		
Bellingham	160	13	Arnold	Daniel		1				1		1					3		
Bellingham	160	14	Thayer	Luther	2			1					1				4		
Bellingham	160	15	Thayer	Silas	1	1	2		1			1		1			7		
Bellingham	160	16	Bullard	Daniel	1		1		1	1	1	1					6		
Bellingham	160	17	Kilburne	Simeon	1			1		3			1				6		
Bellingham	160	18	Holbrook	Peter	3	1		1		1	1		1				8		
Bellingham	160	19	Rockwood	Levi		2			1			1		1			5		
Bellingham	160	20	Paine	Gideon				1				1		1			3		
Bellingham	160	21	Paine	Thomas			1	1		1	2		1				6		
Bellingham	160	22	Darling	Samuel 2d	1	1	1	1		2	1		1				8		
Bellingham	160	23	Burr	Asa				1				1		1			3		
Bellingham	160	24	Morse	James		1							1				2		
Bellingham	160	25	Jones	David				1			1		2				4		
Bellingham	160	26	Jones	Daniel		1		1					1				3		
Bellingham	160	27	Bullard	Elisha	1	3			1	2		1	1				9		
Bellingham	160	28	Thayer	Elias		1		1	1					1			4		
Bellingham	160	29	Thayer	Elias Junr		1		1					1				3		
Bellingham	160	30	Slocum	Simon	1	1	1		1	2	1		1				8		
Bellingham	161	1	Chilson	Joseph	2			1			1	1	1				6		
Bellingham	161	2	Chilson	Joshua	4	1		1		1	1		2				10		
Bellingham	161	3	Thayer	Philo			1					1					2		

10

TOWN	PG#	LN#	HEADS OF HOUSEHOLD		FREE WHITE MALES					FREE WHITE FEMALES					TOTAL ALL OTHER	TOTAL SLAVES	TOTALS	DISTRICT/ TOWNSHIP	NOTES
			LAST NAME	FIRST NAME	under 10	10 to 16	16 to 26	26 to 45	45 and over	under 10	10 to 16	16 to 26	26 to 45	45 and over					
Bellingham	161	4	Chase	Allen	1			1		1			1				4		
Bellingham	161	5	Cook	Noah				1					1	1			3		
Bellingham	161	6	Albee	Alpheus			1			1		1					3		
Bellingham	161	7	Pratt	Joseph	3	1		1		1			1				7		
Bellingham	161	8	Alden	Noah			1		1		1	3		1			7		
Bellingham	161	9	Cook	Ziba	2		1	1		1			1				6		
Bellingham	161	10	Cook	Ezekiel					1				1	1			3		
Bellingham	161	11	Whitley	William					1			1	1				3		
Bellingham	161	12	Scott	Samuel		1	4		1			2	1	1			10		
Bellingham	161	13	Pickering	Simon	1			1		3			1				6		
Bellingham	161	14	Hall	Asa	1		1							1			3		
Bellingham	161	15	Scott	Saul	2		1	1		3	3	1	1				12		
Bellingham	161	16	Scott	Jonathan	1		1		1	1		1	1				6		
Bellingham	161	17	Kelly	Elisha	1		2		1				1	2			7		
Bellingham	161	18	Cook	Elisha			1						1				2		
Bellingham	161	19	King	John			1	1					1				3		
Bellingham	161	20	Pickering	Samuel			1		1			2	1	1			6		
Bellingham	161	21	Paine	Dan	1			1		1	1	1	1				6		
Bellingham	161	22	Vorce	Amariah	3			2					1				6		
Bellingham	161	23	Darling	Rachael	1								1				2		
Bellingham	161	24	Darling	Jacob			3							1			4		
Bellingham	161	25	Freeman	Nathan				1						1			2		
Bellingham	161	26	Bosworth	Ichabod	2			1		2				1			6		
Bellingham	161	27	Bates	Laban	1	1	3		1	1	1	3		1			12		
Bellingham	161	28	Sheepee	Hoppin				1					1				2		
Bellingham	161	29	Bates	Eli	1		2	1		2			1				7		
Bellingham	161	30	Aldrich	Laban	1	1	1		1		2	2	1				9		
Bellingham	162	1	Phillips	Joshua	1		1		1	2	2	1	1				9		
Bellingham	162	2	Chilson	John	3	1	1		2	1	1		1				10		
Bellingham	162	3	Perry	Lot		1			1	1				1			4		
Bellingham	162	4	Darling	Jerusha	1					1			1				3		
Bellingham	162	5	Darling	Cornelius					1			1		1			3		
Bellingham	162	6	Thayer	Ebenezer	1			1					1				3		
Bellingham	162	7	Darling	Joshua			1	1	1	1		1		1			6		
Bellingham	162	8	Darling	Samuel				1						1			2		
Bellingham	162	9	Cook	Benjamin	2	1		1		1		2		1			8		
Bellingham	162	10	Darling	Seth			2							1			3		
Bellingham	162	11	Cook	Zi*	1		1	1		3			1				7		
Bellingham	162	12	Scott	John		1	1		1			2	1	1			7		
Bellingham	162	13	Scott	Sylvanus		2		1		1			1				5		
Bellingham	162	14	Shearman	Nehemiah				1						1			2		
Bellingham	162	15	Shearman	Nathan			1					1					2		
Bellingham	162	16	Shearman	Seth			2	1	1	3	1			1			9		
Bellingham	162	17	Whitacer	William			1		1			1	1				4		
Bellingham	162	18	Draper	Jonathan		1	1		1	1			2	1			7		
Bellingham	162	19	Cushman	Martha	1	1	1				1	1		1			6		
Bellingham	162	20	Metcalf	Hepzibah								1		1			2		
Bellingham	162	21	Hill	Jesse				1					1				2		
Bellingham	162	22	Metcalf	Stephen	1	1	2	1				1	1				7		

TOWN	PG#	LN#	LAST NAME	FIRST NAME	M <10	M 10-16	M 16-26	M 26-45	M 45+	F <10	F 10-16	F 16-26	F 26-45	F 45+	TOTAL ALL OTHER	TOTAL SLAVES	TOTALS	DISTRICT/TOWNSHIP	NOTES
Braintree	66	1	Allen	Joseph	2	1	1		1	2	2	3		1			13		
Braintree	66	2	Allen	Jacob		2	1		1				1				5		
Braintree	66	3	Allen	Lemuel			1			2	1		1	1			6		
Braintree	66	4	Arnold	John V.	1		1	1		2			1				6		
Braintree	66	5	Arnold	Moses			1										1		
Braintree	66	6	Arnold	Ruth Wid.		1					1		2				4		
Braintree	66	7	Allen	Abigail Wid.	1					2			1	1			5		
Braintree	66	8	Blanchard	Ephraim				1		1		1					3		
Braintree	66	9	Bowditch	William	1			1		2			1				5		
Braintree	66	10	Bowditch	Jona	1	1	1	1		3							7		
Braintree	66	11	Bowditch	John			2		1			1		1			5		
Braintree	66	12	Burrill	Peter	1	1		1		3	1		1				8		
Braintree	68	1	Belcher	Uriah		1		1		1	2		1				6		
Braintree	68	2	Burnell	Ephraim			1				1						2		
Braintree	68	3	Booth	William				1		1			1				3		
Braintree	68	4	Blanchard	Samuel	2			1					1				4		
Braintree	68	5	Barrett	John	2	1			1	1		1	1	1			8		
Braintree	68	6	Bates	*	1			1					1	1			4		
Braintree	68	7	Clark	Hobart				1									1		
Braintree	68	8	Copeland	Seth		1		1					1				3		
Braintree	68	9	Copeland	Asa			1			2		1					4		
Braintree	68	10	Curtis	Saml			1	1		1		1		1			5		
Braintree	68	11	Capen	Nathl				1		1		1					3		
Braintree	68	12	Capen	Saml	1		2	1		2	1		1				8		
Braintree	68	13	Clark	Ebenz	2				1	2	2	1	1		1		10		
Braintree	68	14	Cheesman	Stephen	1			1		1	1	1	1	1			7		
Braintree	68	15	Colson	Bolter	1	1			1	3			1				7		
Braintree	68	16	Clap	Barnard	1		1			1				1			4		
Braintree	68	17	Cheesman	Saml	1			1					1	1			4		
Braintree	68	18	Cheesman	M Wid.		1				2		1	1				5		
Braintree	68	19	Capron	Thomas				1					1	1			3		
Braintree	68	20	Curtis	Job	1		1		1				1	1			5		
Braintree	68	21	Clark	John				1						1			2		
Braintree	68	22	Cheesman	Mary Wid						1	1	1					3		
Braintree	68	23	Clark	Hannah Wid						1	2	1	1				5		
Braintree	68	24	Dyer	Peter	3	1	2	1			2		1	2			12		
Braintree	68	25	Dyer	Peter 2d			1							2			3		
Braintree	68	26	Denton	Ebenezer	3			1		2	1	2	1				10		
Braintree	68	27	Denton	Jacob	2	2		1		1	1		1	2			10		
Braintree	68	28	Derby	Jonathan			1	1		3	1		1				7		
Braintree	68	29	French	Moses		1		1		2		1		1			6		
Braintree	68	30	French	Caleb		1	1				1		2				5		
Braintree	68	31	French	Silvanus			1			1			1				3		
Braintree	68	32	French	Asa			1			1		1					3		
Braintree	69	1	French	Elisha				1			1		1				3		
Braintree	69	2	French	Elisha Junr	3		2	1					1				7		
Braintree	69	3	French	Silence Wid		1	1			1			1				4		
Braintree	69	4	French	Ahaz	1	1		1		3	1		1				8		
Braintree	69	5	French	Josiah	1				1	1	1		1				5		
Braintree	69	6	French	James			1			1		1					3		
Braintree	69	7	Fanon	Caleb				1		3			1	1			6		
Braintree	69	8	Fanon	James	2	1	1		1		1			1			7		
Braintree	69	9	Fanon	Azariah				1						1			2		
Braintree	69	10	Fanon	Asaph		1	1	1		1	1	1	1				7		
Braintree	69	11	French	Saml 2d	1	1		1		1			1				5		
Braintree	69	12	French	Samuel	3		1	1		1			1				7		
Braintree	69	13	Fagg	Daniel	2	1		1		2	1		2				9		
Braintree	69	14	Hayward	Daniel		1			1	1				1			4		
Braintree	69	15	Hayward	John	3	2		1		1	1	1	1				10		
Braintree	69	16	Hayward	Nathl	2		1	1		1			1				6		
Braintree	69	17	Hayward	David P	1	1		1	1	1		1		1			7		
Braintree	69	18	Hayward	Debh Wid	2		1					1	1				5		
Braintree	69	19	Hollis	John		1		1					2	1			5		
Braintree	69	20	Hollis	Nathl	1		1		2	1			1	1			7		
Braintree	69	21	Hollis	Joseph	2			1		2	1		1				7		
Braintree	69	22	Hollis	John Junr	1			1		3		1	1	1			8		
Braintree	69	23	Hollis	James		2	1		2			2		3			10		
Braintree	69	24	Holbrook	John	1		2	1		2	1	1		1			9		
Braintree	69	25	Holbrook	Elisha	1		1			2		1					5		
Braintree	69	26	Holbrook	Joseph	1		1	1				1					4		
Braintree	69	27	Hobart	John	1		1		1	3	1	1	1	1			10		
Braintree	69	28	Hobart	Adam		1			1			1		1			4		
Braintree	69	29	Hobart	Adam Junr		1						1					2		
Braintree	69	30	Hobart	Abraham	1		1					1					3		
Braintree	69	31	Hollis	Thomas	1		1		1		1	2		1			7		
Braintree	69	32	Hollis	Thomas Jun			1			3	1		1				6		
Braintree	69	33	Hollis	Silas	3	2	2		1		1	1		1			11		
Braintree	69	34	Hayden	Eli	4			1	1	1		1	1				9		
Braintree	69	35	Hayden	Benj Junr	2		1	1		2			1	1			8		

TOWN	PG#	LN#	HEADS OF HOUSEHOLD		FREE WHITE MALES					FREE WHITE FEMALES					TOTAL ALL OTHER	TOTAL SLAVES	TOTALS	DISTRICT/ TOWNSHIP	NOTES
			LAST NAME	FIRST NAME	under 10	10 to 16	16 to 26	26 to 45	45 and over	under 10	10 to 16	16 to 26	26 to 45	45 and over					
Braintree	69	36	Hayden	Thomas				1		4	1	1					7		
Braintree	70	1	Hobart	William		1	2	1		1				1			6		
Braintree	70	2	Hayden	Robert		1	4	1	1			1	1	1			10		
Braintree	70	3	Hunt	Elihu	1			1					1				3		
Braintree	70	4	Holbrook	David	2		1	1	1	2		1	2				10		
Braintree	70	5	Holbrook	James	2	2	2		1	3	1		2	1			14		
Braintree	70	6	Holbrook	Nathl	1	1	2	1		1	2	1	1				10		
Braintree	70	7	Holbrook	Thomas	1		3		1	2	1	2		1			11		
Braintree	70	8	Holbrook	Abel	3			1		2			1	1			8		
Braintree	70	9	Holbrook	Eben	2	1	1	1		2	1		1				10		
Braintree	70	10	Holbrook	Nehel				1		1		1		1			4		
Braintree	70	11	Holbrook	Nehel Junr	2			1					1				4		
Braintree	70	12	Holbrook	Caleb		1		1					1				3		
Braintree	70	13	Holbrook	Joshua	1			1		1		1					4		
Braintree	70	14	Harmon	William				1						1			2		
Braintree	70	15	Harmon	Ebenz	1			1					1				3		
Braintree	70	16	Hayden	Nehe			2		1	1				1			5		
Braintree	70	17	Hayden	Clement	1			1		1				1			4		
Braintree	70	18	Hunt	Thomas			1					1		1			3		
Braintree	70	19	Hayden	Levi	1	2		1		2				1			7		
Braintree	70	20	Hayden	Oliver	2			1		1			1				5		
Braintree	70	21	Hayden	Amin*				1		4	1		1				7		
Braintree	70	22	Hayden	Job			1			2		1					4		
Braintree	70	23	Holbrook	Esther Wid.							1	1					2		
Braintree	70	24	Hayden	Nehel	2			1		1	2		1				7		
Braintree	70	25	Hollis	Daniel			1						1				2		
Braintree	70	26	Hayden	Nathl	1			1		2			1				5		
Braintree	70	27	Hayden	Stephen	1		1					1					3		
Braintree	70	28	Holbrook	Peter	1		1			1		1					4		
Braintree	70	29	Holbrook	John 2d	1		1					1					3		
Braintree	70	30	Hayden	Ebenz	2			1						1			4		
Braintree	70	31	Hudson	Adonian	1	1		1		1		2	1				7		
Braintree	70	32	Jordan	Peleg		1	1	1				1	1				5		
Braintree	70	33	Jones	Abraham	1	3		1		3		1	1				10		
Braintree	70	34	Loring	Daniel	1	2		3		2		1	1				10		
Braintree	70	35	Ludden	Silvanus				1			1		2				4		
Braintree	70	36	Lovell	Eben			1										1		
Braintree	70	37	Lufkin	Jacob	2			2		1			1				6		
Braintree	70	38	Lane	John	1		1	1				2					5		
Braintree	70	39	Lovell	Stephen	1			1		2			1				5		
Braintree	70	40	Lovell	Jacob			1			1		1					3		
Braintree	70	41	Lovell	Silas				1					2				3		
Braintree	71	1	Milton	Robert		1		1		1				1			4		
Braintree	71	2	Mansfield	Zenas	2		1					1					4		
Braintree	71	3	Newcomb	Ebenz			1	1						1			4		
Braintree	71	4	Newcomb	Saml		1	1	1		1	1			1			6		
Braintree	71	5	Newcomb	Bryant	4	2		1		2	1		1				11		
Braintree	71	6	Newcomb	Remember	3			1		2		1	1				8		
Braintree	71	7	Newcomb	Abraham	1			1				1					3		
Braintree	71	8	Newcomb	Jona	1		3			2		1					7		
Braintree	71	9	Newcomb	Micah			1	1						2			4		
Braintree	71	10	Nash	Benjm		2		1		4			1				8		
Braintree	71	11	Nash	Asa	1			1		2		1					5		
Braintree	71	12	Nash	Marcy Wid			1							1			2		
Braintree	71	13	Nash	Miriam Wid		1							1				2		
Braintree	71	14	Nightingale	Elisha	2		1					1					4		
Braintree	71	15	Penniman	Stephen				1			3		1				5		
Braintree	71	16	Penniman	Stephen Junior	3		1			1		1					6		
Braintree	71	17	Penniman	William		3	1	1				1		1			7		
Braintree	71	18	Penniman	Barzilla	3	1	1					1					6		
Braintree	71	19	Penniman	Ezra				1						1			2		
Braintree	71	20	Penniman	Samuel	3		1			2		1					7		
Braintree	71	21	Penniman	Asa	1		2					1					4		
Braintree	71	22	Penniman	Ebenz	1			1					1	1			4		
Braintree	71	23	Penniman	Ebenz Junr				1		1			1				3		
Braintree	71	24	Pratt	Jesse		1		1						2			4		
Braintree	71	25	Pratt	Saml	2			1					1				4		
Braintree	71	26	Peck	Elijah			1						1				2		
Braintree	71	27	Pool	Thomas	1			1		2			1				5		
Braintree	71	28	Reed	William		1		1			2	2		1			7		
Braintree	71	29	Reed	William Junr			1			1		1					3		
Braintree	71	30	Salisbury	Ambrose	1			1		2	2	1		1			8		
Braintree	71	31	Sampson	Joshua	2			1		1			2				6		
Braintree	71	32	Sampson	Joshua Junior	1		1			1		1					4		
Braintree	71	33	Spear	Deering	2			1					1	1			5		
Braintree	71	34	Shear	Stephen	1		1						1				3		
Braintree	72	1	Stetson	Amos		1	3					1					5		
Braintree	72	2	Soper	Edmund			1			2		2	1				6		
Braintree	72	3	Thayer	Ebenz		2	5	1	1			1		1			11		

TOWN	PG#	LN#	LAST NAME	FIRST NAME	under 10	10 to 16	16 to 26	26 to 45	45 and over	under 10	10 to 16	16 to 26	26 to 45	45 and over	TOTAL ALL OTHER	TOTAL SLAVES	TOTALS	DISTRICT/ TOWNSHIP	NOTES
							FREE WHITE MALES					FREE WHITE FEMALES							
Braintree	72	4	Thayer	Amos					1					1			2		
Braintree	72	5	Thayer	Philip	2	1		1		1		1		1			7		
Braintree	72	6	Thayer	Solomon 2d	1		2	1			1	1		1			7		
Braintree	72	7	Thayer	William			1	1		5	2	1	1	1			12		
Braintree	72	8	Thayer	Richard	1		1	1	1			3		1			8		
Braintree	72	9	Thayer	Elijah	2		1	1		2	2		1				9		
Braintree	72	10	Thayer	Stephen		1	1	1		2		1	1	1			8		
Braintree	72	11	Thayer	Uriah	3		1		1	1	1	2	1				10		
Braintree	72	12	Thayer	Josiah	1			1					1				3		
Braintree	72	13	Thayer	Saml W	2	1	1	1		2	1		1				9		
Braintree	72	14	Thayer	Jonathan					1				2				3		
Braintree	72	15	Thayer	Nehem					1	1	1		1				4		
Braintree	72	16	Thayer	Jonathan Junr	2	1	1	1	1	2	1		1				10		
Braintree	72	17	Thayer	Abraham	3			1		2	1	1	1	1			10		
Braintree	72	18	Thayer	Isaac				1		3			1				5		
Braintree	72	19	Thayer	Caleb	2			1			2						5		
Braintree	72	20	Thayer	Nathl		1		1		1	2	1	1	1			8		
Braintree	72	21	Thayer	Nathl 2d	3			1				1	1				6		
Braintree	72	22	Thayer	Calvin	2	1		1					1				5		
Braintree	72	23	Thayer	Timothy	1	1		1		1			1				5		
Braintree	72	24	Thayer	Elijah				1						1			2		
Braintree	72	25	Thayer	Elijah 2d		1		1		1				1			4		
Braintree	72	26	Thayer	Betty Wid.			1				2	2		1			6		
Braintree	72	27	Thayer	Job	1			1		1	1		1				5		
Braintree	72	28	Thayer	Gideon				1						1			2		
Braintree	72	29	Thayer	Gideon Junr			1					1					2		
Braintree	72	30	Thayer	Silvanus			1						1				2		
Braintree	72	31	Thayer	John				1		1			1				3		
Braintree	72	32	Thayer	Benjm	3	2		1			1		1				8		
Braintree	72	33	Thayer	Levi	2	1	1	1		1	1		1				8		
Braintree	72	34	Thayer	Zachl M.				2		1		1	1				5		
Braintree	72	35	Tower	James	2		2	1		3	2		2				12		
Braintree	72	36	Thayer	Solomon				1		2			1				4		
Braintree	72	37	Thomas	Nat. Robbins	1	1	7			1		2					12		
Braintree	72	38	Taylor	Benjm			1			3			1				5		
Braintree	72	39	Thayer	Minott									2				2		
Braintree	72	40	Tower	John	1			1		1	1			2			6		
Braintree	72	41	Thayer	Demetrius		1		1					1				3		
Braintree	72	42	Thayer	Zachariah				1						1			2		
Braintree	73	1	Tant	Seth															Enumeration left blank
Braintree	73	2	Vinton	Josiah	1		3	1		3	1		1				10		
Braintree	73	3	Vinton	John			1	1				1	1				4		
Braintree	73	4	Vinton	John Junr	2			1		3	1		1				8		
Braintree	73	5	Veazie	Benjm				1				2	1				4		
Braintree	73	6	Veazie	Lemuel		1	1	1		1			1				5		
Braintree	73	7	Veazie	Leml Junr	1			1		2		1					5		
Braintree	73	8	Veazie	Joseph	3			1		2			1				7		
Braintree	73	9	Vose	Mark	2		1	1		1	1			1			7		
Braintree	73	10	Veazie	Silas				1		2							3		
Braintree	73	11	Vinton	Jemima Wid	1		1				1			1			4		
Braintree	73	12	White	Alexander	1	1	2		1		2			1			8		
Braintree	73	13	White	Elihu	3			1		1	1		1	1			8		
Braintree	73	14	Wales	Nathl		1	1	1			1		1	1			6		
Braintree	73	15	Wales	Benjm	1	2		1		1		1	1	1			8		
Braintree	73	16	Wild	William Junr	1	1	1	1				1	1				6		
Braintree	73	17	Wild	Elijah	3			1	1	1			1				7		
Braintree	73	18	Wild	Silas		1			1			1		1			4		
Braintree	73	19	Wild	Jonathan			1	1		2	2		1				7		
Braintree	73	20	Wild	Paul	1	2		1		3			1				8		
Braintree	73	21	Wild	Silas Junior	2	2		1		4			1	1			11		
Braintree	73	22	Wild	Levi				1				1	1				3		
Braintree	73	23	Wild	Thomas	3			1		1		1					6		
Braintree	73	24	Wade	Lot	1			1		3		1					6		
Braintree	73	25	Wild	Person	1		1	1		2			1	1			7		
Braintree	73	26	White	Benjm				1					1				2		
Braintree	73	27	Weld	Ezra	1			1		2		1	1				6		
Braintree	73	28	Whitmarsh	Saml				1		1			1				3		
Braintree	73	29	Coffen	Robert											3		3		
Braintree	73	30	Coleman	William											2		2		
Braintree	73	31	Turner	Plato											1		1		

TOWN	PG#	LN#	HEADS OF HOUSEHOLD — LAST NAME	FIRST NAME	FREE WHITE MALES — under 10	10 to 16	16 to 26	26 to 45	45 and over	FREE WHITE FEMALES — under 10	10 to 16	16 to 26	26 to 45	45 and over	TOTAL ALL OTHER	TOTAL SLAVES	TOTALS	DISTRICT/ TOWNSHIP	NOTES
Brookline	114	1	Ayers	Ebenezer	2		1	2		1			1				7		
Brookline	114	2	Harvey	Jacob					1					1			2		
Brookline	114	3	Jackson	Abraham					1			1					2		
Brookline	114	4	Ayers	Jonathan	2			1				1					4		
Brookline	114	5	Brown	Jeremiah	1			1		3	1		1				7		
Brookline	114	6	Child	Solomon		1	1	1	1		1		1	1			7		
Brookline	114	7	Ellis	Amasa		1	1	1			1		1				5		
Brookline	114	8	Harris	John		2	2		1	1		2	2	1			11		
Brookline	114	9	Harris	Elizabeth								1		1			2		
Brookline	114	10	Child	Elijah		1			1				1				3		
Brookline	114	11	Herren	Jesse		1		1		1			1				4		
Brookline	114	12	Winchester	Nathaniel	2	2	2		1			2	1	1			11		
Brookline	114	13	Meriam	Abel	1		3						1				5		
Brookline	114	14	Cabett	George Esq			3		1			2	2	1			9		
Brookline	114	15	Murdock	Nathaniel	1		3	1		2			1	1			9		
Brookline	114	16	Boylston	Joshua					1				1	2			4		
Brookline	114	17	Dascom	Daniel			2	1		3			1				7		
Brookline	114	18	Clark	Samuel		1	2		1	2	1	1	2	1			11		
Brookline	114	19	Peirce	John Rev		1	1	1					1				4		
Brookline	114	20	Fryman	Hannah						1			1	1			3		
Brookline	114	21	Slack	Samuel	1	1	1	2		1			1	1			8		
Brookline	114	22	Jordon	Josiah	2	2		1		1	1	1	1				9		
Brookline	114	23	Davis	Ebenezer	3		3	1		1		1	1		1		11		
Brookline	114	24	Howe	John	1		1			1			1				4		
Brookline	114	25	Dana	Jonathan	1		3		1		1	1	1				8		
Brookline	114	26	Holden	James	2		1	1		1			1				6		
Brookline	114	27	King	William		1	1		1		2			1			6		
Brookline	114	28	Dana	Daniel					2				2				4		
Brookline	114	29	Toleman	Jonas			1	1		1			1				4		
Brookline	114	30	Corey	Elijah	2	1	2	1					2				8		
Brookline	114	31	Corey	Timothy			3		1		2	2		1			9		
Brookline	114	32	Withington	Enos	1			1					1				3		
Brookline	114	33	Gilman	Lucy				1				2	1		1		5		
Brookline	114	34	Robinson	John		2		1		2		1	1				7		
Brookline	114	35	Sharp	Stephen		1	4	1	1			1	1	1	1		11		
Brookline	114	36	Sharp	Sarah									1	1			2		
Brookline	114	37	Griggs	Samuel	3	2	1	1		2			1	1			11		
Brookline	114	38	Leverett	William	1		1	1				1					4		
Brookline	115	1	Hart	Jacob			3						1				4		
Brookline	115	2	Griggs	Joshua	1	1	1	2		3			2	1			11		
Brookline	115	3	Learnard	Daniel	2		2		1	1	3	1					11		
Brookline	115	4	Brooks	Samuel	4		1	1				1					7		
Brookline	115	5	Aspenwall	John	3	1	4	2				1	1				12		
Brookline	115	6	Aspenwall	Lucy								1	1				2		
Brookline	115	7	Whitney	Elijah		1	3	2		1		1			1		9		
Brookline	115	8	Aspenwall	William Doc		3	4		1	1	1	1	2		4		17		

TOWN	PG#	LN#	LAST NAME	FIRST NAME	FREE WHITE MALES under 10	10 to 16	16 to 26	26 to 45	45 and over	FREE WHITE FEMALES under 10	10 to 16	16 to 26	26 to 45	45 and over	TOTAL ALL OTHER	TOTAL SLAVES	TOTALS	DISTRICT/ TOWNSHIP	NOTES
Canton	129	1	Allen	Thomas	2			1				1	1				5		
Canton	129	2	Allen	Beth*				1		1		1					3		
Canton	129	3	Bailey	Henry				1				2	1				4		
Canton	129	4	Bailey	Israel		1	1	1					2				5		
Canton	129	5	Bailey	Samuel			1					1					2		
Canton	129	6	Bailey	Dudley		1	1	1					1				4		
Canton	129	7	Bailey	Eunice									1				1		
Canton	129	8	Belcher	Joseph	2	1		1		2	1	1	1				9		
Canton	129	9	Belcher	Elisha		1				2		1					4		
Canton	129	10	Bent	William		1	1	1		1	1		1				6		
Canton	129	11	Bemis	Joseph		1	1						1				3		
Canton	129	12	Billing	Roger				1				1	1				3		
Canton	129	13	Billing	Jonathan	1		1	1		3	1		1				8		
Canton	129	14	Billing	Isaac			1	1					1				4		
Canton	129	15	Billing	Samuel			1				1		1				3		
Canton	129	16	Billing	Stephen	1		2	1		1		1	1	1			8		
Canton	129	17	Billing	John	1	1		1		1			1				5		
Canton	129	18	Billing	Jacob			1	1					1				3		
Canton	129	19	Billing	Peter				1		4	2	1					8		
Canton	129	20	Billing	Nathl	1			1					1				3		
Canton	129	21	Billing	Mary Wid.		1							1	1			3		
Canton	129	22	Billing	Rebecca Wid.	1	1	2			1		1	1				7		
Canton	130	1	Billing	Beulah Wid.										2			2		
Canton	130	2	Blackman	Adam				1			2	1	1		1		6		
Canton	130	3	Blackman	Saml		1		1		2	1		1				6		
Canton	130	4	Blackman	John	1			1		2			1				5		
Canton	130	5	Blackman	Ruth Wid.		1					1		1				3		
Canton	130	6	Blake	Stephen		1		1			1		1				4		
Canton	130	7	Briggs	Betty									3				3		
Canton	130	8	Bussey	Benjamin				1					1				2		
Canton	130	9	Bussey	Basheba Wid.								1	1				2		
Canton	130	10	Burr	Seymour											1		1		
Canton	130	11	Capen	Andrew	2	1		1		1			1	1			7		
Canton	130	12	Capen	Christopher		1		1					1	1			4		
Canton	130	13	Capen	Samuel			2	1					2				5		
Canton	130	14	Capen	John		1	2	1		1		2					7		
Canton	130	15	Canterbury	Samuel	2			1					1				4		
Canton	130	16	Carrel	Samuel			1			1			1				3		
Canton	130	17	Chandler	Joseph		1	1	1		2	1		1				7		
Canton	130	18	Crane	Abner		1					1		1				3		
Canton	130	19	Crane	Silas				1		2		1					4		
Canton	130	20	Crane	Year*			1					1					2		
Canton	130	21	Crane	Friend	1		1					1					3		
Canton	130	22	Crane	Nathan	1	1	2		1	2	2	1	3				13		
Canton	130	23	Crane	Henry	1					2		1	1				5		
Canton	130	24	Crane	William			7	1	1	2	1	2		1			15		
Canton	130	25	Crane	Peter		1		1		2	1	1	1				7		
Canton	130	26	Crane	Calvin		1	1	1			1		1				5		
Canton	130	27	Crane	Elijah	1	2	3	1		2		1	1				11		
Canton	130	28	Crane	Amariah				1				2	1	1			5		
Canton	130	29	Crosman	George	1		1	1		1	1	1	1				7		
Canton	130	30	Davenport	Jesse	2	1		1		1	2		1				8		
Canton	130	31	Davenport	Samuel		2	1	1		1	1	2	1				9		
Canton	130	32	Dickerman	Enoch	1	1	1	1				2	1				7		
Canton	130	33	Dickerman	Ezra				1		1	2	1	1				6		
Canton	130	34	Downs	Jesse	2	1		1		3	1		1				9		
Canton	130	35	Downs	Oliver	1	1		1		3			1				7		
Canton	130	36	Drake	John	3	1		1		2			1				8		
Canton	130	37	Dunbar	Elijah		1	1			2	1		1				7		
Canton	130	38	Dunlap	John		1		1					1				3		
Canton	131	1	El*nes	Benjamin		1						1					2		
Canton	131	2	Endicott	Abigail Wid.			2						1	1			4		
Canton	131	3	Estey	John	2			1		1	1		1				6		
Canton	131	4	Everenden	Mary Wid.	1							2	1				4		
Canton	131	5	Everenden	Benja	2	1		1		3			1				8		
Canton	131	6	Farrington	Jonathan				1					1				2		
Canton	131	7	Farrington	Abel	1			1					1				3		
Canton	131	8	Fenns	Elijah		1	2	1		1	1		1	1			8		
Canton	131	9	Fenns	Charles				1			1		1				3		
Canton	131	10	Fenns	Sarah Wid.									1				1		
Canton	131	11	Fisher	Ezekiel		1		1		2		1	1	1			7		
Canton	131	12	Fisher	Lemuel		1	2	1		3	1	1	1				10		
Canton	131	13	Fisher	Experience Wid.								1		1			2		
Canton	131	14	Fisher	Jabin	3			2		2			1				8		
Canton	131	15	Fisher	Elijah	2		1	1		2		2					8		
Canton	131	16	Fisher	Abel	1	1		1		2	1		1				7		
Canton	131	17	Fisher	Samuel		1	1	1				1	1				5		
Canton	131	18	French	Thomas	1	1	1		1		1		1				6		
Canton	131	19	French	Samuel	1		2	1		3			1				8		

TOWN	PG#	LN#	LAST NAME	FIRST NAME	FREE WHITE MALES under 10	10 to 16	16 to 26	26 to 45	45 and over	FREE WHITE FEMALES under 10	10 to 16	16 to 26	26 to 45	45 and over	TOTAL ALL OTHER	TOTAL SLAVES	TOTALS	DISTRICT/ TOWNSHIP	NOTES
Canton	131	20	French	Jason	3			1				1					5		
Canton	131	21	French	Nathl			1			1		1					3		
Canton	131	22	Fuller	Lemuel			1					1					2		
Canton	131	23	Gill	Benjamin			2	1		1		1	1				6		
Canton	131	24	Gill	Elijah	1	2	1	1		2		2	1				10		
Canton	131	25	Gill	Benjamin Jr	2	1	1	1		1			1				7		
Canton	131	26	Gill	Nathan			1			1			1				3		
Canton	131	27	Gill	John	1		1	1				1					4		
Canton	131	28	Gooch	Samuel	3		1			2	1		1				8		
Canton	131	29	de la Goix	Cloude				1					1		1		3		
Canton	131	30	Hartwell	John				1					1				2		
Canton	131	31	Hartwell	David	2			1	1		1	1	1				7		
Canton	131	32	Hawse	Sarah Wid.	4	1				1	1	1	1				9		
Canton	131	33	Hawse	Jonathan	1	3		1		2			1				8		
Canton	131	34	Hayward	Rachel			1						1				2		
Canton	131	35	Henry	William		1		1			1	1	1				5		
Canton	131	36	Henry	Joseph				1		2	1		1				5		
Canton	132	1	Hill	John				1				1	1				3		
Canton	132	2	Hill	Joses	1			1		2		1	1	1			7		
Canton	132	3	Hill	Washington			1			1		1	1				4		
Canton	132	4	Hill	Nathaniel	1			1		2			1				5		
Canton	132	5	Holmes	Joseph	1	1		1		1			1				5		
Canton	132	6	Holmes	Unity Wid.		1	1					1		1			4		
Canton	132	7	Howard	Zechariah Rev.	1		1	1					1				4		
Canton	132	8	Hunt	Ephraim			1			2	1		1				5		
Canton	132	9	Hunt	John	2		1			2			1				6		
Canton	132	10	Holden	Joel											2		2		
Canton	132	11	Johnson	Ezekiel	1	2		1		1	1		1				7		
Canton	132	12	Jones	Ephraim				1					1				2		
Canton	132	13	Jordan	George	1	1		1		3			1				7		
Canton	132	14	Jones	Hannah Wid.									1	1			2		
Canton	132	15	Jordan	Nathl	1			1		1			1				4		
Canton	132	16	Jordan	Mary Wid.						1			1	1			3		
Canton	132	17	Kenney	Nathl				1					1				2		
Canton	132	18	Kenney	John				1					1	1			3		
Canton	132	19	Kenney	Nathan			1					1					2		
Canton	132	20	Kenney	David				1					1				2		
Canton	132	21	McKendry	Archibald	2			1		2	1		1				7		
Canton	132	22	McKendry	Ruth Wid.								1	1				2		
Canton	132	23	Kingsbury	Fisher		2		1					1				4		
Canton	132	24	Kingsbury	Joseph	2			1					1				4		
Canton	132	25	Kinsley	Adam	1	1	4	2		1	1	1	2				13		
Canton	132	26	Kinsley	Silas	2			1		1			1	1			6		
Canton	132	27	Leonard	Enoch		1	2		1			1		2			7		
Canton	132	28	Leonard	Uriah	3			1		1		2	1	1			9		
Canton	132	29	Lewis	James H.				1		1			1	2			5		
Canton	132	30	Lewis	Saban		1		1					1	1			4		
Canton	132	31	Lewis	Benjamin	2			1		1			1				5		
Canton	132	32	Lyon	Ruth Wid.									1				1		
Canton	132	33	Madden	John			1	1		2			1	1			6		
Canton	132	34	May	Luther	2	1		2		1		2					8		
Canton	132	35	May	Rebecca Wid.									1				1		
Canton	133	1	Maxwell	Thompson	1			1		2	1		1				6		
Canton	133	2	Means	John	1			1		2	1	1					6		
Canton	133	3	Morse	Saml	1	1		1		1		1	1				6		
Canton	133	4	Morse	Samuel Junr	1			1					1				3		
Canton	133	5	Morse	John			1	1					1				3		
Canton	133	6	Morse	Asa	3	1		1		1			1				7		
Canton	133	7	Morse	Henry			1	1		2	3		1				8		
Canton	133	8	Montgomery	John	1			1		2			1				6		
Canton	133	9	Patrick	Deborah Wid.									1				1		
Canton	133	10	Pierce	Jesse	1			1		1			1				4		
Canton	133	11	Pitcher	Eliakim		1		1					1				3		
Canton	133	12	Pitcher	Abijah		1				1		1					3		
Canton	133	13	Pettingill	Elkhanah				1				1	1				3		
Canton	133	14	Pitter	Nathl	2			1					1				4		
Canton	133	15	Puffer	John		1		1	2				1				5		
Canton	133	16	Reed	James	3	1		1					1				6		
Canton	133	17	Reed	William	1			1				1					3		
Canton	133	18	Shaller	Ebenezer				1					1				2		
Canton	133	19	Shaller	Michael	2		1	2		2			2				9		
Canton	133	20	Shaller	Isaac	1			1		1		1					4		
Canton	133	21	Shales	Elizabeth Wid.								1	1				2		
Canton	133	22	Shepard	William E		1	1		1			1		1			5		
Canton	133	23	Shepard	Jesse	1			1		3			1				6		
Canton	133	24	Shepard	Basheba Wid.		1	1					1		1			4		
Canton	133	25	Shepard	Thomas	2			1		1		1					5		
Canton	133	26	Shepard	Oliver	1			1		1			1				4		
Canton	133	27	Shepard	Nathaniel	2			1					1				5		

TOWN	PG#	LN#	LAST NAME	FIRST NAME	FREE WHITE MALES under 10	10 to 16	16 to 26	26 to 45	45 and over	FREE WHITE FEMALES under 10	10 to 16	16 to 26	26 to 45	45 and over	TOTAL ALL OTHER	TOTAL SLAVES	TOTALS	DISTRICT/TOWNSHIP	NOTES
Canton	133	28	Silvester	Benjamin	1				1		1		1	1			5		
Canton	133	29	Smith	Ephraim					1					1			2		
Canton	133	30	Smith	James	1	2			1	2	1		1				8		
Canton	133	31	Smith	Lemuel	3			1		1		1					6		
Canton	133	32	Smith	Ephraim Jr		1			1	2	1		1	1			7		
Canton	133	33	Spear	Eliza		1								1			2		
Canton	133	34	Spear	Olive Wid.	2			1					1	1			5		
Canton	133	35	Stetson	Isaac				1		1			1				3		
Canton	133	36	Stickney	Susanna Wid.										2			2		
Canton	133	37	Stoddard	Mercy Wid.	1			1		2			1	1			6		
Canton	133	38	Stone	George	2			1		1			1				5		
Canton	133	39	Strowbridge	Samuel				1					1				2		
Canton	133	40	Strowbridge	Seth			1	1					1				3		
Canton	134	1	Slade	Phillis											4		4		
Canton	134	2	Tant	John	1		1		1	1				1			5		
Canton	134	3	Tant	John Jr	1			1		2		1					5		
Canton	134	4	Tant	Samuel		1				1		1					3		
Canton	134	5	Tant	Levi	1				1	1				1			4		
Canton	134	6	Talbot	David					1	1		1		1			4		
Canton	134	7	Thompson	Sarah Wid.									1	1			2		
Canton	134	8	Thompson	William			1			3		1					5		
Canton	134	9	Thayer	Asa	1		2					1					4		
Canton	134	10	Tilden	Nathl				1						1			2		
Canton	134	11	Tilden	Nathl Junr			3	1		3	1		1				9		
Canton	134	12	Tilden	Josiah	1	1		1		3			1				7		
Canton	134	13	Tilden	Ezra	1		2		2	2	1			2			10		
Canton	134	14	Topliff	Abigail Wid.							1	1	1				3		
Canton	134	15	Tucker	James			1		1	1	2			2			7		
Canton	134	16	Tucker	Benja		1	1		1				1	1			5		
Canton	134	17	Tucker	John	1	2			1	2	1	1	1				9		
Canton	134	18	Tucker	Daniel	2		2		1				1				6		
Canton	134	19	Tucker	Samuel	2	2	1		1	1	1		1				9		
Canton	134	20	Tucker	Simeon	2			1	2	2			1	1			9		
Canton	134	21	Tucker	Lemuel	1		1						1				3		
Canton	134	22	Upham	Abijah					1					1			2		
Canton	134	23	Upham	Amos	1	2		1		2			1	1			8		
Canton	134	24	Upham	Jonathan			1			1			1				3		
Canton	134	25	Upham	Nathan			1			1		2					4		
Canton	134	26	Wheeler	William				1						1			2		
Canton	134	27	Wheeler	Samuel				1					1				2		
Canton	134	28	Wheeler	Hannah										1			1		
Canton	134	29	Wadsworth	David	1	1		1		3			1				7		
Canton	134	30	Wadsworth	Elisha	3			1		1			1				6		
Canton	134	31	Wentworth	Judith Wid.										1			1		
Canton	134	32	Wentworth	Jerusha Wid.	1			1				1		1			4		
Canton	134	33	Wentworth	Joseph	3			1		2			1				7		
Canton	134	34	Wentworth	Seth	1		1	1			1	1		1			6		
Canton	134	35	Wentworth	Oliver	1		1	1		1	1		1				6		
Canton	134	36	Wentworth	Nathl	2			1		1			1				5		
Canton	134	37	Wentworth	Obed	1			1		1			1				4		
Canton	134	38	Wentworth	John Jr	1	1	3	1		3	1			1			11		
Canton	134	39	Wentworth	Susanna Wid.						2			1	1			4		
Canton	134	40	Wentworth	Ebenezer	2	1		1		2		1	1				8		
Canton	134	41	Wentworth	Benjamin				1									1		
Canton	134	42	Wentworth	Rachel						2			1				3		
Canton	134	43	Wentworth	Paul				1					1	2			4		
Canton	134	44	Wentworth	Simeon		1				1		1					3		
Canton	134	45	Wild	Richard	1			1		2	1		1				6		
Canton	134	46	Withington	Henry B.			1	1			1			1			4		
Canton	134	47	Withington	Mather	1	1	1		1	1	1	1	1				8		
Canton	134	48	Withington	John	2	1		1		1		1	1				7		
Canton	134	49	Withington	Edward				1						1			2		
Canton	134	50	Withington	Samuel	1			1			1			1			4		
Canton	134	51	Whydon	Comfort	1			1	1	1			1	1			6		
Canton	134	52	Whydon	Nathaniel	1			1									2		
Canton	134	53	Burrell	David			1		1					1			3		
Canton	134	54	Burrell	Samuel	1			1		1		1					4		

| | | | HEADS OF HOUSEHOLD | | FREE WHITE MALES | | | | | FREE WHITE FEMALES | | | | | | | | | |
TOWN	PG#	LN#	LAST NAME	FIRST NAME	under 10	10 to 16	16 to 26	26 to 45	45 and over	under 10	10 to 16	16 to 26	26 to 45	45 and over	TOTAL ALL OTHER	TOTAL SLAVES	TOTALS	DISTRICT/ TOWNSHIP	NOTES
Cohasset	152	1	Lathrop Esq	Thomas					1					1			2		
Cohasset	152	2	Doane	Elisha Esq	1	3	1	2		2		1	3				13		
Cohasset	152	3	Bates	Samuel			2	1	1	1	1	2		1			9		
Cohasset	152	4	Bordman	Micajah	2			1			1		2				6		
Cohasset	152	5	Bates	Joseph					1			2		1			4		
Cohasset	152	6	Nichols	John	1	1		1		2		1					7		
Cohasset	152	7	Newrich	Hezekiah					1					1			2		
Cohasset	152	8	Lathrop	Anselam	1			1		1	1		1				5		
Cohasset	152	9	Humphrey	Jonathan	3	2		1		2			1				9		
Cohasset	152	10	Lambert	Henry		1			1			1		1			4		
Cohasset	152	11	Beers	Mary										1			1		
Cohasset	152	12	Beal	Jacob				1						2			3		
Cohasset	152	13	Beal	John	3		2	1		2			1				9		
Cohasset	152	14	Cushing	Timothy					1			2		2			5		
Cohasset	152	15	Oliver	Timothy		1			1	1	1	1		1			6		
Cohasset	152	16	Nichols	Maria									1	1			2		
Cohasset	152	17	Bevins	Peter	1		1					1					3		
Cohasset	152	18	James	Galen	2	3			1			2	1				9		
Cohasset	152	19	Souther	Joseph Jr		1		1	1	1	1			1			6		
Cohasset	152	20	Power	Jesse	1	1		1		3	1	1		1			9		
Cohasset	152	21	Burbanks	John	1		1		1	1		2		1			7		
Cohasset	152	22	Burbanks	Timothy	2	1		1		1			1	1			7		
Cohasset	152	23	Souther	Nathan				1				1					2		
Cohasset	152	24	Mcorble	Priscilla										1			1		
Cohasset	152	25	Lincoln	Elisha	2	1		1		1			1				6		
Cohasset	152	26	Souther	Sarah	3					1			1				5		
Cohasset	152	27	Pritchit	Theodore				1			1			1			3		
Cohasset	152	28	Stephenson	Reuben	2	1	1	1		2			1				8		
Cohasset	152	29	Lincoln	Christopher	1			1		2		1	1	1			7		
Cohasset	152	30	Beorker	Maria										2			2		
Cohasset	152	31	Tower	Bethiah	2				1			1		1			5		
Cohasset	152	32	Brown	Samuel			1					2					3		
Cohasset	152	33	Stowel	Adam	2		1	2		3			1				9		
Cohasset	152	34	Oaks	Josiah Widow			1	1				1			1		4		
Cohasset	152	35	James	Christopher	2	1		1					1				6		
Cohasset	152	36	Stodder	James	1	1		1		2			1				6		
Cohasset	152	37	Warwick	Saban	2			1		2			1				6		
Cohasset	152	38	Trent	John		1		1		3			1				6		
Cohasset	152	39	Pratt	Thomas	1		2	2	1			1	2	1			10		
Cohasset	152	40	Cushing	Job	1			2		1		1	1	1			7		
Cohasset	152	41	Nichols	Caleb	2		1		1	1		1	1				7		
Cohasset	152	42	Bates	Theodore		2			1	2	1		2				8		
Cohasset	152	43	Lincoln	Jerom	2	2	1		1	2			1				9		
Cohasset	152	44	Stephenson	Luther Jun		1		1					1	1			4		
Cohasset	152	45	Orcutt	Ignatious		1		1	1				1				4		
Cohasset	152	46	Sutton	John				1		5	1	1	1				9		
Cohasset	152	47	Lincoln	Abraham	2	2	2		1			1		1			9		
Cohasset	152	48	Prescott	Caleb	1				1	1		1		1			5		
Cohasset	153	1	Willcutt	Jesse					1			1		1			3		
Cohasset	153	2	Marble	Ephraim	2			1		1				1			5		
Cohasset	153	3	Bates	Ambrose	1			1		3	1	2	1				9		
Cohasset	153	4	Wheelwright	Gershom	1	1	2		1	3	1	1	1				11		
Cohasset	153	5	Wheelwright	John					1					1			2		
Cohasset	153	6	Joze	Amos					1					1			2		
Cohasset	153	7	Joze	Olive		1	1					2	1				5		
Cohasset	153	8	Willcutt	John	1			1	1	1			1				5		
Cohasset	153	9	Pratt	Aaron Junr	1		1	1		3	1		1				8		
Cohasset	153	10	Bates	Joshua	1	1	1		1		1			1			6		
Cohasset	153	11	Souther	Joseph		1		1						1			3		
Cohasset	153	12	Pratt	Joseph	2			1	1	1			2	3			11		
Cohasset	153	13	Pratt	John		1	1							1			3		
Cohasset	153	14	Whitcomb	Job	1	1	1		1	1			1	1			7		
Cohasset	153	15	Stodder	Lydia										2			2		
Cohasset	153	16	Lichfield	Job	1	1		1		3			1				7		
Cohasset	153	17	Lichfield	Noah	1	1		1		2	1		1				7		
Cohasset	153	18	Whitcomb	Lott	1	1			1			1	2	1			7		
Cohasset	153	19	Whitcomb	Joseph	1		1	1	1			1	2	1			8		
Cohasset	153	20	Whitcomb	Israel		1			1			1	1	1			5		
Cohasset	153	21	Wheelwright	Micah			1						1				2		
Cohasset	153	22	Lincoln	Obediah					1					1			2		
Cohasset	153	23	Herd	George	2			1	1				1				5		
Cohasset	153	24	Bartles	James	1	1	1	1		1	1		1	1			8		
Cohasset	153	25	Lincoln	Mordiecia					1				2	3			6		
Cohasset	153	26	Lincoln	Sarah			1					1		1			3		
Cohasset	153	27	Lincoln	Uriah		1	1				1	2		1			7		
Cohasset	153	28	Lincoln	James	1			1		2	1		1				6		
Cohasset	153	29	Osier	Martha								1		1			2		
Cohasset	153	30	Stephenson	Martin			1			3			1				5		
Cohasset	153	31	Pratt	Aaron		1	1	3	1		1	2					9		

TOWN	PG#	LN#	LAST NAME	FIRST NAME	FREE WHITE MALES					FREE WHITE FEMALES					TOTAL ALL OTHER	TOTAL SLAVES	TOTALS	DISTRICT/ TOWNSHIP	NOTES
					under 10	10 to 16	16 to 26	26 to 45	45 and over	under 10	10 to 16	16 to 26	26 to 45	45 and over					
Cohasset	153	32	Pratt	Samuel		1		1		5			1				8		
Cohasset	153	33	Briggs	Ichabod	1				1	1	1			1			5		
Cohasset	153	34	Oakes	Jonah			1			3	1	2	1				8		
Cohasset	153	35	Lincoln	Fanny	1					1			1				3		
Cohasset	153	36	Bates	Daniel	2		1						1				4		
Cohasset	153	37	Hayden	Ezra		1			1		1			1			4		
Cohasset	153	38	Jones	Catherine						1			2	3			6		
Cohasset	153	39	Hudson	Ibroke			1			3			1				5		
Cohasset	153	40	Beal	Thomas		1			1		1			1			4		
Cohasset	153	41	Beal	David		1	1	1		3		2					8		
Cohasset	153	42	Beal	Hezekiah			1			5			1				7		
Cohasset	153	43	Lincoln	Hezekiah		1			1	2			1				5		
Cohasset	153	44	Lincoln	Zenas	2	1		1		2	1		1				8		
Cohasset	153	45	Willcutt	Thomas	2	1		1		2	1	2	1				10		
Cohasset	153	46	Pratt	Ephraim	3			1		1			1				6		
Cohasset	153	47	Nichols	Enoch	2			1		1		1		1			6		
Cohasset	153	48	Willcutt	John		1		1		1	1	1		1			6		
Cohasset	153	49	Willcutt	Hannah									1				1		
Cohasset	153	50	So*	Elille	1	2		1				1					6		
Cohasset	154	1	Tower	Mary								1		1			2		
Cohasset	154	2	Stodder	Matthew		1		1				3	1				6		
Cohasset	154	3	Beal	Joseph				1		1			1				3		
Cohasset	154	4	Bates	Anna		1	1		1	2	1	1		1			8		
Cohasset	154	5	Bates	Jonathan	2	1	1	1		1			1				7		
Cohasset	154	6	Howard	Gideon			1	1				1					3		
Cohasset	154	7	Tower	Levi	2	1	1	1		1	1	2	1				10		
Cohasset	154	8	Hall	James	3	3		1		1		1	1				10		
Cohasset	154	9	Turner	Job	1	1		1		1	2	1			1		8		
Cohasset	154	10	Nichols	Peter		1		1		2	2	1		1			8		
Cohasset	154	11	Stephenson	Luther	1			1				1		1			4		
Cohasset	154	12	Hudson	Ebenezer			1			1		1					3		
Cohasset	154	13	Nichols	Thomas	2			1		1			1				5		
Cohasset	154	14	Beal	Lewis Alias	1			1				1					3		
Cohasset	154	15	Bates	Bella	2			1		1			1				5		
Cohasset	154	16	Bourne	Thomas				1		3	1	1		1			8		
Cohasset	154	17	Nichols	Percie Jones	2			1		1			1				5		
Cohasset	154	18	Lewis	Susannah		1				2	1	1					5		
Cohasset	154	19	Briggs	Seth			1	1				1	1				4		
Cohasset	154	20	Briggs	Joseph	2			1		1	2		1				7		
Cohasset	154	21	Willcutt	Joel	2		2	1		2	1		1				9		
Cohasset	154	22	Mann	George				1		1	1		1	1			5		
Cohasset	154	23	Marble	Noah				1						1			2		
Cohasset	154	24	Hunphrey	Sally	1							1		1			3		
Cohasset	154	25	Bates	Robert	1			1		2		1					5		
Cohasset	154	26	Bent	Abel				1		1		1		1			4		
Cohasset	154	27	Nichols	Ambrose	1		1			1	1		1				5		
Cohasset	154	28	Lothrop	John	3	1		1		1			1				7		
Cohasset	154	29	Nichols	Doc Israel		1		1				2		1			5		
Cohasset	154	30	Nichols	Daniel	1			1			1	1	1				5		
Cohasset	154	31	Tower	John				1					1				2		
Cohasset	154	32	Beal	Joshua		1		1					1				3		
Cohasset	154	33	Joze	Asa	1	1				1		1					4		
Cohasset	154	34	Cushing	Benjamin			1	1		1			1				4		
Cohasset	154	35	Nichols	David	3	1		1		1		1	1				8		
Cohasset	154	36	Nichols	Lott	1		1		1	2	2	1					9		
Cohasset	154	37	Nichols	Aaron	3	1		1		1			1	1			8		
Cohasset	154	38	Nichols	Nathaniel		1			1	1	1	1	1				6		
Cohasset	154	39	Lincoln	Abraham	1			1		1		1	1				5		
Cohasset	154	40	Lincoln	Ephraim	1	1		1		2	1		1	1			8		
Cohasset	154	41	Nichols	Nathaniel Junr				1				2					4		
Cohasset	154	42	Hudson	Ford	3			1		1		1					6		
Cohasset	154	43	Joze	Susannah	1							1		1			3		
Cohasset	154	44	Beal	Abel	1			1				1		1			4		
Cohasset	154	45	Beal	Seth	3					1			1				6		
Cohasset	154	46	Beal	Daniel			2	1					1				4		
Cohasset	154	47	Beal	Andrew	1		1					1					3		
Cohasset	154	48	Hudson	Ezra				1									1		
Cohasset	155	1	Lincoln	John				1					1				2		
Cohasset	155	2	Berter	Thomas	1	1		1		2	2		1				8		
Cohasset	155	3	Creed	Olive	1								1				2		
Cohasset	155	4	Wilson	Lucy		1							1				2		
Cohasset	155	5	Frent	Abel Jr	3			1					1				5		

20

TOWN	PG#	LN#	HEADS OF HOUSEHOLD		FREE WHITE MALES					FREE WHITE FEMALES					TOTAL ALL OTHER	TOTAL SLAVES	TOTALS	DISTRICT/ TOWNSHIP	NOTES
			LAST NAME	FIRST NAME	under 10	10 to 16	16 to 26	26 to 45	45 and over	under 10	10 to 16	16 to 26	26 to 45	45 and over					
Dedham	136	1	Ames	Luther Esq	2		4	1		2	2		1				12		
Dedham	136	2	Ames	Nathaniel Esq			1		1			1		1			4		
Dedham	136	3	Avery	Jonathan			1		1			2		1			5		
Dedham	136	4	Betile	Betsey						1			1				2		
Dedham	136	5	Atherton	Abner			3						1				4		
Dedham	136	6	Berry	James	1			1		1			1				4		
Dedham	136	7	Brooks	Timothy				1									1		
Dedham	136	8	Bullard	William	3		2	2					1	1			9		
Dedham	136	9	Bedlam	William		1			1	1			1				4		
Dedham	136	10	Babcock	Jason	1		3	1					1				6		
Dedham	136	11	Baker	Eliphalet 3d	1		3	1				1	1				7		
Dedham	136	12	Baker	Daniel				1				2	4				7		
Dedham	136	13	Bates	Samuel	1	2					1	1	1				6		
Dedham	136	14	Bullard	John	2	2		1		2	2	2	1	1			13		
Dedham	136	15	Bullard	Isaac				1		1	1	1	1				5		
Dedham	136	16	Bedlam	Lemuel			1			1	3	1					6		
Dedham	136	17	Briggs	Solomon			1			1	1	1					4		
Dedham	136	18	Clap	Jesse		1		3		1	1	1					7		
Dedham	136	19	Clail	Joseph	2			1		1			1				5		
Dedham	136	20	Clark	Jacob		1	2						1				4		
Dedham	136	21	Child	Francis			3	1					1				5		
Dedham	136	22	Crehore	Elisha	1			1		2		1	1	1			7		
Dedham	136	23	Capen	Nathaniel	1			1		2	1		1				6		
Dedham	136	24	Cain	Paul	1		1		1	3	1		1				8		
Dedham	136	25	Colburn	Nathan Junr				1									1		
Dedham	136	26	Columbia	Leuia	2			1		2			1				6		
Dedham	136	27	Dean	John		1	1		1				1				4		
Dedham	137	1	Draper	William	2			1			1	1	1	2			8		
Dedham	137	2	Draper	Ira	2	2		1		1		1	2				9		
Dedham	137	3	Draper	Desire									1				1		
Dedham	137	4	Damon	Jonathan		1	2	1	1	2	1		2				10		
Dedham	137	5	Damon	David	2		1	1		2			1	1			8		
Dedham	137	6	Doggett	Isaac				1					1				2		
Dedham	137	7	Dean	Joseph			1	1	1			2	1	1			7		
Dedham	137	8	Doggett	Samiel	1		1		1		1			1			5		
Dedham	137	9	Dowes	Edward			1		1		1		1	2			6		
Dedham	137	10	Dana	David	2		2	1	1	1	1	1	1	1			11		
Dedham	137	11	Day	Jonathan				1					1				2		
Dedham	137	12	Davis	Joshua G.	1			1				1	1				4		
Dedham	137	13	Everett	Israel Junr				1			2	2					5		
Dedham	137	14	Eaton	Isaac		1	1		1	1		1		1	1		7		
Dedham	137	15	Eaton	John		1		1				1	1				4		
Dedham	137	16	Ellis	Abner			1	1		2			1				5		
Dedham	137	17	Eaton	Desire			1										1		
Dedham	137	18	Eaton	Thomas		1	1		1			1					4		
Dedham	137	19	Eaton	Luther	1			1		2	1		1				6		
Dedham	137	20	Ellis	Joseph	2			1		2			1				6		
Dedham	137	21	Everett	Isreal & son Wm	1	2			2	1							6		
Dedham	137	22	Endicut	John				1		1	1		1				4		
Dedham	137	23	Eagens	James	2			1		1			1				5		
Dedham	137	24	Furrington	Nathaniel								1		1			2		
Dedham	137	25	Fairbanks	Oliver				1		2		1	1	1			6		
Dedham	137	26	Fairbanks	Ebenezer Jun	1	1	2	1	1	2	1	2	1	1			13		
Dedham	137	27	Furrington	Ebenezer		1	2	1		1	1	2					8		
Dedham	137	28	Furrington	Stephen	1		3	1		1			1		1		8		
Dedham	137	29	Fairbanks	Isreal				1									1		
Dedham	137	30	Fairbanks	Isreal Junr	1	1			1	1	1		1				6		
Dedham	137	31	Fales	Joshua G.	1	2			1			1	1				6		
Dedham	137	32	Fales	Margrett									1				1		
Dedham	137	33	Fisher	Josiah		1			1				1				3		
Dedham	137	34	Fisher	Sarah Wid	1			2	1	1	1		2	1			9		
Dedham	137	35	Fuller	Aaron		1	1		1			1		1			5		
Dedham	137	36	Fuller	Lidia Wid	1							1		1			3		
Dedham	137	37	Furrington	Benjamin	1		1				1	1		2			7		
Dedham	137	38	Fairbanks	Samuel				1					1				2		
Dedham	137	39	Furrington	Ebenezer	2			1		1		1	1				6		
Dedham	137	40	Fales	Samuel		1			1	1	1			2			6		
Dedham	137	41	Fales	Nehemiah	1	2			1	1	1	2		1			9		
Dedham	137	42	Fisher	Timothy	3			1		2	1		2	1			11		
Dedham	138	1	Gorthorp	William				1					1				1		
Dedham	138	2	Gay	Timothy			3	3	1		2			1			10		
Dedham	138	3	Greenwood	Isaac				1			1	1	1				4		
Dedham	138	4	Guild	Ruben			4	1		2		1	1	1			10		
Dedham	138	5	Guild	Amasa	2		2	1		1			1				7		
Dedham	138	6	Guild	Calvin			3				1	1					5		
Dedham	138	7	Gay	Daniel	1			1		1			1	1			5		
Dedham	138	8	Gould	George Maj			1	1	1				2				5		
Dedham	138	9	Guild	John		1	1	1		1			1				5		
Dedham	138	10	Gay	David & Ichabod	1		1	1		1			1	1			6		

21

TOWN	PG#	LN#	LAST NAME	FIRST NAME	FREE WHITE MALES under 10	10 to 16	16 to 26	26 to 45	45 and over	FREE WHITE FEMALES under 10	10 to 16	16 to 26	26 to 45	45 and over	TOTAL ALL OTHER	TOTAL SLAVES	TOTALS	DISTRICT/ TOWNSHIP	NOTES
Dedham	138	11	Guild	Sarah Wid		1						1		2			4		
Dedham	138	12	Haven	Jason Rev			1		1				1	1			4		
Dedham	138	13	Haven	Samuel Esq				1		1	1	1	1				5		
Dedham	138	14	Hensey	Elijah			1			1	1	1	1				5		
Dedham	138	15	Harris	Enoch	1	1	4	1			2		2				11		
Dedham	138	16	Howe	Thomas Junr	2		1			2		2					7		
Dedham	138	17	Howe	Thomas				1			1		1				3		
Dedham	138	18	Howe	William	1		6	2	1	2		2	2				16		
Dedham	138	19	Howe	Joseph	2		1					1					4		
Dedham	138	20	Hawes	Shuba Wid							1		2				3		
Dedham	138	21	Howe	Joseph & Hemon Bostick			2	2									4		
Dedham	138	22	Jones	Henry				1					1				2		
Dedham	138	23	Hadley	Simon	1			1	1				1				4		
Dedham	138	24	Holmes	Ebenezer	1		3	1		2	1	1	1				10		
Dedham	138	25	Jourdan	Richard		1	3						1				5		
Dedham	138	26	Kingsbury	Keziah Wid	1		1			1		1	1				5		
Dedham	138	27	Kingsbury	Joshua G.				1					1				2		
Dedham	138	28	Kingsbury	Moses		1		1		1		2					5		
Dedham	138	29	Kingsbury	Ezekeil	2	1		1		1		2					7		
Dedham	138	30	Kingsbury	Noah	1					3		1	1				6		
Dedham	138	31	Lewis	Joseph Junr	1		3	3		1		1	2				11		
Dedham	138	32	Lealand	Isaac		1		1		3		1	2				8		
Dedham	138	33	Lewis	Paul		1		1				1					3		
Dedham	138	34	Lewis	Abner		1		1					1				3		
Dedham	138	35	Lewis	Joseph	2		2		1			2	1	1			9		
Dedham	138	36	Lowder	Samuel		1	1	1		1		1	1	3			9		
Dedham	138	37	Lewis	Samuel		1		1		1		1	1				5		
Dedham	138	38	Mash	Martin	1		3					2					6		
Dedham	138	39	Mason	Thadues	2		1	1		1		1	1				7		
Dedham	138	40	Mason	William		1			1				1	2			5		
Dedham	138	41	Mann	Robert		1			1				1				3		
Dedham	138	42	Metcalf	Wid Ruth									1				1		
Dedham	138	43	Metcalf	Joseph	1	1		1		1		1					5		
Dedham	138	44	Montague	Rev William				1									1		
Dedham	138	45	Morrell	Elikim	1	1		1			1	1		2			7		
Dedham	138	46	Mann	Harmon	3		1	2		1		1	1				9		
Dedham	138	47	Newell	Ruben Maj	1		1			1			1				3		
Dedham	139	1	Noyes	James			1			1							2		
Dedham	139	2	Noyes	Nathaniel			1			1		1					3		
Dedham	139	3	Orion	Anna Wid		2	2					1	1	1			7		
Dedham	139	4	Paul	Ebenezer		1	3	1				1		1			7		
Dedham	139	5	Pond	Jonas		1		1		2		1		1			6		
Dedham	139	6	Pratt	William	1			1		2			2	1			7		
Dedham	139	7	Pond	Eliphalet Capt	1	1	1		1	1	1		1	2			9		
Dedham	139	8	Persons	Eli		2	5		1			1					9		
Dedham	139	9	Poor	Daniel	1	1	2	1		1	1		1				8		
Dedham	139	10	Richards	Jabez		1	1			2		2					6		
Dedham	139	11	Richards	Jesse	3		1			2		1					7		
Dedham	139	12	Richards	Luther	1					2	1	1	1				6		
Dedham	139	13	Richards	Samuel	1	3		1		2	1	1	1				10		
Dedham	139	14	Richards	Timothy	1	1			1			1		1			5		
Dedham	139	15	Richards	Ruben	1	1	2	1				1	1				7		
Dedham	139	16	Richards	Jonathan	1	1		2		2	1	1	1				9		
Dedham	139	17	Richards	Abiather				1					1				2		
Dedham	139	18	Richards	Abiather Junr	2	1	2		1	3	1	1	1				12		
Dedham	139	19	Richards	Abigail Wid							1	1	1				3		
Dedham	139	20	Richards	Joseph	2			1		1			1				5		
Dedham	139	21	Pond	Moses	1			1		3	1	1	1	1			9		
Dedham	139	22	Pond	Samuel	1			1		2		1					5		
Dedham	139	23	Swan	Joseph Junr		1	1			2		1	1				7		
Dedham	139	24	Smith	William		1	1	1		1	1	2					7		
Dedham	139	25	Spear	John	2		1			2		1	1				7		
Dedham	139	26	Smith	Henry		1		1					1				3		
Dedham	139	27	Sprague	Esther Wid		2	2				1	1	1	1			8		
Dedham	139	28	Sprague	Rebeca Wid	1		2			1	1	2		1			8		
Dedham	139	29	Swan	Joseph				1		1		1					3		
Dedham	139	30	Shuttleworth	Jeremiah		1	1		1		2						5		
Dedham	139	31	Starr	Jonathan		1		1	2			2					6		
Dedham	139	32	Sisk	Edward			1						1				2		
Dedham	139	33	Stowell	Lemuel	1	2		1					1				5		
Dedham	139	34	Stowell	Isaac				1			1		1				3		
Dedham	139	35	Stowell	Jesse			3					1					4		
Dedham	139	36	Stowell	Timothy		1		1				1	1				4		
Dedham	139	37	Stowell	Joel	2		1			1	1						5		
Dedham	139	38	Smith	Thomas				1					1				2		
Dedham	139	39	Smith	Nathaniel		1		1	1	1	2		1				6		
Dedham	139	40	Smith	Sarah									1				1		
Dedham	139	41	Smith	Lemuel		1		1		1			1	1			5		
Dedham	139	42	Smith	Naham	2		1			1			1				5		

TOWN	PG#	LN#	LAST NAME	FIRST NAME	M under 10	M 10-16	M 16-26	M 26-45	M 45+	F under 10	F 10-16	F 16-26	F 26-45	F 45+	TOTAL ALL OTHER	TOTAL SLAVES	TOTALS	DISTRICT/TOWNSHIP	NOTES
Dedham	139	43	Smith	Abner	1		1	1				1	1				5		
Dedham	139	44	Smith	Barach	1				1	2	1		1				6		
Dedham	139	45	Stowell	Fisher			1			1		1					3		
Dedham	139	46	Smith	John	2			1		1		1	1				6		
Dedham	140	1	Turner	James	1	1	1				1	1	1	1			73		
Dedham	140	2	Townsend	Horatio Esq	1			1	1	2		1	1	1	2		10		
Dedham	140	3	Stevens	Jane		1	1					1		1			4		
Dedham	140	4	Wight	Henry	1		2		1	1		1		1			7		
Dedham	140	5	Whiting	Abner			2			1	2	1					6		
Dedham	140	6	Whiting	Samuel				1					1				2		
Dedham	140	7	Whiting	Joshua			1	1		1	2	1					6		
Dedham	140	8	Weatherbee	Benjamin	1	2		2				1	1				7		
Dedham	140	9	Whiting	William		1	1		1			1	2				6		
Dedham	140	10	Whiting	Rufus	1			1		2	2	1					7		
Dedham	140	11	Whiting	Hannah Wid		1			1	1	2		1				6		
Dedham	140	12	Whiting	Moses	1	1	2	1	1		1		1	1			9		
Dedham	140	13	Whiting	Joseph & Paul	1		2			2		1	1				7		
Dedham	140	14	Whiting	Hezekiah	1			1		1		1	1				5		
Dedham	140	15	Whiting	Joseph Dr.			1	1			1		2				5		
Dedham	140	16	Whiting	Stephen		1		1					2				4		
Dedham	140	17	Whiting	Timothy & Solomon		1		2		1	1	1	1	1	1		9		
Dedham	140	18	Whiting	Calvin	2	1	1	1		2		1	1	1			10		
Dedham	140	19	Wheeton	Jesse			1					1	1		3		6		
Dedham	140	20	Wight	Ebenezer Esq	2	3		1	1	1		1	1	1			11		
Dedham	140	21	Wight	Joseph	2		3		1		2		1				9		
Dedham	140	22	Webb	Daniel		1	1					1	1	1			5		
Dedham	140	23	Wilson	John	1	1	1		1			1		1			6		
Dedham	140	24	Whiting	Edward		1		1				2					4		
Dedham	140	25	Wakfield	George				1		1	1	1					4		
Dedham	140	26	Woodward	Deborough		1	1			1	1		1				5		
Dedham	140	27	Weatherbee	Joseph			1	1		1		1	1				6		
Dedham	140	28	Wheelock	Timothy		1		1			1		1				4		
Dedham	140	29	Weatherbee	Comforth	1		2	1		2		1	1				8		
Dedham	140	30	Parker	Jonathan	1		1	1		1		1	1				6		
Dedham	140	31	Pettengill	John	1			1				1					3		
Dedham	140	32	Jones	Walter				1									1		
Dedham	140	33	Stacy	Persons				1									1		
Dedham	140	34	Gorham	David				1									1		
Dedham	140	35	Alonso	House	2			2		2		2	4	4			16		
Dedham	140	36	Garish	Jack												5	5		
Dedham	141	1	Andrews	David			1					1					2	1st Parish	
Dedham	141	2	Briggs	Sarah									1				1	1st Parish	
Dedham	141	3	Bullard	Abigail									1				1	1st Parish	
Dedham	141	4	Billings	Elkanah	1	1		1				1					4	1st Parish	
Dedham	141	5	Coney	William		1	2		1				1				5	1st Parish	
Dedham	141	6	Cobbett	Phillip	1	1	1		1	1	1		1				7	1st Parish	
Dedham	141	7	Chickering	Jabez Rev		1			1	1		2					5	1st Parish	
Dedham	141	8	Colburn	Lemuel	1			1		3			1				6	1st Parish	
Dedham	141	9	Chamberland	Isaac	2		1					1	1				5	1st Parish	
Dedham	141	10	Cobbett	Daniel	2		1	1			1		1		1		7	1st Parish	
Dedham	141	11	Dean	William			1		1				1				3	1st Parish	
Dedham	141	12	Dean	Benjamin				1						1			2	1st Parish	
Dedham	141	13	Dean	Phinehas E.			1			2		1					4	1st Parish	
Dedham	141	14	Dean	Samuel W.	1			1		1	1	1					5	1st Parish	
Dedham	141	15	Dean	Francis		1		1				2					4	1st Parish	
Dedham	141	16	Dean	John	1		1	1		2		1		1			7	1st Parish	
Dedham	141	17	Everett	Asa	1	1			1	1	1		1				6	1st Parish	
Dedham	141	18	Everett	Ebenezer		2			1		1		2				6	1st Parish	
Dedham	141	19	Everett	Ebenezer Jun	3			1					1				5	1st Parish	
Dedham	141	20	Everett	Abel			1		1	3	2	1	1				9	1st Parish	
Dedham	141	21	Everett	William	3	1		1		2		1	1				10	1st Parish	
Dedham	141	22	Ellis	John	1		2		1		2	1	1	1	1		10	1st Parish	
Dedham	141	23	Ellis	Lemuel	1			1		1		1					4	1st Parish	
Dedham	141	24	Ellis	John Junr				1		3		1					5	1st Parish	
Dedham	141	25	Everett	Josiah				1					1				2	1st Parish	
Dedham	141	26	Fisher	Oliver Junr	3			1			1						5	1st Parish	
Dedham	141	27	Fuller	Eliphilet	2	1		1		1		1					6	1st Parish	
Dedham	141	28	Fuller	Jonathan		2		1		2		2	1				8	1st Parish	
Dedham	141	29	Fisher	Oliver	1			1		1			1				4	1st Parish	
Dedham	141	30	Fisher	Eliphilet				1			1		1				3	1st Parish	
Dedham	141	31	Fairbanks	Abner	2			1					1				4	1st Parish	
Dedham	141	32	Fairbanks	David	1	1	1					1					5	1st Parish	
Dedham	141	33	Fales	Eliphilet	1	1	1	1	1		1			1			7	1st Parish	
Dedham	141	34	Fairbank	William	1	1			1		1	1	1				5	1st Parish	
Dedham	141	35	Furrington	David	2		1			1		1	1				6	1st Parish	
Dedham	141	36	Guild	Aaron Majr		1			1					1			3	1st Parish	
Dedham	141	37	Guild	Aaron Junr	1	1			1					1			4	1st Parish	
Dedham	141	38	Guild	Jacob		1		1			1		1				4	1st Parish	
Dedham	141	39	Guild	Oliver		1		1			1		1				4	1st Parish	

			HEADS OF HOUSEHOLD		FREE WHITE MALES					FREE WHITE FEMALES									
TOWN	PG#	LN#	LAST NAME	FIRST NAME	under 10	10 to 16	16 to 26	26 to 45	45 and over	under 10	10 to 16	16 to 26	26 to 45	45 and over	TOTAL ALL OTHER	TOTAL SLAVES	TOTALS	DISTRICT/ TOWNSHIP	NOTES
Dedham	141	40	Guild	Abner	2	1	1	1		2	1	1	1				10	1st Parish	
Dedham	141	41	Guild	Moses	3	1	1	1		2		1	1				10	1st Parish	
Dedham	141	42	Guild	Joel	4		1	1		1			1				8	1st Parish	
Dedham	141	43	Gay	Jesse		1	1		1	1	1		1				6	1st Parish	
Dedham	141	44	Gay	Charles	1			1			2						4	1st Parish	
Dedham	142	1	Gay	Ichabod					1								1	1st Parish	
Dedham	142	2	Gay	Oliver		1	1	1					1				4	1st Parish	
Dedham	142	3	Gay	Wilks	1		1				2						4	1st Parish	
Dedham	142	4	Gay	Ichabod Junr	1			1		2		1					5	1st Parish	
Dedham	142	5	Gay	Ebenezer		1			1	1	1		1				5	1st Parish	
Dedham	142	6	Gay	Nathaniel				1			1		1	1			4	1st Parish	
Dedham	142	7	Grover	George W.	1			1		1			1				4	1st Parish	
Dedham	142	8	Harmon	Michel				1		1			1				3	1st Parish	
Dedham	142	9	Kingsbury	James		1	1				2		1				5	1st Parish	
Dedham	142	10	Lewis	Hannah Wid		1							2				3	1st Parish	
Dedham	142	11	Lewis	Joseph			1						1				2	1st Parish	
Dedham	142	12	Lewis	Jabez	1		1						1				3	1st Parish	
Dedham	142	13	Lewis	Nathaniel			1						1	1			3	1st Parish	
Dedham	142	14	Lewis	Rachel Wid		1				4			2				7	1st Parish	
Dedham	142	15	Morse	Mehitable	1	1					1	1	1				6	1st Parish	
Dedham	142	16	Morse	Sarah Wid									2				2	1st Parish	
Dedham	142	17	Rhoads	Wid									2				2	1st Parish	
Dedham	142	18	Morse	John				1					1		1		3	1st Parish	
Dedham	142	19	Morse	John Junr	2	1		1		1			1				6	1st Parish	
Dedham	142	20	Morse	George		1		1		1	1	1					5	1st Parish	
Dedham	142	21	Morse	Seth	1	2	2		1		1		1				8	1st Parish	
Dedham	142	22	Morse	David	1	1		1		1	1	1					6	1st Parish	
Dedham	142	23	Morse	Oliver			1	1				1		1			4	1st Parish	
Dedham	142	24	Peniman	Jacob				1					1				2	1st Parish	
Dedham	142	25	Rhoads	Eleazer	1		1		1			1		1			5	1st Parish	
Dedham	142	26	Palmer	Anna								1					1	1st Parish	
Dedham	142	27	Phipps	William		1		1					1				3	1st Parish	
Dedham	142	28	Shuttleworth	Ebenezer				1					2				3	1st Parish	
Dedham	142	29	Sumner	Nathaniel				1				1	1				3	1st Parish	
Dedham	142	30	Sumner	Ebenezer		2		1		1			1				5	1st Parish	
Dedham	142	31	Sumner	Margrett Wid		1				3	1		1				6	1st Parish	
Dedham	142	32	Sumner	Nathaniel Junr	3	1		1		1	1	1	1				9	1st Parish	
Dedham	142	33	Sumner	William	2		1			2	1	1					7	1st Parish	
Dedham	142	34	Shephard	John	3		4	1		3	3		1				15	1st Parish	
Dedham	142	35	Savel	William			4	1		1	1		1				8	1st Parish	
Dedham	142	36	Smith	Jacob	2			1		1	1		1				8	1st Parish	
Dedham	142	37	Talbert	Enoch			1				1		1	1			6	1st Parish	
Dedham	142	38	Talbert	Ebenezer	1	1		1		1	1		1				6	1st Parish	
Dedham	142	39	Thorpe	Eliphilet		1		1				1		1			4	1st Parish	
Dedham	142	40	Turner	Joseph				1				1					2	1st Parish	
Dedham	142	41	Turner	Hezekiah	1			1		1	1		1				5	1st Parish	
Dedham	142	42	Weatherbee	Benjamin				1					1				2	1st Parish	
Dedham	142	43	Weatherbee	David	1	1	1				1						4	1st Parish	
Dedham	142	44	White	Ebenezer		1		1					1				4	1st Parish	
Dedham	142	45	White	George	1			1		1	1		1				5	1st Parish	
Dedham	142	46	White	Thomas			1	1					1				3	1st Parish	
Dedham	142	47	White	James				1									1	1st Parish	
Dedham	142	48	W*son	Joseph				1					1				2	1st Parish	
Dedham	143	1	Smith	Abigail							1		1				2	1st Parish	
Dedham	143	2	Baker	Mary Wid									1				1	2nd Parish	
Dedham	143	3	Baker	Jeremiah		1	1	1		2	1		2				8	2nd Parish	
Dedham	143	4	Baker	Joseph		1	1	1		1	1	2		1			8	2nd Parish	
Dedham	143	5	Baker	Eliphalet				1			1		1				3	2nd Parish	
Dedham	143	6	Baker	John	2	1		1					1				6	2nd Parish	
Dedham	143	7	Baker	Eliphalet Jun	1			1		1		1		1			5	2nd Parish	
Dedham	143	8	Baker	Timothy		2		1		1		1	1	1			7	2nd Parish	
Dedham	143	9	Boyden	Benjamin		1		1		1		1	1				5	2nd Parish	
Dedham	143	10	Boyden	Benjamin Junr	1		2					1					4	2nd Parish	
Dedham	143	11	Buckmaster	Edward	2			1		1			1				5	2nd Parish	
Dedham	143	12	Carby	Carolina									1	1			2	2nd Parish	
Dedham	143	13	Colburn	Eliphalet	2			1				1	1				5	2nd Parish	
Dedham	143	14	Colburn	Isaac				1									1	2nd Parish	
Dedham	143	15	Colburn	Isaac Junr	1			1		5	1		1				9	2nd Parish	
Dedham	143	16	Colburn	Timothy		1		1	1			1	1				5	2nd Parish	
Dedham	143	17	Colburn	Phinehas		1		1		1			1				4	2nd Parish	
Dedham	143	18	Colburn	Jonathan	2		1					1					4	2nd Parish	
Dedham	143	19	Colburn	Ichabod		1	1		1	1	1	1	1				7	2nd Parish	
Dedham	143	20	Colburn	Nathan				1									1	2nd Parish	
Dedham	143	21	Colburn	Benjamin	1		2					2					5	2nd Parish	
Dedham	143	22	Colburn	Seth	1		1			1	1						4	2nd Parish	
Dedham	143	23	Colburn	Lewis	1			1		2		1		1			6	2nd Parish	
Dedham	143	24	Colburn	Richard	1		1	2	1	3			1	1			10	2nd Parish	
Dedham	143	25	Colburn	Thomas	1			1		3		1	1				7	2nd Parish	
Dedham	143	26	Colburn	Comforth									1				1	2nd Parish	
Dedham	143	27	Dean	Joseph	1			1		1			1				4	2nd Parish	

TOWN	PG#	LN#	LAST NAME	FIRST NAME	FREE WHITE MALES					FREE WHITE FEMALES					TOTAL ALL OTHER	TOTAL SLAVES	TOTALS	DISTRICT/ TOWNSHIP	NOTES
					under 10	10 to 16	16 to 26	26 to 45	45 and over	under 10	10 to 16	16 to 26	26 to 45	45 and over					
Dedham	143	28	Draper	Daniel	2	1		1						1			5	2nd Parish	
Dedham	143	29	Draper	Joseph	1	1	2		1	1	1	3	1	1			12	2nd Parish	
Dedham	143	30	Ellis	Oliver	1	1	1		1	1	1		1	1			8	2nd Parish	
Dedham	143	31	Ellis	Abner		1	2	2		1		1	1				8	2nd Parish	
Dedham	143	32	Everett	Isaac		1			1					2			4	2nd Parish	
Dedham	143	33	Ellis	Ichabod			2		1		1	1		1			6	2nd Parish	
Dedham	143	34	Ellis	David				1	1			2		1			5	2nd Parish	
Dedham	143	35	Ellis	George	1			1			1	1	1				5	2nd Parish	
Dedham	143	36	Ellis	Nathan					1		2			1			4	2nd Parish	
Dedham	143	37	Ellis	William		1	2	1	1			1	2	1			9	2nd Parish	
Dedham	143	38	Ellis	Aaron	1				1					1			3	2nd Parish	
Dedham	143	39	Fisher	Asa		1			1			1		1			4	2nd Parish	
Dedham	143	40	Fairbanks	Benjamin			1		1		1	2					5	2nd Parish	
Dedham	143	41	Fairbanks	Benjamin Junr	1		1	1		1		1	1				6	2nd Parish	
Dedham	143	42	Fisher	Ebenezer		1		1					1				3	2nd Parish	
Dedham	143	43	Fisher	Nathaniel				1			1		1				3	2nd Parish	
Dedham	144	1	Fisher	John		1		2			1		1				5	2nd Parish	
Dedham	144	2	French	Samuel	1	1			1	1	1		1				6	2nd Parish	
Dedham	144	3	French	Benjamin				1		2	1		1				5	2nd Parish	
Dedham	144	4	French	Benjamin Junr		1				1			1				3	2nd Parish	
Dedham	144	5	Fisher	Benjamin		3						1					4	2nd Parish	
Dedham	144	6	Gay	Ichabod Dr		1		1				1	1	2			6	2nd Parish	
Dedham	144	7	Gay	William	1	3		1		2		1	1				9	2nd Parish	
Dedham	144	8	Gay	Joseph	1		2	1		1	2						7	2nd Parish	
Dedham	144	9	Gay	Josiah				1						2			3	2nd Parish	
Dedham	144	10	Gay	Moses		1	1	1						2			5	2nd Parish	
Dedham	144	11	Gay	Hannah Wid										2			2	2nd Parish	
Dedham	144	12	Glover	David		1				1		1					3	2nd Parish	
Dedham	144	13	Glover	Henry								1	2				3	2nd Parish	
Dedham	144	14	Graham	William				1					1				2	2nd Parish	
Dedham	144	15	Gay	Seth		1		1			1	1	1				5	2nd Parish	
Dedham	144	16	Gay	Luther	4		2	1					2				9	2nd Parish	
Dedham	144	17	Gay	Thadues	2			1		1	1		1				6	2nd Parish	
Dedham	144	18	Gay	Willard	1	2		3		1		1	2				10	2nd Parish	
Dedham	144	19	Gay	Lemuel	1		1	1		1		1	1				6	2nd Parish	
Dedham	144	20	Gay	Colburn			1	1				1					3	2nd Parish	
Dedham	144	21	Gould	John Doc		1		1		1	2	1	1				7	2nd Parish	
Dedham	144	22	Herring	Peletiah	1			1		1			1				4	2nd Parish	
Dedham	144	23	Holmes	John				1		1	1	1					4	2nd Parish	
Dedham	144	24	Kingsbury	Enoch			1	2					1				4	2nd Parish	
Dedham	144	25	Kingsbury	Nathaniel	1		1	1				1	1				5	2nd Parish	
Dedham	144	26	Kingsbury	Nathaniel Junr	1		1					1	1				4	2nd Parish	
Dedham	144	27	Lewis	Meletia									1				1	2nd Parish	
Dedham	144	28	Lewis	Andrew	1			1		1	1		1				5	2nd Parish	
Dedham	144	29	Lenley	Levi	1			1		1		1	1				5	2nd Parish	
Dedham	144	30	Mason	William Junr	1	1		1		2	1		1				7	2nd Parish	
Dedham	144	31	Orion	Elihu	3			1		1		1	1	1			8	2nd Parish	
Dedham	144	32	Pettee	Samuel		1		1					1				3	2nd Parish	
Dedham	144	33	Richards	John				1					2		1		4	2nd Parish	
Dedham	144	34	Richards	Abel	1		2	1		1		1	1				7	2nd Parish	
Dedham	144	35	Richards	Fredrick		1	1					1					3	2nd Parish	
Dedham	144	36	Starr	Elizabeth		1	1			1	1	1	1				6	2nd Parish	
Dedham	144	37	Thacher	Thomas Revd		1	1	1					1				4	2nd Parish	
Dedham	144	38	Whiting	Nathaniel		2	1		1	2	1	3	1				11	2nd Parish	
Dedham	144	39	Whiting	Daniel Col				1									1	2nd Parish	
Dedham	144	40	White	Jacob	1			1				1					3	2nd Parish	

TOWN	PG#	LN#	LAST NAME	FIRST NAME	FREE WHITE MALES					FREE WHITE FEMALES					TOTAL ALL OTHER	TOTAL SLAVES	TOTALS	DISTRICT/ TOWNSHIP	NOTES
					under 10	10 to 16	16 to 26	26 to 45	45 and over	under 10	10 to 16	16 to 26	26 to 45	45 and over					
Dorchester	51	1	Adams	Seth	3	1		2		1		2	1	1			11		
Dorchester	51	2	Anderson	James	1			1					1				3		
Dorchester	51	3	Andrews	Jno			1			2			1				4		
Dorchester	51	4	Atherton	Jemima						2				2			4		
Dorchester	51	5	Bowdoin	James		2	2	3	1			2	1	3			14		
Dorchester	51	6	Badlam	Steph		1	5		1	1		2		1	1		12		
Dorchester	51	7	Baker	James					1			2		1			4		
Dorchester	51	8	Baker	Jno		1	1		1				1	1			5		
Dorchester	51	9	Blake	Nathl	2	2	1	1				2	1				9		
Dorchester	51	10	Bordman	Wm				1		1	1	2					5		
Dorchester	51	11	Belcher	Saml	1		3		1		2	2	2				11		
Dorchester	51	12	Billings	Oliver		1	1		1				1	1			5		
Dorchester	51	13	Billings	Oliver Jr	1			1					2				4		
Dorchester	51	14	Billings	Moses				1		1			2				4		
Dorchester	51	15	Baker	Saml 3d	1		1						1				3		
Dorchester	51	16	Blackman	Leml	2	1		1		1			1	1			7		
Dorchester	51	17	Bird	Benjamin	1		1			1		1					4		
Dorchester	51	18	Bird	Oliver				4					1				5		
Dorchester	52	1	Bisbee	Jona				1		1			1				3		
Dorchester	52	2	Bird	Mary										1			1		
Dorchester	52	3	Beales	Jacob	3			2		1	1		1				8		
Dorchester	52	4	Bird	Samuel			2		2			2	1				7		
Dorchester	52	5	Bird	Elizabeth									1	1			2		
Dorchester	52	6	Bird	Sarah	1		1			1		1	2	1			7		
Dorchester	52	7	Blake	Rachel									2				2		
Dorchester	52	8	Bird	Edward	2	1		1		1	2	1					9		
Dorchester	52	9	Bird	Jona Jr		1	1	2					1	2			7		
Dorchester	52	10	Burrill	Benj	1			1		3			1				6		
Dorchester	52	11	Blake	James					1		1			1			3		
Dorchester	52	12	Bird	Aaron Jr	3		1	1		1	2		1				9		
Dorchester	52	13	Blackman	Jona	2			1		1			1				5		
Dorchester	52	14	Bird	Wm	2		1	1				1					5		
Dorchester	52	15	Bird	Aaron		1	1	1	1					2			6		
Dorchester	52	16	Baker	James			1		1					2			4		
Dorchester	52	17	Baker	Saml		1	1			1			1				5		
Dorchester	52	18	Bussey	Jno	2	1	1		1		1		1	1	2		10		
Dorchester	52	19	Baker	James Jr	2			1		1			1				5		
Dorchester	52	20	Blake	Enos	1		1		1	1	1		1				6		
Dorchester	52	21	Beales	Zebulon	1		1						1				3		
Dorchester	52	22	Blake	Seth	3				1	1			1				6		
Dorchester	52	23	Budge	David			1			1		1					3		
Dorchester	52	24	Baker	Edmund	3		1						2				6		
Dorchester	52	25	Baker	Abigail						1			1	1			3		
Dorchester	52	26	Blagge	Saml		1	1	1		3	1		1		1		9		
Dorchester	52	27	Baker	George				3		1		1	1				6		
Dorchester	52	28	Baker	Susan			1			1		1		1	1		5		
Dorchester	52	29	Baxter	Edw. W.	3	1	2	1		1			1				9		
Dorchester	52	30	Bird	Calvin			1			1		1					3		
Dorchester	52	31	Blackman	Unite	4			1		1	1		1				8		
Dorchester	52	32	Blanchard	Fran.		1			1	3				1			6		
Dorchester	52	33	Blackman	James	1		3				1	1					6		
Dorchester	52	34	Blackman	Saml Jr	1	1		1		1			1				5		
Dorchester	53	1	Blackman	Saml	2				1					3			6		
Dorchester	53	2	Bird	Jona		1	1		1			1	1	1			6		
Dorchester	53	3	Bird	Jona Jr	1			1					1				3		
Dorchester	53	4	Brigden	Zachr	2		1				1	1		1			6		
Dorchester	53	5	Badlam	Ezra			2			1			1				4		
Dorchester	53	6	Bird	George	1		1	1					1				4		
Dorchester	53	7	Bird	Henry		1	1		3	1		2		1			9		
Dorchester	53	8	Bird	Saml	4	1		1			1	1	1				9		
Dorchester	53	9	Clap	Eben Esq.	4	1	1		4	1	1	2	1				15		
Dorchester	53	10	Clap	Lemuel		1	3		1			2		1			8		
Dorchester	53	11	Coxil	Jno		1	4	1		1		1					8		
Dorchester	53	12	Carter	Josiah			1			1		1					3		
Dorchester	53	13	Capen	Saml		1	2	2		3	1		1	1			11		
Dorchester	53	14	Clap	Saml	1	1	8	1					2	1			14		
Dorchester	53	15	Clap	Saml 3rd		1	1	1					1				4		
Dorchester	53	16	Coolidge	Eliz		1						1		1			3		
Dorchester	53	17	Collier	Saml	3			1				1		1			6		
Dorchester	53	18	Clap	Charles		1	1	1					1				4		
Dorchester	53	19	Clap	Roger	2			1	1				1	1			6		
Dorchester	53	20	Clap	Ezekiel	3		1	1					1	1			7		
Dorchester	53	21	Clap	Nathl	2	1		1	1	2	1		2				10		
Dorchester	53	22	Clap	Ann								1		1			2		
Dorchester	53	23	Clap	Pen Jr	2		1			1			1				5		
Dorchester	53	24	Clap	Pen 3d			1			3			1				5		
Dorchester	53	25	Clap	Jona	1			1					1	2			5		
Dorchester	53	26	Clap	David			1						1				2		
Dorchester	53	27	Clap	Saml Jr			1						1				2		

TOWN	PG#	LN#	HEADS OF HOUSEHOLD		FREE WHITE MALES					FREE WHITE FEMALES					TOTAL ALL OTHER	TOTAL SLAVES	TOTALS	DISTRICT/ TOWNSHIP	NOTES
			LAST NAME	FIRST NAME	under 10	10 to 16	16 to 26	26 to 45	45 and over	under 10	10 to 16	16 to 26	26 to 45	45 and over					
Dorchester	53	28	Clap	Seth				1		1			1				3		
Dorchester	53	29	Crane	Isaac	1		1	1	1	1			1				6		
Dorchester	53	30	Crehore	Saml	2	2	3	1		1		1	1				11		
Dorchester	53	31	Clap	Joseph	2	1	2		1	2	1			4			13		
Dorchester	53	32	Cole	Wm				1		1			1				3		
Dorchester	53	33	Cox	Samuel			1			1			1				3		
Dorchester	53	34	Cook	Russell	1	2			1	1	1	3		1			10		
Dorchester	53	35	Capen	Saml Jr	1		1	1				1	1	1			6		
Dorchester	54	1	Clap	Joseph Jr			1			2		1					4		
Dorchester	54	2	Curen	Jno 3d		1		1	1			2		1			6		
Dorchester	54	3	Capen	Ebenz	2	1			2			2		1			8		
Dorchester	54	4	Clap	James	2			1		1		1					5		
Dorchester	54	5	Clap	Thomas					2					2			4		
Dorchester	54	6	Capen	Jno Jr	2	1	4		1	2	2	1		2			15		
Dorchester	54	7	Cox	Capt. Henry	2	2	4	1			1	1					11		
Dorchester	54	8	Capen	Jno			1		1	1			1				4		
Dorchester	54	9	Crane	Leml	3		1	1		1			2				8		
Dorchester	54	10	Champney	James		1		1		2			1				5		
Dorchester	54	11	Champney	Caleb				1						1			2		
Dorchester	54	12	Champney	Jno			1		1	1				2			5		
Dorchester	54	13	Draper	Phillip	2			1					1	1			5		
Dorchester	54	14	Davenport	Ebenz		1	2	1	1	1				2			8		
Dorchester	54	15	Davenport	Elisha	1		1		1	1		3		1			8		
Dorchester	54	16	Deune	Ebenz		1	4	1				1		1			8		
Dorchester	54	17	Deluce	Jno	2			1		2		1					6		
Dorchester	54	18	Davenport	Eben Jr			2					1					3		
Dorchester	54	19	Deluce	Francis				1						1			2		
Dorchester	54	20	Dolbear	Jno				1		1			1	1			4		
Dorchester	54	21	Dorrine	James	1		1			1		1					4		
Dorchester	54	22	Davenport	Saml				1	1	5	2		1				10		
Dorchester	54	23	Davenport	Isaac	2	1		1		1	1		1				7		
Dorchester	54	24	Dickerman	Rebe										2			2		
Dorchester	54	25	Davenport	Jno				1		1			1				3		
Dorchester	54	26	Davenport	Ephm	4			1		1			1				7		
Dorchester	54	27	Davenport	Dan	2			1		2			1	1			7		
Dorchester	54	28	Dodge	Richard											5		5		
Dorchester	54	29	Everett	Oliver	2	2	1		1	2		1	1				10		
Dorchester	54	30	Everett	Moses	3	2	3		1	1		1	2	1			14		
Dorchester	54	31	Everett	Sam H			1	1				2					4		
Dorchester	54	32	Evans	Jeremh			1	1					1				3		
Dorchester	54	33	Eaton	Pearson		2			2	1	1	1					7		
Dorchester	55	1	Ellis	Abel		1	1	1		1	1		1				6		
Dorchester	55	2	Fales	Stephen	1	1	1		1			1		3			8		
Dorchester	55	3	Foster	Timothy		1		1				1		1			4		
Dorchester	55	4	Foster	Edward	2	2			1	2		2	1				10		
Dorchester	55	5	Field	Thomas	1			1		2			1				5		
Dorchester	55	6	Farrington	Jno	1			1				1					3		
Dorchester	55	7	Farrington	Jno				1					1				2		
Dorchester	55	8	Field	Timothy	2	1		1		2	1		1				8		
Dorchester	55	9	Foster	Jacob		1	1			2			1				5		
Dorchester	55	10	Fowler	Saml	2			1		3	1	2	2	1			12		
Dorchester	55	11	Field	Issac H.	3	2	1	1	1	2		1	1	1			13		
Dorchester	55	12	Fuller	Amasa	2	1	1	2				1	1				8		
Dorchester	55	13	Fisher	Ebene			1	1				1	1				4		
Dorchester	55	14	Glover	Alexand	3	1		1			1		1				7		
Dorchester	55	15	Glover	Alex 3d	1		1	1		1		1					5		
Dorchester	55	16	Glover	Alex Jr	2			1		1	1			1			6		
Dorchester	55	17	Greenleaf	Benj				1				1					2		
Dorchester	55	18	Glover	Edw	4			1	5	1	1		2	4			18		including the poor of the town
Dorchester	55	19	Gleason	James	1			1		2			1				5		
Dorchester	55	20	Gibson	Saml	2			1					1				4		
Dorchester	55	21	Gould	Alzah	3		1	1	2	3	1	1	1				13		
Dorchester	55	22	Glover	Josh				1		2		1					4		
Dorchester	55	23	Glover	Edward		1			2	2			1	1			7		
Dorchester	55	24	Glover	Ebenz				1		1	1		1	1			5		
Dorchester	55	25	Glover	Saml Jr			2			1			1				4		
Dorchester	55	26	Glover	Saml	1	1		1					1				4		
Dorchester	55	27	Gurley	Jno	2		1			1		1		2			7		
Dorchester	56	1	Glover	Enoch			1	1	1					1			4		
Dorchester	56	2	Glover	Enoch Jr			1	1						1			3		
Dorchester	56	3	Garvin	Patrick	1			1					1				3		
Dorchester	56	4	Harris	Thad. M	2	2	1	1		1		1	1	1			10		
Dorchester	56	5	Hitchborn	Benj			1	1	1				3	1	3		10		
Dorchester	56	6	How	Relief										2			2		
Dorchester	56	7	How	Abraham	2		3	4	1	1		1	2	1			15		
Dorchester	56	8	How	Joseph	1		1						1				3		
Dorchester	56	9	How	Elizabeth					1					1			2		
Dorchester	56	10	How	Isaac		2	4		1	1		1	1	1			11		
Dorchester	56	11	Hearsy	Stephen	1			1		1			1				4		
Dorchester	56	12	How	Isaac Jr		1	1						1				3		

TOWN	PG#	LN#	LAST NAME	FIRST NAME	FREE WHITE MALES					FREE WHITE FEMALES					TOTAL ALL OTHER	TOTAL SLAVES	TOTALS	DISTRICT/ TOWNSHIP	NOTES
					under 10	10 to 16	16 to 26	26 to 45	45 and over	under 10	10 to 16	16 to 26	26 to 45	45 and over					
Dorchester	56	13	Hunt	Jeremiah	1				1					1			3		
Dorchester	56	14	Howe	James B.	1	1	3	2				2					9		
Dorchester	56	15	Howe	Moses			1			2	1						4		
Dorchester	56	16	Howe	Jno		1	2		1		1		1	1			7		
Dorchester	56	17	Hall	Solomon	4		1			2			1				8		
Dorchester	56	18	Hearsy	Zerub			1						1				2		
Dorchester	56	19	Holden	Steph			1						1				2		
Dorchester	56	20	Holden	Justin	2	1		1					1	1			6		
Dorchester	56	21	Holden	Saml					1				1	1			3		
Dorchester	56	22	Holden	Phin			1		1	1			2	1			6		
Dorchester	56	23	Holden	Wm					1					1			2		
Dorchester	56	24	Humphrey	James	2		5	1		3	3		1	2			17		
Dorchester	56	25	Humphrey	Wm		1		1				1	1	1			5		
Dorchester	56	26	Howard	Jno C.			1			1	1				2		5		
Dorchester	56	27	Humphrey	Sus.			2	1				2		1			6		
Dorchester	56	28	Holden	Jno	2			1		2			1	1			7		
Dorchester	56	29	Hawes	Jno					1					1			2		
Dorchester	57	1	Herrington	Rus.	3		1	1					1	1			7		
Dorchester	57	2	Holmes	Ilsach	2			1		1			1				5		
Dorchester	57	3	Hanes	Edward			1			2			1				4		
Dorchester	57	4	Hitchings	Wm		1	1		1	2		2		1			8		
Dorchester	57	5	Holden	Ezekiel			1						1				2		
Dorchester	57	6	Hawes	Saml			1						1				2		
Dorchester	57	7	Hawes	Jesse	1		1						1				3		
Dorchester	57	8	Hearsy	Bela	2			1		1			1				5		
Dorchester	57	9	How	Jno Jun	1	1		1		1	1		1				6		
Dorchester	57	10	Humphrey	Abij				1		1			1	1			4		
Dorchester	57	11	Henly	Wm		1	1			2	1		1				6		
Dorchester	57	12	Hall	Richard		1	1		1			2		2			7		
Dorchester	57	13	Hall	Hopestill			1					1		1			3		
Dorchester	57	14	Hall	Jno	2	1		1		1			1	1			7		
Dorchester	57	15	Hall	Jno			1						1				2		
Dorchester	57	16	Hearsy	Amos	1			1				2		1			5		
Dorchester	57	17	Hawes	Joseph		1			1		1	1	2	1			7		
Dorchester	57	18	Jacobs	Benj	1	1	1	1		1		1	1		1		8		
Dorchester	57	19	Johnson	David	2			1		1	1	1					7		
Dorchester	57	20	Jordan	Oliver	2		2					1		1			6		
Dorchester	57	21	Jones	Eben				1					2				3		
Dorchester	57	22	Jones	Delivernc									2				2		
Dorchester	57	23	Jones	Elijah	2	1		1				1		1			6		
Dorchester	57	24	Kilton	James				1	1	1		1		1			4		
Dorchester	57	25	King	William	1		1			1		1					4		
Dorchester	57	26	Kent	Eliz	1									4			5		
Dorchester	57	27	Kilton	Ebenz	2			2					1	1			6		
Dorchester	57	28	Kilton	Eben Jr	4		1			2			1				8		
Dorchester	57	29	Kilton	Edward	2		1			1			1				5		
Dorchester	57	30	Kilton	Thankfull						2		1		1			4		
Dorchester	57	31	Lyon	Saml B.	4	3	1	1		1		1	1				12		
Dorchester	57	32	Leeds	Saml Jr	1			1		3		1	1	1			8		
Dorchester	57	33	Leeds	Saml					1					1			2		
Dorchester	58	1	Leeds	Saml 3rd	2			1		2			1				6		
Dorchester	58	2	Leeds	Miguel			4	1				2	1		1		9		
Dorchester	58	3	Litchfield	Josiah				1									1		
Dorchester	58	4	Lunders	Wm	1			1					1				3		
Dorchester	58	5	Leeds	Thomas	2	1		1	1	3			1				9		
Dorchester	58	6	Leeds	Josiah	2	1		1					1				5		
Dorchester	58	7	Leeds	Mary						1			2				3		
Dorchester	58	8	Leeds	Nathan		1		1					1				3		
Dorchester	58	9	Lewis	Jacob	1	1	1	1			1	1	1		5		12		
Dorchester	58	10	Leeds	Benj. B.	2		1	1	1	1			1				7		
Dorchester	58	11	Leeds	Jno				1					1				2		
Dorchester	58	12	Leeds	Susan			1					1		1			3		
Dorchester	58	13	Lyon	Thomas	1		1	1		1				1			5		
Dorchester	58	14	Leonard	*			3						1				4		
Dorchester	58	15	Low	Catharine		1				2		1	1				5		
Dorchester	58	16	Lemish	Jno	2	1		1		2	1		1				8		
Dorchester	58	17	Lewis	James	1			1		2	2		1				7		
Dorchester	58	18	Lyon	Benj	4			1		1			1				7		
Dorchester	58	19	Lapham	Elisha	2			1		2			2				7		
Dorchester	58	20	Morton	Perez				3		3	1	1	1		3		12		
Dorchester	58	21	Minott	George	1		2	1		1	1	1		2			10		
Dorchester	58	22	Minott	Jno		1	1	1	1	2	1	2					9		
Dorchester	58	23	Munro	Wm			1					1					2		
Dorchester	58	24	Munro	Saml					1					1			2		
Dorchester	58	25	Munro	Thom.			1			1	1		1				5		
Dorchester	58	26	Mann	Ephrm				1		1			1				3		
Dorchester	58	27	Marshall	Moses			1			2			1				4		
Dorchester	58	28	Mosely	Thom.	2	1	1	1		1	2	1	1	1			11		
Dorchester	58	29	Mann	Wm		1	1	1		2	1	1	1	1			9		

TOWN	PG#	LN#	HEADS OF HOUSEHOLD		FREE WHITE MALES					FREE WHITE FEMALES					TOTAL ALL OTHER	TOTAL SLAVES	TOTALS	DISTRICT/ TOWNSHIP	NOTES
			LAST NAME	FIRST NAME	under 10	10 to 16	16 to 26	26 to 45	45 and over	under 10	10 to 16	16 to 26	26 to 45	45 and over					
Dorchester	58	30	Miller	H.K.	3	1		2		1		1	1				9		
Dorchester	58	31	McCurney	Mic.					1	1				1			3		
Dorchester	58	32	Mosely	P.M.			1										1		
Dorchester	59	1	Morton	Henry					1	1			1				3		
Dorchester	59	2	Marshal	Joseph					1			1	1				3		
Dorchester	59	3	McIntosh	James	2		1			1		1					5		
Dorchester	59	4	Manning	George	1	1		1		2			1				6		
Dorchester	59	5	Morse	Jno			1			2	1						4		
Dorchester	59	6	Melish	Saml	1				1	1	1		1	1			6		
Dorchester	59	7	Mellish	Jno		1		1		5	1	2	1				11		
Dorchester	59	8	Minott	G.R.	1			1		1		1		1			5		
Dorchester	59	9	Mansfield	Shu	2		2	1		2		1	1				9		
Dorchester	59	10	Merrifield	Sam		1		1					1				3		
Dorchester	59	11	Merrifield	Abij.			1							2			3		
Dorchester	59	12	McIntosh	Steph.	3	1		1					1				6		
Dorchester	59	13	McIntosh	Jerem	1	1	1		1	3	1	1		1			10		
Dorchester	59	14	Mann	Wm	2			1		1	1		1				6		
Dorchester	59	15	Nicholson	Jno			2	1		3		1	2				9		
Dorchester	59	16	Neuman	Henry	3			1		2			1	1			8		
Dorchester	59	17	Niles	Ebenz	3	2	2	1		2			2				12		
Dorchester	59	18	Pierce	Saml		1	2	1	1	1	1		1				8		
Dorchester	59	19	Pierce	Edward	2	2	1	1	1	1		3	2				13		
Dorchester	59	20	Pierce	Joseph			2	1		1		1	1				6		
Dorchester	59	21	Pierce	Robert				1		1			1				3		
Dorchester	59	22	Pierce	Thom.	2	1		1		2	3		1				10		
Dorchester	59	23	Payson	Saml				1					1				2		
Dorchester	59	24	Payson	George	1	1		1		4			1				8		
Dorchester	59	25	Preston	Edwd	1	1	2	2		2	1	1	1				11		
Dorchester	59	26	Pope	John		1		1	1	1			1	2			7		
Dorchester	59	27	Pope	Elijah				1				2	1	1			5		
Dorchester	59	28	Pope	Fred & Wm	2		3	1		1		2					9		
Dorchester	59	29	Payson	Saml	2		2	1		1	1	1		1	1		10		
Dorchester	59	30	Pierce	Benj		1	2	1					2	1			7		
Dorchester	60	1	Pierce	Heph	1		1	1					2				5		
Dorchester	60	2	Preston	Jno		3		1		3			1				8		
Dorchester	60	3	Parker	Sally				1					1				2		
Dorchester	60	4	Pierce	Abrahm		1	1			3			1				6		
Dorchester	60	5	Preston	Sarah				1						3			4		
Dorchester	60	6	Palfrey	Jno	3			1		1	1	1					7		
Dorchester	60	7	Perry	Thom.	2				1	1		1					5		
Dorchester	60	8	Pierce	Jno		1	2	1	1	2	4		1				12		
Dorchester	60	9	Pratt	Phebe			7	2					1				10		
Dorchester	60	10	Paul	Wm	1			1		2			1				5		
Dorchester	60	11	Pierce	Jno	1	1	4		1		1	1		1			10		
Dorchester	60	12	Randall	Robt			1			2			1				4		
Dorchester	60	13	Robinson	Jas. Maj.		1	7	2		1	1		3	1			16		
Dorchester	60	14	Russel	Jno	1	1		3					1				6		
Dorchester	60	15	Robinson	Edwd	1	1	6	3				1	1				13		
Dorchester	60	16	Robinson	James	1		2	1	1				1				6		
Dorchester	60	17	Robinson	Jerus.	1			1					3	1	1		7		
Dorchester	60	18	Robertson	Jno		1			1			1	1		3		7		
Dorchester	60	19	Robinson	Thom		1		1					1				3		
Dorchester	60	20	Richards	Saml	1			1		1	1		1				5		
Dorchester	60	21	Richards	Wm		1	1		1	1	1		1				6		
Dorchester	60	22	Randal	Saml		1		1		3	2	1		1			9		
Dorchester	60	23	Rine	Dennis	1			1					1				3		
Dorchester	60	24	Robinson	Sukey									1	2			3		
Dorchester	60	25	Skinner	Jno	1	1		1	2			1	2	1			9		
Dorchester	60	26	Stetson	Thad	2			1	1			2					6		
Dorchester	60	27	Shepard	Ralph	2		4						1				8		
Dorchester	60	28	Spear	Aaron	3			1			1	2	1				8		
Dorchester	60	29	Sweetland	Rebec.						1		4					5		
Dorchester	60	30	Simmons	Benj	2			1		1			1				5		
Dorchester	61	1	Spear	Lem Jr	1		1			1			1				4		
Dorchester	61	2	Spear	Leml				1					1				2		
Dorchester	61	3	Spear	James	4			1					1				6		
Dorchester	61	4	Straton	Jona		1							1				2		
Dorchester	61	5	Swift	Nathl		1	1	1				2					5		
Dorchester	61	6	Smith	Saml			1		2				1	2			6		
Dorchester	61	7	Sumner	Wm	2	3	5	3	2	2	2	2	1		1		23		
Dorchester	61	8	Savil	Jno			1			1		1					3		
Dorchester	61	9	Thayer	Arodi				1				2		1			4		
Dorchester	61	10	Travis	Joshua	2			1		2			1				6		
Dorchester	61	11	Tolman	Ebenz			1	1	2			1		2			7		
Dorchester	61	12	Tolman	Jonas			1					2	1				5		
Dorchester	61	13	Tolman	John	2	1	1		1			1		1			7		
Dorchester	61	14	Tolman	Ezckl	1		2		1					1			5		
Dorchester	61	15	Tolman	Leml				1				1					2		
Dorchester	61	16	Tileston	Thom	1		1	1	3	1							8		
Dorchester	61	17	Tileston	Elisha					1				1	1			3		

TOWN	PG#	LN#	LAST NAME	FIRST NAME	FREE WHITE MALES					FREE WHITE FEMALES					TOTAL ALL OTHER	TOTAL SLAVES	TOTALS	DISTRICT/ TOWNSHIP	NOTES
					under 10	10 to 16	16 to 26	26 to 45	45 and over	under 10	10 to 16	16 to 26	26 to 45	45 and over					
Dorchester	61	18	Tileston	Eben		1		1			1	1	1	1			6		
Dorchester	61	19	Tileston	Timo			2		1					1			4		
Dorchester	61	20	Townsend	David	2				2	1	1	1	2				9		
Dorchester	61	21	Turner	Elisha		1		1		1			1				4		
Dorchester	61	22	Talbot	Benj			1	1					1				3		
Dorchester	61	23	Talbot	Hannah								1		1			2		
Dorchester	61	24	Thayer	Benj			1			1			1				3		
Dorchester	61	25	Thayer	Zach	2			1		3			1	1			8		
Dorchester	61	26	Tucker	Alh*	2		1	1					1				5		
Dorchester	61	27	Tolman	Ann	1		2	1		1			1				6		
Dorchester	61	28	Topliff	Saml Jr				1		2	1	1					5		
Dorchester	61	29	Tolman	Saml					1					1			2		
Dorchester	61	30	Tolman	Saml Jr	1			1		1		1					4		
Dorchester	62	1	Tolman	Wm	1			1		1	1		1				5		
Dorchester	62	2	Topliff	Saml		1	1	2	1	1	1		1				8		
Dorchester	62	3	Tucker	Elijah			2	1			1	1	1				6		
Dorchester	62	4	Tileston	Ezekiel	2	1			1	1			1	1			7		
Dorchester	62	5	Tucker	Phinehas				1		2		1	1				5		
Dorchester	62	6	Tileston	Euclid	3	1	2	1		1		1	1	1			11		
Dorchester	62	7	Trow	Richard			3	1		2			2				8		
Dorchester	62	8	Tolman	Benj D	1			1		2			1				5		
Dorchester	62	9	Tolman	James	1		1	1		1	1	1					6		
Dorchester	62	10	Trescott	Eben			2		1			1		1			5		
Dorchester	62	11	Trescott	Jona					1					1			2		
Dorchester	62	12	Trott	Luke			1		1	1			1	1			5		
Dorchester	62	13	Thatcher	Ceaser											2		2		
Dorchester	62	14	Underwood	Rufus			2			1		1					4		
Dorchester	62	15	Vaughn	Jno					1				1				2		
Dorchester	62	16	Vaughn	Mary								1		1			2		
Dorchester	62	17	Vinson	Benj	3			1		3			1	1			9		
Dorchester	62	18	Vose	William	3	1	1	1		2		1	1	2			12		
Dorchester	62	19	Vanicar	Henry	2			1		3			1				7		
Dorchester	62	20	Wales	Eben Esq.		2			1		1	3					7		
Dorchester	62	21	Withington	Saml		1	1	4	1	1		3	1				12		
Dorchester	62	22	Withington	Eb Jr	1	1	2		1			3		2			10		
Dorchester	62	23	Withington	Lem		2			1			2	1				6		
Dorchester	62	24	Withington	Noah			1			2			1				4		
Dorchester	62	25	Withington	Jno	1			1					1				3		
Dorchester	62	26	Withington	Edwd	2		4	3	1	1	1	3	1				16		
Dorchester	62	27	Withington	Thom	1			1				1		1			4		
Dorchester	62	28	Withington	Eliz										2			2		
Dorchester	62	29	Withington	Danl	3	2	2	1		1	1		1				11		
Dorchester	62	30	Withington	I.W.	2	1		1		1			1				6		
Dorchester	62	31	Withington	Phil.				1	1				1	1			4		
Dorchester	63	1	Withington	Eben				1	1	1			1	1			5		
Dorchester	63	2	Wentworth	Moses	1			1						1			3		
Dorchester	63	3	Wilson	Wm	3			1				1	1				6		
Dorchester	63	4	Wales	Eben Jun	2		1	1	1	2			2				9		
Dorchester	63	5	Wales	Stephen	1		1	1		2			1	1			7		
Dorchester	63	6	Wood	Rebeckah	2								1				3		
Dorchester	63	7	White	Mary		1	2							1			4		
Dorchester	63	8	White	Abijah					2	1				2			5		
Dorchester	63	9	Williams	Jno	4				1			2	1				8		
Dorchester	63	10	Wiswell	Jno	1			2		1			1				5		
Dorchester	63	11	White	Jno Jun	1			1		3			1				6		
Dorchester	63	12	White	John					1			1		2			4		
Dorchester	63	13	Wilson	Abiathar	1			1		1				1			4		
Dorchester	63	14	Wheelock	Abel	5				1	1	1	1	1				10		
Dorchester	63	15	Walker	Wm	1	1	1		1		1			1			6		
Dorchester	63	16	Walker	Spencer	1				1	7	2			1			12		
Dorchester	63	17	Whitney	Moses	1	1	1			1		1					5		
Dorchester	63	18	Williams	Eben			2	1						1			4		
Dorchester	63	19	Wiswell	Jno		1	1	1				1		3			7		
Dorchester	63	20	Wiswell	Ichabod	1			1		1	1		1				6		
Dorchester	63	21	Welch	Wm	2			1		2			1				6		
Dorchester	63	22	Williams	Caleb				1					1				2		
Dorchester	63	23	Williams	Thom	2		1	1			1		1				6		
Dorchester	63	24	Wild	Joseph			1	1		1	2	1					6		
Dorchester	63	25	Wiswell	Daniel	1	1			1	1	1			1			6		

TOWN	PG#	LN#	LAST NAME	FIRST NAME	FREE WHITE MALES					FREE WHITE FEMALES					TOTAL ALL OTHER	TOTAL SLAVES	TOTALS	DISTRICT/ TOWNSHIP	NOTES
					under 10	10 to 16	16 to 26	26 to 45	45 and over	under 10	10 to 16	16 to 26	26 to 45	45 and over					
Dover	149	1	Allen	Timothy		2	3		2			1		1	1		10		
Dover	149	2	Allen	Eleazer		1		1									2		
Dover	149	3	Allen	Perez	1		1			2		1					5		
Dover	149	4	Allen	Mary Wid.								1	1				2		
Dover	149	5	Ayers	Jesse	3		1			1		1					6		
Dover	149	6	Allen	Fisher		1	1	1				1		1			5		
Dover	149	7	Ayers	Eleazer	2		1					1					4		
Dover	149	8	Battle	Ebenzer		1		1				1		1			4		
Dover	149	9	Battle	John				2					2				4		
Dover	149	10	Battle	Ebenezer Jr	3	1		1			2		1				8		
Dover	149	11	Battle	Josiah	3	1		1			1	1	1				8		
Dover	149	12	Battle	Hezekiah	1	1		1		1	1		1				6		
Dover	149	13	Battle	Jonathan	1	2		1		2	1		1				8		
Dover	149	14	Bacon	William			1	1						1			3		
Dover	149	15	Bacon	Silas	3	1		1		1	1		1				8		
Dover	149	16	Baker	Jabez	1	1	1	1	1	1		1	2	2			11		
Dover	149	17	Baker	Jabez Jr	2		1					1					4		
Dover	149	18	Bacon	Josiah				1					2				3		
Dover	149	19	Burridge	John	1		1			2		1					5		
Dover	149	20	Barridge	Abigail Wid.		1	1				1	1	1				5		
Dover	149	21	Brown	John	2	1		1		2	1		1				8		
Dover	149	22	Battle	Nathaniel	1	1		1		2			1				6		
Dover	149	23	Bacon	Josiah Jr	3	2		1				1	1				8		
Dover	149	24	Bacon	Aaron			1			3		1					5		
Dover	149	25	Guy	Bethsheba										1			1		
Dover	149	26	Chickering	Nathaniel	5	2	1		2	1			1				12		
Dover	149	27	Cheney	Simon		1		1				1		1			4		
Dover	149	28	Chickering	Jesse	4			1		1			1				7		
Dover	150	1	Cheney	Joseph	2	1						1	1	1			7		
Dover	150	2	Chickering	John		1						1		1			3		
Dover	150	3	Chickering	John Jr	1		1					1					3		
Dover	150	4	Cleveland	David		2		1		1	3		1				8		
Dover	150	5	Carryl	George Doc	1		1	1		1		1	1	1			7		Rev. Benjamin Carryl included
Dover	150	6	Cheney	John	2			1		3			1				7		
Dover	150	7	Colburn	Danforth			1					1					2		
Dover	150	8	Chickering	David	1		1			2		1					5		
Dover	150	9	Draper	John & Nolten	1		2	1		1			2	1			8		
Dover	150	10	Draper	Jesse	1	1		1		1	1	1					6		
Dover	150	11	Draper	Michel		1	1	1		2			1				6		
Dover	150	12	Draper	Josiah	1			1			1		1	1			5		
Dover	150	13	Day	Ralph	1			1		3	1		1				7		
Dover	150	14	Dean	Luke	2	1			1	2			1				7		
Dover	150	15	Draper	Lidia Wid.								1	1				2		
Dover	150	16	Ellis	Jonathan			2	2		3			3	1			11		
Dover	150	17	Ellis	Rebecca										3			3		
Dover	150	18	Fisher	Jesse			1		2	1	3			1			8		
Dover	150	19	Fisher	Samuel	2	2	1	1			1		1				8		
Dover	150	20	Fisk	Nathaniel	1			1					1				3		
Dover	150	21	Fuller	David					1					1			2		
Dover	150	22	Fuller	David Jr	2	1		1		1	1		1				7		
Dover	150	23	Fisher	Mary Wid.										1			1		
Dover	150	24	Fisher	Moses	1		1			1		1					4		
Dover	150	25	Gooking	Daniel	1	1		1						1			4		
Dover	150	26	Gray	Benjamin		2	1			1		1		1			7		
Dover	150	27	Gay	Stephen	1			1		4			1				7		
Dover	150	28	Guy	Jonathan				1		1							2		
Dover	150	29	Haven	Joseph & Noah		1		1	1		1		1				5		
Dover	150	30	Hartshorn	Obed	1	1	1										3		
Dover	150	31	Hayns	Aaron	1	4		4		2			1	1			13		
Dover	150	32	Harden	Elias		1	1	1		1	2		1				7		
Dover	150	33	Jones	John Col & son Adam	1		1	1		1	2		1	1			8		
Dover	150	34	Jepson	John	2		1			1	2		1				7		
Dover	150	35	King	Solomon		1				1		1					3		
Dover	150	36	Leatherbee	Thomas		1		1					1				3		
Dover	150	37	Mason	John			1	1				1	1				4		
Dover	150	38	Mann	James		1	2	1				1	1				6		
Dover	150	39	Newell	Jesse	2		1			3		1					7		
Dover	150	40	Newell	Jonathan		2						1					3		
Dover	150	41	Petterlow	Eve									1	1			2		
Dover	150	42	Perry	Samuel	4		1	1		2		1	1				10		
Dover	150	43	Richards	Lemuel				1		1	1		1				4		
Dover	150	44	Richards	William		1		1			1		1				4		
Dover	150	45	Richards	Solomon	1	1		1		1	1		1				6		
Dover	150	46	Richards	Richard		1	1	1	1	1			1	1			7		
Dover	150	47	Ruggles	John		1		1		1			1				4		
Dover	150	48	Reed	John	2			2		1			1				6		
Dover	150	49	Richards	Joseph	4	1		1					1				7		
Dover	150	50	Richards	Josiah		1		1									2		
Dover	150	51	Robbins	Nathaniel	1			1		1			1				4		
Dover	150	52	Smith	Ebenezer		1	2	1		1		2		1			8		

TOWN	PG#	LN#	LAST NAME	FIRST NAME	FREE WHITE MALES					FREE WHITE FEMALES					TOTAL ALL OTHER	TOTAL SLAVES	TOTALS	DISTRICT/ TOWNSHIP	NOTES
					under 10	10 to 16	16 to 26	26 to 45	45 and over	under 10	10 to 16	16 to 26	26 to 45	45 and over					
Dover	150	53	Smith	Asa		1		1		1			1				4		
Dover	150	54	Tisdale	Billings			1		1			1	1				4		
Dover	150	55	Tisdale	Henry			1	2	1			2	1	1			8		
Dover	150	56	Wight	Amos					1			1	1				3		
Dover	151	1	Wilson	Epperaim			2		1					1			4		
Dover	151	2	Wilson	Samuel					1				2				3		
Dover	151	3	Whiting	William		1	1	1	1			2		1			7		
Dover	151	4	Williams	John			1						1				2		
Dover	151	5	Wight	Caleb	1		1				1						3		
Dover	151	6	Whiting	Aaron	4	1	2		1	2				1			11		
Dover	151	7	Whiting	Ellis				1					1				2		

TOWN	PG#	LN#	LAST NAME	FIRST NAME	FREE WHITE MALES					FREE WHITE FEMALES					TOTAL ALL OTHER	TOTAL SLAVES	TOTALS	DISTRICT/ TOWNSHIP	NOTES
					under 10	10 to 16	16 to 26	26 to 45	45 and over	under 10	10 to 16	16 to 26	26 to 45	45 and over					
Foxborough	22	1	Billings	Samuel		1		1	1	1	1	1					6		
Foxborough	22	2	Belcher	Eleazer		1	2	1						1			5		
Foxborough	22	3	Belcher	Eleazer Jr			1			1			1				3		
Foxborough	23	1	Boyden	Amos	1	1		1		1				1			5		
Foxborough	23	2	Boyden	Seth	2	1		1		3			1	1			9		
Foxborough	23	3	Baker	Samuel				1						1			2		
Foxborough	23	4	Bales	John		1		1				1		1			4		
Foxborough	23	5	Boyden	Elijah	3		1	1		1			1				7		
Foxborough	23	6	Billings	Jacob				1		3	1		1				6		
Foxborough	23	7	Belcher	Samuel	1			1		2			1				5		
Foxborough	23	8	Clark	Nathaniel			2	1	1		1			1			6		
Foxborough	23	9	Clark	Nathaniel				1						1			2		
Foxborough	23	10	Clark	William		1		1	1	1		3		1			7		
Foxborough	23	11	Clark	Elbridge	1			1					1				3		
Foxborough	23	12	Clark	Nathaniel Jr	2			1		1	1		1				6		
Foxborough	23	13	Carpenter	Sarah Wd									1	1			2		
Foxborough	23	14	Carpenter	Peter	3		1	1					1				6		
Foxborough	23	15	Carpenter	John	1	1		1		1			1				5		
Foxborough	23	16	Carpenter	Ezra	2	1			1	1	1	2	1				9		
Foxborough	23	17	Comee	John				1						1			2		
Foxborough	23	18	Comee	John Jr	1	2			1	3	1	1		1			10		
Foxborough	23	19	Comee	Oliver	2	2		1		2			1				8		
Foxborough	24	1	Comee	Benjamin			1	1		2	1		1				6		
Foxborough	24	2	Clap	Thomas	2		1	1	1	3			1	1			10		
Foxborough	24	3	Clark	Elkanah	3			1		1			1				6		
Foxborough	24	4	Clark	Jacob				1						1			2		
Foxborough	24	5	Clark	Thacher	4			1		1	1		1				8		
Foxborough	24	6	Clap	William	1	1	1	2		2	1	1	1				10		
Foxborough	24	7	Daniels	Francis					1	1	1		2				5		
Foxborough	24	8	Daufance	Martin		2			1	1				1			5		
Foxborough	24	9	Daniels	James	1			1		1			1				4		
Foxborough	24	10	Everett	Aaron		1	2		1		2	1		1			8		
Foxborough	24	11	Everett	Millie		1	2						1	1			5		
Foxborough	24	12	Everett	Joseph	2	1		1	1	1			1				7		
Foxborough	24	13	Everett	Richard		1		1				1	1	1			5		
Foxborough	24	14	Everett	Jesee				1		2			1				4		
Foxborough	24	15	Forrist	Samuel				1						1			2		
Foxborough	24	16	Forrist	Ebenezer				1		2	1		1				5		
Foxborough	24	17	Forrist	Amos				1					1				2		
Foxborough	24	18	Freeman	James			2		1	2	4			1			10		
Foxborough	24	19	Fisher	Ruth W						1		2	1				4		
Foxborough	24	20	Farrington	Eliph	3			1		1	1		1				7		
Foxborough	24	21	Guild	Elias	1	2	1	1		1	1		1				8		
Foxborough	24	22	Grover	Jabez			1	1			1		1				4		
Foxborough	24	23	Grover	Amasa	2	2		1		1			1	1			8		
Foxborough	24	24	Henry	Joseph		1	2		1	1				1			6		
Foxborough	24	25	Hewes	John	1	1		1		1	4		1				9		
Foxborough	24	26	Hodgers	Spencer	1	1	2		1			1		1			7		
Foxborough	24	27	Hartshorn	Jeremiah	1	2			1	1	1	1	1				8		
Foxborough	24	28	Hartshorn	Jesee	1			1		1		2	1				6		
Foxborough	24	29	Henry	Joseph V			1			2			1				4		
Foxborough	24	30	Jones	Frances	3		1	1		1	1		1				8		
Foxborough	24	31	Leonard	Mehitible W	1	1	1				1			1			5		
Foxborough	24	32	Leonard	Jacob	2		1	1		2			1				7		
Foxborough	24	33	Kingsbury	Nathan				1			2		1				4		
Foxborough	24	34	Morse	Margaret										1			1		
Foxborough	24	35	Morse	Daniel				1						1			2		
Foxborough	24	36	Morse	Elisha		1		1						2			4		
Foxborough	24	37	Morse	Solomon				1					1	1			3		
Foxborough	24	38	Morse	Timothy				1			1			1			3		
Foxborough	24	39	Morse	Jacob		1		1				1		1			4		
Foxborough	24	40	Morse	Jedediah				1		1				1			3		
Foxborough	24	41	Morse	Simon				1		1				1			3		
Foxborough	24	42	Morse	Amos		1	1	1		1	2			1			7		
Foxborough	24	43	Morse	Adam			2	1	1					1			5		
Foxborough	25	1	Morse	*	1	2		1		1		2	1				8		
Foxborough	25	2	Miller	Helfon	1			1		1	2	2		1			8		
Foxborough	25	3	Metcalf	Cornelius			1				1		1				3		
Foxborough	25	4	Morse	Jarvis			1			1			1				3		
Foxborough	25	5	Morse	John			1					1	1				3		
Foxborough	25	6	Morse	Samuel		1		1		1				1			4		
Foxborough	25	7	Morse	Asa		1		1						1			3		
Foxborough	25	8	Morse	Head	3			1		1			1				6		
Foxborough	25	9	Morse	Oliver	2			1					1				4		
Foxborough	25	10	Mason	Elias	2			1		1			1	1			6		
Foxborough	25	11	Paine	William		1		1					2	1			5		
Foxborough	25	12	Paine	Asa	3			1		1		1	1				7		
Foxborough	25	13	Paine	Anna Wd	1	2							1				4		
Foxborough	25	14	Plimpton	Asa	1	2	1		1			1	1	2			9		

TOWN	PG#	LN#	LAST NAME	FIRST NAME	FREE WHITE MALES					FREE WHITE FEMALES					TOTAL ALL OTHER	TOTAL SLAVES	TOTALS	DISTRICT/ TOWNSHIP	NOTES
					under 10	10 to 16	16 to 26	26 to 45	45 and over	under 10	10 to 16	16 to 26	26 to 45	45 and over					
Foxborough	25	15	Plimpton	Elijah	1	2			1				1				5		
Foxborough	25	16	Pettee	Benjamin		1	1		1				1	1			5		
Foxborough	25	17	Pettee	Hezekiah	3			1		2	1		1				8		
Foxborough	25	18	Pettee	David	1			1		1			1				4		
Foxborough	25	19	Pettee	William				1						1			2		
Foxborough	25	20	Pettee	Simon	1	1	2		1	2				1			8		
Foxborough	25	21	Payson	Swift			1		1		1	1		1			5		
Foxborough	25	22	Payson	Phillips		1	1			2			1				5		
Foxborough	25	23	Pratt	Isaac		1			1	1	1	1	1				6		
Foxborough	25	24	Pratt	Sarah Wd	1			1					3	1			6		
Foxborough	25	25	Pratt	Jessee					1	3	1		1				6		
Foxborough	25	26	Pratt	Abijah	2	1		1		1	1		1				7		
Foxborough	25	27	Pratt	Levi	1			1			1			1			4		
Foxborough	25	28	Paine	Stephen	1		1						1				3		
Foxborough	25	29	Patten	David		1			1	3			1	1			7		
Foxborough	25	30	Paine	Abial	3	1			1		1	2	1				9		
Foxborough	25	31	Paine	Enoch		1	1		1	1	1		1				6		
Foxborough	25	32	Paine	Jacob	3	2	2		1	1		1		1			11		
Foxborough	25	33	Pettee	Oliver	1	1	1	1		1	1		1				7		
Foxborough	25	34	Robins	Eleazer				1						1			2		
Foxborough	25	35	Robinson	Seth		1	1		1			2	1	1			7		
Foxborough	25	36	Rhods	Stephen	1			1		2	1		1				6		
Foxborough	25	37	Sumner	John				1				1		1			3		
Foxborough	25	38	Sumner	John Jr	3	1		1					1				6		
Foxborough	25	39	Sumner	William	2	1		1		1			1	1			9		
Foxborough	25	40	Stratton	James			2		1	1	2	1		1			8		
Foxborough	25	41	Stearns	Joshua	1	1			2		1	2		1			8		
Foxborough	25	42	Sumner	Roger	2			1		1			1				5		
Foxborough	25	43	Shephard	John		2			2	2				1			7		
Foxborough	25	44	Shephard	Jacob		2	2		1	2	2			1			11		
Foxborough	25	45	Shephard	Joseph			1		1		1	2		1			6		
Foxborough	25	46	Shephard	Joseph Jr				1		1			1				3		
Foxborough	25	47	Shephard	Ephraim	2	2	1		1		1			1			8		
Foxborough	26	1	Shearman	Job		2			1	2			1	1			6		
Foxborough	26	2	Stratton	George	1	1	1	1				2		1			7		
Foxborough	26	3	Stratton	Robert	1			1					1				3		
Foxborough	26	4	Shaw	Asa	1			1		3		1	1				7		
Foxborough	26	5	Shaw	George				1		1			1				3		
Foxborough	26	6	Shelley	Jonathan Jr	2			1		1			1	1			6		
Foxborough	26	7	Shelley	Jonathan			1	1					1	1			4		
Foxborough	26	8	Shaw	Thomas				1					1	1			3		
Foxborough	26	9	Shearman	Obed	1		1			2			1	1			6		
Foxborough	26	10	Shearman	John	1		1			1		1					4		
Foxborough	26	11	Stratton	Joseph			1			3		1	1				6		
Foxborough	26	12	Tiffany	Joseph		1		1		1			1				4		
Foxborough	26	13	Tiffany	Isaac			1				1						2		
Foxborough	26	14	Titus	Ruben		1			1				1				3		
Foxborough	26	15	Warren	Ebenezer	1	1		1	1	2	1	4		1			12		
Foxborough	26	16	Winston	Shadrack	4	2			1			1	1				9		
Foxborough	26	17	Wilson	Daniel	1	1			1		1	2					7		
Foxborough	26	18	Willis	Job		1			1				1	2			5		
Foxborough	26	19	Wood	Bridget Wd				1		1		2	1				5		
Foxborough	26	20	Wright	Lemuel				1				1	1				3		
Foxborough	26	21	Wright	Jonathan				1					1				2		
Foxborough	26	22	Wilbor	Elisha	1	1		1		1		1					5		
Foxborough	26	23	White	Asa	1			1			1						3		
Foxborough	26	24	Welman	Oliver	1			1			1	1	1				5		
Foxborough	26	25	White	Simeon	2			1		1	1		1				6		
Foxborough	26	26	Wight	Lemuel Jr	3			1		1	1						6		
Foxborough	26	27	Worse	Joel			4	1			1		1				8		
Foxborough	26	28	Foalhing		7			4	1	3	3	2	2	2			24		First name blank
Foxborough	26	29	Howe	Zadack		1			1			2		1					

TOWN	PG#	LN#	LAST NAME	FIRST NAME	FREE WHITE MALES					FREE WHITE FEMALES					TOTAL ALL OTHER	TOTAL SLAVES	TOTALS	DISTRICT/ TOWNSHIP	NOTES
					under 10	10 to 16	16 to 26	26 to 45	45 and over	under 10	10 to 16	16 to 26	26 to 45	45 and over					
Franklin	163	1	Whiting	John	2			2		1	1		2				8		
Franklin	163	2	Rockwood	Seth	1				1			1		2			4		
Franklin	163	3	Pond	Jamotis	2			1				1		2			6		
Franklin	163	4	Blake	Phillip	1		1		1		1		1	1			6		
Franklin	163	5	Pond	Oliver N.	1		1	1		2			1				6		
Franklin	163	6	Emmons	Nathaniel		1	2		1	1	1	2		1	1		10		
Franklin	163	7	Fisher	Asa	1	2		1		1			1				6		
Franklin	163	8	Metcalf	Hanan		1		1		1			1				4		
Franklin	163	9	Hartshorn	David	1		2	1		1			1	1			7		
Franklin	163	10	Fisher	Joseph	1		1	1		1			1				6		
Franklin	163	11	Fisher	Jabez				3		1			1				5		
Franklin	163	12	Allen	Abijah	2	1	3	1		1	1		1				10		
Franklin	163	13	Fisher	Daniel C.	1		1			2			1				5		
Franklin	163	14	Metcalf	Timothy	2	1		1		1			1				6		
Franklin	163	15	Metcalf	Ebenezer				1									1		
Franklin	163	16	Richardson	Amasa	2	1	1						1				5		
Franklin	163	17	Whiting	Asa		1	1			1	1	1					5		
Franklin	163	18	Adams	Thaddeus	1	1	1		1	1	1		1				7		
Franklin	163	19	Richardson	Daniel	2	1	2		1	3			1				10		
Franklin	163	20	Baker	Abijah	1		1	1		1	1						5		
Franklin	163	21	Gay	Timothy	4			1					1				6		
Franklin	163	22	Morse	Darius	3		1	1					1	1			7		
Franklin	163	23	Thurston	Daniel	2	1		1		1			1				6		
Franklin	163	24	Bacon	Charlotte									3				3		
Franklin	163	25	Gay	Thomas		2		1					1				4		
Franklin	163	26	Richardson	Ezekiel	1			1		2			1				5		
Franklin	163	27	Richardson	Leva			1			3	2		1				7		
Franklin	163	28	Adams	Nehemiah	2	2		2		1	2						9		
Franklin	163	29	Smith	Oliver N.	1		1	1		1			1				5		
Franklin	163	30	Adams	Nathaniel		1		1		1			2				5		
Franklin	163	31	Richardson	Eli		1	2	1					1	1			6		
Franklin	163	32	Adams	Wiliiam	1	2		1				1	2	1			8		
Franklin	164	1	Metcalf	Titus	1			1					1				3		
Franklin	164	2	Metcalf	James				1					1		1		3		
Franklin	164	3	Metcalf	Abijah	1		1	1		1	1		1				6		
Franklin	164	4	Hawkins	Sarah						1			1				2		
Franklin	164	5	Harding	Elisha		1		1		1			1				4		
Franklin	164	6	Harding	Asa	1		1	1		1			1				5		
Franklin	164	7	Lawrence	Ozias	1			1		1			1				4		
Franklin	164	8	Hills	Joseph					1				1				2		
Franklin	164	9	Hills	Jason	3			1		2			1				7		
Franklin	164	10	Hills	Joseph Jun	2			1					1				4		
Franklin	164	11	Gilmore	Mary						1			1				2		
Franklin	164	12	Gillmore	William	5			1				1					7		
Franklin	164	13	Miller	Joseph					1			1	1				3		
Franklin	164	14	Miller	Jesse	2			1		1		1					5		
Franklin	164	15	Gillmore	James					1			1		1			3		
Franklin	164	16	Gillmore	Robert		2		1		1		1					5		
Franklin	164	17	Pearce	John	3			1		1		1					6		
Franklin	164	18	Gillmore	James 2nd			1			1		1					3		
Franklin	164	19	Gillmore	David				1					1				2		
Franklin	164	20	Gillmore	Joseph	1			1					1	1			4		
Franklin	164	21	Mann	Susannah				1				2	1				4		
Franklin	164	22	Fisher	Timothy		1		1					2	1			5		
Franklin	164	23	Fisher	Timothy Junr	3	1		1		1	1		1				8		
Franklin	164	24	Guild	Samuel	1	1	1	1		2	2		1	1			10		
Franklin	164	25	Guild	Ebenezer	1		2		1	2		2		1			9		
Franklin	164	26	Keaton	Thankful	1		1	1		1	1		1				6		
Franklin	164	27	Woodward	Nathan	1			1			1		1	1			5		
Franklin	164	28	Woodward	James	2	1		1		1	2		1				8		
Franklin	164	29	Hawes	Josiah				1			1						2		
Franklin	164	30	Hawes	Levi		1		1		2		1	1				6		
Franklin	164	31	Ware	Jabez				1					1				2		
Franklin	165	1	Ware	Phinehas		2	1	1		1		2	1				8		
Franklin	165	2	Hawes	Joseph					1			1	1				3		
Franklin	165	3	Hawes	Amos	1	1	1	1			1		2				7		
Franklin	165	4	Metcalf	Hannah									1				1		
Franklin	165	5	Fisher	Levi		1		1		2	3		1				8		
Franklin	165	6	Metcalf	Calvin	2		1	1				1	1				8		
Franklin	165	7	Adams	Peter					1				1	1			3		
Franklin	165	8	Adams	James	1		1	1		1		1	1				6		
Franklin	165	9	Dean	Ebenezer					1				1				2		
Franklin	165	10	Dean	Ichabod		1	2	1				2	1				7		
Franklin	165	11	Parkhurst	Moses	1			1		2			1				5		
Franklin	165	12	Adams	Moses	1	2		1		1		1	1				7		
Franklin	165	13	Whiting	Peter		1	1	1							1		4		
Franklin	165	14	Fairbanks	Asa				1					1	1			3		
Franklin	165	15	Fairbanks	Asa Junr	1	1	1	1		2	2		1				9		
Franklin	166	1	Harding	James	1			1			2		1				5		

TOWN	PG#	LN#	HEADS OF HOUSEHOLD		FREE WHITE MALES					FREE WHITE FEMALES					TOTAL ALL OTHER	TOTAL SLAVES	TOTALS	DISTRICT/ TOWNSHIP	NOTES
			LAST NAME	FIRST NAME	under 10	10 to 16	16 to 26	26 to 45	45 and over	under 10	10 to 16	16 to 26	26 to 45	45 and over					
Franklin	166	2	Ware	Jesse			1	1	1	1		1	1	1			7		
Franklin	166	3	Ware	Amariah	1		2	1			1		1	1			7		
Franklin	166	4	Blake	Abraham Jr	3			1	1	1			1		1		8		
Franklin	166	5	Bailey	Prince											2		2		
Franklin	166	6	Pond	Oliver Junr	1			1		2			2				6		
Franklin	166	7	Rockwood	Timothy	1	1			1		1	1	1				6		
Franklin	166	8	Rockwood	Samuel			1		1	1	1			2			6		
Franklin	166	9	Pond	Oliver					1				1	1			3		
Franklin	166	10	Pond	Goldsbury	1	1		1					1				4		
Franklin	166	11	Daniels	Joel		1		1		1			1				4		
Franklin	166	12	Thurston	Abijah		1	1		1	1	2			1			7		
Franklin	166	13	Thurston	Elizabeth									1	1			2		
Franklin	166	14	Metcalf	Nathan	2	1	1	1		2			1				8		
Franklin	166	15	Metcalf	Asa		1		1	1	1	1		1				5		
Franklin	166	16	Lawrence	Cephas	4	1		1		3			1				10		
Franklin	166	17	Daniels	Joseph	2			1		2		1					6		
Franklin	166	18	Daniels	Unity							1	1	1				3		
Franklin	166	19	Blake	Solomon		1		1					1	1			4		
Franklin	166	20	Pond	Elihu	2		1	1		1	1		1	2			9		
Franklin	166	21	Metcalf	Billy		1	2		1		1		1				8		
Franklin	166	22	Pond	Timothy	2			1		2			1				6		
Franklin	166	23	Pond	Benajah	2			1		2			1				6		
Franklin	166	24	Pond	Hezekiah		1		1		1			1	2			6		
Franklin	166	25	Pond	Ichabod	1			1					1				3		
Franklin	166	26	Pond	Bejamin				3	1								4		
Franklin	166	27	Ellis	Royal	1			1				1					3		
Franklin	166	28	Partridge	Eleazer		1			1	1	1	1		1			6		
Franklin	166	29	Bacon	Joseph		1	1			1			1				4		
Franklin	166	30	Bacon	ruth						1			2				3		
Franklin	166	31	Bacon	Seth		1		1					1				3		
Franklin	166	32	Fisher	Jason	2	2		1		1	1	1	1				9		
Franklin	166	33	Jackson	William			1						2				3		
Franklin	166	34	Adams	John	1	2	2		1	3	1	1		1			12		
Franklin	166	35	Lathbridge	Samuel		1		1		1	1		2				6		
Franklin	166	36	Lathbridge	James			1		1	1			1				3		
Franklin	167	1	Lincoln	William	1			1					3	1			6		
Franklin	167	2	Perry	Simeon		1	1			1		1					4		
Franklin	167	3	Blake	Calvin		1		1		2	1		1				6		
Franklin	167	4	Blake	Robert Jun	1		1		1			1		1			5		
Franklin	167	5	Daniels	Amariah		1		1			1		1				4		
Franklin	167	6	Clark	Asa				1					1				2		
Franklin	167	7	Cleavland	Samuel	1		1					1					3		
Franklin	167	8	Fisher	Eleazer Jun	2		1	1	1	1	1		1				8		
Franklin	167	9	Smith	G*	1	1		1					1				4		
Franklin	167	10	Pond	Solomon	1			1	1				2				6		
Franklin	167	11	Torry	John				1				3	1				5		
Franklin	167	12	Metcalf	John		1	2	1			1		1				6		
Franklin	167	13	Ellis	Daniel	1			1		2			1				5		
Franklin	167	14	Lawrence	Daniel	2			1		1			1				5		
Franklin	167	15	Fisher	Lewis	2	1		1	1	1		1	1		1		9		
Franklin	167	16	Fuller	Augustine	1			1		1			1				4		
Franklin	167	17	Lathbridge	Samuel Junr		2	1		1	1	1			1			7		
Franklin	167	18	Kingsbury	Timothy	1		1		1				1	1			5		
Franklin	167	19	Kingsbury	James	2			1					1				4		
Franklin	167	20	Boyd	Willard				1		2			2		1		6		
Franklin	167	21	Turner	Calvin	2			1		1		1	1				6		
Franklin	167	22	Perrigo	James Junr	2			1					1				4		
Franklin	167	23	Miller	Nathaniel	1		1	1				1					4		
Franklin	167	24	Boyd	John				1					1				2		
Franklin	167	25	Williams	Abigail	3						2		1				6		
Franklin	167	26	Kingsbury	Aaron		1				1	1	1					4		
Franklin	167	27	Kingsbury	Elizabeth		1				1			1				3		
Franklin	167	28	Kingsbury	Benjamin	2		1	1		2		1					7		
Franklin	167	29	Whiting	Joseph				1			1		1				3		
Franklin	167	30	Metcalf	James Junr		1	1	1		2		2	1				8		
Franklin	167	31	Kingsbury	Stephen	1		2		1	1			1				6		
Franklin	167	32	Clark	Dyer		1	2	1					1				5		
Franklin	167	33	Clark	Dyer Jun				1		2			1				4		
Franklin	167	34	Fairbanks	Willard		1		1				1					3		
Franklin	168	1	Morse	Sarah			1				1		1	1			4		
Franklin	168	2	Pond	Robert				1					1	1			3		
Franklin	168	3	Pond	Robert Junr	3		1	1		1	1	2	1				10		
Franklin	168	4	Daniels	Nathan	1	2			1	2			1	1			8		
Franklin	168	5	Daniels	Adams			1	1				1	1				4		
Franklin	168	6	Richardson	Abigail		1						3	1	1			6		
Franklin	168	7	Rockwood	Benjamin	1				1	1				1			4		
Franklin	168	8	Fisher	Caleb	2		2	1		1		2	1				9		
Franklin	168	9	Fisher	Hezekiah				1					1				2		
Franklin	168	10	Fisher	Amos	1			1		1			1				5		

TOWN	PG#	LN#	LAST NAME	FIRST NAME	FREE WHITE MALES					FREE WHITE FEMALES					TOTAL ALL OTHER	TOTAL SLAVES	TOTALS	DISTRICT/ TOWNSHIP	NOTES
					under 10	10 to 16	16 to 26	26 to 45	45 and over	under 10	10 to 16	16 to 26	26 to 45	45 and over					
Franklin	168	11	Fisher	Nathan					1					1			2		
Franklin	168	12	Pond	Malkiah		1	1	1	1					1			5		
Franklin	168	13	Pond	Samuel			2	2						1			5		
Franklin	168	14	Pond	William	2			1		1	1		1				6		
Franklin	168	15	Fisher	Moses	1		1			3			1				6		
Franklin	168	16	Dean	Seth		1	1	1				1	1				5		
Franklin	168	17	Ellis	Joseph				1						1			2		
Franklin	168	18	Ellis	Timothy	1	1	2	1		1	1	1	1	1			10		
Franklin	168	19	Allen	John		2	5		1	1		2		1			12		
Franklin	168	20	Metcalf	Samuel		1	1	1	1	1		2		1			8		
Franklin	168	21	Metcalf	Jonathan	1		2	1		4		1	1				10		
Franklin	168	22	White	Elihu			1							1			2		
Franklin	168	23	White	Jonathan	1		1			1			1				4		
Franklin	168	24	Norcrose	Asa	1			1						2			4		
Franklin	168	25	Metcalf	Silence	1							1	1				3		
Franklin	168	26	White	Nathan	1			1		2	1	1					6		
Franklin	168	27	Brown	Joseph	3	1		1		1	1	1	1				9		
Franklin	168	28	Hewes	Solomon	1		2	1						1			5		
Franklin	168	29	Clark	Samuel	1		2	1			1	1	1	1			8		
Franklin	168	30	Daniels	Henry				1					1	1			3		
Franklin	168	31	Daniels	David	4		1	1					1	1			8		
Franklin	168	32	Daniels	Eleazer	1	1		1	1	2			1	1			8		
Franklin	168	33	Makepiece	William	1			1		1			1				4		
Franklin	168	34	Seaver	Ichabod		1		1		1	1	1	1				6		
Franklin	168	35	Cobb	Luther	1			1				1	1				4		
Franklin	168	36	Thayer	Nathaniel	2	1	2	1		1	1	1	1				10		
Franklin	169	1	Knapp	Moses	3	1	5	3	1	1	1	1	1				17		
Franklin	169	2	Scott	Ichabod	1			1		1				1			4		
Franklin	169	3	Cook	Jaire	3			1			1	1	1	1			8		
Franklin	169	4	Richardson	John				1				1		1			3		
Franklin	169	5	Richardson	John W.	1		1			1		1					4		
Franklin	169	6	Ware	Eli	1		3	1				1	1	3			10		
Franklin	169	7	Aldis	Ebenezer				1				2		1			4		
Franklin	169	8	Smith	Samuel			1	1		2	1		1				6		
Franklin	169	9	Freeman	Otis	3	1								1			5		
Franklin	169	10	Ware	Billy	1			1					1	1			4		
Franklin	169	11	Scott	David				1					1				2		
Franklin	169	12	Sayles	Daniel	2	2	1	1		1	1	2	1				11		
Franklin	169	13	Cook	Whipple	2		1			1			1				5		
Franklin	169	14	Darling	Benjamin	1		1			1			1				4		
Franklin	169	15	Braly	Silence										1			1		
Franklin	169	16	Herrington	James	2		1			2	2		1				8		
Franklin	169	17	Heaton	Samuel	2			1		2	2		1	1			9		
Franklin	169	18	Mann	Elias	1			1				2	1	1			6		
Franklin	169	19	Mann	Thomas	2	1	1	1		1	1	1	1				9		
Franklin	169	20	Mann	Nathan		1		1		1	1	2		1			7		
Franklin	169	21	Whiting	Elizabeth										1			1		
Franklin	169	22	Whiting	Joseph 2nd	3	1	1	1		1			2				9		
Franklin	169	23	Gould	Peter A.	2			1					1		1		5		
Franklin	169	24	Treddle	Syer											4		4		
Franklin	169	25	Pond	Barzilla	1	1		1		2	1	1	2				9		
Franklin	169	26	Woodward	Holland	3			1			1		1				6		
Franklin	169	27	Terry	John Junr			1			1	1	2					5		
Franklin	169	28	Morse	Jason	3		1	1		1	1		1				8		
Franklin	169	29	Fisher	Peter		1	3	1		1	1	1	1	1			10		
Franklin	169	30	Butterworth	Noah	1		1	1		3	2		1				9		
Franklin	169	31	Adams	Timothy			1				1	1					3		

TOWN	PG#	LN#	HEADS OF HOUSEHOLD		FREE WHITE MALES					FREE WHITE FEMALES					TOTAL ALL OTHER	TOTAL SLAVES	TOTALS	DISTRICT/ TOWNSHIP	NOTES
			LAST NAME	FIRST NAME	under 10	10 to 16	16 to 26	26 to 45	45 and over	under 10	10 to 16	16 to 26	26 to 45	45 and over					
Medfield	85	1	Adams	Thomas				2	1		1		1	1			6		
Medfield	85	2	Adams	Elijah		2			1	1	1	1		1			7		
Medfield	85	3	Admas	Elijah Jun	1			1		1		1					4		
Medfield	85	4	Adams	Gershom	1				1		1			1	1		5		
Medfield	85	5	Adams	George W.				1		1			1	1			4		
Medfield	85	6	Adams	Darius	1			1		1			1				4		
Medfield	85	7	Allen	Noah				1					1				2		
Medfield	85	8	Allen	Jonathan				1				1	1				3		
Medfield	85	9	Allen	Phinehas	4			1		1		2	1				9		
Medfield	85	10	Allen	Nathan			2	1				1	1				5		
Medfield	85	11	Allen	Sarah									1				1		
Medfield	85	12	Allen	James		1		1		1		2	2				7		
Medfield	85	13	Allen	Eliakim				1					1				2		
Medfield	85	14	Allen	Sarah Jun	1								1				2		
Medfield	85	15	Allen	William	3	1		1		1			1				7		
Medfield	85	16	Alby	Asa			1	1					1				3		
Medfield	85	17	Armsby	Ader									2				2		
Medfield	85	18	Archelus	James											2		2		
Medfield	86	1	Baxter	John	1		2			1	1		2				8		
Medfield	86	2	Boyden	Asa		1		1			1	1	1				5		
Medfield	86	3	Boyden	Silas	1			1		2			1				5		
Medfield	86	4	Boyden	Amos	3			1					1				5		
Medfield	86	5	Breck	Joseph		1	1	1		1		2	1				7		
Medfield	86	6	Breck	Jonathan	4	1		1		1			1				8		
Medfield	86	7	Breck	Edward	2			1		1			1				5		
Medfield	86	8	Bradford	Walter	1	1		1		2		1					6		
Medfield	86	9	Bullen	Moses			2	1				1	1				5		
Medfield	86	10	Bullen	Ichabod				1					1				2		
Medfield	86	11	Bullard	Silas	1			1		1	1		1				5		
Medfield	86	12	Bullard	John			1						2				3		
Medfield	86	13	Bran	Lucy											1		1		
Medfield	86	14	Clark	Edward				1			1		1				3		
Medfield	86	15	Clark	Joseph				1					1				2		
Medfield	86	16	Clark	Seth			1	1					1				3		
Medfield	86	17	Clark	Ebenezer	1	1	1	1		1	1		1	1	1		9		
Medfield	86	18	Clark	Joseph Jun		1	1					1					3		
Medfield	86	19	Clark	Elias				1			1		1				3		
Medfield	86	20	Clark	Jacob				1					1				2		
Medfield	86	21	Clark	Elisha	1			1		1			1				4		
Medfield	86	22	Clark	David		1		1				1	1	1			5		
Medfield	86	23	Clark	Aaron	2			1				1					4		
Medfield	86	24	Clark	Abigail			1						1				?		
Medfield	86	25	Clark	William	1	1		1	1	1	1	2	1				9		
Medfield	86	26	Cheney	Timothy	1	2			1	1		1	1				7		
Medfield	86	27	Cheny	Levi				1		1			1	1			4		
Medfield	86	28	Chenery	Oliver	3		1	1		1	1		1				8		
Medfield	86	29	Chenery	Ephraim			2	1	1	1	1		1				7		
Medfield	86	30	Chenery	Simeon	1	1			1	2	1			2			8		
Medfield	86	31	Chenery	Elisha		1		1					1				2		
Medfield	87	1	Cleveland	Edward		1		1				1		1			4		
Medfield	87	2	Cleveland	Zimri	4	1		1			2	1	1				10		
Medfield	87	3	Cole	Asa	2			1		1			1	1			6		
Medfield	87	4	Cutler	Simeon					2	1		2		1			6		
Medfield	87	5	Cutler	Oliver	1			1		1	1		1				5		
Medfield	87	6	Daniels	Noah	1		2	1		1	1		1				7		
Medfield	87	7	Ellis	Abner	2			1					1				4		
Medfield	87	8	Ellis	Jemima				1					1				2		
Medfield	87	9	Ellis	Nathan				1					1				2		
Medfield	87	10	Ellis	Obed			1						1				2		
Medfield	87	11	Ellis	Oliver			1			1			1	1			4		
Medfield	87	12	Ellis	George	1	1		1		1	1		1				6		
Medfield	87	13	Ellis	Sarah								2		1			3		
Medfield	87	14	Ellis	Abigail									1				1		
Medfield	87	15	Fisher	John			1	1					1	1			4		
Medfield	87	16	Fisher	Obed		1		1		1	1		1				5		
Medfield	87	17	Fisher	Luther	1			1		2	1		1				6		
Medfield	87	18	Fisher	Paul	1		1	1		2	1		1				7		
Medfield	87	19	Fisher	Dorcas									1				1		
Medfield	87	20	Fisk	Jonathan			1	1		1			1				4		
Medfield	87	21	Fuller	Elizabeth								1	1				2		
Medfield	87	22	Fuller	John	1	1			1	1	2		1				7		
Medfield	87	23	Fisher	Mary			1	1					1				3		
Medfield	87	24	Gay	Jason	1			1		1			2				5		
Medfield	87	25	Green	Warwick											7		7		
Medfield	87	26	Hamant	Asa			1	1					1				3		
Medfield	87	27	Hamant	Asa Jun			1										1		
Medfield	87	28	Hamant	Francis			2		1				1				4		
Medfield	87	29	Hamant	Timothy			1					1					2		
Medfield	88	1	Harding	Keziah								1		1			2		

TOWN	PG#	LN#	LAST NAME	FIRST NAME	FREE WHITE MALES under 10	10 to 16	16 to 26	26 to 45	45 and over	FREE WHITE FEMALES under 10	10 to 16	16 to 26	26 to 45	45 and over	TOTAL ALL OTHER	TOTAL SLAVES	TOTALS	DISTRICT/ TOWNSHIP	NOTES
Medfield	88	2	Harding	Moses B.		1		1		1		1	1				5		
Medfield	88	3	Harding	Abraham	2			1			1		2				6		
Medfield	88	4	Harding	Nathan		1	1		1			1		1			5		
Medfield	88	5	Harthorn	Moses	4		1	1		2	1		1				10		
Medfield	88	6	Hill	Mary	1									1			2		
Medfield	88	7	Hinsdale	Abigail										1			1		
Medfield	88	8	Hosker	William				1						1			2		
Medfield	88	9	Jerauld	James		1		1	1			1					4		
Medfield	88	10	Johnson	Joseph		2		1	1	1		1		1			7		
Medfield	88	11	Kingsbury	Amos			1	1					1	1			4		
Medfield	88	12	Kitterage	Peter											4		4		
Medfield	88	13	Lovell	David				1									1		
Medfield	88	14	Lovell	David Jun				1					1	1			3		
Medfield	88	15	Lovell	Dyer		1		1					3	1			6		
Medfield	88	16	Lovell	Moses	1	2		2				2	1	1			9		
Medfield	88	17	Lawrence	Elihu	1			1		3	2	1	1				9		
Medfield	88	18	Mann	Elias		1				1				1			3		
Medfield	88	19	Mann	Rufus	2		1	1			1	1	1				7		
Medfield	88	20	Mason	Asa			1	1					1	1			4		
Medfield	88	21	Mason	Amos		1	1		1			2		1			6		
Medfield	88	22	Mason	Johnson	3			1		1		1	1				7		
Medfield	88	23	Mason	Alpheus	1	1	2	1		1	1	1	1		1		10		
Medfield	88	24	Morse	Eliakim		1		1					2				4		
Medfield	88	25	Morse	Eliakim Jun	1		1	1		1	1		1				6		
Medfield	88	26	Morse	Thaddeus				1		3			1				5		
Medfield	88	27	Morse	James		1		1	1					1			4		
Medfield	88	28	Onion	David	1	2		1					1	1			6		
Medfield	89	1	Partridge	Nathan				1						2			3		
Medfield	89	2	Partridge	Oliver	2			1					1				4		
Medfield	89	3	Peters	Adam				1				1					3		
Medfield	89	4	Peters	William		1	2	1		1		1					6		
Medfield	89	5	Peters	Jethro				1				1					2		
Medfield	89	6	Perry	Daniel		1	1	1					2	2			7		
Medfield	89	7	Perry	Eleazer				1		2	1		1				5		
Medfield	89	8	Plimpton	Ruth										1			1		
Medfield	89	9	Plimpton	Silas		2		1				2					5		
Medfield	89	10	Plimpton	Amos				1					1				2		
Medfield	89	11	Plimpton	Abigail			1							1			2		
Medfield	89	12	Plimpton	Sarah			1							2			3		
Medfield	89	13	Plimpton	Augustus		1	1						1	1			4		
Medfield	89	14	Plimpton	David				2		2		1		1	1		7		
Medfield	89	15	Plimpton	David Jun	2			1		2	1		1				7		
Medfield	89	16	Plimpton	Joseph				1		1			1				3		
Medfield	89	17	Prentiss	Thomas Rev	3	1	2	1	1	4	1	1	1	2			17		
Medfield	89	18	Pratt	Dan	2	1	1						1				5		
Medfield	89	19	Ruggels	Josiah	1			1		3			1				6		
Medfield	89	20	Seaver	Joshua		1		1						1			3		
Medfield	89	21	Seabry	Elijah	1		1			1		1					4		
Medfield	89	22	Smith	Isaiah	2			1		3			1				7		
Medfield	89	23	Smith	Lebbens	1			1		2	1		1				6		
Medfield	89	24	Smith	Drucilla	2					2		2	1				7		
Medfield	89	25	Smith	John				1	1				4	1			7		
Medfield	89	26	Smith	John Jun				1					1				2		
Medfield	89	27	Smith	Rachel				1		1			1				3		
Medfield	89	28	Smith	Ephraim	1			1		1	1		1				5		
Medfield	89	29	Smith	Jonathan	1	1		1			1	1		1			6		
Medfield	89	30	Smith	Jeremiah			1			1			1				3		
Medfield	89	31	Smith	Titus	2			1		2	1		1				7		
Medfield	90	1	Smith	Enos	1	1		1				1	1				5		
Medfield	90	2	Smith	Aaron				1		2			1				4		
Medfield	90	3	Smith	Amos				1	1	1	1	2	1				7		
Medfield	90	4	Stearns	Nathaniel	1			1		4			1	1			8		
Medfield	90	5	Theboult	John				1						2			3		
Medfield	90	6	Thompson	John	1			1		2			1				5		
Medfield	90	7	Tilden	Stephen	1		1					2					4		
Medfield	90	8	Townsend	Sarah				1		1				1			3		
Medfield	90	9	Turner	Calvin	3			1		2			1				7		
Medfield	90	10	Turner	George				1		1	1			1			4		
Medfield	90	11	Wheelock	Eleazer				1						1			2		
Medfield	90	12	Wheelock	Ephraim		1	2	1					1	1			6		
Medfield	90	13	Wheelock	Oliver			1						1				2		
Medfield	90	14	Wight	Jonathan			1		1	1		1	1	2	1		8		
Medfield	90	15	Wight	Jonathan Junr	3			1		1			2				7		
Medfield	90	16	Wight	Nathan		1	1						1				3		
Medfield	90	17	Wight	Moses	1	2		1		1	1	1	1				8		
Medfield	90	18	Wight	Asa				1		2			1				4		
Medfield	90	19	Wheelock	Seth		1	1			2	1						5		
Medfield	90	20	Woodward	Artemas			3	1		1	1	1	1				8		

TOWN	PG#	LN#	LAST NAME	FIRST NAME	FREE WHITE MALES					FREE WHITE FEMALES					TOTAL ALL OTHER	TOTAL SLAVES	TOTALS	DISTRICT/ TOWNSHIP	NOTES
					under 10	10 to 16	16 to 26	26 to 45	45 and over	under 10	10 to 16	16 to 26	26 to 45	45 and over					
Medway East Parish	91	1	Abbee	Joseph	1	1		1		2			1				6		
Medway East Parish	91	2	Adams	Oliver		1		1			1		1				4		
Medway East Parish	91	3	Adams	Silvanus	1			1					1		1		4		
Medway East Parish	91	4	Adams	Jonathan 3rd		1	1	1					1				4		
Medway East Parish	91	5	Adams	Jasper	2			1		1		1	1				6		
Medway East Parish	91	6	Adams	Jonathan Jun				1					1				2		
Medway East Parish	91	7	Adams	Silas	2			1					1				4		
Medway East Parish	91	8	Adams	Micah	2			1		2			2				7		
Medway East Parish	91	9	Adams	Jonathan					1				1				2		
Medway East Parish	91	10	Ballou	Thomas	2			1		1			1				5		
Medway East Parish	91	11	Bullen	Daniel				1		1	1		1				4		
Medway East Parish	91	12	Bullen	Jonathan		1	1	1		2			2				7		
Medway East Parish	91	13	Bullen	Jeduthun	2	1		1		1			1				6		
Medway East Parish	91	14	Bullard	Abigail		1						1	1				3		
Medway East Parish	91	15	Bullard	Timothy			1					1					2		
Medway East Parish	91	16	Bullard	Ralph	1		1					1					3		
Medway East Parish	91	17	Bullard	Adam		1		1		1	2		1				6		
Medway East Parish	91	18	Bullard	Liberty	1	1						1					3		
Medway East Parish	91	19	Barber	George					1		3	1		1			6		
Medway East Parish	91	20	Barber	Seneca	1			1		1			1				4		
Medway East Parish	91	21	Boyden	Jairus	1		1	1		1			1	1			6		
Medway East Parish	91	22	Broad	Ephraim			1						1				2		
Medway East Parish	91	23	Bridges	Elijah	1		1					1					3		
Medway East Parish	91	24	Clark	Elijah			1	1					1				3		
Medway East Parish	91	25	Clark	Theodire		1		1			1	1			1		5		
Medway East Parish	91	26	Clark	Timothy			1	1	1				1				4		
Medway East Parish	91	27	Clark	Stephen		1	1	1		2	1	1	1	2			10		
Medway East Parish	91	28	Clark	John Jun			1			1			1				3		
Medway East Parish	91	29	Clark	John 3rd	2		1	1					1				5		
Medway East Parish	91	30	Clark	Oliver	1			1		1			1				4		
Medway East Parish	91	31	Chenery	Benjamin	1		1	1		3			1				7		
Medway East Parish	91	32	Coffee	Ishmael											5		5		
Medway East Parish	92	1	Curtis	Jeremiah	2	1	1	1		2			1				8		
Medway East Parish	92	2	Curtis	Rachel									1				1		
Medway East Parish	92	3	Daniels	Jeremiah				1					1				2		
Medway East Parish	92	4	Daniels	Jeremiah Jun		3		1					1				5		
Medway East Parish	92	5	Daniels	Abigail		1	1					1	1				4		
Medway East Parish	92	6	Daniels	Moses			2	1			2		1				6		
Medway East Parish	92	7	Daniels	Amos			1						1				2		
Medway East Parish	92	8	Daniels	Joseph				1					1				2		
Medway East Parish	92	9	Daniels	Lemuel	1	1		1				1	1				5		
Medway East Parish	92	10	Daniels	Asa		1		1					1				3		
Medway East Parish	92	11	Daniels	Asa Jun		1		1		1			1				4		
Medway East Parish	92	12	Daniels	Jesse			1			1	2		1				5		
Medway East Parish	92	13	Daniels	Henry				1					1				2		
Medway East Parish	92	14	Daniels	Henry Jr		1		1		1			1				4		
Medway East Parish	92	15	Daniels	Sabin	1			1					1				3		
Medway East Parish	92	16	Ellis	Henry				1				1		1			3		
Medway East Parish	92	17	Ellis	Henry Jun				1		1		1					3		
Medway East Parish	92	18	Ellis	Samuel	1			1		1		1					4		
Medway East Parish	92	19	Ellis	Ebenezer			1	1					2	1			5		
Medway East Parish	92	20	Ellis	John				1					1	1			3		
Medway East Parish	92	21	Ellis	John Jun		1	1	1		1	1		1				6		
Medway East Parish	92	22	Ellis	Abner		1		1		1		2	1				6		
Medway East Parish	92	23	Ellis	Seth				1					1				2		
Medway East Parish	92	24	Ellis	Simeon	1			1		1		1	1				5		
Medway East Parish	92	25	Ellis	Luther			1			2							3		
Medway East Parish	92	26	Fairbanks	Silas	1	1		1		3		1	1				8		
Medway East Parish	92	27	Fisher	Elihu			2			2	2						6		
Medway East Parish	92	28	Gould	Joshua				1			2		1				4		
Medway East Parish	92	29	Gould	Esther									1				1		
Medway East Parish	92	30	Grout	Nathan	1	1		1		1	1		1				6		
Medway East Parish	93	1	Harding	Stephen	3	1	1			1		1	1				8		
Medway East Parish	93	2	Harding	Theodore			1	1				1	1				4		
Medway East Parish	93	3	Harding	Theophilus	1		1					1					3		
Medway East Parish	93	4	Harding	Uriah		1		1		1	1		1				5		
Medway East Parish	93	5	Harding	Timothy	1	1		1		2			1				6		
Medway East Parish	93	6	Harding	Thomas	2	2		1		2		2		1			10		
Medway East Parish	93	7	Harding	Abraham		1	2	1		1	1		1				7		
Medway East Parish	93	8	Harding	Asa	2	1		1			2		1				7		
Medway East Parish	93	9	Hamant	Timothy			1	1					1				3		
Medway East Parish	93	10	Hill	Timothy			1			1			1				3		
Medway East Parish	93	11	Hill	Simon				1				1	1				3		
Medway East Parish	93	12	Hill	Simon Jun	1			1		2			1				5		
Medway East Parish	93	13	Hill	Samuel		1		1					1				3		
Medway East Parish	93	14	Hill	Reuben	1		1					1					3		
Medway East Parish	93	15	Hill	Moses			1	1	1	1		1	1				6		
Medway East Parish	93	16	Hill	Moses Jun			1					1					2		
Medway East Parish	93	17	Hill	Jonathan				1		1			1				3		

TOWN	PG#	LN#	HEADS OF HOUSEHOLD		FREE WHITE MALES					FREE WHITE FEMALES					TOTAL ALL OTHER	TOTAL SLAVES	TOTALS	DISTRICT/ TOWNSHIP	NOTES
			LAST NAME	FIRST NAME	under 10	10 to 16	16 to 26	26 to 45	45 and over	under 10	10 to 16	16 to 26	26 to 45	45 and over					
Medway East Parish	93	18	Jones	Thomas					2					1			3		
Medway East Parish	93	19	Jones	Simson		1	1	1		2			1	1			7		
Medway East Parish	93	20	Jones	Nathan		1		2	1	1		2	1				8		
Medway East Parish	93	21	Kingsbury	Zibina				1					1				2		
Medway East Parish	93	22	Lovell	Joseph					1					1			2		
Medway East Parish	93	23	Lovell	Nathaniel		1	3		1					1	1		7		
Medway East Parish	93	24	Mason	Abner			1		1					2			4		
Medway East Parish	93	25	Mason	Harding	2			1					1				4		
Medway East Parish	93	26	Metcalf	Philip	2			1		1			1				5		
Medway East Parish	93	27	Morse	Thomas	1				1	1	1	1		3			8		
Medway East Parish	93	28	Morse	Benoni Jun		1		1	1	3	1	1	1				9		
Medway East Parish	93	29	Partridge	Samuel	1	1			1	2	2	2		1			10		
Medway East Parish	93	30	Partridge	Joshua					1			1		1	2		5		
Medway East Parish	94	1	Partridge	Seth					1					1			2		
Medway East Parish	94	2	Partridge	Ziba	1		1	1		1			1				5		
Medway East Parish	94	3	Partridge	Darius		1		1					1				3		
Medway East Parish	94	4	Parnel	Benjamin		1			1		2			2			6		
Medway East Parish	94	5	Penniman	James					1				1	1			3		
Medway East Parish	94	6	Philips	Jedidiah	1	1			1	1		2		1			7		
Medway East Parish	94	7	Plimpton	Ezekiel	1	1			1	2		1		1			7		
Medway East Parish	94	8	Pond	Moses			1	1	1	1			1	1			6		
Medway East Parish	94	9	Puffer	William					1					1			2		
Medway East Parish	94	10	Puffer	Job	4			1		1			1				7		
Medway East Parish	94	11	Richardson	Abijah	1		2		1	2	2	1	1				10		
Medway East Parish	94	12	Richardson	Joseph	1		1			2		1					5		
Medway East Parish	94	13	Richardson	Oliver				1			1			1			3		
Medway East Parish	94	14	Richardson	Simeon	1	1	1		1	3	1	1		2			11		
Medway East Parish	94	15	Richardson	Moses			1		1			1	1				4		
Medway East Parish	94	16	Richardson	Moses Jun			1			1		1					3		
Medway East Parish	94	17	Richardson	Elisha	1		2		1	3				1			8		
Medway East Parish	94	18	Richardson	Asa P		1			1			1		1			4		
Medway East Parish	94	19	Richardson	Asa	1			1		3		1					6		
Medway East Parish	94	20	Richardson	Ezra	2	1	1	1		2	1	2	1				11		
Medway East Parish	94	21	Rockwood	Amos	1		1	1	1	1			1				6		
Medway East Parish	94	22	Royall	Prince	1								1		1		3		
Medway East Parish	94	23	Turner	Amos	2	3		1		2			1				9		
Medway East Parish	94	24	Thayer	Nahum		1		1		1		1					4		
Medway East Parish	94	25	Walker	Comfort	2		1	1		2		1	1				8		
Medway East Parish	94	26	Wheeler	Lewis		1	1	1		2	1		1				7		
Medway East Parish	94	27	Whitney	Joshua			2		1			1		1			5		
Medway East Parish	94	28	Williams	Levi	2			1				1					4		
Medway East Parish	94	29	Wright	Luther Rev.				1					1				2		

TOWN	PG#	LN#	LAST NAME	FIRST NAME	FREE WHITE MALES under 10	10 to 16	16 to 26	26 to 45	45 and over	FREE WHITE FEMALES under 10	10 to 16	16 to 26	26 to 45	45 and over	TOTAL ALL OTHER	TOTAL SLAVES	TOTALS	DISTRICT/ TOWNSHIP	NOTES
Medway West Parish	95	1	Adams	Eliakim	1	1	2	1		1	2	1					9		
Medway West Parish	95	2	Adams	John				1					1				2		
Medway West Parish	95	3	Adams	Hezekiah				1		2			1				4		
Medway West Parish	95	4	Adams	Obadiah		2		1		1		2	1	1			8		
Medway West Parish	95	5	Adams	Moses				1						1			2		
Medway West Parish	95	6	Adams	Aaron	1		1	1				1	1				5		
Medway West Parish	95	7	Adams	Mary								2		1			3		
Medway West Parish	95	8	Adams	Ezra			1						1				2		
Medway West Parish	95	9	Adams	Thomas	3	1			1	2	1	1		1			10		
Medway West Parish	95	10	Albee	John	1		1		1	1				2			6		
Medway West Parish	95	11	Allen	Mary	2			1					1	1			5		
Medway West Parish	95	12	Allen	Nathaniel			1	1		2			1				5		
Medway West Parish	95	13	Albee	Amos	1	1		1		1			1				5		
Medway West Parish	95	14	Barber	Joseph				1						1			2		
Medway West Parish	95	15	Barber	Joseph Jun	3			1		1			1				6		
Medway West Parish	95	16	Bullard	Isaac		1	2	1				1	3	1			9		
Medway West Parish	95	17	Bullard	Malichi	1		1	1		1	1						5		
Medway West Parish	95	18	Bullen	Elizabeth				1		1	1	2		1			6		
Medway West Parish	95	19	Clark	Samuel	2		1	1				2					6		
Medway West Parish	95	20	Clark	Martha										1			1		
Medway West Parish	95	21	Clark	Asa				1						1			2		
Medway West Parish	95	22	Clark	John	3		1	1				1	1				7		
Medway West Parish	95	23	Cutler	Calvin	2		1	1		2		1	1				8		
Medway West Parish	95	24	Cutler	Simon		1		1				2		2			6		
Medway West Parish	95	25	Cutler	Simon Jun			1			1			1				3		
Medway West Parish	95	26	Cutler	Elisha				1		1	1			1			4		
Medway West Parish	95	27	Cutler	Nathaniel	2		1	1		1	1		1				7		
Medway West Parish	95	28	Cleveland	Samuel	1		1	1		1			1	1			6		
Medway West Parish	95	29	Darling	Abel	2			1		3			1				7		
Medway West Parish	96	1	Ellis	Abijah	2			1		2		1	1				7		
Medway West Parish	96	2	Ellis	Oliver		1		1		1			1				4		
Medway West Parish	96	3	Fales	James	1		1	1				1					4		
Medway West Parish	96	4	Feltt	William		1		1					2				4		
Medway West Parish	96	5	Feltt	Moses	1							1					2		
Medway West Parish	96	6	Fisher	Simon				1					1				2		
Medway West Parish	96	7	Fisher	John	1			1		2			1				5		
Medway West Parish	96	8	Fisher	Joel		1		2		1		1		1			6		
Medway West Parish	96	9	Fuller	Asa				1					1				2		
Medway West Parish	96	10	Gibbs	James				1					1				2		
Medway West Parish	96	11	Green	John	1		1			1			1	1			5		
Medway West Parish	96	12	Green	Luther	2			1		1			1				5		
Medway West Parish	96	13	Grant	Joshua	2			1	1	1		1					6		
Medway West Parish	96	14	Harding	Job	3	1		1		1			1				7		
Medway West Parish	96	15	Hawes	Joel	2	1	1	1		2	1	1	1				10		
Medway West Parish	96	16	Haywood	Nahum	1		1	1				1					4		
Medway West Parish	96	17	Hixson	Seth				1					2				3		
Medway West Parish	96	18	Hixson	Isaac	3	1		1				1	1				7		
Medway West Parish	96	19	Hixson	Reuben	1			1		2	2						6		
Medway West Parish	96	20	Holbrook	Partridge	1		1	2		1			1				6		
Medway West Parish	96	21	Hixson	Asa	3			1		1			1				6		
Medway West Parish	96	22	Ide	Daniel	2		1	1					1				6		
Medway West Parish	96	23	Kibbee	Isaac	1	1	1		1	1	1			1			7		
Medway West Parish	96	24	Kimbel	Nathaniel	2			1					1				4		
Medway West Parish	96	25	Lawrence	David	1			1		1			1				4		
Medway West Parish	96	26	Lewitt	Peter		2		1		2			1				6		
Medway West Parish	96	27	Loverain	Thaddeus	3		1	1				1	1				7		
Medway West Parish	97	1	Mann	Ralph	2	1	1		1		1		1				7		
Medway West Parish	97	2	Metcalf	Luther	1	1	6	1				1	2				12		
Medway West Parish	97	3	Morse	Abner	1	1	1	1		2	1	1	1	1			10		
Medway West Parish	97	4	Morse	Henry				1				1		1			3		
Medway West Parish	97	5	Morse	Benoni				1				1		1			3		
Medway West Parish	97	6	Partridge	Joel	1		1		1	2	1		1				7		
Medway West Parish	97	7	Partridge	Elijah	1			1		1		1	1				5		
Medway West Parish	97	8	Partridge	Simeon		2		1					1				4		
Medway West Parish	97	9	Partridge	Nathaniel				1				1		1			3		
Medway West Parish	97	10	Partridge	Ezekiel			2						1				3		
Medway West Parish	97	11	Pike	Elijah	2			1		1			1				5		
Medway West Parish	97	12	Plimpton	Job			1	1		1				1			4		
Medway West Parish	97	13	Richardson	James	2			1		3		1	1	1			9		
Medway West Parish	97	14	Richardson	Abigail				1					1	2			4		
Medway West Parish	97	15	Richardson	Amos			2			1		2		1			6		
Medway West Parish	97	16	Rockwood	Moses Jun	1	1		1	1				1				5		
Medway West Parish	97	17	Rose	Samuel											2		2		
Medway West Parish	97	18	Sanford	David Rev				1				1	1	1			4		
Medway West Parish	97	19	Sanford	Philo	2	2	1	1		3	1		1				11		
Medway West Parish	97	20	Shumway	Jabez		1		1		1		2		1			6		
Medway West Parish	97	21	Thompson	Ebenezer	1	1		1		1	2						6		
Medway West Parish	97	22	Thompson	Abigail										1			1		
Medway West Parish	97	23	Twiss	Samuel		1		1				1					4		

TOWN	PG#	LN#	LAST NAME	FIRST NAME	FREE WHITE MALES					FREE WHITE FEMALES					TOTAL ALL OTHER	TOTAL SLAVES	TOTALS	DISTRICT/ TOWNSHIP	NOTES
					under 10	10 to 16	16 to 26	26 to 45	45 and over	under 10	10 to 16	16 to 26	26 to 45	45 and over					
Medway West Parish	97	24	Ware	Joseph	3	1		1		1			1				7		
Medway West Parish	97	25	Wight	James					2				1				3		
Medway West Parish	97	26	Wight	Aaron	3		1		1	1	3	3	1		1		14		
Medway West Parish	97	27	Whiston	Ezra			1		1					1			3		
Medway West Parish	97	28	Whiting	Timothy	1			1		1			1				4		
Medway West Parish	97	29	Whiting	Elias	3				1	1	1		1				7		
Medway West Parish	97	30	White	Elijah	3			1						1			5		

TOWN	PG#	LN#	HEADS OF HOUSEHOLD LAST NAME	FIRST NAME	FREE WHITE MALES under 10	10 to 16	16 to 26	26 to 45	45 and over	FREE WHITE FEMALES under 10	10 to 16	16 to 26	26 to 45	45 and over	TOTAL ALL OTHER	TOTAL SLAVES	TOTALS	DISTRICT/ TOWNSHIP	NOTES
Milton	44	1	Amory	Jno	1			1		1	1	2					6		
Milton	44	2	Alleyne	Abel	3		1	1		2	1	2	1	1			12		
Milton	44	3	Adams	Moses			1						1				2		
Milton	44	4	Adams	Saml	1	1	1		1	1	1		1				7		
Milton	44	5	Adams	Jno		1	1	1	1	1	1		1				7		
Milton	44	6	Alexander	Best											2		2		
Milton	44	7	Bronsden	Benj	2	1			1	2		1					7		
Milton	44	8	Briggs	Daniel	3	2	6	6	3		1	4	1				26		
Milton	44	9	Bidge	Joseph	1			2		1	1	2					7		
Milton	44	10	Badcock	Wm	1		1		1				1				4		
Milton	44	11	Badcock	Wm Jun	1		1	1		1	1						5		
Milton	44	12	Bent	Jno			1		1	1	1		1				5		
Milton	44	13	Bent	Shepherd	2			1					1				4		
Milton	44	14	Belcher	Moses		1		1		1	2		1				6		
Milton	44	15	Collum	Baker			1			3			1				5		
Milton	44	16	Blade	James				1			1		2				4		
Milton	44	17	Badcock	Thomas	1			1		1	1	1					5		
Milton	44	18	Bowman	James	2	1		1		2	1		1				8		
Milton	45	1	Bent	Josiah	1	1	2	1	1	2		2					10		
Milton	45	2	Billings	Joseph	2		2	1			1	2	1				9		
Milton	45	3	Bronsden	Jno B.	2	2		1		1		1		2			9		
Milton	45	4	Bradley	Stephen	2	1		1				1		1			6		
Milton	45	5	Badcock	Leml				1		2	1	1		1			6		
Milton	45	6	Baker	Thomas				1					1				2		
Milton	45	7	Baggs	Seth	3		1	1				1	1	1			8		
Milton	45	8	Boris	L.L.		2		3	1		1	1	2		1		11		
Milton	45	9	Blake	Liba				1					1				2		
Milton	45	10	Brewer	Wid.							1			1			2		
Milton	45	11	Bent	Joseph			1	1		1	2		1				6		
Milton	45	12	Cabot	Samuel	2	3		2		2	2		3				14		
Milton	45	13	Crane	Thom Esq		1	1		1			1	1				5		
Milton	45	14	Coats	Ezra	1			1		2	4		2				10		
Milton	45	15	Crehore	Jno			2	1		2	1		1				7		
Milton	45	16	Crehore	Benj		1	1	1		1			1				5		
Milton	45	17	Canady	Benj	1		2		1	3	1		1				9		
Milton	45	18	Crane	Seth		2		1			1		1				5		
Milton	45	19	Crehore	Wm B.	1		4		1	2			2				10		
Milton	45	20	Cotton	Joseph											5		5		
Milton	45	21	Copeland	Ephrm				1					1				2		
Milton	45	22	Childs	Wm	1		1			2		1					5		
Milton	45	23	Crane	Vose				1					3	1			5		
Milton	45	24	Crane	Jerem	1		1	1		2		1	2				8		
Milton	45	25	Crehore	Thomas	4		5	1		1	1	3	1				16		
Milton	45	26	Clarke	George	1			1					1				3		
Milton	45	27	Crehore	Wm			1	1					3				5		
Milton	45	28	Crehore	Jno S.	3		1	1		1			1				7		
Milton	45	29	Copeland	Isaac	4		1	1		1		1	1				9		
Milton	45	30	Davenport	Isaac		1	3	1		1	1	1	2				10		
Milton	45	31	Davenport	Nath		1	2	1	1	1	1		1	1	1		9		
Milton	45	32	Davis	Amos				1		1			1				3		
Milton	46	1	Dunmore	Arch.	3			1					1				5		
Milton	46	2	Dingley	Jno	1			1	1				1				4		
Milton	46	3	Davenport	Wm		2			1	1		1		1			6		
Milton	46	4	Davis	Lemuel		3			1			1					5		
Milton	46	5	Dixon	Robert	3			1		2		1					7		
Milton	46	6	Drue	Jno											2		2		
Milton	46	7	Drue	Wm											4		4		
Milton	46	8	Davenport	Adam		1	1		1	3							6		
Milton	46	9	Everett	Isachar				1				2					3		
Milton	46	10	Ford	James	1	2		1	4			1	1				10		
Milton	46	11	Ford	Waitstill		1						2	2	1			6		
Milton	46	12	Fenne	Mary	1					1	1						3		
Milton	46	13	Farrington	Jona	2			1		1			1				5		
Milton	46	14	French	David		2			1				1				4		
Milton	46	15	Ford	Jessaniah	2		1	1		1		2	1		1		9		
Milton	46	16	Felt	Benjamin	2	2	1		1	1	1	1		1			10		
Milton	46	17	Gill	Jacob	1		1		1	1	1	1		1			7		
Milton	46	18	Grover	Sam K		2	3	1	1		1		2	1			11		
Milton	46	19	Gardner	Jno	1			1			2						4		
Milton	46	20	Grover	Nathl	1				1				1				3		
Milton	46	21	Grover	Thomas				1					1				2		
Milton	46	22	Gulliver	Nathl				1					1				2		
Milton	46	23	Gibbins	Jno	3			1		1			1				6		
Milton	46	24	Gay	Jno	2			1					1				4		
Milton	46	25	Gulliver	Rufus	2			1		2			1				6		
Milton	46	26	Gay	Asa	1			1		1	2		1				6		
Milton	46	27	Gulliver	Jno				1									1		
Milton	46	28	Gulliver	Leml			1						1				2		
Milton	46	29	Gulliver	Cornelius		2		1			2		1				6		

44

TOWN	PG#	LN#	LAST NAME	FIRST NAME	FWM under 10	FWM 10 to 16	FWM 16 to 26	FWM 26 to 45	FWM 45 and over	FWF under 10	FWF 10 to 16	FWF 16 to 26	FWF 26 to 45	FWF 45 and over	TOTAL ALL OTHER	TOTAL SLAVES	TOTALS	DISTRICT/ TOWNSHIP	NOTES
Milton	46	30	Gould	Sarah										1			1		
Milton	46	31	Holbrook	Amos	1				1	2	1	1	1		1		8		
Milton	47	1	Harling	Thomas			1		1				2				4		
Milton	47	2	Humphrey	Nath	1	1			1				1				4		
Milton	47	3	Hunt	Lemuel	3	1		1		3			1				9		
Milton	47	4	Hunt	Samuel	3			2	1	1			1	3			11		
Milton	47	5	Horten	Steph		1			1	1	1			1			5		
Milton	47	6	Horten	Patience					1				1	1			3		
Milton	47	7	Hunt	Abner					1								1		
Milton	47	8	Houghton	Jno		1		2					1				4		
Milton	47	9	Hooker	Wm	2			1		2			1	1			7		
Milton	47	10	Hunt	Isaac				1			1		1				3		
Milton	47	11	Houghton	Jason	5	1		1		1			1				9		
Milton	47	12	Houghton	Ralph				1						1			2		
Milton	47	13	Hunt	Gideon			2						1				3		
Milton	47	14	Henshaw	Han	1			1				1	1	1			5		
Milton	47	15	How	Margaret	1	1				1	1		1				5		
Milton	47	16	Hubbert	Caleb	2		2	1		1			1	1			8		
Milton	47	17	Houghton	Silas		1		1						1			3		
Milton	47	18	Houghton	Oliver			1						2				3		
Milton	47	19	Horton	Samuel		2		1				1		1			5		
Milton	47	20	Joy	Elizabeth		1							2	1			4		
Milton	47	21	Jones	Nathan	1			1		1	1		1				5		
Milton	47	22	Jones	Joseph				1						1			2		
Milton	47	23	Kneeland	Susan			1				1		1				3		
Milton	47	24	Keyes	Nathanl				1						1			2		
Milton	47	25	Lillie	Jno May	3			1		1	3		1		1		10		
Milton	47	26	Lamb	Moses	1	2	2	1		1			1	1			9		
Milton	47	27	Lyon	Jacob	1			1			1		1				4		
Milton	47	28	McKean	Joseph			1					3					4		
Milton	47	29	McLean	Agnes								1		2	1		4		
Milton	47	30	Mitchel	Andrew	2	1	1	1					2				7		
Milton	47	31	Morton	Thad	2	1		1					1				5		
Milton	47	32	Marshal	Jno		1			1	1				1			4		
Milton	48	1	May	Joseph	1				1	4				1			7		
Milton	48	2	Murray	Jno				1					1				2		
Milton	48	3	Mills	Fuller	2			1		2			1				6		
Milton	48	4	Pope	Joseph		1		1		2		1					5		
Milton	48	5	Proctor	Waren	1			1		1		1					4		
Milton	48	6	Pinchbeck	Wm F.	1			1		1	1		1				5		
Milton	48	7	Parker	Solom			1	1		1			1				4		
Milton	48	8	Perry	Nehemh	3			1					1				5		
Milton	48	9	Pierce	Charles	3	2		1	1	1			1	1			10		
Milton	48	10	Pierce	Lettrice								1	1				2		
Milton	48	11	Pierce	Rufus	2		1		1	1	2	3	1				11		
Milton	48	12	Pierce	Wm	3	1		1		1	1		1				8		
Milton	48	13	Pierce	Jno				1					2				3		
Milton	48	14	Pratt	Joel	1	1							1				3		
Milton	48	15	Pollock	Susan								1	2	1			4		
Milton	48	16	Robbins	Ed H.	2			1		2	3		1		2		11		
Milton	48	17	Ramsen	Dyar		2			1	2		1	1	1			8		
Milton	48	18	Reed	Josiah	1				1	2			1				5		
Milton	48	19	Ruggles	Jno			1	1		1	1		1	1			6		
Milton	48	20	Raven	James				1						1			2		
Milton	48	21	Reed	Noah	1			1		1	1		1				5		
Milton	48	22	Reed	James			1	1		1				1			4		
Milton	48	23	Swift	Jno		3	2	1			2		1		1		10		
Milton	48	24	Sullivan	Jno	1	2	1	1		1		1					7		
Milton	48	25	Sumner	Jesse	2		2	1		1		1	1				8		
Milton	48	26	Sloane	Peter				1					1				2		
Milton	48	27	Smith	Isaac	3			1		2		1	1				8		
Milton	48	28	Smith	Henry								1					1		
Milton	49	1	Swift	Saml	2	2			2	2	1		1				10		
Milton	49	2	Sherman	Jno	1	2			1	2	1		1				8		
Milton	49	3	Smith	Seth	1			1						1			3		
Milton	49	4	Silvester	Benj	2		1						1				4		
Milton	49	5	Sumner	David		2		1		4		3	2				12		
Milton	49	6	Sumner	Mercy								1	1	1			3		
Milton	49	7	Sumner	Seth			1	1					1	1			4		
Milton	49	8	Sumner	Jabez	2			1		1				3			7		
Milton	49	9	Stimpson	Josph	1			1		1				1			4		
Milton	49	10	Sumner	Lydia								1	1	1			3		
Milton	49	11	Sumner	Sarah			1				1			1			3		
Milton	49	12	Tucker	David	1	1			1		1	1		1			6		
Milton	49	13	Tucker	Isaac			1	1		2	1			1			6		
Milton	49	14	Tucker	Nathl	1	1	2	2				1	2	1			10		
Milton	49	15	Turrill	Benj					1				1	1			3		
Milton	49	16	Turner	Elisha	2	1		1		2	1		1				8		
Milton	49	17	Talbot	George	1				1	3	1	1		1			8		

TOWN	PG#	LN#	LAST NAME	FIRST NAME	FREE WHITE MALES					FREE WHITE FEMALES					TOTAL ALL OTHER	TOTAL SLAVES	TOTALS	DISTRICT/ TOWNSHIP	NOTES
					under 10	10 to 16	16 to 26	26 to 45	45 and over	under 10	10 to 16	16 to 26	26 to 45	45 and over					
Milton	49	18	Tidd	Adam											4		4		
Milton	49	19	Tucker	Saml	3	1	1		1		1	2		1			10		
Milton	49	20	Tucker	Jereh				2				2		1			5		
Milton	49	21	Thayer	Beza	2	1		1		3			1				8		
Milton	49	22	Turner	Benj	2			1					1				4		
Milton	49	23	Tucker	Eben		1		1					1				3		
Milton	49	24	Thompson	Sam		2	2	1		2	1		1				9		
Milton	49	25	Tailor	Wm			4				1	1					6		
Milton	49	26	Tailor	Thom	1		1				1	1	1				5		
Milton	49	27	Tucker	Jaret		1	1	1		1	1	1					6		
Milton	49	28	Tucker	Amal	1		1	1		1			1				5		
Milton	49	29	Tucker	Tim		1		1	1				2	1			6		
Milton	49	30	Tucker	Tim Jr			1						1				2		
Milton	49	31	Tucker	James	2	1		1		1			2				7		
Milton	49	32	Tucker	George		1		1					1				3		
Milton	50	1	Vose	Daniel			1		1		1	1		1	1		6		
Milton	50	2	Vose	Lewis	1		1						1				3		
Milton	50	3	Vose	Stephen				1					1				2		
Milton	50	4	Vose	Alexa	2	1		1		1			1				6		
Milton	50	5	Vose	Saml				1						1			2		
Milton	50	6	Vose	Saml Jr			1			2		1	1				5		
Milton	50	7	Vose	Hannh										1			1		
Milton	50	8	Vose	Mary										1			1		
Milton	50	9	Vose	Lydia	1		1			1			1	1			5		
Milton	50	10	Vose	Elijah	3	1		1		1	1	1	1	2			11		
Milton	50	11	Vose	Nathan		2		1		1	2	1		1			8		
Milton	50	12	Vose	Sarah									2				2		
Milton	50	13	Vose	Joseph			1	1			1	1	1		1		6		
Milton	50	14	Vose	Moses	1			1		1			1				4		
Milton	50	15	Vose	Benj		1	1	1		2			1		2		8		
Milton	50	16	Vose	Wm		2		1		2			1				6		
Milton	50	17	Ward	Joshua	1			1		3			2	1			8		
Milton	50	18	White	Elizabeth	3						1		1				5		
Milton	50	19	Wadsworth	Wm	1		2	1		1			1				6		
Milton	50	20	Wadsworth	Josh	1			1		2	1		1				6		
Milton	50	21	Wadsworth	Benj	3			1		2	1		1				8		
Milton	50	22	White	Jno	1		1					2					4		
Milton	50	23	Wild	Joseph				1				3		1			5		
Milton	50	24	Wadsworth	Jno	1	1	2	2					1	1			8		
Milton	50	25	Williams	Sam	2			1		2			1				6		
Milton	50	26	Williams	Zebh	1	1		1		2			2				7		
Milton	50	27	Young	Jno	1			1					1				3		

TOWN	PG#	LN#	LAST NAME	FIRST NAME	FREE WHITE MALES					FREE WHITE FEMALES					TOTAL ALL OTHER	TOTAL SLAVES	TOTALS	DISTRICT/ TOWNSHIP	NOTES
					under 10	10 to 16	16 to 26	26 to 45	45 and over	under 10	10 to 16	16 to 26	26 to 45	45 and over					
Needham	145	1	Alden	Silas Col.	1		1		1	2				1			6		
Needham	145	2	Alden	Henry				1						1			2		
Needham	145	3	Alden	William	3		1			1		1		1			7		
Needham	145	4	Alden	Silas Junr	3			1					1				5		
Needham	145	5	Atherton	Jesse			1						1				2		
Needham	145	6	Browd	Timothy		1	1		1				1	1			5		
Needham	145	7	Brown	Joshua				1		2	2			1			6		
Needham	145	8	Bacon	Ephriam				1		3			1				5		
Needham	145	9	Bacon	Moses	2		1				1	1	1				6		
Needham	145	10	Brown	William				1						1			2		
Needham	145	11	Bright	Michel		1		1						1			3		
Needham	145	12	Blackinton	Othniel		1	1						2				4		
Needham	145	13	Bullen	Amaziah	1	1			1	1	1	2	1				8		
Needham	145	14	Bird	Ebenezer	1			1	1			1	1				5		
Needham	145	15	Bird	Benjamin	1		1	1		3		1	1				8		
Needham	145	16	Bullard	Epheriam		1			1			1		2			5		
Needham	145	17	Bullard	Nathaniel	2	1	1	1		2	1	1		1			10		
Needham	145	18	Browd	Thodore				1		1				1			3		
Needham	145	19	Brown	Samuel		1			1				1	1			4		
Needham	145	20	Bracket	Lemuel	1		1			3	1	1	1				9		
Needham	145	21	Bodridge	Galen		1	1			1		2		1			6		
Needham	145	22	Blodgett	Simon				1					1	1			3		
Needham	145	23	Brown	Jacob	1	1		1					1				4		
Needham	145	24	Caffree	John				1		1				1			3		
Needham	145	25	Cook	Elikim				1				1			1		3		
Needham	145	26	Cook	Elikiam Junr		1		1				1					3		
Needham	146	1	Clark	Ebenezer		1		1		1			1	1			5		
Needham	146	2	Clark	William	1	2		1		1	1	1	1				8		
Needham	146	3	Clough	John				1				1		1			3		
Needham	146	4	Colburn	Joseph			1			1		1					3		
Needham	146	5	Devenport	Benjamin		1		1		1		2		1			6		
Needham	146	6	Devenport	Enoch	1			1		1				2			5		
Needham	146	7	Dewing	Henry	1			1	1	1		1	1	1			7		
Needham	146	8	Day	John		1		1		1	1		1	1			6		
Needham	146	9	Dewing	Timothy	1	1		1		1	1						6		
Needham	146	10	Dewing	Nathan	1	2	1	1		1	1		1				8		
Needham	146	11	Dewing	Martha										1			1		
Needham	146	12	Daniels	Joseph		1	1		1			1		1			5		
Needham	146	13	Daniels	Jeremiah			1	1		2		1	1				6		
Needham	146	14	Daniells	Timothy				1									1		
Needham	146	15	Deming	Charles	2		1			2		1					6		
Needham	146	16	Dana	Luther	1			1					1				3		
Needham	146	17	Daggett	Asa		1		1					1				3		
Needham	146	18	Deming	Rebaca Wid.									1	1			2		
Needham	146	19	Edes	John			1		1			1	1	1			5		
Needham	146	20	Edes	Amos		1	1		1	2	1	1					8		
Needham	146	21	Eaton	William	1			1		2			1	1			6		
Needham	146	22	Flagg	Solomon				1									1		
Needham	146	23	Fuller	Enoch			3					1					4		
Needham	146	24	Fisher	Joseph			1		1		2	1		1			6		
Needham	146	25	Fisher	George	1	1	5	2		1		2	1				13		
Needham	146	26	Fisher	Nathaniel		1			1				2	1			5		
Needham	146	27	Fisher	Samuel			1		1	1	2			2			7		
Needham	146	28	Fisher	Zubia Wid										1			1		
Needham	146	29	Fisher	Aaron	3	2			1				1				7		
Needham	146	30	French	Timothy	3			2		1		1	1				8		
Needham	146	31	Farria	Alexander				1					1	1			3		
Needham	146	32	Fuller	Solomon		1	2		1				1	2			7		
Needham	146	33	Fuller	Amos		2		1	1				1	1			6		
Needham	146	34	Fuller	Eleazer		1			1			1		2			5		
Needham	146	35	Fuller	Robert	1			1						1			3		
Needham	146	36	Flagg	Elishua	1		1	1		1		2					6		
Needham	146	37	Floyd	Phillip	1	1	1	1	1	3	1		1				10		
Needham	146	38	Fisk	Enoch	3		1		1	1	3	2	1				12		
Needham	146	39	Fisk	Peter Doct			1										1		
Needham	146	40	Fuller	Jonathan			1			2			1				4		
Needham	146	41	Fuller	William Esq			2		1	2	1		1	1			8		
Needham	146	42	Fuller	William Junr		1		1				1	1				4		
Needham	146	43	Fuller	Abigail Wid									1				1		
Needham	146	44	Fuller	Jerusha Wid			1	1		1				1			4		
Needham	146	45	Fairbanks	David	1			1		2	1		1				6		
Needham	146	46	Felton	Daniel		1	1		1				1	1			5		
Needham	146	47	Fuller	Elishua	2	1		1		1	1		1				7		
Needham	146	48	Fales	Daniel	1		1					1					3		
Needham	146	49	Gurnet	Susana	1							1		2			4		
Needham	146	50	Greenwood	Samuel	4	1		1		1	1	1					9		
Needham	146	51	Gay	Jonathan		2	1		2			2		2			9		
Needham	146	52	Gay	Jonathan Junr			1			1		1	1				4		
Needham	146	53	Garfield	Moses		1	2	1	1		1	1	1				8		

TOWN	PG#	LN#	LAST NAME	FIRST NAME	FREE WHITE MALES under 10	10 to 16	16 to 26	26 to 45	45 and over	FREE WHITE FEMALES under 10	10 to 16	16 to 26	26 to 45	45 and over	TOTAL ALL OTHER	TOTAL SLAVES	TOTALS	DISTRICT/ TOWNSHIP	NOTES
Needham	147	1	Glover	Henry	1	1		1		4			1				8		
Needham	147	2	Gill	William	2			4		1			1				8		
Needham	147	3	Gibson	James			1			1		1					3		
Needham	147	4	Hawes	Esther										1			1		
Needham	147	5	Harrison	Joseph	1	1	1	1		2	1	1	1				9		
Needham	147	6	Hamond	Peter			1										1		
Needham	147	7	Hunting	Daniel			1		1	2	1		1				6		
Needham	147	8	Hawes	Joseph		1			1		1			1			4		
Needham	147	9	Hunting	Israel	3		1	1		1	1	1	1				9		
Needham	147	10	Harris	Michel		1	1		1	3		2		1			9		
Needham	147	11	Hunting	Hezekiah		1							1				2		
Needham	147	12	Hawes	Samuel	1	1				2			1				5		
Needham	147	13	Jackson	Phinehas				1		2	2		1				6		
Needham	147	14	Jourden	Jesse	2			1		2	1		1				7		
Needham	147	15	Jackson	Epheraim		1	2	1			1	2	1				8		
Needham	147	16	Kingsbury	Jonathan Col.		2		1	1			2		1			7		
Needham	147	17	Kingsbury	Moses Junr	1	1		1		1			1				5		
Needham	147	18	Kingsbury	Joseph		2	2		1		1	1	1				8		
Needham	147	19	Kingsbury	Samuel	1			1		2			1				5		
Needham	147	20	Kingsbury	Sarah										1			1		
Needham	147	21	Kingsbury	Timothy		1		2	1				1	1			6		
Needham	147	22	Kingsbury	Moses		2		2				1		1			6		
Needham	147	23	Kingsbury	Jonathan		2		1			1		1	1			6		
Needham	147	24	Kingsbury	Joseph Junr	1	1	1	1					1				5		
Needham	147	25	Fuller	Hannah Wid.		1								1			2		
Needham	147	26	Kingsbury	Daniel		1		1		2	1		1				6		
Needham	147	27	Kingsbury	Iasiah	2			1		2	1		1				7		
Needham	147	28	Kingsbury	David		1			1	1	1			1			5		
Needham	147	29	Kingsbury	Asa			1						1				2		
Needham	147	30	Lyon	Peter		3	2			3		1	1				10		
Needham	147	31	Lewis	Joshua			2		1	1	2	1		1			8		
Needham	147	32	Lovel	Joseph	2	1		1					1				5		
Needham	147	33	Miller	James	1			1						1			3		
Needham	147	34	Morse	Amos	1			1						1			3		
Needham	147	35	Marshal	Jacob	1			1		1			1				4		
Needham	147	36	Mansfield	Epes	1			1		3	1		1				7		
Needham	147	37	Morrall	Isaac Doct	1	2	1		2	1		1	1	2			11		
Needham	147	38	Mills	David	1			1			1			2			5		
Needham	147	39	Mills	Ezra	3			1		3			1				8		
Needham	147	40	Mills	Oliver	1	2		1	1	1		1	1	1			9		
Needham	147	41	Mills	William				1						1			2		
Needham	147	42	Mills	Benjamin			1						1				2		
Needham	147	43	Mills	Lemuel	2		1		1	1	2		1				8		
Needham	147	44	McIntosh	William Col.		1		1						1			3		
Needham	147	45	Mann	Moses Col.		2	1		2	2	1		1				9		
Needham	147	46	McIntosh	Royal	1	1		1		4			1	1			9		
Needham	147	47	McIntosh	Gideon		1			1	1			1				4		
Needham	147	48	McIntire	Sarah Wid.	2			1					1	1			5		
Needham	147	49	McIntire	Jemima									1	1			2		
Needham	147	50	Mills	Enoch				1		1			1				3		
Needham	147	51	*	Elab	1			1						2			4		
Needham	148	1	McIntosh	Ebenezer	3		1	2	1				1				8		
Needham	148	2	Noyes	Thomas Revd.		1											1		
Needham	148	3	Newell	Elizabeth Wid.										1			1		
Needham	148	4	Newell	Josiah		1	1		2		2	1		1			8		
Needham	148	5	Newell	George	1			1		1			1				4		
Needham	148	6	Ockinton	David		1		1				1		1			4		
Needham	148	7	Obrine	Richard				1		3			1				5		
Needham	148	8	Palmer	Stephen Revd.	1		2	1		2	1	1	1				9		
Needham	148	9	Parker	Nathaniel				1						1			2		
Needham	148	10	Paine	Epheriam	1			1		1	1			1			5		
Needham	148	11	Pratt	Samuel		1	2	1					1	1			6		
Needham	148	12	Peirce	Elikem	3		1	1		1			1				7		
Needham	148	13	Parker	Jacob				2						1			3		
Needham	148	14	Parker	Samuel	2		1						1				4		
Needham	148	15	Parker	William	3			1		3			1				8		
Needham	148	16	Parker	Olive Wid.		1				4	1	1					7		
Needham	148	17	Robbins	Jeremiah		1				1	1						3		
Needham	148	18	Richardson	Timothy	1	1		1		1			1	1			6		
Needham	148	19	Richardson	Ebenezer				1						1			2		
Needham	148	20	Russell	Thomas	1	2		1		1			1	1			7		
Needham	148	21	Smith	Joel	1		1					1					3		
Needham	148	22	Smith	Cristopher				1		1			1	1			4		
Needham	148	23	Smith	Luther			1										1		
Needham	148	24	Smith	George	1		1	1		1		1					5		
Needham	148	25	Steadman	Joseph	1	1			1	1	1			1			6		
Needham	148	26	Smith	Jonathan				1						1			2		
Needham	148	27	Smith	Jonathan Junr	2	3		1		1		1	1	1			10		
Needham	148	28	Stevens	Epheriam			3	1		1							9		

TOWN	PG#	LN#	LAST NAME	FIRST NAME	FREE WHITE MALES					FREE WHITE FEMALES					TOTAL ALL OTHER	TOTAL SLAVES	TOTALS	DISTRICT/ TOWNSHIP	NOTES
					under 10	10 to 16	16 to 26	26 to 45	45 and over	under 10	10 to 16	16 to 26	26 to 45	45 and over					
Needham	148	29	Steadman	Ebenezer	1	1			1	1	1			1			6		
Needham	148	30	Smith	David		1			1	1				1			4		
Needham	148	31	Smith	David Junr	1	1	1	1		1	1		1				7		
Needham	148	32	Stevens	Epheriam Junr		1		2		1		1	1				6		
Needham	148	33	Stevens	Abijamin			1			1		1					3		
Needham	148	34	Smith	Aaron				1		3	1	1	1				7		
Needham	148	35	Smith	Benjamin			1			4			1				6		
Needham	148	36	Smith	Peletiah	1		1					2					4		
Needham	148	37	Smith	Daniel		1	1		1				1	1			4		
Needham	148	38	Sheperd	Isaac			1	2	1	2	1			1			8		
Needham	148	39	Smith	James	1	1		1		1		1					5		
Needham	148	40	Smith	William		1		1						2			4		
Needham	148	41	Smith	Robert			1	1					1	1			4		
Needham	148	42	Smith	Timothy	1	2		1				1		1			6		
Needham	148	43	Smith	Phinehas			1					1					2		
Needham	148	44	Sawing	Levi	1		1	1		4	1		1				9		
Needham	148	45	Smith	Jason	3		1			1	1		1				7		
Needham	148	46	Slack	Elizabeth										1			1		
Needham	148	47	Slack	Benjamin	1		1	1		2	1		1				7		
Needham	148	48	Tolman	John		1		1				1		1			4		
Needham	148	49	Walker	Azariah	4			2		1	1	1	1	1	1		12		
Needham	148	50	Ware	Daniel	2	2		1		1	1		2				9		
Needham	148	51	Woodcock	Samuel	2	2		1		2		2		1			10		
Needham	148	52	Wilson	Nathaniel	1		1						1				3		
Needham	148	53	Woodward	Asa			1	1		1			1				4		
Needham	149	1	Whiting	Mary Wid.		1				1	1			1			4		
Needham	149	2	Ware	Nathaniel				1						1			2		
Needham	149	3	Ware	Epherim		1	1	1				1	1				5		
Needham	149	4	Ware	Elijah				1		1	2		1				5		
Needham	149	5	Ware	Jonathan		1		1				1	1				4		
Needham	149	6	Wilson	Nathaniel Junr		1	1			1		1					4		
Needham	149	7	Ware	Nathaniel Junr	1			1		3			1				6		
Needham	149	8	Williams	Asa	1			1					1				3		
Needham	149	9	Swazey	Manuel	2			1					1				4		
Needham	149	10	Simon	Edward				1		1		1					3		
Needham	149	11	Skiner	Job	1			1		1		1					4		
Needham	149	12	Smith	Cristopher Junr		1		1		1			1				4		
Needham	149	13	Lott	David				1		1	1		1				4		
Needham	149	14	Ware	Luther				1		1	1		1				4		
Needham	149	15	Watkins	David	1			1					1				3		
Needham	149	16	Ware	Joseph	1				1	1	1		1				5		
Needham	149	17	Muze	Benoi	1		1			2		1					5		

TOWN	PG#	LN#	LAST NAME	FIRST NAME	FREE WHITE MALES under 10	10 to 16	16 to 26	26 to 45	45 and over	FREE WHITE FEMALES under 10	10 to 16	16 to 26	26 to 45	45 and over	TOTAL ALL OTHER	TOTAL SLAVES	TOTALS	DISTRICT/ TOWNSHIP	NOTES
Quincy	39	1	Adams	John		5	3	1		1	1	3	1	2			17		President of the United States
Quincy	39	2	Adams	Peter B. Esq	1		2	1	1		1	2					8		
Quincy	39	3	Arnold	Jos N	2	1		1		2	1		1				8		
Quincy	39	4	Arnold	Daniel	2			1		1			1				5		
Quincy	39	5	Adams	Jedediah	2	1		1		1			1	1			7		
Quincy	39	6	Alleyne	Josiah				1						1			2		
Quincy	39	7	Adams	Micajah	2		2	1		2			1				8		
Quincy	39	8	Adams	Eliz Wid.			1						1				2		
Quincy	39	9	Adams	Willm				1					1				2		
Quincy	39	10	Adams	Thomas		1		1		1		1	1				5		
Quincy	39	11	Apthorp	P.H.	1	1	1			2		3	1	2	*		11		
Quincy	39	12	Adams	Ebenz			1				2		1	1			5		
Quincy	39	13	Adams	Josiah	1		1			1	2		1				6		
Quincy	40	1	Beule	Benj Esq				1				2	1		1		5		
Quincy	40	2	Bass	Saml		1							1				2		
Quincy	40	3	Black	Moses		3		1		1		3	1		2		11		
Quincy	40	4	Baxter	Joseph		1		1				2	1				5		
Quincy	40	5	Bass	Seth			1			1			1				3		
Quincy	40	6	Beale	Jona	2	1						1	1		1		7		
Quincy	40	7	Burrell	Seth		1	1						1	1			4		
Quincy	40	8	Briesler	Jno	1		1				1		1				4		
Quincy	40	9	Beale	Hannah									1				1		
Quincy	40	10	Black	Rachel								2	1				3		
Quincy	40	11	Beale	Richard			1			2		2	1				6		
Quincy	40	12	Bracket	James J	1		2			1		2			1		7		
Quincy	40	13	Bracket	Peter		2		3		2			1				8		
Quincy	40	14	Baxter	Ed W	3		1	1		1	3		1				10		
Quincy	40	15	Bent	Nedebiah	1	1	1		1	1	1	2		1			9		
Quincy	40	16	Bent	Lemuel			1			2			1				4		
Quincy	40	17	Baxter	Jona		1		2	2	2			1				8		
Quincy	40	18	Baxter	Jona Jun			2	1		1			1				5		
Quincy	40	19	Baxter	Saml	1			1					1				3		
Quincy	40	20	Baxter	Thompson		1			3				1		2		7		
Quincy	40	21	Bracket	James J			2		1			1	1				5		
Quincy	40	22	Bicknelll	Peter	1	2	2	1		5		2	1				14		
Quincy	40	23	Brown	Saml	1	1	1		1			2	1				7		
Quincy	40	24	Bass	David		2		1				1	1				5		
Quincy	40	25	Bass	Josiah	1	1		2	1	1			1	1			8		
Quincy	40	26	Billings	Edmd	1		1	1				3	1		2		9		
Quincy	40	27	Billings	Jno	2	2			1		2	1	1	1			10		
Quincy	40	28	Beule	Lillie						3	2	2		1			8		
Quincy	40	29	Belcher	Sam Jun	3	1		2		1			1				8		
Quincy	40	30	Baxter	Wm	2		2	2		1			2				9		
Quincy	40	31	Bass	Jona Deac	3		2	1		2			1	1			10		
Quincy	40	32	Bracket	Joseph			2		1			1		2			6		
Quincy	40	33	Bass	Hezekiah			1	1	1				1				4		
Quincy	40	34	Bass	Benj Esq		1		3					2	1			7		
Quincy	40	35	Butch	Jno	2			1		1			1				5		
Quincy	40	36	Clark	Wm. Rev.			1			1		1			1		4		
Quincy	40	37	Copeland	Saml		2		1		3	1		2				9		
Quincy	41	1	Copeland	Sarah							1		1				2		
Quincy	41	2	Crane	Thomas	1			1			1		1				4		
Quincy	41	3	Clark	Saml							1		1	1	1		2		
Quincy	41	4	Cleverly	Thom		1		1		1			1		1		4		
Quincy	41	5	Cleverly	Jno	1			1	1	2			1				6		
Quincy	41	6	Cleverly	Benj 2d	2			1		2		1					6		
Quincy	41	7	Chandler	Wm	2	2		1		2			1				8		
Quincy	41	8	Cook	Thomas	3	1		1		3			1				9		
Quincy	41	9	Carey	Alpheus	3	1	2	1		1	2	1					12		
Quincy	41	10	Cox	Saml	2	2		1		1		1	1				8		
Quincy	41	11	Clark	Mary Wid.			2				1		1				4		
Quincy	41	12	Cranch	Richa Esq		1			1		2	1	1	1			7		
Quincy	41	13	Cleverly	Joseph	2			1	1	1		3					8		
Quincy	41	14	Curtis	Noah	3	3	1	1			2		1				11		
Quincy	41	15	Crane	Elisha L.	1	1		1		1							4		
Quincy	41	16	Catin	Peter	1		1			2			1				5		
Quincy	41	17	Crane	Ebenz	2			1		2			1	1			7		
Quincy	41	18	Curtis	Edwd	3			1		1	1		1	1			8		
Quincy	41	19	Chandler	Elipht	2			1		1	1	1	1				6		
Quincy	41	20	Dwelly	Jno		1	3	2			1	2					9		
Quincy	41	21	Davis	Rufus	1			1					1				3		
Quincy	41	22	Dwelly	Leml	2			1				1					4		
Quincy	41	23	Everson	Wm P.	1			1					1				4		
Quincy	41	24	Field	Lydia Wid.	1	1			1		1		1				5		
Quincy	41	25	Field	Jackson	2	1	1		1	3	1		1				10		
Quincy	41	26	French	Lucy Wid.		2							1				3		
Quincy	41	27	Faxon	Benj	3			1			1						5		
Quincy	41	28	Field	James incd the Poor	2	1		1		1			1				6		
Quincy	41	29	Fenno	Jesse	1			1		2			1	1			6		
Quincy	41	30	French	Moses	4		1					1					6		

TOWN	PG#	LN#	LAST NAME	FIRST NAME	FREE WHITE MALES					FREE WHITE FEMALES					TOTAL ALL OTHER	TOTAL SLAVES	TOTALS	DISTRICT/ TOWNSHIP	NOTES
					under 10	10 to 16	16 to 26	26 to 45	45 and over	under 10	10 to 16	16 to 26	26 to 45	45 and over					
Quincy	41	31	Field	Joseph		1			1	2		1	1	1			7		
Quincy	41	32	Fowle	Jacob	3	1	1	1		1	1		1				9		
Quincy	41	33	Field	Gilbert		1		1		3			1				6		
Quincy	41	34	Greenleaf	Danl				2			1	1					4		
Quincy	41	35	Glover	Nathl		1		1			1		1				4		
Quincy	42	1	Glover	Elisha	1		3	1	1				2	1			9		
Quincy	42	2	Glover	Josiah				1					1				2		
Quincy	42	3	Glover	Ebenr				1		1			1				3		
Quincy	42	4	Glover	Benj W.			1						1				2		
Quincy	42	5	Glover	Wm			4		1		1			1			7		
Quincy	42	6	Gay	Henry L.	2			1		2	1		1				7		
Quincy	42	7	Gay	Abigail						2		1	1				4		
Quincy	42	8	Hall	Edward	2			1		1		1					5		
Quincy	42	9	Hartwich	Adam				1		2		1					4		
Quincy	42	10	Hall	Jno		1	2		1			2		1			7		
Quincy	42	11	Hartwich	Peter	2		2	1		3		1					9		
Quincy	42	12	Hunt	Mary			1			3		1		1			6		
Quincy	42	13	Hayden	Abel	1			1		2		1					5		
Quincy	42	14	Hayden	Abel	1			1		2		1					5		
Quincy	42	15	Hubart	Josh		1		2	1		1	1		1			7		
Quincy	42	16	Hubart	Peter	1	1		1		4			1				8		
Quincy	42	17	Hartwich	Fred	2		2	1		1	1	1					8		
Quincy	42	18	Heath	Saml W.			1			2	1		1				5		
Quincy	42	19	Hobart	Saml	2	1		1		2	2		1				9		
Quincy	42	20	Hartwick	Charles	1			1		2		1					5		
Quincy	42	21	Hayden	Caleb	2		1	2		1			2				8		
Quincy	42	22	Hayden	Elisha	2		1						1				4		
Quincy	42	23	Hayden	Caleb Jr	2	1		1		1			1				6		
Quincy	42	24	Hayden	Nathl	4	1							1				7		
Quincy	42	25	Howard	James					1	1	1			2			5		
Quincy	42	26	Horton	Enoch					1	1			1				3		
Quincy	42	27	Hunt	Joseph	1			1		2		1					5		
Quincy	42	28	Johnson	Thomas											3		3		
Quincy	42	29	Jones	Saml					1								1		
Quincy	42	30	Mears	George			1					1					2		
Quincy	42	31	Miller	Eben Esq				2			1		1				4		
Quincy	42	32	Meads	Wm P.	1	1		1		2		1					6		
Quincy	42	33	Miller	Jno				2		2		1					5		
Quincy	42	34	Marsh	Wilson	1	1	1		1	3	3		1				11		
Quincy	42	35	Marsh	Jona	2			1		1	1		1				6		
Quincy	42	36	Merrick	Richd											2		2		
Quincy	42	37	Newcomb	Richd		1		1			1		1				4		
Quincy	42	38	Newcomb	Jno R.	3			1		1			1				6		
Quincy	42	39	Newcomb	Eben Jr.	1			1		1	1		1				5		
Quincy	42	40	Newcomb	Charles	3			1		2	2		1	1			10		
Quincy	42	41	Nightingale	Reg	1		3				1	1					6		
Quincy	42	42	Nightingale	Jos.			2		1			3		1			7		
Quincy	42	43	Nightingale	Saml Jr	3			1		1			1				6		
Quincy	42	44	Nightingale	Dan	1			1		1		1					4		
Quincy	42	45	Nightingale	Jno	1	2		1				2	1				7		
Quincy	42	46	Nightingale	Eben	2	3		1		1			1				8		
Quincy	42	47	Nightingale	Saml	1		1		1			1	1				5		
Quincy	42	48	Newcomb	Jno	5	2	3			1	1	2	1	2			17		
Quincy	42	49	Porter	David				1					1				2		
Quincy	42	50	Pierce	Jonas		1	1					1	1				5		
Quincy	42	51	Pray	Jno	2	2	3	1		2	1	1	1				13		
Quincy	42	52	Pope	Asa	1	1	2			1		1					6		
Quincy	42	53	Pierce	Richd	1			1		2				1			5		
Quincy	42	54	Phipps	Thom	2	1			1	2	1	1	1				9		
Quincy	42	55	Pope	Jno				1		2							4		
Quincy	42	56	Pratt	James	1		1					1					3		
Quincy	42	57	Pray	Samuel				1		1			1				3		
Quincy	42	58	Pray	Benj	3	1		1		2		1	1	1			10		
Quincy	42	59	Quincy	Morton Esq			1	1				1	1	1			5		
Quincy	42	60	Quincy	Josiah Esq			1	1		1		2					5		
Quincy	42	61	Rawson	Jona	2	2		1		3		1					9		
Quincy	42	62	Richard	Jno P.	1		3	1		1		1	1				8		
Quincy	42	63	Ripley	Spencer		1		1			1	1					4		
Quincy	43	1	Shaw	Wm Esq	1	2		3		2	1	2			3		14		
Quincy	43	2	Spear	Daniel		1		1					1	1			4		
Quincy	43	3	Spear	Steph. Jr	2			1					1				4		
Quincy	43	4	Spear	Elijah			1						1				2		
Quincy	43	5	Savel	Edward	1	1		1		2	1	1					7		
Quincy	43	6	Stetson	Amos					1		1			1			3		
Quincy	43	7	Saunders	Jno					1		1	2		1			5		
Quincy	43	8	Spear	Jno	1	1		2	1	2	1		2				10		
Quincy	43	9	Spear	Seth	2	1			3	4	1			1			12		
Quincy	43	10	Spear	Wm		1			1					1			3		
Quincy	43	11	Savil	Saml Jr	1	1	3	1		2	2		2				12		

TOWN	PG#	LN#	LAST NAME	FIRST NAME	FREE WHITE MALES					FREE WHITE FEMALES					TOTAL ALL OTHER	TOTAL SLAVES	TOTALS	DISTRICT/ TOWNSHIP	NOTES
					under 10	10 to 16	16 to 26	26 to 45	45 and over	under 10	10 to 16	16 to 26	26 to 45	45 and over					
Quincy	43	12	Saunders	Wm					1	3				1			5		
Quincy	43	13	Savil	Nathl	3				1					1			5		
Quincy	43	14	Savil	Saml					1					1			2		
Quincy	43	15	Stone	Jno					1					1			2		
Quincy	43	16	Spear	Jedh	2		1	1		1			1				6		
Quincy	43	17	Thayer	Gains	2	1		1		1		1					6		
Quincy	43	18	Turrell	Thom			2			1		1					4		
Quincy	43	19	Turrell	Joseph		1		1					1	1			4		
Quincy	43	20	Trott	Thom		1		1				2	1	2			7		
Quincy	43	21	Trask	Saml				1						1			2		
Quincy	43	22	Turrell	Nathl	2			1		2			1				6		
Quincy	43	23	Underwood	Eben	2		1					1	1				5		
Quincy	43	24	Veesey	Metran				1						2			3		
Quincy	43	25	Veesey	Elijah	2	2	1	1		2	1			2			11		
Quincy	43	26	Veesey	Wm				1						1			2		
Quincy	43	27	Whitney	Peter Rev.			1					1	1				3		
Quincy	43	28	Webb	Jona		1		1		1	2	5		1			11		
Quincy	43	29	White	Man.										2	4		6		
Quincy	43	30	Wilson	Jno				1									1		
Quincy	43	31	Webster	Thom				1						1			2		

TOWN	PG#	LN#	HEADS OF HOUSEHOLD		FREE WHITE MALES					FREE WHITE FEMALES					TOTAL ALL OTHER	TOTAL SLAVES	TOTALS	DISTRICT/ TOWNSHIP	NOTES
			LAST NAME	FIRST NAME	under 10	10 to 16	16 to 26	26 to 45	45 and over	under 10	10 to 16	16 to 26	26 to 45	45 and over					
Randolph	123	1	Alden	Ebenezer	1	1		1	1	1			2				7		
Randolph	123	2	Alden	Silas	4	2	1	1		1		2	1				12		
Randolph	123	3	Alden	Simeon	1			2		2			1				7		
Randolph	123	4	Adams	John	1	1		1		2			1				6		
Randolph	123	5	Allen	Samuel				1		2		1	1				5		
Randolph	123	6	Allen	Benja				1									1		
Randolph	123	7	Bass	Samuel	2	2	2	1			1	1	1	1			11		
Randolph	123	8	Belcher	Nathaniel	2		1	1		2	3		1				10		
Randolph	123	9	Belcher	Richard	1	1	1	1					2				6		
Randolph	123	10	Belcher	Billy	2					3			1				7		
Randolph	123	11	Belcher	Joseph	2		2	1	1			1	2	1			10		
Randolph	123	12	Belcher	Samuel		2	1	1		3	1		1				9		
Randolph	123	13	Belcher	Epgraim	2	1		1		1			1				6		
Randolph	123	14	Belcher	Thomas		1			1		3	1	1				7		
Randolph	123	15	Belcher	Jonathan	1		1	1				1	1				5		
Randolph	123	16	Belcher	John	1			1			1						3		
Randolph	123	17	Belcher	Ebenezer				1									1		
Randolph	123	18	Beals	John	1	1	1			1			1				5		
Randolph	124	1	Beals	Eleazar	2	1	2	1		3	1	1	1				12		
Randolph	124	2	Beals	Iseael				1			1	1					3		
Randolph	124	3	Burres	David	3		1						1				5		
Randolph	124	4	Canady		1					1		1					3		First name left blank
Randolph	124	5	Clark	Barnabas				2		1	1	1	1				6		
Randolph	124	6	Clark	Jacob	3		1			2		1					7		
Randolph	124	7	Clark	Atkins	2	1	1		1	1	1	2		1			10		
Randolph	124	8	Clark	Amasa		1				1		1					3		
Randolph	124	9	Clark	Joshua	1	2		1			1		1				6		
Randolph	124	10	Clark	Eliza Wid							1		1				2		
Randolph	124	11	Cheeseman	Silas	1			1		3		1	1				7		
Randolph	124	12	Curtis	Jonathan		1		1					2				4		
Randolph	124	13	Curtis	Jonathan		1		1					2				4		
Randolph	124	14	Curtis	Samuel		1		1		1			1				4		
Randolph	124	15	French	Joshua	2	1	1	1		2		1	1				9		
Randolph	124	16	French	Zenas	2		1	1		2	1	1	1				9		
Randolph	124	17	French	Jotham	1	1	2	1		1	1	1	1				9		
Randolph	124	18	French	Thomas	1	1	4		1	2	1	2		1	1		14		
Randolph	124	19	French	Luther	2	1	1	1				1	1				7		
Randolph	124	20	French	William	1	2	1	1		1	1		1				8		
Randolph	124	21	French	Nehemiah		1		1				1	1				4		
Randolph	124	22	French	Adonijah	1		1			1		1					4		
Randolph	124	23	French	Esther		1							1				2		
Randolph	124	24	Faxon	Edward	1	3		1		2			1				8		
Randolph	124	25	Faxon	Daniel		1				1		1					3		
Randolph	124	26	Gurney	Giles		1						1					2		
Randolph	124	27	Hayden	Stephen	1	1						1					3		
Randolph	124	28	Hayden	Ziba			1			2	2	1					6		
Randolph	124	29	Howard	Joshua		1		1			1	1					4		
Randolph	124	30	Howard	Aaron	1	1		1				1		1			5		
Randolph	124	31	Howard	Simeon		1		1		1			1				4		
Randolph	124	32	Howard	Zebulon Jr		1		2		2			1				6		
Randolph	124	33	Howard	Eliza Wid									1				1		
Randolph	124	34	Howard	Asa	1		1			1		1					4		
Randolph	124	35	Howard	Ebenezer				1					1				2		
Randolph	125	1	Holbrook	Ichabod	2	2	1	1		1	1		1	2			11		
Randolph	125	2	Holbrook	Thomas	2	2		1		1		1					7		
Randolph	125	3	Hollis	Adam	1		1	1		2			1	1			7		
Randolph	125	4	Hollis	John				1		1			1				3		
Randolph	125	5	Hollis	Ambrose	5		1						1				7		
Randolph	125	6	Hubbard	Enoch		1		1		1			1				4		
Randolph	125	7	Hubbard	Nathl				1				1	1				3		
Randolph	125	8	Hudson	Eli	1		1					1					3		
Randolph	125	9	Hunting	Daniel	2			1					2				5		
Randolph	125	10	Hunting	Joseph		2		1		1	1	2	1	1			9		
Randolph	125	11	Hunting	Nathl		1		1				1		1			4		
Randolph	125	12	Hunting	Hannah Wid	2					1	1	1					5		
Randolph	125	13	Jones	Abraham	1	3		1		3	1		1				10		
Randolph	125	14	Jones	Ransel	3			1		1	1		1				7		
Randolph	125	15	Jones	Mary									1				1		
Randolph	125	16	Jackson	Peter			1						1				2		
Randolph	125	17	Kimbal	William	2		1				1		1				5		
Randolph	125	18	Kingsbury	Joshua		1		1		1			1				4		
Randolph	125	19	Kingman	James				1					1				2		
Randolph	125	20	Lindfield	William				1					1				2		
Randolph	125	21	Lindfield	Wm 2d		1		1			1	2		1			6		
Randolph	125	22	Lindfield	Wm 3d	2		1	1		1	1	1	1				8		
Randolph	125	23	Lindfield	David		1		1				1		1			4		
Randolph	125	24	Lindfield	Saml	1	1	1	1			1	1	1				7		
Randolph	125	25	Lindfield	Benjamin	2			1		1			1				5		
Randolph	125	26	Littlefield	Aaron	2	1		1		1	1		1				7		
Randolph	125	27	Littlefield	Hannah Wid							1		1				2		
Randolph	125	28	Ludden	Hezekiah		1		1					2	2			6		
Randolph	125	29	Ludden	Samuel	1		1	1		3		1	1				8		
Randolph	125	30	Mann	Seth		1	1	1		1		1	2				8		
Randolph	125	31	Mann	Benjamin		2		1		2	1	2		1			9		
Randolph	125	32	Mann	Joseph	1	1	1	1		2			1				7		
Randolph	126	1	Madden	John Jr	2			1		2	1		1				7		
Randolph	126	2	Mark	Josiah	2			1		1			1				5		
Randolph	126	3	Niles	Nathaniel		1		1					1				4		
Randolph	126	4	Niles	Isaac	1			1			1	1		2			6		
Randolph	126	5	Niles	Jacob	1		1			2			2				6		

TOWN	PG#	LN#	HEADS OF HOUSEHOLD LAST NAME	HEADS OF HOUSEHOLD FIRST NAME	FREE WHITE MALES					FREE WHITE FEMALES					TOTAL ALL OTHER	TOTAL SLAVES	TOTALS	DISTRICT/ TOWNSHIP	NOTES
					under 10	10 to 16	16 to 26	26 to 45	45 and over	under 10	10 to 16	16 to 26	26 to 45	45 and over					
Randolph	126	6	Niles	Joshua				1		3			1				5		
Randolph	126	7	Niles	Ebenezer					1			1		1			3		
Randolph	126	8	Noyes	David	1	2	1	1		1	1		1				8		
Randolph	126	9	Nucumb	Samuel				1					1	1			3		
Randolph	126	10	Packard	Samuel		1	1						1				3		
Randolph	126	11	Paine	Zeba	3			1					2				6		
Randolph	126	12	Paine	Benjamin	4	1		1					1	1			8		
Randolph	126	13	Paine	Silas	4			1		1			1	1			8		
Randolph	126	14	Paine	Nathl				1		1			2				4		
Randolph	126	15	Penniman	Enoch				1		2		1		1			5		
Randolph	126	16	Pierce	William	1			1				1					3		
Randolph	126	17	Porter	Abijah				1		1			1				3		
Randolph	126	18	Porter	Joseph	2	2		1		2			1				8		
Randolph	126	19	Reed	Frederick			1			2			1	1			5		
Randolph	126	20	Reed	Asa	1		1						2				4		
Randolph	126	21	Reed	Jesse			1										1		
Randolph	126	22	Sawin	Eliphelet		2		1						2			5		
Randolph	126	23	Sawin	Eunice Wid	1									1			2		
Randolph	126	24	Spear	Nathaniel	1	1	1	1		1	2	1					8		
Randolph	126	25	Spear	Jonathan		2		1					1	1			6		
Randolph	126	26	Spear	Joseph	1	2		1		2	1		1	1			9		
Randolph	126	27	Spear	Joshua	2		1	1		1			1	1			7		
Randolph	126	28	Spear	John										1			1		
Randolph	126	29	Spear	Mary Wid										1			1		
Randolph	126	30	Silvester	Philip	1			1						1			3		
Randolph	126	31	Stone	Timothy	2	1		1		1			1				6		
Randolph	127	1	Spooner	William					1	1				1			3		
Randolph	127	2	Stetson	Benja		1	1	1				1		1			5		
Randolph	127	3	Stetson	William			1			1		1					3		
Randolph	127	4	Stetson	Gideon	1	1	3	1		1	1	1		1			10		
Randolph	127	5	Stetson	Jonathan	1	1	2	1					1				6		
Randolph	127	6	Stetson	Peter			1					1					2		
Randolph	127	7	Smith	Isaac	1	1	2	1		1			2	2			10		
Randolph	127	8	Strong	Jonathan Revd	2	3		1		3			1	1			11		
Randolph	127	9	Stevens	Wid										1			1		
Randolph	127	10	Thayer	Shadrach	2		1							1			4		
Randolph	127	11	Thayer	Paul	1			1				1	2	1			7		
Randolph	127	12	Thayer	Jeremiah	2	1		1		1	1	1					8		
Randolph	127	13	Thayer	Richard		1	1			3	2	1	1				9		
Randolph	127	14	Thayer	Noah	1			1		1				1			4		
Randolph	127	15	Thayer	Meshech	2		1			1			1	1			6		
Randolph	127	16	Thayer	Rufus	1		2						1	1			5		
Randolph	127	17	Thayer	Samuel	1	1	1	1	1				2	1			8		
Randolph	127	18	Thayer	Luther	4	1		1				1		1			8		
Randolph	127	19	Thayer	Zacheus				1	1			2		1			5		
Randolph	127	20	Thayer	Micah				1						1			2		
Randolph	127	21	Thayer	Micah 2d	2			1		1			1				5		
Randolph	127	22	Thayer	Micah 3d			2			1			1				4		
Randolph	127	23	Thayer	Jonathan		2		1		4	1		1				9		
Randolph	127	24	Thayer	Phinehas				1		3	2		1				7		
Randolph	127	25	Thayer	Benja				1						2			3		
Randolph	127	26	Thayer	Levi	2			1		1			1				5		
Randolph	127	27	Thayer	Timothy				1			1		1				3		
Randolph	127	28	Thayer	Robert	3			1		1			1	1			9		
Randolph	127	29	Thayer	Simeon	1	1		1		1	1	1		1			8		
Randolph	127	30	Thayer	Alexander	2			1		2			1				6		
Randolph	127	31	Thayer	Ezra	3	2		1		1			1				9		
Randolph	127	32	Thayer	Levi Junr		1							1				2		
Randolph	127	33	Thayer	Peter	1			1		2			1				5		
Randolph	127	34	Thayer	Peter				1									1		
Randolph	127	35	Turner	Seth		1		1						1			3		
Randolph	127	36	Turner	Seth Junr	1		1	1				1	1				6		
Randolph	127	37	Tower	Gideon	1		1	1				1		1			5		
Randolph	127	38	Tower	Gideon Junr	2	1	1	1		3	2	2	1				13		
Randolph	128	1	Tower	Joseph		1		1				1		1			4		
Randolph	128	2	Tower	Isaac	1	1		1				1					4		
Randolph	128	3	Temple	Samuel	1			1		1			1				4		
Randolph	128	4	Vinton	Oliver	1			1		1			1				4		
Randolph	128	5	Wales	Elisha		1	1	1		2	2	1		1			9		
Randolph	128	6	Wales	Atherton				1						1			2		
Randolph	128	7	Wales	Jonathan	1			1						1			3		
Randolph	128	8	Wales	Jonathan Jun			1										1		
Randolph	128	9	Wales	Ephraim		1	1	1		1	1						5		
Randolph	128	10	Wales	Atherton Jun	2	1		1		1	1	1					7		
Randolph	128	11	Wales	John	1	2						1	2				6		
Randolph	128	12	Wales	Silence Wid									2	1			3		
Randolph	128	13	White	Joseph		1		1		1	1			1			5		
Randolph	128	14	White	Cornelius		1	3	2				1		1			8		
Randolph	128	15	White	Rhoda Wid	2								1				3		
Randolph	128	16	White	Caleb	3			1						1			5		
Randolph	128	17	White	Bailey		1		1		3	1		1				7		
Randolph	128	18	White	Simeon				1		2			1				4		
Randolph	128	19	White	Lot	1			1		1			1				4		
Randolph	128	20	White	Micah	3	1		1		1	2		1				9		
Randolph	128	21	Whitcomb	Jacob		2	3	1		1		2		1			10		
Randolph	128	22	Whitcomb	Phebe		1	1			2	1		1				6		
Randolph	128	23	Whitcomb	John			1			1			1				3		
Randolph	128	24	Whitcomb	Moses	2			1		2	1		1				7		
Randolph	128	25	Whitcomb	Robert	2			1		1	1		1	1			7		
Randolph	128	26	Whiting	William			1					1					2		

TOWN	PG#	LN#	HEADS OF HOUSEHOLD		FREE WHITE MALES					FREE WHITE FEMALES					TOTAL ALL OTHER	TOTAL SLAVES	TOTALS	DISTRICT/ TOWNSHIP	NOTES
			LAST NAME	FIRST NAME	under 10	10 to 16	16 to 26	26 to 45	45 and over	under 10	10 to 16	16 to 26	26 to 45	45 and over					
Randolph	128	27	Whyton	Samuel	2			1		1		1					5		
Randolph	128	28	Wild	John	1	1			1	1	1		1	1			7		
Randolph	128	29	Wild	Joshua	2		1					1					4		
Randolph	128	30	West	Thomas					1	1			1	1			4		
Randolph	128	31	West	John			1					1					2		
Randolph	128	32	Woods	Samuel					1				1	1			3		
Randolph	128	33	Woods	Samuel Junr				1		2			1				4		
Randolph	128	34	Wentworth	Theophilus	1			1		1		1					4		

TOWN	PG#	LN#	LAST NAME	FIRST NAME	FREE WHITE MALES under 10	10 to 16	16 to 26	26 to 45	45 and over	FREE WHITE FEMALES under 10	10 to 16	16 to 26	26 to 45	45 and over	TOTAL ALL OTHER	TOTAL SLAVES	TOTALS	DISTRICT/ TOWNSHIP	NOTES
Roxbury	99	1	Warner	Jonathan	1	1			1	2	1	2		1			9		
Roxbury	99	2	Newell	Abigail								1		1			2		
Roxbury	99	3	Sumner	Clement	2	1	1		1	2	1	2		1			11		
Roxbury	99	4	Woodard	John Chever	1	3	1	1			1	1	1	1			10		
Roxbury	99	5	Worsley	Joseph	2	1	2	3			2		1	1			12		
Roxbury	99	6	Williams	Stedman	2	1	3	1			1	1	1	1			11		
Roxbury	99	7	Sumner	Samuel			4		1		4	1		1			11		
Roxbury	99	8	Burrel	James			1	1		2	1	1	1				7		
Roxbury	99	9	Lethbridge	Fisher		1		1						1			3		
Roxbury	99	10	Leprelete	Deborah		1	1							1			3		
Roxbury	100	1	Juro	French Consul				1						1			2		
Roxbury	100	2	Mayo	Thomas 3d	3			1		2			1				7		
Roxbury	100	3	Gore	Paul	2		4	1		2			1	1			11		
Roxbury	100	4	Curtis	Joseph			4	1			1	1	1	1			9		
Roxbury	100	5	Williams	John D.	2	1	4		4		1	1		1			14		
Roxbury	100	6	Williams	Joseph	1	1	1	2	2		1	2	2	2			14		
Roxbury	100	7	Withington	Lewis	1			1					1	1			4		
Roxbury	100	8	Stilling	Mary						3	1		1				5		
Roxbury	101	1	Davenport	Joseph	1	1		2	1			1	1		1		8		
Roxbury	101	2	Barry	Samuel			8	1			1	1	1				12		
Roxbury	101	3	Hancock	Belcher	3	1	1		1	1	1		2				10		
Roxbury	101	4	Bradley	Lemual	1		1			1		1					4		
Roxbury	101	5	Baker	Eleazer	1			1					1				3		
Roxbury	101	6	Davenport	Benjamin		1								1			2		
Roxbury	101	7	Brewer	William		1	1	3		1	2	1	1	1			11		
Roxbury	101	8	Downer	Eliphalet Decn		5		1		1				1			8		
Roxbury	101	9	Peirce	James	1			1		1			1				4		
Roxbury	101	10	Crehore	Joseph	2	1	1	1		1	1		1				8		
Roxbury	101	11	Wyman	William		1		2		1	2		1				7		
Roxbury	101	12	Faxon	Nathaniel		2		1					1				4		
Roxbury	101	13	Thayer	Ann										2			2		
Roxbury	101	14	Ward	John	1		1		1	1	1		1	1			7		
Roxbury	101	15	Ward	Samuel		1	1	1				1					4		
Roxbury	101	16	Dexter	Willibar	2		1			1		1	1				6		
Roxbury	101	17	Shed	Mary									1				1		
Roxbury	101	18	Dale	John			1			2			1				4		
Roxbury	101	19	Peirce	Eli			1			1			1				3		
Roxbury	101	20	Johnson	Joseph				1		1			1				3		
Roxbury	101	21	Jones	Lewis		1	1			3			1				6		
Roxbury	101	22	Seaver	Susannah								1	1				2		
Roxbury	101	23	Heath	Joseph	1	1		1			1	1					5		
Roxbury	101	24	Hide	Huldah	2						1		1				4		
Roxbury	101	25	Coney	John	2		1			2			1				6		
Roxbury	101	26	Cunningham	William			1	1									2		
Roxbury	101	27	Heath	Peleg			2	1		1	2		1				7		
Roxbury	101	28	Howe	George	2		1	1		1	1		1				7		
Roxbury	101	29	Craft	Abigail	1	1	5					3	1				11		
Roxbury	101	30	Davis	Isaac			5	1			1	1	1				9		
Roxbury	101	31	Gould	Jacob		3	1			2		1	1				8		
Roxbury	101	32	Dudley	Sarah		1							1				2		
Roxbury	101	33	Peirpont	Robert	2	1	2	5		1			1	2			14		
Roxbury	101	34	Harriman	Moses	1		2	1		1	1	1					7		
Roxbury	102	1	Fellows	John M.	1			1		2			1				5		
Roxbury	102	2	Harris	Noah			1			1			1				3		
Roxbury	102	3	Langley	Ester		1	4				1	1		1			8		
Roxbury	102	4	White	Bartholomew			1			1		1					3		
Roxbury	102	5	Faxon	Eleb	2	2	2	1		1		1	1				10		
Roxbury	102	6	Freeman	Samuel			1			4			1				6		
Roxbury	102	7	Duich	Benjamin		1		1			1		2				5		
Roxbury	102	8	Cooper	Isaac			41			1		1					3		
Roxbury	102	9	Tileston	Nathaniel	2			2		1		1	1				7		
Roxbury	102	10	Seaver	William	1		4	1		1		1	1				9		
Roxbury	102	11	McCarthy	William		1	1					1		1			4		
Roxbury	102	12	McCarthy	Sarah								1		1			2		
Roxbury	102	13	Thomas	Caleb			1			2	1		1				5		
Roxbury	102	14	Stiner	John				1		1			1				3		
Roxbury	102	15	Stone	John				1		1			1				3		
Roxbury	102	16	Hendrake	David	1		1			1			1				4		
Roxbury	102	17	Mayo	William	2			1		1			3				7		
Roxbury	102	18	White	James				1		1	1		1				4		
Roxbury	102	19	Hawes	Benjamin		1	2						1				4		
Roxbury	102	20	Bugbee	Edward	2		1			1	1		1				6		
Roxbury	102	21	Prince	Darbee											5		5		
Roxbury	102	22	Minot	Drever											8		8		
Roxbury	102	23	Skillings	Pollidore											5		5		
Roxbury	102	24	Smith	Thaddeus	2		1			1			1				5		
Roxbury	102	25	Domineque				1	1					1				3		First name left blank
Roxbury	102	26	Lewes	James	2		1	1		2		1	1				8		
Roxbury	102	27	Lewes	John		1	1			1		1	1				5		
Roxbury	102	28	Fisher	Lever	1			1		1			1				4		
Roxbury	102	29	Green	John	2	1		1		1	1		1				7		
Roxbury	102	30	Bugbee	Ebenezer	3			1		1	1	2		1			9		
Roxbury	102	31	Seaver	Ebenezer Esq	2	1	5	2	1	3	1	2	1				18		
Roxbury	102	32	Seaver	Tabatha			1				1		1	1			3		
Roxbury	102	33	Parker	William	1		1						1				3		
Roxbury	102	34	Curtis	Isaac		1	2				1	2					6		
Roxbury	102	35	Blaney	Samuel		1	2			1			1				5		
Roxbury	102	36	Davis	John 3d	2		1	1		1			1				6		
Roxbury	102	37	Davis	Jacob		1		1						1			3		
Roxbury	102	38	Fowle	Jonathan	2			1		3	1		1				8		

TOWN	PG#	LN#	HEADS OF HOUSEHOLD LAST NAME	HEADS OF HOUSEHOLD FIRST NAME	FREE WHITE MALES under 10	10 to 16	16 to 26	26 to 45	45 and over	FREE WHITE FEMALES under 10	10 to 16	16 to 26	26 to 45	45 and over	TOTAL ALL OTHER	TOTAL SLAVES	TOTALS	DISTRICT/TOWNSHIP	NOTES
Roxbury	102	39	Everet	Nathaniel				1		1	1		1				4		
Roxbury	103	1	Jordon	John			1						1				2		
Roxbury	103	2	Forbes	Elisha			1	2				2	1				6		
Roxbury	103	3	Wyman	Thomas			1		1				1				3		
Roxbury	103	4	Hoyt	Lewis	2			1		2			1				6		
Roxbury	103	5	Withington	Phinehas	2	1	3	1		2	5	1	1	1			17		
Roxbury	103	6	Fuller	Ebenezer				1		2			1				4		
Roxbury	103	7	Heath	William Esq Honble		1	2		1				1	1	1		7		
Roxbury	103	8	Heath	William Junr	2			1		1			1				5		
Roxbury	103	9	Spooner	Sally	1						1		1				3		
Roxbury	103	10	Wyman	Thomas Junr	3			1		2	1		1				8		
Roxbury	103	11	Saunderson	Daniel				1			1			1			3		
Roxbury	103	12	Burrell	Silvanus	1	1		1		2	1		1				7		
Roxbury	103	13	Heath	Samuel		1	2	1					1				5		
Roxbury	103	14	Lynch	Dennis	5			1		1			1				8		
Roxbury	103	15	Lethbridge	Mary									2				2		
Roxbury	103	16	Whitman	Hannah									1				1		
Roxbury	103	17	Williams	Henry H.			1	1									2		
Roxbury	103	18	Brewer	Nathaniel	1			1		3	1		1				7		
Roxbury	103	19	Gould	Otis		1	2	1		1	1		2				8		
Roxbury	103	20	Nolin	George	1			1		2			1				5		
Roxbury	103	21	Champney	Jonathan				1					1				2		
Roxbury	103	22	As Overseer of the Poor		1				8	1				11			21		
Roxbury	103	23	Ruggles	Nathaniel Esq	1	1	1		1		1	2	1	2			10		
Roxbury	103	24	Magee	James		2	1		1	5	1	1	2	1	3		17		
Roxbury	103	25	Williams	Stephen 3d	2	2	1	1		3	2		2				13		
Roxbury	103	26	Sloan	David	1	1		1		2			1				6		
Roxbury	103	27	Holbrook	Daniel				1									1		
Roxbury	103	28	Read	John Esq			1	1					1	1	1		4		
Roxbury	103	29	Read	John Junr	2	1	1	1		1		1	1				8		
Roxbury	103	30	White	Aaron		4	1	1		1	3		1				11		
Roxbury	103	31	Mayo	Thomas Junr	1		1	1		2			1	1			7		
Roxbury	103	32	Weld	Samuel		1	2	1		1	1	1					7		
Roxbury	103	33	Warren	Samuel					1			1	1				3		
Roxbury	103	34	Davis	Jonathan Doc		1		1			1		1	1			5		
Roxbury	103	35	Bedge	John				1					1				2		
Roxbury	104	1	Langdon	Mary						2	1		1				4		
Roxbury	104	2	Wyman	John	2		1	1		2		1	1	1			9		
Roxbury	104	3	Williams	Hannah		1		2			3	1	1	1	1		9		
Roxbury	104	4	Smith	Joseph				1					1				2		
Roxbury	104	5	Ruggles	Joseph Junr	2		1	1	1	3		1	1				10		
Roxbury	104	6	Ruggles	Martha	1		1	3				2	2	1			10		
Roxbury	104	7	Ruggles	Joseph Esq		1	3	1		1			1	2			9		
Roxbury	104	8	Pratt	Simeon		2	1	1		1	1		1				8		
Roxbury	104	9	Lambert	William				1		3	1		2		2		9		
Roxbury	104	10	Lee	William			1	1		2			1	1			6		
Roxbury	104	11	Roads	Moses		1	1						1				3		
Roxbury	104	12	Williams	Stephen		1	4		1				2	1			9		
Roxbury	104	13	Mears	James Junr				1			1		1				3		
Roxbury	104	14	Seaver	Benjamin	3	1	2	1			1	1	1	1			11		
Roxbury	104	15	Sumner	Elizabeth		1				1			2	1	2		7		
Roxbury	104	16	Poignard	David	1			1			2	1	1				6		
Roxbury	104	17	Dillaway	Samuel	2			1		1		2					6		
Roxbury	104	18	Bartlett	John Doc	1			1		2	2	1	1				8		
Roxbury	104	19	Bicknall	Humphrey	3	1	3	1		1		1	1				11		
Roxbury	104	20	Orr	Mary		1							1	1			3		
Roxbury	104	21	Seaver	Joseph				1				2					3		
Roxbury	104	22	Pratt	William	1		1						1				3		
Roxbury	104	23	Seaver	Nathaniel				1		1			1				3		
Roxbury	104	24	Freeman	Phillip	2			1		2		1	1				7		
Roxbury	104	25	Symms	Stephen	3			1		1	2		1				8		
Roxbury	104	26	Hayden	Abner		1		1		1			1				4		
Roxbury	104	27	Peirce	Lemuel	1		1	2		1			1				6		
Roxbury	104	28	Bird	Samuel			1	1				1					3		
Roxbury	104	29	Fedder	James	1			1		2			1				5		
Roxbury	104	30	Mathews	Gardner				1		1			1				3		
Roxbury	104	31	Clap	Caleb	1	1	5	1		2			1		1		12		
Roxbury	104	32	Murreil	Joseph	1			1	1	3			1				7		
Roxbury	105	1	Davis	Stephen	3			1		3			2				8		
Roxbury	105	2	Dowse	James	2			1		1			1				5		
Roxbury	105	3	Gay	Joel	3		3	2	1	3		3	1				15		
Roxbury	105	4	Mansfield	Stephen	3	1		1		2			1				8		
Roxbury	105	5	Davis	Lemuel	1			1		1		1					4		
Roxbury	105	6	Bowen	Samuel				1									1		
Roxbury	105	7	Bowen	John	2			1		1		1		1			6		
Roxbury	105	8	Levens	Joel			1	2		1			1				5		
Roxbury	105	9	Shepherd	James				1		1		1		1			4		
Roxbury	105	10	Seaver	John	1	1				2			1				5		
Roxbury	105	11	Crane	Nathaniel	1			1					1	1			4		
Roxbury	105	12	Symms	George	2	1		2			1		1				7		
Roxbury	105	13	Smith	Ebenezer	1	1	1		1	1		2	2	1			10		
Roxbury	105	14	Dudley	Elijah	1			1		3	1		1				7		
Roxbury	105	15	Burrell	Jerusha	1	1	1	2		2	3	2		1			13		
Roxbury	105	16	Smith	Ralph	1	3	4	2	1	1		1	2		1	1	17		
Roxbury	105	17	Whiting	Joel	1		2	1			1	1	1				7		
Roxbury	105	18	Hunting	Asa		1		1		1			2	1			6		
Roxbury	105	19	Wait	Benjamin			1	1		2			1				5		
Roxbury	105	20	Wait	Rebecca		1						3	2	1			7		
Roxbury	105	21	Parker	Ruben	1	1	1		3				1				7		
Roxbury	105	22	Dove	John	1	2		1		1		1	1				7		

TOWN	PG#	LN#	LAST NAME	FIRST NAME	FREE WHITE MALES					FREE WHITE FEMALES					TOTAL ALL OTHER	TOTAL SLAVES	TOTALS	DISTRICT/ TOWNSHIP	NOTES
					under 10	10 to 16	16 to 26	26 to 45	45 and over	under 10	10 to 16	16 to 26	26 to 45	45 and over					
Roxbury	105	23	Williams	John F.				1					1				2		
Roxbury	105	24	Wait	Samuel			1	3		1		2		1	2		10		
Roxbury	105	25	Gore	Samuel		1		1	1					1			4		
Roxbury	105	26	Gore	Samuel Junr				1		1		2					4		
Roxbury	105	27	Shed	Grace	2		1					1	1				5		
Roxbury	105	28	Robins	William			1			1		2					4		
Roxbury	105	29	Milet	Samuel			4	1		1	2	2	1				11		
Roxbury	105	30	Whitney	Elisha		1	5		1		1		1	1			10		
Roxbury	105	31	Beduna	Benjamin				1									1		
Roxbury	105	32	Balaney	William	1	2	1	1		1		2	1				9		
Roxbury	105	33	Healey	Sarah	2		2			2	1		1				8		
Roxbury	105	34	Cummins	Cezar											6		6		
Roxbury	106	1	Munroe	Jedediah				1	2		2		1				6		
Roxbury	106	2	Cheney	Thomas		1		1	1	1		1	1				6		
Roxbury	106	3	Turner	Edward		2		1		3	1	1	1				9		
Roxbury	106	4	Munroe	Nehemiah		1	5		1	1		1		1			10		
Roxbury	106	5	Clap	John			3	1		3	1	1	1				10		
Roxbury	106	6	Peirce	Martin	1	1			1	2	1	1	1				8		
Roxbury	106	7	Sumner	Edward	2	1	1	2	1	4	2	2	1				16		
Roxbury	106	8	Williams	John		1		1	1		1	1	1	1			7		
Roxbury	106	9	Hawes	Mary	2	1					1	1	1				6		
Roxbury	106	10	Ramsdell	Masheck				1					1				2		
Roxbury	106	11	Nolen	Thomas			1		1			1					3		
Roxbury	106	12	Bosson	William	3	1	1		1	2		4	1				13		
Roxbury	106	13	Roe	James		1			1		1						3		
Roxbury	106	14	Jackson	Antipas	2		1		1		1						5		
Roxbury	106	15	Payson	Abigail				1				1					2		
Roxbury	106	16	Mellish	Betsey						3		1					4		
Roxbury	106	17	Gore	Joshua			1		1		2	1					5		
Roxbury	106	18	Collins	Hannah		1	1		1			1					4		
Roxbury	106	19	Larvley	Daniel	3	1	1					3					8		
Roxbury	106	20	Seaver	William	2			1	1		1						5		
Roxbury	106	21	Trask	Samuel	3		1		2	1		1					8		
Roxbury	106	22	Smith	Amos			3	2	1			1					7		
Roxbury	106	23	Baker	Mary					1		1						2		
Roxbury	106	24	Alden	Hannah	1			1			1						3		
Roxbury	106	25	Felton	Joshua			1			2	1						4		
Roxbury	106	26	Felton	Nathaniel			1			1	1						3		
Roxbury	106	27	Fox	Ebenezer	1	2	1				1	1					6		
Roxbury	106	28	Adams	Zabdiel	2		4	2		2		1	1				12		
Roxbury	106	29	Williams	Thomas Junr Esq	2		3	2			1	2	2		1		13		
Roxbury	106	30	Howe	Susannah			4	1	1	1	2		2				11		
Roxbury	106	31	Weld	Benjamin	1	1	4	1		2	1	1	1				12		
Roxbury	106	32	Patten	Nathaniel	1	1	2	1		2		1					8		
Roxbury	106	33	Brewer	Ebenezer	2		1			1	1		1				6		
Roxbury	106	34	Davis	Aaron Junr		1	2	1		2		1	2	1	1		11		
Roxbury	106	35	Patten	William			3	1		1			1				6		
Roxbury	106	36	A?ll	Thomas	3	2		1	1	2	1		1				11		
Roxbury	107	1	Davis	William			1			1							2		
Roxbury	107	2	Davis	Moses	1			1		2		1	1		1		7		
Roxbury	107	3	Davis	Susannah		1	1				1	3	1				7		
Roxbury	107	4	Bacon	Joseph	1		1			2		1					5		
Roxbury	107	5	Thayer	Abraham	1		1			2		1					5		
Roxbury	107	6	Samson	Stephen	6	1	1	1		1		2					12		
Roxbury	107	7	Gallope	Richard		1		1		1	1						4		
Roxbury	107	8	Bird	James		2		1		4		1					8		
Roxbury	107	9	Daggett	Jesse	3	2	2	3	1	1	1	1	2				16		
Roxbury	107	10	Cooke	Jonathan	1		1			1		1					4		
Roxbury	107	11	Cuningham	Lois	3						1		1				5		
Roxbury	107	12	Lawrance	Seth		4						1					5		
Roxbury	107	13	Lyon	Jason	2	1		1		1			1				6		
Roxbury	107	14	Gale	Calven	3		3			1		1					8		
Roxbury	107	15	Rumrill	Aaron	1		1			2		1		1			6		
Roxbury	107	16	Gore	Joseph	2			1		1	1	1		1			7		
Roxbury	107	17	Worts	Robert	1		1			2		1	1				6		
Roxbury	107	18	Brown	Joseph	2		1			2	1	1	1				8		
Roxbury	107	19	Barns	William	2		3	2			1	1	1				10		
Roxbury	107	20	Taber	Elnathan	2	1		1				1					5		
Roxbury	107	21	Robinson	Thomas T.		1		1		1		2					5		
Roxbury	107	22	Willard	Simon	3	1	3		1	3		1	1	1			14		
Roxbury	107	23	James	Joseph	1	1	8	1		1		2					14		
Roxbury	107	24	Curtis	Hannah							3	1	1				6		
Roxbury	107	25	Leland	Ebenezer	2	1	1	1		1	1		1	1			9		
Roxbury	107	26	Symms	Samuel			1			2		1					4		
Roxbury	107	27	Davis	Charles	1		1	1			1	3			1		8		
Roxbury	107	28	Bowman	Lucy			4				1		1	1	1		7		
Roxbury	107	29	Leonard	Grant			1		1		1						3		
Roxbury	107	30	Cummins	William	1	1	1			2			1				6		
Roxbury	107	31	Burditt	Nathan			6	1	1	4		1	1				14		
Roxbury	107	32	Hurd	Precilla									1				1		
Roxbury	107	33	Cummins	Jacob				1			3						4		
Roxbury	107	34	Foster	Rufus	1		1				1						3		
Roxbury	107	35	Goddard	Ebenezer	1			1		2	1	1	1				7		
Roxbury	108	1	Newman	Andrew		1	1		1		1		1				5		
Roxbury	108	2	Partridge	Thaddeus				1		1		1		1			3		
Roxbury	108	3	Sawen	John	1		3	2		1		2					9		
Roxbury	108	4	Watson	Nathan		4					1						5		
Roxbury	108	5	Belknap	Charles				1					2				3		
Roxbury	108	6	Child	Aaron	1				1		1						4		
Roxbury	108	7	Knower	Benjamin	1			1		1	2	5		1			11		

TOWN	PG#	LN#	LAST NAME	FIRST NAME	under 10	10 to 16	16 to 26	26 to 45	45 and over	under 10	10 to 16	16 to 26	26 to 45	45 and over	TOTAL ALL OTHER	TOTAL SLAVES	TOTALS	DISTRICT/ TOWNSHIP	NOTES
					FREE WHITE MALES					FREE WHITE FEMALES									
Roxbury	108	8	McIntire	Mary									1				1		
Roxbury	108	9	Young	James	1			1		1		1					4		
Roxbury	108	10	Zeigler	George	2	1	1	1		1	1	1	1				9		
Roxbury	108	11	Dennison	James	1		1	1		1			1				5		
Roxbury	108	12	Whittemore	Nancy		2	2						1	1			6		
Roxbury	108	13	Marshall	Benjamin		1	1					1	1				4		
Roxbury	108	14	Mears	James		1			1	1				1			4		
Roxbury	108	15	Braid	John				1					1				2		
Roxbury	108	16	Packard	Seth		5	1	1		2			1				10		
Roxbury	108	17	Howard	Samuel	1			1		2	1	1					7		
Roxbury	108	18	Craft	Mary		1							4	1			6		
Roxbury	108	19	Goddard	Ebenezer Junr		1				1			1				3		
Roxbury	108	20	Patrick	Phinehas	2			1					1				4		
Roxbury	108	21	Hersey	Zerubable		1				1			1				3		
Roxbury	108	22	Joy	Charles	2	1							1				4		
Roxbury	108	23	James	Charles		2				1			1				4		
Roxbury	108	24	Cutting	Ephraim		3	2						1				6		
Roxbury	108	25	Champney	Elizabeth								1		1			2		
Roxbury	108	26	Kittle	Samuel	3			1		1			1				6		
Roxbury	108	27	Williams	Thomas Doc	1	1	3	3	1				2	2	1		14		
Roxbury	108	28	Marean	Samuel	2			1		1			1				5		
Roxbury	108	29	Pierpont	Ebenezer				1			1		1				3		
Roxbury	108	30	Marvel	Jonathan					1	1			1				3		
Roxbury	108	31	Dimsdell	Charles	2			1		2			1				6		
Roxbury	108	32	Lowell	John Esq Honble		1	2		1			2	2	1	2		11		
Roxbury	108	33	Bruce	Stephen	1	2	1		1	1	1	2	1	1	1		12		
Roxbury	108	34	Colbourn	Thomas				1					1				2		
Roxbury	109	1	Cookson	Samuel				1	1			1	1	1	1		5	2nd Parish	
Roxbury	109	2	Whittemore	Michael	4		1	1		2		1					9	2nd Parish	
Roxbury	109	3	Chenery	Ephraim		1						1					2	2nd Parish	
Roxbury	109	4	Wood	Lemuel	1			1		1		1	1				5	2nd Parish	
Roxbury	109	5	Weld	David	1	1	2	4	1	1		2	1				13	2nd Parish	
Roxbury	109	6	Davis	John		1	2		2	1	1						7	2nd Parish	
Roxbury	109	7	Dunster	Isaiah		2	2	1			2	1					8	2nd Parish	
Roxbury	109	8	Mayo	Thomas		1		1			1	1	1				5	2nd Parish	
Roxbury	109	9	Scott	Judith	1					1	2		1	2			7	2nd Parish	
Roxbury	109	10	Chamberlain	Sarah		1						1	1				3	2nd Parish	
Roxbury	109	11	Chamberlain	Nehemiah	1	1		1		1	1	1					6	2nd Parish	
Roxbury	109	12	Chamberlain	Stephen				1					1				2	2nd Parish	
Roxbury	109	13	Davis	Noah		1	2	2	1		1	3		1			11	2nd Parish	
Roxbury	109	14	Pane	Samuel				1					1				2	2nd Parish	
Roxbury	109	15	Daniels	Richard	1		1			3			1				6	2nd Parish	
Roxbury	109	16	Davis	John Junr		1	1				1	1					4	2nd Parish	
Roxbury	109	17	Draper	Nathan	1		1	1		3	1	1	1				9	2nd Parish	
Roxbury	110	1	Richards	Elizabeth								1					1	2nd Parish	
Roxbury	110	2	Richards	Joseph		2		1			1		1				5	2nd Parish	
Roxbury	110	3	Jones	John		1		1					1				3	2nd Parish	
Roxbury	110	4	Corey	Anna						1	2		1				4	2nd Parish	
Roxbury	110	5	Corey	Hannah									1				1	2nd Parish	
Roxbury	110	6	Griggs	James	2	1			2				1	3			9	2nd Parish	
Roxbury	110	7	Corey	Benjamin		5	2					1	1				9	2nd Parish	
Roxbury	110	8	Talburt	Nathaniel		2		1		1			1				5	2nd Parish	
Roxbury	110	9	Mayo	John	1			1	1			1	1				5	2nd Parish	
Roxbury	110	10	Richards	Edward			1					1					2	2nd Parish	
Roxbury	110	11	Broad	John			2										2	2nd Parish	
Roxbury	110	12	Richards	Joshua	1		3	1		1	1	1					8	2nd Parish	
Roxbury	110	13	Gay	Amasa	1			1		2		1	1				6	2nd Parish	
Roxbury	110	14	Richards	Abigail	1					2		1	1				5	2nd Parish	
Roxbury	110	15	Lyon	Thomas			1	1	1			1	4				8	2nd Parish	
Roxbury	110	16	Lyon	Benjamin			1			2		1	1				5	2nd Parish	
Roxbury	110	17	Richards	Levi			1	1		1		1					4	2nd Parish	
Roxbury	110	18	Draper	William		1	2	2		1	1	1					8	2nd Parish	
Roxbury	110	19	Dudley	Ebenezer	1		3	1		1			1				7	2nd Parish	
Roxbury	110	20	Wilson	Ephraim		2		1		2			1				6	2nd Parish	
Roxbury	110	21	Griggs	William	1	1				2			1	1			7	2nd Parish	
Roxbury	110	22	Davis	Amasa	1		1	1		1	1		1	1			7	2nd Parish	
Roxbury	110	23	Billings	Benjamin		1	3	1		4		2	1				12	2nd Parish	
Roxbury	110	24	Whiting	Ebenezer		1		1	1			1	1	1	2		8	2nd Parish	
Roxbury	110	25	Billings	Lemuel	1	2	3	1				2	1	1			11	2nd Parish	
Roxbury	110	26	Davis	Aaron		1	1	1	3	2	3		1	1			13	2nd Parish	
Roxbury	110	27	Davis	Samuel	1		1	1		1			1				5	2nd Parish	
Roxbury	110	28	Whiting	Seth	1	1	1	1		1	1		1				7	2nd Parish	
Roxbury	110	29	Goodnough	Ephraim	2		2			1		2					7	2nd Parish	
Roxbury	110	30	Draper	Grace		1							1	1			3	2nd Parish	
Roxbury	110	31	White	Luther		1				1			1				3	2nd Parish	
Roxbury	110	32	Harris	Jamima									1				1	2nd Parish	
Roxbury	110	33	Whitney	Jacob					1				1				2	2nd Parish	
Roxbury	110	34	Richards	Rebecca	1								1				2	2nd Parish	
Roxbury	111	1	Prince												2		2	2nd Parish	First name left blank
Roxbury	111	2	Crawley	Abraham	3			1				2	1				7	2nd Parish	
Roxbury	111	3	Dascom	John		1				1		1					3	2nd Parish	
Roxbury	111	4	Posthill	Robert			1	1		1			1	1			5	2nd Parish	
Roxbury	111	5	Wilson	Aaron		1		1					1				3	2nd Parish	
Roxbury	111	6	Griggs	Thomas		1		1			1		1				4	2nd Parish	
Roxbury	111	7	Baker	John			1		1	1	1	1		1			6	2nd Parish	
Roxbury	111	8	Baker	David	2			1		1			1				5	2nd Parish	
Roxbury	111	9	Gookins	Edmund				1					1				2	2nd Parish	
Roxbury	111	10	Smith	Thomas											2		2	2nd Parish	
Roxbury	111	11	May	John				1		2				1			4	2nd Parish	
Roxbury	111	12	Draper	Mary										1			1	2nd Parish	

TOWN	PG#	LN#	LAST NAME	FIRST NAME	FWM under 10	FWM 10 to 16	FWM 16 to 26	FWM 26 to 45	FWM 45 over	FWF under 10	FWF 10 to 16	FWF 16 to 26	FWF 26 to 45	FWF 45 over	TOTAL ALL OTHER	TOTAL SLAVES	TOTALS	DISTRICT/ TOWNSHIP	NOTES
Roxbury	111	13	Fairbanks	Samuel	1			1		1			1				4	2nd Parish	
Roxbury	111	14	Farrington	Stephen	1		1	1		1	2	1					7	2nd Parish	
Roxbury	111	15	Pond	John		2		1			1	1					5	2nd Parish	
Roxbury	111	16	Henshaw	John	2			1		3		1					7	2nd Parish	
Roxbury	111	17	Gay	Samuel				1									1	2nd Parish	
Roxbury	111	18	Loewes	Timothy				1					1				2	2nd Parish	
Roxbury	111	19	Jones	Alden	2		1			1		1					5	2nd Parish	
Roxbury	111	20	Davis	Nathaniel		1	1			4		1		1			8	2nd Parish	
Roxbury	111	21	Baker	John Junr	1			1					1				3	2nd Parish	
Roxbury	111	22	Vose	Oliver		1		1	1				1	1			5	2nd Parish	
Roxbury	111	23	Titterton	Gabriel		1	1			1	2		1	2			8	2nd Parish	
Roxbury	111	24	Child	Abner		1	1			1		1					4	2nd Parish	
Roxbury	111	25	Bradford	John Revd	1	1	1	1				3	2				9	2nd Parish	
Roxbury	111	26	Murdock	Ephraim				1		2	1		1				5	2nd Parish	
Roxbury	111	27	Murdock	Ebenezer	1	1	1	1			1	1					6	2nd Parish	
Roxbury	111	28	Davis	Sarah										2			2	2nd Parish	
Roxbury	111	29	Draper	Moses	1			1		1		1	1				5	2nd Parish	
Roxbury	112	1	McCarthy	Anna			1			1		1	2		1		6	3rd Parish	
Roxbury	112	2	Parker	John	2		2	1		3		2	2				12	3rd Parish	
Roxbury	112	3	Shepherd	William	1			1				1	1				5	3rd Parish	
Roxbury	112	4	Woodard	Josiah	2	1		1		2	1		1	1			9	3rd Parish	
Roxbury	112	5	Munroe	Daniel	1	1		1					1				4	3rd Parish	
Roxbury	112	6	Perry	Benjamin		1	1			1		1					4	3rd Parish	
Roxbury	112	7	Starr	Daniel				1		2			1				4	3rd Parish	
Roxbury	112	8	Gould	John	2		1			1		1					5	3rd Parish	
Roxbury	112	9	Stutivant	Isaac		1		1		2			1				5	3rd Parish	
Roxbury	112	10	Blackman	Sarah		2	1			1			1				5	3rd Parish	
Roxbury	112	11	Woods	George	1			1			1		1				4	3rd Parish	
Roxbury	112	12	Lovering	Joseph		1		1			1		1				4	3rd Parish	
Roxbury	112	13	Brewer	Joseph				1					1				2	3rd Parish	
Roxbury	112	14	Wales	William	1			1		2			1	1			6	3rd Parish	
Roxbury	112	15	Brewer	Sarah	2						1	3	1				7	3rd Parish	
Roxbury	112	16	May	Solomon	1		2	1					1	1			6	3rd Parish	
Roxbury	112	17	Child	Phinehas		2	1	1		2	1	1		1			9	3rd Parish	
Roxbury	112	18	Hatch	Crowell	1		2		1	3	1		1				9	3rd Parish	
Roxbury	112	19	Cutler	Benjamin Clark	1	1		1		2	1		1	1	1		9	3rd Parish	
Roxbury	112	20	Randall	Abraham		1		1				1	1				4	3rd Parish	
Roxbury	112	21	Wheeler	Deborah & Sarah	1						1	2	2				6	3rd Parish	
Roxbury	112	22	Howe	David	3		1		1				1	1			7	3rd Parish	
Roxbury	112	23	Williams	William	3			1		1	1		1				7	3rd Parish	
Roxbury	112	24	Whittemore	Jacob	4	1			2	2	1	2	1				13	3rd Parish	
Roxbury	112	25	Winchester	Gulliver			4	2	1			4	1	1			13	3rd Parish	
Roxbury	112	26	Williams	Isaac	1	1	1	1		1		2		1			8	3rd Parish	
Roxbury	112	27	Williams	Stephen Junr	1	1	1	1				1					5	3rd Parish	
Roxbury	112	28	Weld	Elijah	1	1		1				1	1				5	3rd Parish	
Roxbury	112	29	Thayer	Obed		1	2	1		2		1					7	3rd Parish	
Roxbury	112	30	Dickerman	Lemuel				1		2	1		1				5	3rd Parish	
Roxbury	110	31	Weld	John				1						1			2	3rd Parish	
Roxbury	112	32	Hopkins	Michael	2	1		1		1	1		2				8	3rd Parish	
Roxbury	112	33	Greenough	David	1		2	1	2	2	1		1	1	1		11	3rd Parish	
Roxbury	112	34	Weld	Ebenezer		3	2		2			2	1		1		11	3rd Parish	
Roxbury	112	35	Weld	Nathaniel		1		1					1				3	3rd Parish	
Roxbury	112	36	Weld	Thomas		2	2		1	3	1	1	1		1		12	3rd Parish	
Roxbury	112	37	Weld	Jacob	1		6		1	2	1		2		1		14	3rd Parish	
Roxbury	113	1	Weld	William Gordon	1	1		1					1				4	3rd Parish	
Roxbury	113	2	Weld	Mary						1		1	1	1			4	3rd Parish	
Roxbury	113	3	Trull	Jonathan	1	1		3		2	1		1				9	3rd Parish	
Roxbury	113	4	Davis	Ezra	2	1	1	1	1		1	1					9	3rd Parish	
Roxbury	113	5	Chamberlin	Stephen Junr	2			1		1			1				5	3rd Parish	
Roxbury	113	6	Colbourn	Levi				1					1				2	3rd Parish	
Roxbury	113	7	Payson	Stephen	2	1	4	1				1	1	1			11	3rd Parish	
Roxbury	113	8	Lowder	Henry		2						1					3	3rd Parish	
Roxbury	113	9	Lowder	John				1				2					3	3rd Parish	
Roxbury	113	10	Gray	Thomas Revd	1	1		1		1		1	2	1			8	3rd Parish	
Roxbury	113	11	Woodard	Abigail	3			1		1			1				6	3rd Parish	
Roxbury	113	12	Bacon	Henry		1		1		1	1		1				5	3rd Parish	
Roxbury	113	13	Hammond	Mary						2			1				3	3rd Parish	
Roxbury	113	14	Weld	Sarah									1	1			2	3rd Parish	
Roxbury	113	15	White	David				1		2	1	1		1			6	3rd Parish	
Roxbury	113	16	Loring	Elijah			4	1		1		1	1				8	3rd Parish	
Roxbury	113	17	Hunting	Jabez	1	1	2	2		2		1	1		1		11	3rd Parish	
Roxbury	113	18	Bridgun	Petre											3		3	3rd Parish	
Roxbury	113	19	Child	Stephen	1	2	2	3		3		1	1				13	3rd Parish	
Roxbury	113	20	Stimson	Charles			2						1				3	3rd Parish	
Roxbury	113	21	White	Sarah								1		1			2	3rd Parish	
Roxbury	113	22	Heath	Samuel		1	2			1	1	2	1				8	3rd Parish	
Roxbury	113	23	Brimmer	Martin	1			1	1		6		1		2		12	3rd Parish	
Roxbury	113	24	May	Lemuel		1	2		1	2			1				7	3rd Parish	
Roxbury	113	25	Duballet	John				1			1				1		3	3rd Parish	
Roxbury	113	26	Estey	Lucy	3					1	1		1	1			7	3rd Parish	
Roxbury	113	27	Hoyt	Elna	3	1						1	1	2			9	3rd Parish	
Roxbury	113	28	Scott	Ebenezer	1	1		1		3	2		1				9	3rd Parish	
Roxbury	114	1	Wally	Thomas			1	1		1		2	1				6	3rd Parish	
Roxbury	114	2	Spurr	Eliphalet			2	1		2		3	1				9	3rd Parish	
Roxbury	114	3	Davis	Increase			1		1	1		1					4	3rd Parish	
Roxbury	114	4	Jackson	Thaddeus	3		2	1	1	3	3		1				15	3rd Parish	
Roxbury	114	5	Craft	Caleb		1	6		2			1	1	1	1		13	3rd Parish	
Roxbury	114	6	Parker	Caleb	1			1					1	1			4	3rd Parish	
Roxbury	114	7	Webb	Ebenezer		1			2				1				5	3rd Parish	
Roxbury	114	8	Winship	Joseph				1						1	1		3	3rd Parish	

TOWN	PG#	LN#	HEADS OF HOUSEHOLD LAST NAME	FIRST NAME	FREE WHITE MALES under 10	10 to 16	16 to 26	26 to 45	45 and over	FREE WHITE FEMALES under 10	10 to 16	16 to 26	26 to 45	45 and over	TOTAL ALL OTHER	TOTAL SLAVES	TOTALS	DISTRICT/ TOWNSHIP	NOTES
Roxbury	114	9	Carey	John			1	1		2	2	2	1				9	3rd Parish	
Roxbury	114	10	Peter	John	2				1	2	2		1				8	3rd Parish	
Roxbury	114	11	Higginson	Stephen	1		1		1		1	3	1	1			9	3rd Parish	
Roxbury	114	12	Aldin	Solomon	1		4	1		2	1		1				10	3rd Parish	
Roxbury	114	13	White	Benjamin	1		2		1		1	2	2	2			11	3rd Parish	
Roxbury	114	14	Harbach	Thomas	2	1	1	1		1			1				7	3rd Parish	
Roxbury	114	15	Gardner	Caleb		1	2	1		3		2	1	1			11	3rd Parish	
Roxbury	114	16	Hide	Thaddeus			1		1	1				1			4	3rd Parish	
Roxbury	114	17	Hammon	Jonathan	1	2	1	1		2	1		1				9	3rd Parish	
Roxbury	114	18	Richards	Ebenezer	1		2	1		1		1	1				7	3rd Parish	
Roxbury	114	19	Jackson	Jonathan	1		2		1	2			2				8	3rd Parish	
Roxbury	115	1	Baker	Preserved		1	2	1	1				1				6	3rd Parish	
Roxbury	115	2	Mason	Jonathan Esq	2		1	2		2	2	3	2	2			16	3rd Parish	
Roxbury	115	3	Heath	John		1			1				2	3	1		8	3rd Parish	
Roxbury	115	4	Heath	Ebenezer	1		2	1		3	1	1	1				10	3rd Parish	
Roxbury	115	5	Gardner	Isaac S. Esq	1	1	2	2			2			2			10	3rd Parish	
Roxbury	115	6	Lucas	John	1	1			1			2		1			6	3rd Parish	
Roxbury	115	7	Gibbs	Daniel			2					1					3	3rd Parish	
Roxbury	115	8	White	Samuel			1	1					1	1			3	3rd Parish	
Roxbury	115	9	Akers	William	1	1	1	1	1	1	1	1	1				9	3rd Parish	
Roxbury	115	10	Hyslop	David			2	1	1		1	2	1				8	3rd Parish	
Roxbury	115	11	Sullivan	John L.	1		3	1		1		1	1	1	3		12	3rd Parish	
Roxbury	115	12	Goddard	John				1				1		1			3	3rd Parish	
Roxbury	115	13	Farewell	Abraham			4					1					5	3rd Parish	
Roxbury	115	14	Goddard	Joseph	2	1	2	2	2	3	2	1	1				16	3rd Parish	
Roxbury	115	15	Davis	Benjamin	2		2	2				1	1				8	3rd Parish	
Roxbury	115	16	Craft	Samuel			2		1			1		1	1		6	3rd Parish	
Roxbury	115	17	Thayer	Zephion	4		6	1		1		3					15	3rd Parish	

TOWN	PG#	LN#	LAST NAME	FIRST NAME	FREE WHITE MALES					FREE WHITE FEMALES					TOTAL ALL OTHER	TOTAL SLAVES	TOTALS	DISTRICT/ TOWNSHIP	NOTES
					under 10	10 to 16	16 to 26	26 to 45	45 and over	under 10	10 to 16	16 to 26	26 to 45	45 and over					
Sharon	31	1	Allen	Seth	1				1			1		1			4		
Sharon	31	2	Allen .	James	4	1		1		1			1				8		
Sharon	31	3	Andrews	Darrius	3			1				1					5		
Sharon	31	4	Billings	Jonathn	1		1	1	1	1	1		1	1			8		
Sharon	31	5	Billings	William	1	1		1		1			1				5		
Sharon	31	6	Billings	Leonard	3		3	1		1	1		1				10		
Sharon	31	7	Baker	Elijah	2			1	1				1	1			6		
Sharon	31	8	Billings	Hath*	2			1		2	1		1				7		
Sharon	31	9	Bullard	Silas			1	1		2		1	1				6		
Sharon	31	10	Billings	Elijah		1		1				1		1			4		
Sharon	32	1	Bullard	Benj	2			1		2	2	1	1				9		
Sharon	32	2	Bullard	Judith W									1	1			2		
Sharon	32	3	Billing	James	3			1		2			1				7		
Sharon	32	4	Baker	Elijah Jr		2		1		2		2	1				8		
Sharon	32	5	Billing	James J	3			1		2			1				7		
Sharon	32	6	Billing	Lewis				1		1		1					3		
Sharon	32	7	Billing	Joseph			1	1		2		1	1				6		
Sharon	32	8	Baker	Ebenezer			1					1					2		
Sharon	32	9	Bradshaw	Nathl					1					1			2		
Sharon	32	10	Belcher	Jonathan				1	1					1			3		
Sharon	32	11	Bradshaw	Nathl 2	2	1		1	1	2				1			8		
Sharon	32	12	Billing	Anna W		1		1				1		1			4		
Sharon	32	13	Curtis	Phillip	2	2		1		1			1	1			8		
Sharon	32	14	Clark	Thomas	2		1		1	3	1	1					9		
Sharon	32	15	Clark	Hosea	1			1		1			1				4		
Sharon	32	16	Capin	Elijah				1						1			2		
Sharon	32	17	Clark	Silvanus	1	1			1			1		1			5		
Sharon	32	18	Curtis	Oliver	3			1					1				5		
Sharon	32	19	Capin	Lemuel	1	2			1			1		1			6		
Sharon	32	20	Cobb	Jonathan	1	1						1					4		
Sharon	32	21	Curtis	Calvin	2			1					1				4		
Sharon	32	22	Capin	Ezekiel		1	1	1	1	1			1				6		
Sharon	32	23	Capin	Jerusha Wd			1	1	1			1		1			5		
Sharon	32	24	Cummins	Joseph	2	2		1	1	1		1	1				9		
Sharon	32	25	Coney	Thomas					1					1			2		
Sharon	32	26	Clark	Asa		1		1				2		1			5		
Sharon	32	27	Capin	Oliver			3						2				5		
Sharon	32	28	Curtis	Francis		1	1	1				1					4		
Sharon	32	29	Coney	Joseph					1					1			2		
Sharon	32	30	Clark	Appallus	1			1		2		1					5		
Sharon	32	31	Coney	Ichabod	2	2			1	1		2	1				9		
Sharon	32	32	Callaft	W John			1	1				1	1				4		
Sharon	32	33	Capin	Samuel		1		1		3			1				6		
Sharon	33	1	Coney	Nathaniel			1		1			1	1	1			5		
Sharon	33	2	Clap	Timothy	3			1	1			1		1			7		
Sharon	33	3	Drake	John			1	1				2		1			5		
Sharon	33	4	Drake	Nathaniel	1			1		1		1					4		
Sharon	33	5	Drake	Joseph				1									1		
Sharon	33	6	Drake	Abial	1	1	1			1		2		1			7		
Sharon	33	7	Drake	Nathan	2	1		1		2	1		1				8		
Sharon	33	8	Drake	Spencer	1			1		1	1						4		
Sharon	33	9	Drake	*	1	1	2		1	1		1	1				8		
Sharon	33	10	Drake	George	1	1	1					2		1			6		
Sharon	33	11	Drake	John V		1		1			1			1			4		
Sharon	33	12	Drake	Moses	2	2	1						1				6		
Sharon	33	13	Drake	Hannah	2		1			2			1	1			7		
Sharon	33	14	Everett	Oliver		1		1		2				1			5		
Sharon	33	15	Everett	Edward		1	1	1		1	2	1		1			8		
Sharon	33	16	Estey	Lemuel				1		3	1		1				6		
Sharon	33	17	Estey	Samuel	1			2					1	1			5		
Sharon	33	18	Estey	John				1						1			2		
Sharon	33	19	Fuller	Ebenezer	2			1		2		1					6		
Sharon	33	20	Fuller	Lemuel			1	1				1		1			4		
Sharon	33	21	Fisher	Aaron	2	1		2			1		1	1			8		
Sharon	33	22	Fairbanks	Benj					1					1			2		
Sharon	33	23	Fairbanks	Benj Jr		1		1		1			1				4		
Sharon	33	24	Fisher	David		1		1				1	1	1			5		
Sharon	33	25	Felch	Isaac	4	1		1		1	2			1			10		
Sharon	33	26	Fisher	Jacob		1		1						1			3		
Sharon	33	27	Fairbanks	Jerh	1			1		2			1				5		
Sharon	33	28	Frost	Peter	1	1	2		1	1			1				7		
Sharon	33	29	French	Edward		1		1		3		2	1				7		
Sharon	33	30	Fuller	Jeremiah	2			1					1	1			5		
Sharon	33	31	Forrist	Samuel	2	1		1		2			1				7		
Sharon	33	32	Gannet	Benjamin			1	2	1				1	1			6		
Sharon	33	33	Gould	Simon	1			1		2			1				5		
Sharon	33	34	Gilbert	Solomon	3	1			1		2			1			8		
Sharon	33	35	Gay	Solomon		1	1	1					2	1			6		
Sharon	34	1	Gannet	Joseph		1	1	1		5		2	1	1			12		

TOWN	PG#	LN#	LAST NAME	FIRST NAME	FREE WHITE MALES					FREE WHITE FEMALES					TOTAL ALL OTHER	TOTAL SLAVES	TOTALS	DISTRICT/ TOWNSHIP	NOTES
					under 10	10 to 16	16 to 26	26 to 45	45 and over	under 10	10 to 16	16 to 26	26 to 45	45 and over					
Sharon	34	2	Gould	Ezra	1	1			1		1		1				5		
Sharon	34	3	Gannet	Benjamin J		1		1		1	1	1	1				6		
Sharon	34	4	Glover	Samuel	2			1		2	1	1	1				8		
Sharon	34	5	Gould	Kezia									1	2			3		
Sharon	34	6	Gilbert	Samuel	1		1					1					3		
Sharon	34	7	Gould	Nathaniel	1	1	1	2		1			1				7		
Sharon	34	8	Hervins	Amasa	4			1		1			1				7		
Sharon	34	9	Hervins	William		1			1					1			3		
Sharon	34	10	Hervins	Samuel		1		1				1		1			4		
Sharon	34	11	Hervins	Elijah	1		1		1			1		2			6		
Sharon	34	12	Harlon	N Mathew	1		1		1		2	2		2			9		
Sharon	34	13	Homer	Zebulon V	3	1	1	1		2		1		1			10		
Sharon	34	14	Harlon	Ruth Wd								1	1				2		
Sharon	34	15	Hodgers	Benjamin		2	1	1	1	1		2		1			9		
Sharon	34	16	Hervins	Enock	1	1	1		1	1		1	1				7		
Sharon	34	17	Hixon	Richard	1			1		1		1		1			5		
Sharon	34	18	Holmes	William		1			1	1		1					4		
Sharon	34	19	Holmes	Ebenezer	3			1		1	1		1				7		
Sharon	34	20	Harlon	Ebenezer	2	2		1		1			1				7		
Sharon	34	21	Hewins	Jacob		1	1		1		1			1			5		
Sharon	34	22	Holmes	Samuel			1	1						1			3		
Sharon	34	23	Holmes	Samuel Jr	3			1		3			1				8		
Sharon	34	24	Harlow	Elizabeth Wd								1	1				2		
Sharon	34	25	Hewins	John			1			1		1	1				4		
Sharon	34	26	Hewins	Jacob Jr	1	1		1		3			1				7		
Sharon	34	27	Hewins	F*			1			2		1					4		
Sharon	34	28	Hewins	Ebenezer		1		1	1	1		1		1			6		
Sharon	34	29	Holmes	Zebulon				1						1			2		
Sharon	34	30	Holmes	Benjamin	1			1				2					4		
Sharon	34	31	Hewins	Joseph Esq			1		1		1	1		1			5		
Sharon	34	32	Hewins	Benjamin		1		1	1	1	1	2		1			7		
Sharon	34	33	Hewins	David	1			1		1			1				4		
Sharon	34	34	Holmes	Luther		1						1		1			3		
Sharon	34	35	Hewins	Enock Jr		1		1		3		1	1				7		
Sharon	34	36	Holmes	John				1				1		1			3		
Sharon	35	1	Jonson	John		1		1		2			1				5		
Sharon	35	2	Jonson	Caleb	1	1		1		2			1				6		
Sharon	35	3	Jonson	Obadiah		2		1		2			1				6		
Sharon	35	4	Jonson	Benjamin	2	1		1			1		1	2			8		
Sharon	35	5	Jonson	Joshua	3	3					1	1	1				9		
Sharon	35	6	Jordan	Jacob			1	1		2				1			5		
Sharon	35	7	Jonson	Isaac		2	1	1	1	4	1		1				11		
Sharon	35	8	Ingraham	Benjm	1	1			1			2		1			6		
Sharon	35	9	Kingsbury	Nathaniel				1						1			2		
Sharon	35	10	Kingman	Benjam	1		1							1			4		
Sharon	35	11	Kallock	Thomas	2			1	1	1			2	1			8		
Sharon	35	12	Lovel	Samuel				1						2			3		
Sharon	35	13	Lewis	Job											4		4		
Sharon	35	14	Leonard	Nathl		2	1	2					1				6		
Sharon	35	15	Leonard	Walley	3			1	1	1			1				6		
Sharon	35	16	Laurance	David		2		1		5		1	1				10		
Sharon	35	17	Morse	Ezra		1			1			1		1			4		
Sharon	35	18	Morse	Nathaniel			2		1				1	1			5		
Sharon	35	19	Morse	Joseph		1		1	1				1	1			5		
Sharon	35	20	Morse	Eliphalet		1		1		3	1		1				7		
Sharon	35	21	Morse	Gillead			1		1	1		1		1			5		
Sharon	35	22	Morse	John	1	1		1		2			1				6		
Sharon	35	23	Morse	Levi	1		1	1	1	1		2	1	1			9		
Sharon	35	24	Morse	Joseph Jr	2	1		1					1				5		
Sharon	35	25	Mackintosh	Andrew	1			1		1			1				4		
Sharon	35	26	Morse	Elijah	1			1		2			1				5		
Sharon	35	27	Puffer	Mattathias				1						1			2		
Sharon	35	28	Plimpton	Zeba		2		1		1	1		1				6		
Sharon	35	29	Quinzey	Marquis			1			1		1					3		
Sharon	35	30	Randal	Benjm Esq		1			1	1		1	3	1	1		9		
Sharon	35	31	Richard	William		1	1		1	1							4		
Sharon	35	32	Rhoades	Daniel	3		1	1		2	2	3	1	1			14		
Sharon	35	33	Randal	Joseph		3		1				1					5		
Sharon	35	34	Richard	Daniel	1	1	1	1	1			3	1				9		
Sharon	35	35	Richard	Jeremiah	2			1		2				1			6		
Sharon	35	36	Richard	Ebenezer		1	1	2	2			2		1			9		
Sharon	35	37	Richard	Benjamin		1		1		1				1			4		
Sharon	35	38	Richard	Benjam Jr	1			1		1		1					4		
Sharon	35	39	Ronald	Benjamin	1	1		1		1			1	2			7		
Sharon	35	40	Rhoades	Simeon				1					1				2		
Sharon	35	41	Rapakeel	John				1		2	1			1			5		
Sharon	35	42	Savel	Benjamin			1	1					2	1			5		
Sharon	35	43	Smith	Isaac		1	1		1			1		1			5		
Sharon	36	1	Smith	John	1			1				1					3		

TOWN	PG#	LN#	LAST NAME	FIRST NAME	FREE WHITE MALES					FREE WHITE FEMALES					TOTAL ALL OTHER	TOTAL SLAVES	TOTALS	DISTRICT/ TOWNSHIP	NOTES
					under 10	10 to 16	16 to 26	26 to 45	45 and over	under 10	10 to 16	16 to 26	26 to 45	45 and over					
Sharon	36	2	Swift	Job		2	2		2	1	1		2				10		
Sharon	36	3	Savel	John	1	1	3	1		1		1	1				9		
Sharon	36	4	Savage	William				2				1					3		
Sharon	36	5	Swift	Samuel			1			2			1				4		
Sharon	36	6	Savel	Mary Wd			2						2	1			5		
Sharon	36	7	Spaulding	David	1		1					1					3		
Sharon	36	8	Smith	Huel Jr	2				1	5		1					9		
Sharon	36	9	Shelley	Abner	4	2		1		1				1			9		
Sharon	36	10	Toleman	John			1	1						1			3		
Sharon	36	11	Tisdale	Edward			2	1				1	1				5		
Sharon	36	12	Tolman	William	1	1	1	1		1			1				6		
Sharon	36	13	Tolman	Willm Jr	1		1			1							3		
Sharon	36	14	Tabot	Josiah	2	1		1		2	1	1					8		
Sharon	36	15	Whittemore	Joshua	2	1		1		2	1	1					8		
Sharon	36	16	Willis	Solomon				1					5	1			7		
Sharon	36	17	Witherton	William	1			1	1	2			2				7		
Sharon	36	18	White	David	1	2	2	1			1	1		1			9		
Sharon	36	19	Wood	Joseph	1	1			1	2		1		1			7		
Sharon	36	20	White	Joseph	2	1		1			1	1					6		
Sharon	36	21	Whitaker	Jonathan Revd	2		1	1				1	1				6		
Sharon	36	22	Wentworth	Stephen				1									1		
Sharon	36	23	Whittemore	Edward	2			1				1					4		
Sharon	36	24	Wood	Jethro				1					1				2		

TOWN	PG#	LN#	LAST NAME	FIRST NAME	FREE WHITE MALES					FREE WHITE FEMALES					TOTAL ALL OTHER	TOTAL SLAVES	TOTALS	DISTRICT/ TOWNSHIP	NOTES
					under 10	10 to 16	16 to 26	26 to 45	45 and over	under 10	10 to 16	16 to 26	26 to 45	45 and over					
Stoughton	117	1	Adams	Peter			2	2	1			1		1			7		
Stoughton	117	2	Atherton	Consider					1			1		1			3		
Stoughton	117	3	Atherton	John		2	1		1		1	1		1			7		
Stoughton	118	1	Atherton	John Junr	1			1		1		1					4		
Stoughton	118	2	Agher	Jedidiah	1			1		1		1					4		
Stoughton	118	3	Allen	Tural			1		1			1	1	1			5		
Stoughton	118	4	Battle	Jonathan	2	3			1	1	2		1				10		
Stoughton	118	5	Battle	Curtis	2			1		3			1	1			8		
Stoughton	118	6	Battle	Edward	1		2	1		2			1				7		
Stoughton	118	7	Belcher	Atherton					1	2	1		1				5		
Stoughton	118	8	Belcher	Edward				1		1			1				3		
Stoughton	118	9	Bleker	John				1				1		1			3		
Stoughton	118	10	Belcher	Oliver	1		1	1		1	1						5		
Stoughton	118	11	Belcher	Joseph					1	1			1	1			4		
Stoughton	118	12	Bird	Lemuel	2		1		1	1	2	1		1			9		
Stoughton	118	13	Bird	Isaac	1		1	1	1	2	1	4		1			12		
Stoughton	118	14	Bird	Samuel		1	1		1	2		1		1			7		
Stoughton	118	15	Bird	Asa			1			5			1				7		
Stoughton	118	16	Bird	Abner	1			1		2			1				5		
Stoughton	118	17	Bird	Elizabeth	1					1	1			1			4		
Stoughton	118	18	Bisbee	Benjamin	2		1	1	1	2		1	1	1			10		
Stoughton	118	19	Belknap	Isaac	1				1		1	1	1				5		
Stoughton	118	20	Blanchard	William	2	1	2		1		1		1	1			9		
Stoughton	118	21	Blanchard	Jonathan	6			1					1				8		
Stoughton	118	22	Bracket	Samuel			1	1		1		2		1			6		
Stoughton	118	23	Briggs	Joel Revd	2	2		1		2		1	1				9		
Stoughton	118	24	Briggs	Stephen		1			1	3	1	1	1	1			9		
Stoughton	119	1	Capen	Jonathan					1				1	1			3		
Stoughton	119	2	Capen	Jonathan Jr	1				1	2	3			1			8		
Stoughton	119	3	Capen	John	3	1	1		1					1			7		
Stoughton	119	4	Capen	Samuel					1		1			1			3		
Stoughton	119	5	Capen	William			2			1	1		1				5		
Stoughton	119	6	Capen	Elisha	1			1		2			1				5		
Stoughton	119	7	Capen	Edward			1		1			1		1			4		
Stoughton	119	8	Capen	James	3	1	1	1		2	1		1				10		
Stoughton	119	9	Capen	Edward Junr	3	1		1		1	1		1				8		
Stoughton	119	10	Capen	Uriah			1			1			1				3		
Stoughton	119	11	Capen	Benja & Abraham		1	1	2				1	1				6		
Stoughton	119	12	Clap	John		2	1		2				1	1			7		
Stoughton	119	13	Carr	William	2		1						1				4		
Stoughton	119	14	Crane	Ebenezer		1		1		3			1				6		
Stoughton	119	15	Curtis	Thomas	1	2	1	1				1	1				7		
Stoughton	119	16	Curtis	William Jnr	1	1	2		2	3	1		1				11		
Stoughton	119	17	Curtis	Moses	1		1	1		2	1		1				7		
Stoughton	119	18	Dickerman	John	3		1		1	2	1		1				9		
Stoughton	119	19	Dickerman	John Junr	1			1		1		2					5		
Stoughton	119	20	Dickerman	Peter	2				1	2	1		1				7		
Stoughton	119	21	Drake	Nathan			1		1			1		2			5		
Stoughton	119	22	Drake	Lemuel		1		1				1	2				5		
Stoughton	119	23	Drake	Enoch	2	1		1		3			1				8		
Stoughton	119	24	Drake	William	2	2	1		1	2			2				10		
Stoughton	119	25	Drake	Ziba	2	1		1		1		2	1				8		
Stoughton	119	26	Drake	David	2	1		1		1	1		1				7		
Stoughton	119	27	Dunbar	Peter	1	1	3		1				1	1			8		
Stoughton	119	28	Dunbar	Rebecca Wid									1	1			2		
Stoughton	119	29	Farrington	George L.	1	2		1				1	1				6		
Stoughton	119	30	French	John					1		1			1			3		
Stoughton	119	31	French	John Junr	1			1		1			1				4		
Stoughton	119	32	French	John 2d					1					1			2		
Stoughton	119	33	French	William		1	3		2	2	2			2			12		
Stoughton	119	34	Gay	Aaron		1			1	1				1			4		
Stoughton	119	35	Gay	Nathaniel		2	1			1			1				5		
Stoughton	120	1	Gay	Hezekiah		1	3		1		1	1		2			9		
Stoughton	120	2	Gay	Lemuel	1	2	1		2				1	3			10		
Stoughton	120	3	Gay	Timothy		1	2		1	1		2	1	1			9		
Stoughton	120	4	Gay	Mary Wid		1	1					2	3	1			8		
Stoughton	120	5	Glover	Thomas		1	1		1					1			4		
Stoughton	120	6	Glover	Samuel	1			1			1			1			4		
Stoughton	120	7	Goldthwait	Jacob	1				1					1			3		
Stoughton	120	8	Goldthwait	Jacob Jr	1			1					1				3		
Stoughton	120	9	Goldthwait	Timothy	4	1		1		1			1				8		
Stoughton	120	10	Goldthwait	Lot				1		1			1				3		
Stoughton	120	11	Guild	Elmer					1	2	1			1			5		
Stoughton	120	12	Guild	Israel	2	1		1					1				5		
Stoughton	120	13	Harris	Eliza Wid	1			1		2		1	1	1			7		
Stoughton	120	14	Hawse	Levi	2	1			2	1	2		1				9		
Stoughton	120	15	Hayden	Ebenezer	1	1		1	1	1	2		1	1			9		
Stoughton	120	16	Hayden	Moses		1			1			1	1				4		
Stoughton	120	17	Henry	Michael			1		1	1				1			4		

65

TOWN	PG#	LN#	LAST NAME	FIRST NAME	FREE WHITE MALES under 10	10 to 16	16 to 26	26 to 45	45 and over	FREE WHITE FEMALES under 10	10 to 16	16 to 26	26 to 45	45 and over	TOTAL ALL OTHER	TOTAL SLAVES	TOTALS	DISTRICT/ TOWNSHIP	NOTES
Stoughton	120	18	Hixon	Jeremiah	2	1		1		1			2				7		
Stoughton	120	19	Holbrook	Jason	1			1		2		1					5		
Stoughton	120	20	Holmes	John					1					1			2		
Stoughton	120	21	Holmes	Philip		1		1			1		1	1			5		
Stoughton	120	22	Holmes	Mather	1		1	1		2	2	1	1				9		
Stoughton	120	23	Holmes	Luther		1	1					1	1				4		
Stoughton	120	24	Holmes	Samuel	1		1	1		1	1		1				6		
Stoughton	120	25	Holmes	John 2d	3	1		1		1	1	1	1				9		
Stoughton	120	26	Holmes	Joseph				1				2	1				4		
Stoughton	120	27	Johnson	Nathaniel	2			1		1			1				5		
Stoughton	120	28	Johnson	Lewis			1				1						2		
Stoughton	120	29	Jordan	Abraham					1			1	1				3		
Stoughton	120	30	Jordan	Joseph					1								1		
Stoughton	120	31	Keith	Barnabas		1		1					1				3		
Stoughton	120	32	Kenney	Elijah	4			1					1				6		
Stoughton	120	33	Leach	Lot	1		1	1		2			1	1			7		
Stoughton	120	34	Leeds	Nathaniel	1			1		2	1		1				6		
Stoughton	120	35	Littlefield	Nathl					1			1	1				3		
Stoughton	120	36	Littlefield	Nathl Jr	4			1		1			1				7		
Stoughton	120	37	Littlefield	Samuel	3	1		1		1	1		1				8		
Stoughton	120	38	Lovel	Susanna		1						1	1	1			4		
Stoughton	121	1	Marshall	Benja		2		1		1	1			1			6		
Stoughton	121	2	Merion	Wid Lidia	1	1	1			1	1			1			6		
Stoughton	121	3	Monk	Eliphelet				1					1				2		
Stoughton	121	4	Monk	Eliphelet Jr	2			1		1			1				5		
Stoughton	121	5	Monk	Jacob	2	1		1				1	1				6		
Stoughton	121	6	Monk	George			1			1		1					3		
Stoughton	121	7	Monk	Elijah		1	1		1	2	2	1					8		
Stoughton	121	8	Monk	William				1		1	1						3		
Stoughton	121	9	Monk	Lemuel	2			1			1						4		
Stoughton	121	10	Monk	Christopher	2			1		1	1		1				6		
Stoughton	121	11	Morse	Joseph	1	2	1		1	2	1			1			9		
Stoughton	121	12	Morton	Ambrose	2	3		1			1		1				8		
Stoughton	121	13	Morton	Isaac	1		1	1		1			1				5		
Stoughton	121	14	Morton	Seth		1	1			2			1				5		
Stoughton	121	15	Morton	Eleazar			1			4			1				6		
Stoughton	121	16	Morton	Nathl		2	1						1				4		
Stoughton	121	17	Morton	Abigail Wid									2	1			3		
Stoughton	121	18	Osgood	Samuel		1		1	1	1			1	2			7		
Stoughton	121	19	Page	Charles	2	1	1		1	1	1	3	1	1			12		
Stoughton	121	20	Paul	Samuel	2		1	1		1			1	1			7		
Stoughton	121	21	Packard	Benja	3			1		1	1		1	1			8		
Stoughton	121	22	Packard	Abiezer		3		1				1	2				7		
Stoughton	121	23	Pierce	Seth		1		1		2			1				5		
Stoughton	121	24	Pendergrass	John	1			1		2				1			5		
Stoughton	121	25	Pope	Frederick		1	1		1	1				1			5		
Stoughton	121	26	Pope	Sarah Wid		1	2			2	1			1			7		
Stoughton	121	27	Pope	Ralph					1	1				1			3		
Stoughton	121	28	Pope	Lazarus	2		1	1	1	1	3			1			10		
Stoughton	121	29	Porter	Joseph					2	1	1			1			5		
Stoughton	121	30	Porter	Robert	1	1		1					1				4		
Stoughton	121	31	Porter	Cyrus		1					1						2		
Stoughton	121	32	Porter	Abigail Wid									1				1		
Stoughton	121	33	Reynolds	Philip		1	1			1		1					4		
Stoughton	121	34	Richards	Joseph		2		1		1	1						6		
Stoughton	121	35	Richmond	Edward Revd		1		1		1		1	1				5		
Stoughton	121	36	Ryne	Dennis			1			2			1				4		
Stoughton	121	37	Sargant	Wm B.	3	1		1		2			1				8		
Stoughton	122	1	Shepard	Samuel	1		1	1				2					6		
Stoughton	122	2	Smith	Joseph	2	1	2		1	1		1	1				9		
Stoughton	122	3	Smith	Elijah		1		1					1				3		
Stoughton	122	4	Smith	Jese	1	1	1	1					1	1			6		
Stoughton	122	5	Smith	Jese Junr		1							1				2		
Stoughton	122	6	Smith	Philip				1					1				2		
Stoughton	122	7	Smith	Lemuel		2		1	1			2					6		
Stoughton	122	8	Smith	Nathl	1	1	1	1		2		1	1				8		
Stoughton	122	9	Snow	Uriah		1		1						1			3		
Stoughton	122	10	Southworth	Jedidiah		1		1						1			3		
Stoughton	122	11	Southworth	Jedidiah Junr	2			1		1			1				5		
Stoughton	122	12	Southworth	Consider	1		1					1					3		
Stoughton	122	13	Spear	Simeon		2	1			1	1			1			6		
Stoughton	122	14	Sumner	Roger		1	2	1		1	1			1			7		
Stoughton	122	15	Swan	Robert				1									1		
Stoughton	122	16	Swan	Robert Junr		1	2	1		1	1		1	1			8		
Stoughton	122	17	Swan	James	1	1		1		1			1				5		
Stoughton	122	18	Swan	Luther	1			1		1			1				4		
Stoughton	122	19	Stone	James					1					1			2		
Stoughton	122	20	Smith	Rebekah Wid										1			1		
Stoughton	122	21	Talbot	Samuel	1	2	1		1			1					7		

TOWN	PG#	LN#	LAST NAME	FIRST NAME	FREE WHITE MALES					FREE WHITE FEMALES					TOTAL ALL OTHER	TOTAL SLAVES	TOTALS	DISTRICT/ TOWNSHIP	NOTES
					under 10	10 to 16	16 to 26	26 to 45	45 and over	under 10	10 to 16	16 to 26	26 to 45	45 and over					
Stoughton	122	22	Talbot	Jabez		2			1				1				4		
Stoughton	122	23	Talbot	Richard			1			1		1					3		
Stoughton	122	24	Talbot	Isaac	1				1		1	1		1			5		
Stoughton	122	25	Talbot	Isaac Junr	3			1		1			1				6		
Stoughton	122	26	Thayer	Joseph	3				1					1			5		
Stoughton	122	27	Thayer	Caleb			1		1		1		1				4		
Stoughton	122	28	Tilden	Sarah									1	2			3		
Stoughton	122	29	Tolman	Saml	2	1		1	1	2	1		1	3			12		
Stoughton	122	30	Tolman	Thomas	2		1	1					1	1			6		
Stoughton	122	31	Vose	Jeremiah	2	1	1		1			2	2	1			10		
Stoughton	122	32	Wadsworth	George				1		2	3		1	1			8		
Stoughton	122	33	Wadsworth	Benja		1		1					2				4		
Stoughton	122	34	Wadsworth	Abigail Wid								1		1			2		
Stoughton	122	35	Wales	Samuel		1	1	1		4			1	1			9		
Stoughton	122	36	Wales	Joshua	1	2	3		1	1	1	2	1				12		
Stoughton	122	37	Wales	Nathl	1				1	2				1			5		
Stoughton	122	38	Waters	Asa	1	1		1		1			1				5		
Stoughton	122	39	Waters	Zebulon	1			1		1							3		

TOWN	PG#	LN#	LAST NAME	FIRST NAME	FWM under 10	FWM 10 to 16	FWM 16 to 26	FWM 26 to 45	FWM 45 and over	FWF under 10	FWF 10 to 16	FWF 16 to 26	FWF 26 to 45	FWF 45 and over	TOTAL ALL OTHER	TOTAL SLAVES	TOTALS	DISTRICT/ TOWNSHIP	NOTES
Walpole	26	1	Allen	Joshua			1						1				2		
Walpole	26	2	Allen	Abel		1		2						1			4		
Walpole	26	3	Allen	Nathan		1		1			1	1					4		
Walpole	26	4	Allen	Daniel	1		1					1					3		
Walpole	26	5	Allen	David	1			1		2	1	1					6		
Walpole	26	6	Boyden	Joel			1						1	1			3		
Walpole	26	7	Baker	Ziba		1		1		1	1		1				5		
Walpole	26	8	Boyden	John 3d			1		1	2	1		1				6		
Walpole	26	9	Boyden	Ezekiel				1					1				2		
Walpole	26	10	Boyden	Samuel		2		1						2			5		
Walpole	26	11	Bullard	Seth Esq		1		1				1		1			4		
Walpole	26	12	Bullard	Joel	1			1		2			1				5		
Walpole	26	13	Blake	Ebenezer			1	1				1		1			4		
Walpole	27	1	Boyden	Jonathan	1			1						1			3		
Walpole	27	2	Bullard	William			1	1				1		1			4		
Walpole	27	3	Boyden	Jacob	2	2		1					1				6		
Walpole	27	4	Boyden	Elijah	4		2	1		1	1	1	1				11		
Walpole	27	5	Boyden	Benjamin		1	1	1						1			4		
Walpole	27	6	Boyden	Phinas	3	2		1				1	1				8		
Walpole	27	7	Bacon	William				1				1		1			3		
Walpole	27	8	Boyden	Joshua		1		1				1		1			4		
Walpole	27	9	Boyden	John				1						1			2		
Walpole	27	10	Bruce	David				1		1			1				3		
Walpole	27	11	Boyden	Sarah W		1				1			2				4		
Walpole	27	12	Boyden	Asa	1			1		3			1				6		
Walpole	27	13	Billings	Richard		1	1	1		1		1	1				6		
Walpole	27	14	Barrows	David	3			1		2		1	1	1			9		
Walpole	27	15	Blake	Ebenezer				1					1				2		
Walpole	27	16	Baker	Ebenezer			1					1		1			3		
Walpole	27	17	Barden	Phillip				1						1			2		
Walpole	27	18	Blake	Elizabeth						1	2		1				4		
Walpole	27	19	Bacon	Daniel	1			1		1			1				4		
Walpole	27	20	Bacon	William Jr	2	1		1		1			1				6		
Walpole	27	21	Boyden	John Jr			1	1				1		1			4		
Walpole	27	22	Clap	Joshua Esq				1						1			2		
Walpole	27	23	Clap	Oliver		2		1				1		1			5		
Walpole	27	24	Clap	Eliphalet Jr				1		3			1				5		
Walpole	27	25	Carrol	Jonathan		2	2	1			2		1				8		
Walpole	27	26	Clap	Daniel	1			1					1				3		
Walpole	27	27	Clap	Levi	3	1		1		1			1				7		
Walpole	27	28	Ceaveland	John			1	1	1				1				5		
Walpole	27	29	Clark	Oliver		1		1					1				3		
Walpole	27	30	Clark	Seth Esq	1		1	1				1					4		
Walpole	27	31	Clap	Joshua Jr				1			1		1		1		4		
Walpole	27	32	Clap	Elijah			1						1				2		
Walpole	27	33	Copp	Samuel			1	1				1		2			5		
Walpole	27	34	Clap	Eliphalet	1			1						1			3		
Walpole	27	35	Clap	Ebenezer				1			1			1			3		
Walpole	27	36	Clap	Ebenezer Jr		1		1	1	1			1				5		
Walpole	27	37	Clap	Ichabod		1	1	1					1				4		
Walpole	27	38	Clap	Jacob		2	1	1					1	2			7		
Walpole	27	39	Clap	Elizabeth		1							1				2		
Walpole	27	40	Clap	Oliver Jr	2			1		1			1				5		
Walpole	27	41	Clap	Th*n*			1						1				2		
Walpole	27	42	Clap	Thadeus	2		1	1					1	1			6		
Walpole	27	43	Clap	Eleazer	2	1	1	1		2	1	1	1				10		
Walpole	27	44	Clap	Elipha		1		1		2		1					5		
Walpole	28	1	Clap	Thomas			1	1		1							3		
Walpole	28	2	Clap	Rufus		2		1			1	1	1				6		
Walpole	28	3	Day	Jeremiah		1	1		1		1	1		2			7		
Walpole	28	4	Day	Joseph		1		1			1	1	1				5		
Walpole	28	5	Day	Ebenezer			1			3	1		1				6		
Walpole	28	6	Dupee	James	1	1	1		1		1	1					7		
Walpole	28	7	Dexter	Mary W		2					1		1				4		
Walpole	28	8	Ellis	Eliphalet		1	1	1		2			1				6		
Walpole	28	9	Ellis	John	1		1		1	2	3	1	1				10		
Walpole	28	10	Ellis	Moses		1	2	1			1						5		
Walpole	28	11	Ellis	John Jr	1		1						1				3		
Walpole	28	12	Ellis	Joseph		1		1			1	1	1				5		
Walpole	28	13	Ellis	Oliver	2	1		1		2			1				7		
Walpole	28	14	Ellis	Aaron	1		1			1			1				4		
Walpole	28	15	Foster	Lois									1				1		
Walpole	28	16	Foley	Jonathan	2			1		2		1					6		
Walpole	28	17	Fales	Moses			1						1				2		
Walpole	28	18	Fales	Moses Jr	1	1		1		2	1		1				7		
Walpole	28	19	Fisher	Daniel		2		1					1				4		
Walpole	28	20	Fales	C Aaron	2	1		1		2	1		1				8		
Walpole	28	21	Fisher	Daniel Jr	2			1		1			1				5		
Walpole	28	22	Frizel	John				1					1				2		

68

TOWN	PG#	LN#	LAST NAME	FIRST NAME	FREE WHITE MALES					FREE WHITE FEMALES					TOTAL ALL OTHER	TOTAL SLAVES	TOTALS	DISTRICT/ TOWNSHIP	NOTES
					under 10	10 to 16	16 to 26	26 to 45	45 and over	under 10	10 to 16	16 to 26	26 to 45	45 and over					
Walpole	28	23	Fales	Joseph		1	1		1	2	1	1		1			8		
Walpole	28	24	Fales	Ebenezer	1		1	2	1	1	1	1	1	2			11		
Walpole	28	25	Fuller	Samuel		1			1					1			3		
Walpole	28	26	Fales	Abiather	2	2			1	2	1	1	1				10		
Walpole	28	27	Fisher	Sarah Wd		1								1			2		
Walpole	28	28	Fales	Samuel			1	1				1	1				4		
Walpole	28	29	Frizel	A John		1		1		3			1				6		
Walpole	28	30	Farrington	John		1		1						1			3		
Walpole	28	31	Fales	Sarah Wd						1		1	1				3		
Walpole	28	32	Fales	Sewel			1			1		1					3		
Walpole	28	33	Fales	Stephen		1		1				1	1				4		
Walpole	28	34	Fales	Jabez	1		1					1					3		
Walpole	28	35	Fales	Aaron	1		1		1	1				1			5		
Walpole	28	36	Guild	Samuel					1					1			2		
Walpole	28	37	Guild	Joseph Jr	2			1						1			4		
Walpole	29	1	Guild	Samuel Jr	3			1		1				1			6		
Walpole	29	2	Gay	Benjamin	1				1	1	1	3		1			8		
Walpole	29	3	Gay	Joseph		1			1				1				3		
Walpole	29	4	Gay	Calvin	1				2	1	2		1	1			8		
Walpole	29	5	Guild	Rebeckah	1						1	1		1			4		
Walpole	29	6	Guild	Hathannah	1			1				1	1				4		
Walpole	29	7	Gay	Joel	1		1	1		2			1				6		
Walpole	29	8	Guild	Herman			1										1		
Walpole	29	9	Gallett	Augustin		1	1	2		4	1		2				11		
Walpole	29	10	Guild	Aaron			1						1				2		
Walpole	29	11	Gay	Jacob	3		1		1				1				6		
Walpole	29	12	Guild	Joseph	1			1	1			1		1			5		
Walpole	29	13	Griggs	William	1				1					1			3		
Walpole	29	14	Guild	Jacob	2				1					1			4		
Walpole	29	15	Grayham	William	1		1	1		1		1					5		
Walpole	29	16	Gould	Lincon		1		1					1				3		
Walpole	29	17	Hanes	Benjamin		2	2		1		1	1		1			8		
Walpole	29	18	Hartshorn	Timothy				1					1	1			3		
Walpole	29	19	Hartshorn	Richard		1	1		1				2	1			6		
Walpole	29	20	Hartshorn	Asa	1	1		1		1			3				7		
Walpole	29	21	Hartshorn	Samuel	1	3			1	1		1	1				8		
Walpole	29	22	Hartshorn	Ebenezer	1				1		2		2				6		
Walpole	29	23	Hartshorn	Lewis	3			1		1			1				6		
Walpole	29	24	Hall	John	1	1			1	1		1		1			6		
Walpole	29	25	Hall	Josiah	3	2			1	1			1				8		
Walpole	29	26	Harris	Nicholas				1									1		
Walpole	29	27	Hill	George	1				1	1			2	1			6		
Walpole	29	28	Hartshorn	John			1				1		1				3		
Walpole	29	29	Hill	Josiah			1			1			1				3		
Walpole	29	30	Hartshorn	Fisher	1		1		1	2	1	1	1				8		
Walpole	29	31	Kingsbury	William			1			2		1					4		
Walpole	29	32	Kingsbury	Seth				1						1			2		
Walpole	29	33	Kingsbury	Daniel	1		1	1	1	2			1				7		
Walpole	29	34	Kingsbury	Seth Jr	1				1				1				3		
Walpole	29	35	Kingsbury	Nathan				1						1			2		
Walpole	29	36	Kingsbury	Solomen	1	1			1	3		1	1				8		
Walpole	29	37	Kingsbury	Joseph	2			1		1		1	1				6		
Walpole	29	38	Kendal	Jonathan		1			1		1			1	1		5		
Walpole	30	1	Kingsbury	Jacob			1			1							2		
Walpole	30	2	Kingsbury	Samuel	1			1		2		1					5		
Walpole	30	3	Kingsbury	Asa	1			1				1	3				6		
Walpole	30	4	Keith	John	1			1		3		1					6		
Walpole	30	5	Lewis	Isaac		1	1	1		1			1				5		
Walpole	30	6	Lewis	David	1			1		2		1	1				6		
Walpole	30	7	Morse	Ezekiel	1			1		2		1					5		
Walpole	30	8	Morse	Jotham			1		1		1			2			5		
Walpole	30	9	Morse	Joshua			1	1						1			3		
Walpole	30	10	Morse	Richard	1	1		1					1				4		
Walpole	30	11	Mann	Timothy			1	1		1			1	1			5		
Walpole	30	12	Mann	Benjamin	3	1			1				1	1			7		
Walpole	30	13	Morey	George Revd	2	1			1	2	1		1				8		
Walpole	30	14	Morse	Aaron		1							1				2		
Walpole	30	15	Morse	Obadiah		1		1		2			1				5		
Walpole	30	16	Morse	Agnes Wd		1			1	1				1			4		
Walpole	30	17	Marshal	John	2	1	2	1		2	1		1				10		
Walpole	30	18	Marsh	Caleb	3			1					1				5		
Walpole	30	19	Miriam	Ebenezer				1		1			1				3		
Walpole	30	20	Mann	Seth		1				1					1		3		
Walpole	30	21	Messinger	James				1									1		
Walpole	30	22	Needham	John			1	1	2		1	1	2				8		
Walpole	30	23	Nason	Willaby	2				1	1		1		1			6		
Walpole	30	24	Nason	Jesse		1	1					1					3		
Walpole	30	25	Nason	Nathanael	1				1					1			3		
Walpole	30	26	Pond	Nathan				1									2		

TOWN	PG#	LN#	LAST NAME	FIRST NAME	FREE WHITE MALES					FREE WHITE FEMALES					TOTAL ALL OTHER	TOTAL SLAVES	TOTALS	DISTRICT/ TOWNSHIP	NOTES
					under 10	10 to 16	16 to 26	26 to 45	45 and over	under 10	10 to 16	16 to 26	26 to 45	45 and over					
Walpole	30	27	Pond	Nathan Jn	3	2		1		2			1				9		
Walpole	30	28	Pond	Eli	1			1			1		1				4		
Walpole	30	29	Partridge	Henry					1					1			2		
Walpole	30	30	Partridge	Otis	4	2		1	1	2	1		1				12		
Walpole	30	31	Partridge	Henry Jr	1	1	1			2	1	1		1			8		
Walpole	30	32	Pattee	Benjamin		1			1		2	1		1			6		
Walpole	30	33	Payton	Kezia Wd			1							1			2		
Walpole	30	34	Page	Joseph		1		1		1	2		1	1			7		
Walpole	30	35	Page	Asa				1				4	1	1			7		
Walpole	30	36	Palley	Nathael		1	2		1	2	1		2	1			10		
Walpole	30	37	Page	Oliver	1		1						1				3		
Walpole	30	38	Richard	John		1			1				1				3		
Walpole	30	39	Robbins	William		1			1		1	1		1			5		
Walpole	30	40	Rhoade	Eliphalet		1	1		1	3	1	1	1				9		
Walpole	31	1	Rhoade	Eleazer				1		3			1				5		
Walpole	31	2	Smith	Moses	2			1	1	2			1	1			8		
Walpole	31	3	Smith	Samuel				1		1				1			3		
Walpole	31	4	Smith	Samuel Jr	1			1			1		1				4		
Walpole	31	5	Smith	Henry				1		1				1			3		
Walpole	31	6	Smith	Seth			1		1		1		1				4		
Walpole	31	7	Smith	Asa					1	1	1			1			4		
Walpole	31	8	Smith	John	3	2		1					1				7		
Walpole	31	9	Smith	Isaac	1	1	1		1	2				1			7		
Walpole	31	10	Smith	Jeremiah	1	2			1	1		2	1				8		
Walpole	31	11	Smith	Peter	2			1					1				4		
Walpole	31	12	Smith	Liffee	3		2	1		1			1	1			9		
Walpole	31	13	Smith	Eleazer	3			1		1				1			6		
Walpole	31	14	Studson	Joshua	1		1	1				1					4		
Walpole	31	15	Smith	Abigail Wd								1		1			2		
Walpole	31	16	Smith	Royal			1						1				2		
Walpole	31	17	Smith	Timothy			1										1		
Walpole	31	18	Thomas	John		1		1		3			1				6		
Walpole	31	19	Thompson	Elijah	1	1		1	1	1	1		1	1			8		
Walpole	31	20	Turner	Abner				1			1			1			3		
Walpole	31	21	Turner	Nathan	1	1		1		1	2		1	1			8		
Walpole	31	22	Tisdale	James		1	1		1		1		1				5		
Walpole	31	23	Turner	Jacob		2			1	4			1				8		
Walpole	31	24	Turner	Joseph				1									1		
Walpole	31	25	Wallet	Andrew	2	1		1	1		1	1		1			8		
Walpole	31	26	Wild	Jonathan	3	1		1	1	1	1		2		1		11		
Walpole	31	27	Allen	Amos	1			1		1				1			4		
Walpole	31	28	Boyden	Daniel	1		1			1	1	1					5		

TOWN	PG#	LN#	LAST NAME	FIRST NAME	FREE WHITE MALES under 10	10 to 16	16 to 26	26 to 45	45 and over	FREE WHITE FEMALES under 10	10 to 16	16 to 26	26 to 45	45 and over	TOTAL ALL OTHER	TOTAL SLAVES	TOTALS	DISTRICT/ TOWNSHIP	NOTES
Weymouth	74	1	Arnold	Samuel			2		1			1	1				5	North Parish	
Weymouth	74	2	Arnold	Alexander	1			1		1							3	North Parish	
Weymouth	74	3	Arnold	Saml Junior	1		4			1	1	1					8	North Parish	
Weymouth	74	4	Beals	Hannah									1				1	North Parish	
Weymouth	74	5	Burrill	Peter Widw of	*	*	*	*	*	*	*	*	*	*			*	North Parish	
Weymouth	74	6	Bates	Levi	4	1	1	1		3	2		1				13	North Parish	
Weymouth	74	7	Blanchard	Ann		1	2				1	1		1			6	North Parish	
Weymouth	74	8	Badlam	Saml			2		1		1	2		1			7	North Parish	
Weymouth	74	9	Badlam	Unity										2			2	North Parish	
Weymouth	74	10	Bicknell	Benjm		1	1		1			1		1			5	North Parish	
Weymouth	74	11	Burrell	Joseph	1	1		1		2			1				6	North Parish	
Weymouth	74	12	Bates	Elnathan		1	1	1	1			2		1			7	North Parish	
Weymouth	74	13	Bates	Silvanus	2	1		1		1			1				6	North Parish	
Weymouth	74	14	Bates	Joshua		1		2	1	2	1	1					8	North Parish	
Weymouth	74	15	Bicknell	Zachariah				1				1		1			3	North Parish	
Weymouth	74	16	Burrell	Asa	1		1			1			1				4	North Parish	
Weymouth	74	17	Bates	Jesse	2			1		3		2	1				10	North Parish	
Weymouth	74	18	Bates	Alpheus	1	2	1	1		3			1				9	North Parish	
Weymouth	74	19	Beals	Lazarus A.	1			1				1		1			4	North Parish	
Weymouth	74	20	Blanchard	David	2		1	1		4	3	1	1				13	North Parish	
Weymouth	74	21	Bates	Urban		1	2	1	1			2		1			8	North Parish	
Weymouth	74	22	Bicknell	Bathsheba	1					2			1	2			6	North Parish	
Weymouth	74	23	Bates	Elisha	3			1		2	1		1				8	North Parish	
Weymouth	74	24	Bates	Eunice									1	1			2	North Parish	
Weymouth	74	25	Beales	Nathl				1				1					2	North Parish	
Weymouth	74	26	Binney	Joshua	2			1		1		1					5	North Parish	
Weymouth	74	27	Binney	Elkanah		1		1						1			3	North Parish	
Weymouth	74	28	Beal	Azariah				1						1			2	North Parish	
Weymouth	74	29	Bates	William				1				1		1			3	North Parish	
Weymouth	74	30	Cushing	Er	2	1	1		1	1		2		1			9	North Parish	
Weymouth	74	31	Cleverly	Jona		1	1					1					3	North Parish	
Weymouth	74	32	Cushing	Saml	1			1					1				3	North Parish	
Weymouth	74	33	Cushing	Thomas	1	1		1		2			1	1			7	North Parish	
Weymouth	74	34	Cushing	Thomas Junr	3		1	1					1				6	North Parish	
Weymouth	74	35	Cowen	Howland	3	1		1				2	1				8	North Parish	
Weymouth	74	36	Copeland	Gershom	1		1		1			1		1			5	North Parish	
Weymouth	74	37	Canterbury	John	2		1	2		2			1				8	North Parish	
Weymouth	74	38	Copeland	Gershom Junr	1	1		1		2		1					6	North Parish	
Weymouth	74	39	Cushing	Bela			1			3		1					5	North Parish	
Weymouth	74	40	Cushing	John	3		1			1		1					6	North Parish	
Weymouth	74	41	Cushing	Zenas			1										1	North Parish	
Weymouth	75	1	Colson	Thomas Junr		1		1				1					3	North Parish	
Weymouth	75	2	Cushing	Reg* Junr	2		1			1		1					5	North Parish	
Weymouth	75	3	Cushing	Grace										2			2	North Parish	
Weymouth	75	4	Copeland	John			1					1					2	North Parish	
Weymouth	75	5	Dyer	Asa		1		1				1		1			4	North Parish	
Weymouth	75	6	Dyer	Benjamin				1		2			1	1			5	North Parish	
Weymouth	75	7	Dyer	Samuel	1			1		3	1		1				7	North Parish	
Weymouth	75	8	Dyer	Ruth						1			1				2	North Parish	
Weymouth	75	9	Dyer	Asa Junior	1			1		2			1				5	North Parish	
Weymouth	75	10	Dyer	Joseph				1		1			1	2			5	North Parish	
Weymouth	75	11	Dyer	Solomon	1	1		1		1	1		1				6	North Parish	
Weymouth	75	12	Dyer	William	2			1					1				4	North Parish	
Weymouth	75	13	Damon	Jonathan	2			1		2	1	1		1			8	North Parish	
Weymouth	75	14	Dyer	Susanna								1		1			2	North Parish	
Weymouth	75	15	Dyer	Releaf		1						1		1			3	North Parish	
Weymouth	75	16	Dyer	Jacob	3		1	1		1	1		1		1		9	North Parish	
Weymouth	75	17	Ford	David	1			1		4			1				7	North Parish	
Weymouth	75	18	Fenno	Saml	1			1		1			1				4	North Parish	
Weymouth	75	19	Humphrey	James			1	1						1			3	North Parish	
Weymouth	75	20	Hunt	Asa	3			1		1	2		1	1			9	North Parish	
Weymouth	75	21	Hunt	Zachariah	1	1		1					1				4	North Parish	
Weymouth	75	22	Holbrook	Josiah			1	1				1		2			8	North Parish	
Weymouth	75	23	Hunt	Ebenz	1		1	1		1		1		1			6	North Parish	
Weymouth	75	24	Hunt	Ebenz Jun	1	1	1						1				5	North Parish	
Weymouth	75	25	Harding	James	3			1		1		1	1				7	North Parish	
Weymouth	75	26	Humphrey	Silence Wid	1		1	1					3	1			7	North Parish	
Weymouth	75	27	Humphrey	Saml				1		1				1			3	North Parish	
Weymouth	75	28	Humphrey	James 3d			1			3			1				5	North Parish	
Weymouth	75	29	Humphrey	Joseph	3			1		2			1				7	North Parish	
Weymouth	75	30	Holbrook	Elisha		1		1				2		1			5	North Parish	
Weymouth	75	31	Humphrey	James 2d	1		3		1	2	2			1			10	North Parish	
Weymouth	75	32	Hill	Ebenezer				1						1			2	North Parish	
Weymouth	75	33	Humphrey	Josiah				1				1		1			3	North Parish	
Weymouth	75	34	Humphrey	Saml	2			1				1		1			5	North Parish	
Weymouth	76	1	Holbrook	Abizer				1						1			2	North Parish	
Weymouth	76	2	Humphrey	William	2			1		1			1				5	North Parish	
Weymouth	76	3	Hunt	Saml	1			1		1	1		1				5	North Parish	
Weymouth	76	4	Holbrook	John	2		1	1		2			1				7	North Parish	
Weymouth	76	5	Holbrook	Silvanus	3			1		1			1				6	North Parish	
Weymouth	76	6	Jones	Elisha		1			1				1	1			4	North Parish	
Weymouth	76	7	Jones	James		1		1					1				3	North Parish	
Weymouth	76	8	Jones	Elisha Junior	1			1		2			1				5	North Parish	
Weymouth	76	9	Joyce	Thomas			2	1		1		1					5	North Parish	
Weymouth	76	10	Jeffs	John				1			1			1			3	North Parish	
Weymouth	76	11	Kingman	Ebenz	4			1	1	1			1	1			9	North Parish	
Weymouth	76	12	Lovell	Solomon				1									1	North Parish	
Weymouth	76	13	Lovell	James		1		2			1	1	1				6	North Parish	
Weymouth	76	14	Lincoln	Frederick	1	1			1		3			1			7	North Parish	
Weymouth	76	15	Larabee	Asa			1			2			1				4	North Parish	

TOWN	PG#	LN#	LAST NAME	FIRST NAME	FREE WHITE MALES: under 10	10 to 16	16 to 26	26 to 45	45 and over	FREE WHITE FEMALES: under 10	10 to 16	16 to 26	26 to 45	45 and over	TOTAL ALL OTHER	TOTAL SLAVES	TOTALS	DISTRICT/TOWNSHIP	NOTES
Weymouth	76	16	Loud	Silvanus	3	2		1		3	1	1	1				12	North Parish	
Weymouth	76	17	Lewis	Jonathan			1			2			1	1			5	North Parish	
Weymouth	76	18	Loud	Eliot			3		1		2			1			7	North Parish	
Weymouth	76	19	Loud	Joseph				1					1				2	North Parish	
Weymouth	76	20	Lovell	David	2			1					1	2			6	North Parish	
Weymouth	76	21	Lovell	Yardly			1					1	1	1			4	North Parish	
Weymouth	76	22	Lovell	David	1	1		1					1	1			5	North Parish	
Weymouth	76	23	Norton	Jacob Revd	4	1		1					2				8	North Parish	
Weymouth	76	24	Nash	Moses	1	1	1		1	2	1	1		1			9	North Parish	
Weymouth	76	25	Nash	Job	2	2			1	1	1	1		1			9	North Parish	
Weymouth	76	26	Nash	Elisha				1									1	North Parish	
Weymouth	76	27	Nash	Ezra	1	1		1		3	1			1			8	North Parish	
Weymouth	76	28	Nash	Zichri	3	1	1	1						2			8	North Parish	
Weymouth	76	29	Nash	Joseph				1				1		1			3	North Parish	
Weymouth	76	30	Nash	Joseph Junr	4	1		1	1	1	2		1				11	North Parish	
Weymouth	76	31	Nash	Timothy	1		1	1		1		2	1				7	North Parish	
Weymouth	76	32	Nash	Zadoc		1	2	1						1			5	North Parish	
Weymouth	76	33	Nash	Charles	1			1		2			1				5	North Parish	
Weymouth	76	34	Nash	Ebenezer	1		1						1				3	North Parish	
Weymouth	76	35	Pratt	Jonathan		1			1	1	1	1		1			6	North Parish	
Weymouth	76	36	Pratt	James	1		1		1	1		1		1			6	North Parish	
Weymouth	76	37	Pratt	Ichabod	1	1			1	1		1		1			6	North Parish	
Weymouth	76	38	Pratt	Stephen		1	1			1			1	2			6	North Parish	
Weymouth	76	39	Pratt	Silvanus				1			1		1				3	North Parish	
Weymouth	76	40	Pratt	Benjamin 2d		1		1		2	1	1					6	North Parish	
Weymouth	76	41	Pratt	Peter		1			1			1	1				4	North Parish	
Weymouth	76	42	Pratt	Jona Junior	2			1		1			1				5	North Parish	
Weymouth	77	1	Phillips	William				1									1	North Parish	
Weymouth	77	2	Pratt	Joshua		2	1	1		1			1	1			7	North Parish	
Weymouth	77	3	Plumber	Joseph				1					1				2	North Parish	
Weymouth	77	4	Peakes	Joseph	1		1		1	1	1	1		1			7	North Parish	
Weymouth	77	5	Pratt	Abiah	1	1		1		2	1		1				7	North Parish	
Weymouth	77	6	Porter	Jonathan		1			1			2		2			6	North Parish	
Weymouth	77	7	Porter	Abner				1						1			2	North Parish	
Weymouth	77	8	Porter	William				1						1			2	North Parish	
Weymouth	77	9	Pratt	Samuel	3	1	2			1	2			1			10	North Parish	
Weymouth	77	10	Pratt	Samuel Junr	1		1					1					3	North Parish	
Weymouth	77	11	Pratt	Robert	2			1		1			1				5	North Parish	
Weymouth	77	12	Pratt	Benjamin Junr		1	1	1		1	1	1	1				7	North Parish	
Weymouth	77	13	Pratt	Stephen		1	1							2			5	North Parish	
Weymouth	77	14	Pratt	Benjm	1			1					1	1			4	North Parish	
Weymouth	77	15	Phillips	William Junr				1		2			1				4	North Parish	
Weymouth	77	16	Pratt	Asa	3			1		2			1				7	North Parish	
Weymouth	77	17	Pratt	Abner		2				1		1		1			5	North Parish	
Weymouth	77	18	Porter	Joseph Junr	1		1						1				3	North Parish	
Weymouth	77	19	Pratt	Laban	3	1		1			1		1				7	North Parish	
Weymouth	77	20	Reed	Samuel		1		1				2		1			5	North Parish	
Weymouth	77	21	Rice	David				1			1		1				3	North Parish	
Weymouth	77	22	Rice	John		1		1		3			1				8	North Parish	
Weymouth	77	23	Rice	Jonah		1	1		1	2	1	2	2				10	North Parish	
Weymouth	77	24	Richards	Nathl Junr		1	1		1	1	2		1				6	North Parish	
Weymouth	77	25	Rice	David Junr	3			1		2	1		1				8	North Parish	
Weymouth	77	26	Ripley	William				1						2			3	North Parish	
Weymouth	77	27	Reed	Thomas				1		4			1				6	North Parish	
Weymouth	77	28	Tufts	Cotton		1		1	1	1		1	1	1			7	North Parish	
Weymouth	77	29	Tufts	Cotton Junr	1	1	2			2		1	1				8	North Parish	
Weymouth	77	30	Torrey	Sarah1		1		1	1	1			1				5	North Parish	
Weymouth	77	31	Tirrell	Noah			1	1						2			4	North Parish	
Weymouth	77	32	Torrey	Phillip	1			1				2		2	1		6	North Parish	
Weymouth	77	33	Tirrell	Levi			1			3			1				5	North Parish	
Weymouth	77	34	Tirrell	Noah Junr	2	2		1		3			1				9	North Parish	
Weymouth	77	35	Torrey	Daniel				1				2		1			4	North Parish	
Weymouth	77	36	Torrey	James			1										1	North Parish	
Weymouth	77	37	Turner	Jacob		1		1		1				1			4	North Parish	
Weymouth	77	38	Torrey	Benj				1		1	1						3	North Parish	
Weymouth	77	39	White	John	2			2		2	1	1	1				9	North Parish	
Weymouth	77	40	White	Ja*	2			1					1				4	North Parish	
Weymouth	77	41	Weston	Deboh Wd			1				1	2		2			6	North Parish	
Weymouth	77	42	Whitman	Abiah		1	1						1	1			4	North Parish	
Weymouth	77	43	White	Nathl	2	4	1			2	1	1					11	North Parish	
Weymouth	77	44	Webb	Thomas		1		2				1		3			7	North Parish	
Weymouth	77	45	Wilds	William	2	1				1		1	1				7	North Parish	
Weymouth	78	1	White	Abiel	3	2	1	1		1	1	1	2	2			14	North Parish	
Weymouth	78	2	White	Asa		1		1			1			1			4	North Parish	
Weymouth	78	3	Whitmark	Peter	1	1	1			1		2		1			7	North Parish	
Weymouth	78	4	Webb	Saml Junr			2	2			1		1	2			8	North Parish	
Weymouth	78	5	Waterman	Hannah Wid		1					1	1		1			4	North Parish	
Weymouth	78	6	Whitmark	Saml	2			1	1				1	1			8	North Parish	
Weymouth	78	7	Waterman	David	2			1		3			1				7	North Parish	
Weymouth	78	8	White	Lurania						1		1					2	North Parish	
Weymouth	78	9	Webb	Thomas		1	1	1		1	2	1	1				9	North Parish	
Weymouth	78	10	Agar	Benjm				1									1	South Parish	
Weymouth	78	11	Agar	Jonan	2	1		1		2		1					7	South Parish	
Weymouth	78	12	Bailey	Nathl				1					1				2	South Parish	
Weymouth	78	13	Bailey	Saml		2		1		2			1				6	South Parish	
Weymouth	78	14	Blanchard	Danl Wid			3	1				1	1	1			7	South Parish	
Weymouth	78	15	Blanchard	Nathl	3	1		1		4			1				10	South Parish	
Weymouth	78	16	Blanchard	Bela			2					1					3	South Parish	
Weymouth	78	17	Blanchard	Daniel		2	1	1				1					6	South Parish	
Weymouth	78	18	Blanchard	Saml			1	1						1			3	South Parish	

TOWN	PG#	LN#	LAST NAME	FIRST NAME	FREE WHITE MALES under 10	10 to 16	16 to 26	26 to 45	45 and over	FREE WHITE FEMALES under 10	10 to 16	16 to 26	26 to 45	45 and over	TOTAL ALL OTHER	TOTAL SLAVES	TOTALS	DISTRICT/ TOWNSHIP	NOTES
Weymouth	78	19	Blanchard	Saml 2d				1	1			1					3	South Parish	
Weymouth	78	20	Blanchard	Nicholas				1			1			1			3	South Parish	
Weymouth	78	21	Blanchard	Nichos Junior	2	1		1		3			1				8	South Parish	
Weymouth	78	22	Baily	Edward				1						1			2	South Parish	
Weymouth	78	23	Bates	Thaddeus	1	1		1		3			1				7	South Parish	
Weymouth	78	24	Beales	Uriah	1			1		1		1	1	1			6	South Parish	
Weymouth	78	25	Burrell	Reuben Wid	1					2			1				4	South Parish	
Weymouth	78	26	Burrell	Saml				1			1			1			3	South Parish	
Weymouth	78	27	Burrell	Saml Junr	1			1		1		1		1			5	South Parish	
Weymouth	78	28	Bates	Robert	1	1		1		1	1	1	1	1			8	South Parish	
Weymouth	78	29	Blanchard	Abner				1					1				2	South Parish	
Weymouth	78	30	Blanchard	Thomas			1		1		1	3	1				7	South Parish	
Weymouth	78	31	Blanchard	Josiah	1			1		1			1				4	South Parish	
Weymouth	78	32	Blanchard	John	1	1	1		1	1	1			1			7	South Parish	
Weymouth	78	33	Bates	Saml 2d	2	2	1	2		2			1	1			11	South Parish	
Weymouth	78	34	Bates	John Ward	4			1		1	2	1	1	1			11	South Parish	
Weymouth	78	35	Bates	Saml		2	2	1		2				2			11	South Parish	
Weymouth	78	36	Beales	Sarah										3			3	South Parish	
Weymouth	78	37	Burrell	Robert	2			1		3			1				7	South Parish	
Weymouth	78	38	Bailey	Abraham			1					1					2	South Parish	
Weymouth	78	39	Burrell	Daniel				1						1			2	South Parish	
Weymouth	78	40	Colson	Josiah			1	1					1	1			4	South Parish	
Weymouth	78	41	Colson	Thomas 3d			1	1						1			3	South Parish	
Weymouth	79	1	Cushing	Adam	1	3	1	1		1			1				8	South Parish	
Weymouth	79	2	Cheesman	Hosea	1	1		1				2	1	1			7	South Parish	
Weymouth	79	3	Copeland	John			1						1				2	South Parish	
Weymouth	79	4	Cushing	Beale			1			3			1				5	South Parish	
Weymouth	79	5	Dyer	John	1	1	1	1		1	1	1					7	South Parish	
Weymouth	79	6	Derby	Jona				1						1			2	South Parish	
Weymouth	79	7	Derby	Abner	3			1		1			1				6	South Parish	
Weymouth	79	8	French	Jacob	1	1				2			1				6	South Parish	
Weymouth	79	9	Hollis	Jesse			1			2		1					4	South Parish	
Weymouth	79	10	Hunt	Nancy Wid						2			1				3	South Parish	
Weymouth	79	11	Holbrook	Jerusa Wid		1	2	1			1		1	1			7	South Parish	
Weymouth	79	12	Holbrook	Nathl		1	2	1			1			1			6	South Parish	
Weymouth	79	13	Hunt	Robert	2	1	2		1	2	1	2		2			13	South Parish	
Weymouth	79	14	Holbrook	John	2			1		1			1	3			8	South Parish	
Weymouth	79	15	Holbrook	Abner	1			1				1					3	South Parish	
Weymouth	79	16	Holbrook	Benja				1					1				2	South Parish	
Weymouth	79	17	Holbrook	David		1	1										2	South Parish	
Weymouth	79	18	Holbrook	Nathl Junr	2	1	2	1		1		1	1				9	South Parish	
Weymouth	79	19	Hollis	Hosea	1		1					1					3	South Parish	
Weymouth	79	20	Holbrook	Silvanus	2		1			1			1				5	South Parish	
Weymouth	79	21	Hawes	John	1			1		1	1			1			5	South Parish	
Weymouth	79	22	Hawes	John Junior	1	1	1	1		1		1					6	South Parish	
Weymouth	79	23	Hawes	Joseph			1			2		1					4	South Parish	
Weymouth	79	24	Hollis	Betty Wid		1						1	1				3	South Parish	
Weymouth	79	25	Joy	William		2		1				1	1				5	South Parish	
Weymouth	79	26	Joy	Nehemiah				1				2	1				4	South Parish	
Weymouth	79	27	Joy	Ebenezer				1		1			1				3	South Parish	
Weymouth	79	28	Joy	David				1				2	1				5	South Parish	
Weymouth	79	29	Joy	Turner	1			1					1				3	South Parish	
Weymouth	79	30	Joy	David Junr	1			1		3			1				6	South Parish	
Weymouth	79	31	Joy	Benjm	1	1		1			1		1				5	South Parish	
Weymouth	79	32	Jeff	James	1		1						1				3	South Parish	
Weymouth	79	33	Kingman	Zachariah		1	1					1					3	South Parish	
Weymouth	79	34	Kingman	John	1				1					1			3	South Parish	
Weymouth	79	35	Kingman	John 2nd		1			1			1		1			4	South Parish	
Weymouth	79	36	Loud	David	2	1	3	1			1		1				9	South Parish	
Weymouth	80	1	Loud	William				1				1		1			3	South Parish	
Weymouth	80	2	Loud	Jacob		1						1					2	South Parish	
Weymouth	80	3	Loud	Hulda Wid	2	1					1		1				5	South Parish	
Weymouth	80	4	Loud	Eliphalet	3			1		2	3	1	1				11	South Parish	
Weymouth	80	5	Loud	Benjamin	1		1	2		3			1				8	South Parish	
Weymouth	80	6	Loud	Daniel	3			1		2			1				7	South Parish	
Weymouth	80	7	Lovell	John			1							1			2	South Parish	
Weymouth	80	8	Lovell	Lemuel	2	1	1						1				5	South Parish	
Weymouth	80	9	Loud	Wm Junr				1		1	1						4	South Parish	
Weymouth	80	10	Nash	Joshua	1	1	1		1	1				1			6	South Parish	
Weymouth	80	11	Nash	John					1								1	South Parish	
Weymouth	80	12	Norton	John			1				1		1				3	South Parish	
Weymouth	80	13	Orcutt	Andrew				1						1			2	South Parish	
Weymouth	80	14	Orcutt	Moses	2		1	1		2	2		1				9	South Parish	
Weymouth	80	15	Pratt	Ezra			3		1		1	1	2	1			9	South Parish	
Weymouth	80	16	Porter	Isaac Wid of								2	1	1			4	South Parish	
Weymouth	80	17	Pratt	Zenas	2	1	1	1		2		1	1				9	South Parish	
Weymouth	80	18	Pratt	Isaac	1	1				3	1		1				7	South Parish	
Weymouth	80	19	Pool	Thomas			1		1				1	1			4	South Parish	
Weymouth	80	20	Pratt	Matthew	2	1		1		2		2	1				10	South Parish	
Weymouth	80	21	Pratt	Matthew Junr			1						1				2	South Parish	
Weymouth	80	22	Porter	Joseph				1					2	1			4	South Parish	
Weymouth	80	23	Pratt	Joseph	3			1		1	2		1				8	South Parish	
Weymouth	80	24	Pool	Gardner		1				1							2	South Parish	
Weymouth	80	25	Pratt	Mary Wid		1							1	1			3	South Parish	
Weymouth	80	26	Rogers	John			1			1		2		2			6	South Parish	
Weymouth	80	27	Richards	Nath				1				1		1			3	South Parish	
Weymouth	80	28	Richards	James	1		1	1	1				1	1			6	South Parish	
Weymouth	80	29	Richards	Jacob	2			1		3	1		1				8	South Parish	
Weymouth	80	30	Richards	James 2d	1			1		2		1					5	South Parish	
Weymouth	80	31	Reed	Frederick	1			1			1			1			4	South Parish	

TOWN	PG#	LN#	LAST NAME	FIRST NAME	FREE WHITE MALES under 10	10 to 16	16 to 26	26 to 45	45 and over	FREE WHITE FEMALES under 10	10 to 16	16 to 26	26 to 45	45 and over	TOTAL ALL OTHER	TOTAL SLAVES	TOTALS	DISTRICT/ TOWNSHIP	NOTES
Weymouth	80	32	Reed	Ezra	2	1	2	1		2		1	1	1			11	South Parish	
Weymouth	80	33	Ripley	Eliphalet				1		4	2		1				8	South Parish	
Weymouth	80	34	Richards	Thomas	1			1		1	1	1					5	South Parish	
Weymouth	80	35	Richards	Phebe Wid	1					1		1					3	South Parish	
Weymouth	80	36	Richards	Robert			1			2			1				4	South Parish	
Weymouth	80	37	Shaw	David	2			1		1			1				5	South Parish	
Weymouth	80	38	Shaw	John & Jesse	1	1	1	1	1	2	1		3				11	South Parish	
Weymouth	80	39	Shaw	Jeremiah	2			1		2			1				6	South Parish	
Weymouth	81	1	Shaw	Nathaniel	2		2	1		2		2					9	South Parish	
Weymouth	81	2	Stoddard	Hezekiah		1						1					2	South Parish	
Weymouth	81	3	Smith	Lemuel	2	2		1		2	1		2				10	South Parish	
Weymouth	81	4	Stoddard	Jesse	2		1					1	1				5	South Parish	
Weymouth	81	5	Smith	William	1		2		1	1				1			6	South Parish	
Weymouth	81	6	Torrey	David				1			2			1			4	South Parish	
Weymouth	81	7	Thayer	Obediah				1			1			1			3	South Parish	
Weymouth	81	8	Thayer	Richard			1	1		3			1	1			7	South Parish	
Weymouth	81	9	Tirrell	Joseph		1	1	1						2			5	South Parish	
Weymouth	81	10	Torrey	James		1			1	2	2	1		1			8	South Parish	
Weymouth	81	11	Tirrell	John	2	2	1		1	2	1			1			10	South Parish	
Weymouth	81	12	Thomas	John	2			1		2				1			6	South Parish	
Weymouth	81	13	Tirrell	Vinson		1	1	1		1	1		1	2			8	South Parish	
Weymouth	81	14	Trufant	Jonathan	1	1			1	1				2			6	South Parish	
Weymouth	81	15	Trufant	Joshua			1										1	South Parish	
Weymouth	81	16	Trufant	David	1			1		2			2				6	South Parish	
Weymouth	81	17	Thayer	Luther	4			1					2				7	South Parish	
Weymouth	81	18	Tirrell	Benj	4			1		1			1				7	South Parish	
Weymouth	81	19	Thayer	Zenas	2			1		4	1		1				9	South Parish	
Weymouth	81	20	Tirrell	James 2d	2	1	2	1	1	1		1	1	1			11	South Parish	
Weymouth	81	21	Tirrell	Jacob 2d	1			1		4			1				7	South Parish	
Weymouth	81	22	Torrey	James Gershom	1		1					1					3	South Parish	
Weymouth	81	23	Torrey	Samuel	3	2		1				1	1	1			9	South Parish	
Weymouth	81	24	Thayer	Randal	1		1					1					3	South Parish	
Weymouth	81	25	Thayer	Barnabas	2	2		1		2	2		1				10	South Parish	
Weymouth	81	26	Vinson	John		1			1					1			3	South Parish	
Weymouth	81	27	Vinson	John Junr	1	2		1	1	3	1	2	1				12	South Parish	
Weymouth	81	28	Vining	David			2		1		1	1	1	1			7	South Parish	
Weymouth	81	29	Vining	Joseph	1			1					1				3	South Parish	
Weymouth	81	30	Vining	Joseph Junr	1	1	1			2	1		1				7	South Parish	
Weymouth	81	31	Vining	James	1		1					1					3	South Parish	
Weymouth	81	32	Vining	Deboh Wid							1		1				2	South Parish	
Weymouth	81	33	Vinson	Thomas			1					1					2	South Parish	
Weymouth	81	34	Vining	Saml Holbk	1			1		1			1				4	South Parish	
Weymouth	81	35	Vining	Bela		1	1					1					3	South Parish	
Weymouth	81	36	Williams	Revd Simeon		2			1	1	1	1	1	1			8	South Parish	
Weymouth	81	37	White	Hezekiah			1	1	1				1	1			5	South Parish	
Weymouth	81	38	Wade	Amasa	1			1		2			1				5	South Parish	
Weymouth	81	39	White	Silas			1		1	1				1			4	South Parish	
Weymouth	81	40	White	Daniel				1						1			2	South Parish	
Weymouth	81	41	White	James	3			1		2			1				7	South Parish	
Weymouth	81	42	White	Benjm				1						1			2	South Parish	
Weymouth	81	43	White	David	1	1	1		1	2	1	1		1			9	South Parish	
Weymouth	82	1	White	Asa			1			1			1				3	South Parish	
Weymouth	82	2	White	Aaron				1						1			2	South Parish	
Weymouth	82	3	White	David		2				1		1	1				5	South Parish	
Weymouth	82	4	White	Jeremiah	1		1					1					3	South Parish	
Weymouth	82	5	White	Jonathan	1	1		1		1		1	1				6	South Parish	

TOWN	PG#	LN#	HEADS OF HOUSEHOLD LAST NAME	FIRST NAME	FREE WHITE MALES under 10	10 to 16	16 to 26	26 to 45	45 and over	FREE WHITE FEMALES under 10	10 to 16	16 to 26	26 to 45	45 and over	TOTAL ALL OTHER	TOTAL SLAVES	TOTALS	DISTRICT/ TOWNSHIP	NOTES
Wrentham	170	1	Messenger	John					1					1			2		
Wrentham	170	2	Messenger	John Junr	5			1					1				7		
Wrentham	170	3	Fisher	William	2			1		1	1	1	1				7		
Wrentham	170	4	Brastow	Beriah	1	2	1		1	2		2		1			10		
Wrentham	170	5	Brewer	Edward	1			1			1		1				4		
Wrentham	170	6	Messenger	Ebenezer	1		1	1			2		1				6		
Wrentham	170	7	Shaw	Mason	1			1			1	1					4		
Wrentham	170	8	Druce	Samuel	1	2		4		1		1	1		2		12		
Wrentham	170	9	Mann	James			3	2		2			2	1	1		11		
Wrentham	170	10	Francour	John				1		2	1				3		8		
Wrentham	170	11	Day	Jeremiah			2	2				2	2	1			9		
Wrentham	170	12	Smith	James	1	1	1		1			2		1			7		
Wrentham	170	13	Cobb	Joseph Junr			1			2		1					4		
Wrentham	170	14	Force	Elijah				1		2			1				4		
Wrentham	170	15	Bowdella	M.	1					1	1	1			3		7		
Wrentham	170	16	Jenks	Luke	1		1			1		2					5		
Wrentham	170	17	Ballou	Pelatiah	1		1						1				3		
Wrentham	171	1	Cook	Ruben			1			2		1					4		
Wrentham	171	2	Cook	Aaron	1	1	2		1	1		2	1	1			10		
Wrentham	171	3	Thurber	Ozias	1			1		1			1				4		
Wrentham	171	4	Jenks	William				1				2		1			4		
Wrentham	171	5	Jenks	Job	2		1	1		1		1					6		
Wrentham	171	6	Cook	Abner Junr	2			1		2			1				6		
Wrentham	171	7	Ballou	Elizabeth	1		1					1		1			4		
Wrentham	171	8	Cook	Abner Junr			2		1			1	2	1			7		
Wrentham	171	9	Ballou	Flavius	1		1						1				3		
Wrentham	171	10	Ballou	Mary						1		1					2		
Wrentham	171	11	Grant	Beriah	1				1	2			1				5		
Wrentham	171	12	Grant	Rhodes			1							2			3		
Wrentham	171	13	Metcalf	Thomas	2	1	3		1	2	2	1					13		
Wrentham	171	14	Metcalf	Silas			1	1	1		1			1			5		
Wrentham	171	15	Metcalf	Lewis	1			1				1					3		
Wrentham	171	16	Comstock	Nathan		1		3	1	4		1	1	1			12		
Wrentham	171	17	Cole	Noah	1	1		1		2			1				6		
Wrentham	171	18	Ballou	Darius	1			1		4	2	1					9		
Wrentham	171	19	Hawes	David	1			1	1	1	1	1		1			7		
Wrentham	171	20	Hawes	Elisha	2				1	3		1	1				8		
Wrentham	171	21	Ray	Mary	2	2						1	1				6		
Wrentham	171	22	Clark	Frederick	1			1					1				3		
Wrentham	171	23	Taylor	Elizabeth								1	1	1			3		
Wrentham	171	24	Fisher	Lewis	4			1		1			1				7		
Wrentham	171	25	Morse	Keturah	1					2			1				4		
Wrentham	171	26	Howard	John	2		1	1					1				5		
Wrentham	171	27	Williams	Williams	1	2	3		1			1		1			9		
Wrentham	171	28	Hall	Amariah	1	2		1		3			1				8		
Wrentham	171	29	Tillingham	Allen	1		2	1		2		1			1		8		
Wrentham	171	30	Clark	Stephen		1	1		1	2				1			6		
Wrentham	171	31	Clark	Onismus			1						1				2		
Wrentham	171	32	Ray	Enos		1		1		2		1	1				6		
Wrentham	171	33	Crowning	Clifford Junior	2			1		2		1					6		
Wrentham	171	34	Aldrich	Asa		2	1		1		1			1			6		
Wrentham	172	1	Aldrich	Nathaniel	2			1					1				4		
Wrentham	172	2	Grant	Joshua	3		2	2		1	1		2				11		
Wrentham	172	3	Grant	Moses		1	2		2			2		2			9		
Wrentham	172	4	Grant	Luther	1		1					1					3		
Wrentham	172	5	Grant	Joseph		1		1		1			1				4		
Wrentham	172	6	Grant	Benjamin				1				1	1				3		
Wrentham	172	7	Grant	David	2	1		1					1				5		
Wrentham	172	8	Day	Samuel	3	1		1		2	1	1		3			14		
Wrentham	172	9	Fairbanks	Molly	1					2	1	1					5		
Wrentham	172	10	Hartshom	Silas	1			1			1		1				4		
Wrentham	172	11	Ware	Benjamin		1		1	1			1		1			5		
Wrentham	172	12	Ware	David				1	2			1		1			5		
Wrentham	172	13	Pond	Reuben			1					1		1			4		
Wrentham	172	14	Bacon	Elias					1		1	2	1				5		
Wrentham	172	15	Ware	Nathaniel		2	3		1		1	2		4			13		
Wrentham	172	16	Bliss	Isaac	2				1	1			1				5		
Wrentham	172	17	Craige	Moses		1	1		1	3		1					7		
Wrentham	172	18	Walton	Amos		2			1				1	1			5		
Wrentham	172	19	Whiting	Lewis			2				1	1	1	1			7		
Wrentham	172	20	Barber	George			1						1				2		
Wrentham	172	21	Witherell	Abel		1			1			1		2			5		
Wrentham	172	22	Mann	George		1	1	1						1			4		
Wrentham	172	23	Whiting	John		1	1	2	2		1	2	2				11		
Wrentham	172	24	Mann	Amherst	1			2		1		1	1				6		
Wrentham	172	25	Day	Benjamin				1						1			2		
Wrentham	172	26	Dunton	Ambrose			1						1				2		
Wrentham	172	27	Blake	Asa					2					1			3		
Wrentham	172	28	Blake	Ebenezer	2	1		1				1		1			6		

75

TOWN	PG#	LN#	LAST NAME	FIRST NAME	M under 10	M 10 to 16	M 16 to 26	M 26 to 45	M 45 and over	F under 10	F 10 to 16	F 16 to 26	F 26 to 45	F 45 and over	TOTAL ALL OTHER	TOTAL SLAVES	TOTALS	DISTRICT/ TOWNSHIP	NOTES
Wrentham	172	29	Barrons	William	2		1			2			1				6		
Wrentham	172	30	Ferrigo	James		1		1				2	2				6		
Wrentham	172	31	Tucker	Ebenezer	1			1		1			1				4		
Wrentham	172	32	Tucker	Ebenezer Junr			1			2			2				5		
Wrentham	172	33	Cleavland	John		1		1		1		1					4		
Wrentham	173	1	Holbrook	David	1	2	1		1		1			1			7		
Wrentham	173	2	Pond	David		1	1		1					3			6		
Wrentham	173	3	Pond	Pellue	1	1		1		1	2	1					7		
Wrentham	173	4	Holbrook	Abigail	1							1		1			3		
Wrentham	173	5	Blake	Darius	1			1		1			1				4		
Wrentham	173	6	Morse	Otis	1			1		2			1				5		
Wrentham	173	7	Wilson	Jared	1	1		1		1			1				5		
Wrentham	173	8	Day	Robert	1	1		1			2		2				7		
Wrentham	173	9	Turner	Isaiah	1		1	1		1	2		1				7		
Wrentham	173	10	Armsby	Unity	2	1	1				2		1				7		
Wrentham	173	11	Holbrook	Mary	2		1	1			2				1		7		
Wrentham	173	12	Holbrook	Daniel				2		1		1		1			5		
Wrentham	173	13	Blake	John				1						1			2		
Wrentham	173	14	Farrington	Josiah	2			1		1			1				5		
Wrentham	173	15	Ware	Oliver		2		1		1	1		1				6		
Wrentham	173	16	Fisher	Leonard	4			1		1			1				7		
Wrentham	173	17	Blinn	George		1		1		2	1		1				6		
Wrentham	173	18	Boyaden	Richard	1	1	2		1		2		1				8		
Wrentham	173	19	Sayles	Elisha	1		2		1	1			1				6		
Wrentham	173	20	Boyaden	James		1	1		1			1		1			5		
Wrentham	173	21	Boyaden	James Junr	1	1		1		1			1				5		
Wrentham	173	22	Holbrook	James	1	1			1			1		1			5		
Wrentham	173	23	Holbrook	Samuel			1			1			1				3		
Wrentham	173	24	Richardson	Samuel				1			1		1	1			4		
Wrentham	173	25	Richardson	Jason		1		1		2		1	1	1			7		
Wrentham	173	26	Smith	Christopher		1	1			2			1				5		
Wrentham	173	27	Dunbar	Simeon	1		1				1						3		
Wrentham	173	28	Fales	Nathan	1		1	1		2		1	1	1			8		
Wrentham	173	29	Thompson	Jason			1			1			2				4		
Wrentham	173	30	Ware	Joel		2		1		2	1		1				7		
Wrentham	173	31	Fairbanks	George				1		1	1		1				4		
Wrentham	173	32	Ware	Nathan			2	1	1		2	1	1				8		
Wrentham	173	33	Vince	Moses		1		1		1	1		1				5		
Wrentham	173	34	Mann	Moses		1	1		1		1	2		1			7		
Wrentham	174	1	Holbrook	Henry	1	1		1						1			4		
Wrentham	174	2	Gould	Daniel				1					1	1			3		
Wrentham	174	3	Ware	Asa	2		1		1	2		1	1				8		
Wrentham	174	4	Blake	Jeremiah		1		1	1	1	1		2				8		
Wrentham	174	5	Frost	Jonathan		1	1			1		1					4		
Wrentham	174	6	Hawes	William	1		1	1		3		4	1				11		
Wrentham	174	7	Blake	Abijah				1					1				2		
Wrentham	174	8	Blake	Samuel	2		1			1	1		1				6		
Wrentham	174	9	Blake	Solomon		1		1				1		1			4		
Wrentham	174	10	Blake	Enoch		1						1					2		
Wrentham	174	11	Ware	Josiah	1		1	1		1	1			1			6		
Wrentham	174	12	Ware	Samuel	1	1	1		1	1	1			1			7		
Wrentham	174	13	Fisher	Seth	3			1					1				5		
Wrentham	174	14	Cook	Daniel		2							1	1			4		
Wrentham	174	15	Frost	Moses				1					1				2		
Wrentham	174	16	Gould	Cyrus	1	1	3	1		1		2	1	1			11		
Wrentham	174	17	Farrington	Oliver	1		2	1		2		1	1	1			9		
Wrentham	174	18	Hewes	George R.T	1	1			1	1			1				5		
Wrentham	174	19	Fisher	David Junr	2		4	2		1	1	1					11		
Wrentham	174	20	Farrington	Daniel				1					1				2		
Wrentham	174	21	Kallock	Cornelius		1		1				1	1				4		
Wrentham	174	22	Hawes	Benjamin		1		1	1			1		1	1		6		
Wrentham	174	23	Fisher	Abijah		1			1	1			1				4		
Wrentham	174	24	Pond	Abner Junr	2			1					1				4		
Wrentham	174	25	Ware	Abiel	1					2			1				4		
Wrentham	174	26	Ware	Timothy			1					1					2		
Wrentham	174	27	Rhodes	Timothy	2	2	1	1		1		1	2	1			11		
Wrentham	174	28	Grant	Justus	1		1					1					3		
Wrentham	174	29	Thayer	Obadiah A.		1	1	1		2			1				6		
Wrentham	174	30	Thayer	Noah		1		1				1		1			4		
Wrentham	174	31	Walcott	Ebenezer	2	1	1	1		2			1				8		
Wrentham	174	32	Hancock	Dolly		1	1	1		1			1				5		
Wrentham	174	33	Ware	Joseph				1						1			2		
Wrentham	174	34	Chever	Royal			1				2						3		
Wrentham	174	35	Chever	Daniel				1			3		1				5		
Wrentham	175	1	Chever	Amos				1				1	2	1			5		
Wrentham	175	2	Chever	Amos Junr			1						1				2		
Wrentham	175	3	Knowlton	Benjamin				1		1	1			2			5		
Wrentham	175	4	Blake	Andrew		1		1				1		1			4		
Wrentham	175	5	Blose	Samuel	1			1		1			2				7		

TOWN	PG#	LN#	LAST NAME	FIRST NAME	FREE WHITE MALES					FREE WHITE FEMALES					TOTAL ALL OTHER	TOTAL SLAVES	TOTALS	DISTRICT/ TOWNSHIP	NOTES
					under 10	10 to 16	16 to 26	26 to 45	45 and over	under 10	10 to 16	16 to 26	26 to 45	45 and over					
Wrentham	175	6	Alverson	David					1					1			2		
Wrentham	175	7	Darling	Elias	2		1			1			1				5		
Wrentham	175	8	Hathaway	Peleg			1			1			1				3		
Wrentham	175	9	Whiting	John 3d	3		2	1		2			1				9		
Wrentham	175	10	Chever	Ebenezer					1				1	2			4		
Wrentham	175	11	Chever	James			1						1				2		
Wrentham	175	12	Chever	Cyrus		1				3		1					5		
Wrentham	175	13	Hayden	Jerusha		2								1			3		
Wrentham	175	14	Hayden	Isaac	1		1			1		1					4		
Wrentham	175	15	Blake	Samuel	4		1	1		1			1				8		
Wrentham	175	16	Brown	Asa	1		1	2	1			1		1			7		
Wrentham	175	17	Chever	James 2nd		2								2			4		
Wrentham	175	18	Newell	Silas	1		1			1			1				4		
Wrentham	175	19	Sprague	Amos	1		1			2			1				5		
Wrentham	175	20	Whiting	Otis	1	1	1	1		2	1		1				8		
Wrentham	175	21	Whiting	Elkanah	2	1		1	1		1		1				7		
Wrentham	175	22	Whiting	Marjory		1							1				2		
Wrentham	175	23	Whiting	Jerusha	1	1	1			1	2	1	1				8		
Wrentham	175	24	Follett	Luther			1			1		1					3		
Wrentham	175	25	Shepardson	Isaac	3	2		1		1	1		1				9		
Wrentham	175	26	Peck	Solomon		1			1					1			3		
Wrentham	175	27	Peck	Jesse	1		1						1				3		
Wrentham	175	28	Shepardson	Nathaniel		1		1					1				3		
Wrentham	175	29	Trask	Edward					1				1	1			3		
Wrentham	175	30	Guild	Samuel	2	1	1	1			1		1	1			8		
Wrentham	175	31	Blackington	George			1		1		1	1		1			5		
Wrentham	175	32	Franklin	John		1	1		1					1			4		
Wrentham	175	33	Franklin	Solomon	3		1			1			1				6		
Wrentham	175	34	Wight	Thomas	2				1	1		1		1			6		
Wrentham	176	1	Rhodes	Simeon			1		1		1			1			4		
Wrentham	176	2	Ware	Ichabod			1		1					2			4		
Wrentham	176	3	Hunt	Ephraim	2	1	1		1	4	1		1				11		
Wrentham	176	4	George	Thomas Junr				1		1			1				3		
Wrentham	176	5	Whight	Edward		1	3		1			1	1	1			8		
Wrentham	176	6	Whight	William	1		1					1					3		
Wrentham	176	7	Cummings	Benoni	2	1		1		3			1	1			9		
Wrentham	176	8	Jerauld	Mary										1			1		
Wrentham	176	9	Fisher	Isaac	1		1		1					1			4		
Wrentham	176	10	Guild	Ebenezer	1	1			1	2		2		1			8		
Wrentham	176	11	Cobb	Jeremiah	1	1	1		1	1		1		1			7		
Wrentham	176	12	Gillmore	James	3	1		1		1	1		1				8		
Wrentham	176	13	Turner	Samuel	2		1			1			1	3			8		
Wrentham	176	14	Tucker	Jeremiah	1			1		1			1				4		
Wrentham	176	15	Fisher	Samuel	1	1		1				1	1	1			6		
Wrentham	176	16	Robinson	Benjamin				1					1				2		
Wrentham	176	17	Gould	Whiting			1			2			1	1			5		
Wrentham	176	18	Bishop	Seth	1		1						1				3		
Wrentham	176	19	Slack	Joel	2		1	1		2			1	1			8		
Wrentham	176	20	Read	Jesse					1		1						2		
Wrentham	176	21	Chever	John					1				1	1			3		
Wrentham	176	22	Chever	John Junr	1		1	1			1		1				5		
Wrentham	176	23	Fairbanks	James	1	1			2	1		2	1				8		
Wrentham	176	24	Partridge	Timothy	1			1		3			1				6		
Wrentham	176	25	Mann	Jason	1			1		2			1	1			6		
Wrentham	176	26	Cobb	John Junr	2			1				1					4		
Wrentham	176	27	Cobb	Otis			1			5			1				7		
Wrentham	176	28	Bowdich	Samuel	2		2	1		2	1		1	1			10		
Wrentham	176	29	Porter	John	2			1			1	1		1			6		
Wrentham	176	30	Robbins	Comfort			1						1	1			4		
Wrentham	176	31	Robbins	Experience									1	1			2		
Wrentham	176	32	Nicholson	John		1			1					1			3		
Wrentham	177	1	Ware	Paul	2		2	1		1			1	1			8		
Wrentham	177	2	Read	Zachariah		1	2		1				1	1			6		
Wrentham	177	3	Richardson	Daniel	1			1					1	1			4		
Wrentham	177	4	George	Thomas	1		2		1	1	2	2		1			10		
Wrentham	177	5	Ide	James			1			1			1	1			4		
Wrentham	177	6	George	John		1	1		1			1	1		1		6		
Wrentham	177	7	Pond	William			1			4			1				6		
Wrentham	177	8	Cobb	John		1			1			1	1	1			5		
Wrentham	177	9	Boyd	Bethuel	1			1		2			1				5		
Wrentham	177	10	Hancock	Mathew									1	1			2		
Wrentham	177	11	Hancock	Henry		1		1	1		1		1	1			6		
Wrentham	177	12	Everett	Daniel	1	1	1	2		3	3	1	1	1			14		
Wrentham	177	13	Everett	Timothy		1		1		1	1		1				5		
Wrentham	177	14	Whiting	David	2			1		2			1	1			7		
Wrentham	177	15	Shepard	Jonathan			2	1			1	2		1			7		
Wrentham	177	16	Bowers	Isaac											3		3		
Wrentham	177	17	Messenger	Swicher		1			1					1			3		
Wrentham	177	18	Claflin	Noah		1		1	1	1				1			5		

TOWN	PG#	LN#	LAST NAME	FIRST NAME	FWM under 10	FWM 10 to 16	FWM 16 to 26	FWM 26 to 45	FWM 45 over	FWF under 10	FWF 10 to 16	FWF 16 to 26	FWF 26 to 45	FWF 45 over	TOTAL ALL OTHER	TOTAL SLAVES	TOTALS	DISTRICT/ TOWNSHIP	NOTES
Wrentham	177	19	Messenger	George W.	1			1		1	1		1				5		
Wrentham	177	20	Chever	Timothy			1	1						1			3		
Wrentham	177	21	Shepard	Benjamin		1	2		2				6	1			12		
Wrentham	177	22	Cowden	John				1					1				2		
Wrentham	177	23	Shepard	Benjamin Junr	1			1				2					4		
Wrentham	177	24	Hall	Abijah	1			1		1		1					4		
Wrentham	177	25	Blake	Jacob	1			1		3			2	1			8		
Wrentham	177	26	Bugbee	Samuel			1	1									2		
Wrentham	177	27	Ambler	John	2			1		1			1				5		
Wrentham	177	28	Hawes	John	1	2	1		1					1			6		
Wrentham	177	29	Blake	Ebenezer					1		1			1			3		
Wrentham	177	30	Blake	Luther			1					1					2		
Wrentham	177	31	Pond	Timothy					1			1		1			3		
Wrentham	177	32	Pond	Jabez	1			1		1			1				4		
Wrentham	177	33	Pond	William				1		3	1		1				6		
Wrentham	177	34	Cobb	Ebenezer			3	1	1	1	2						8		
Wrentham	178	1	Heaton	Nathaniel			1	1					1	1			4		
Wrentham	178	2	Guild	Joseph			1	1				3		1			6		
Wrentham	178	3	Chever	Elias	1			1		1			1				4		
Wrentham	178	4	Blake	Robert		3	2		1	1	1			2			10		
Wrentham	178	5	Blake	Ezra	2	1	2		1	1	2	1		1			11		
Wrentham	178	6	Thurston	Samuel		1		1	1				1	1			5		
Wrentham	178	7	Hawes	Ebenezer	1			1	1	1		1	1	1			7		
Wrentham	178	8	Day	Jesse			1	1		2	3		1				8		
Wrentham	178	9	Gay	Joseph	2			1	1	1			1				6		
Wrentham	178	10	Guild	Richard				1					1				2		
Wrentham	178	11	Guild	Lansen	1			1					1				3		
Wrentham	178	12	Guild	Richard Junr	1			1		1			1				4		
Wrentham	178	13	Hawes	Nathan		1	1		2	1	1	1		1			8		
Wrentham	178	14	Ware	Hezekiah			1						1				2		
Wrentham	178	15	Hawes	George	1		2	1		1	1		1				7		
Wrentham	178	16	Guild	Benjamin				1						2			3		
Wrentham	178	17	Guild	John	1		1	1		1	1	1	1				7		
Wrentham	178	18	Coleman	Job			1	1	1	1		1	1				6		
Wrentham	178	19	Norton	Jerusha	1		1			2			1				5		
Wrentham	178	20	Frost	Samuel	1			1		1	2	3		1			9		
Wrentham	178	21	Tyler	David			1		3				1				5		
Wrentham	178	22	Fales	Samuel	3	1		1		3			1				9		
Wrentham	178	23	Blake	Alpheus			1			1			1				3		
Wrentham	178	24	White	Luther	2			1		1			1				5		
Wrentham	178	25	Mann	Jeremiah			1						1				2		
Wrentham	178	26	Ware	Daniel	1	1			1	1			1				5		
Wrentham	178	27	Mann	Thomas				1					8				9		
Wrentham	178	28	Mann	jacob		2			1				1		1		5		
Wrentham	178	29	Porter	Libbeus	1			1		2	1		1	1			7		
Wrentham	178	30	Pond	Abijah		1	2		2	2	3	3		1			14		
Wrentham	178	31	Pond	Jacob				1						1			2		
Wrentham	178	32	Pond	Elijah	4			1				1		1			7		
Wrentham	178	33	Fales	David				1						1			2		
Wrentham	178	34	Fales	David Junr	4		2		5	1		2					14		
Wrentham	179	1	Metcalf	David	1	1		1		2	1	1	1	1			9		
Wrentham	179	2	Everett	John				1			1			1			3		
Wrentham	179	3	Daggett	Ebenezer	1	1		1		1			1				5		
Wrentham	179	4	Pond	Joseph				1						2			3		
Wrentham	179	5	Pond	Barnard	2			1		1	1		1				6		
Wrentham	179	6	Ruggles	Joel	4	3		1	1	2	1		1	1			14		
Wrentham	179	7	Gillmore	Andrew			1		1				1				3		
Wrentham	179	8	Gillmore	Lemuel		1	1	1		2	2	2	1				10		
Wrentham	179	9	Gillmore	Daniel	2			1		4			1				8		
Wrentham	179	10	Gillmore	Andrew Junr	4	2		1		1			1				9		
Wrentham	179	11	White	Eliphalet	1		1	1		1	1		1				6		
Wrentham	179	12	Read	Jonathan			1		1	1	1			1			5		
Wrentham	179	13	Pond	Jeremiah				1						2			3		
Wrentham	179	14	Fisher	Timothy	2			1		1	1	1					6		
Wrentham	179	15	Pond	Oliver			1	2	1			1	2	1			8		
Wrentham	179	16	Pond	Increase	1	1		1				1		1			5		
Wrentham	179	17	Fales	John				1			1			1			3		
Wrentham	179	18	Blake	Nathan	1			1		2	2			1			7		
Wrentham	179	19	Everett	Marcus			1			1			1				3		
Wrentham	179	20	Tilson	Nehemiah	1		1	1		2			1				6		
Wrentham	179	21	Blake	Jacob			1	1					1				3		
Wrentham	179	22	Blake	Daniel	1			1		2		1	1				6		
Wrentham	179	23	Dupee	Charles Junr	1	1	2	1		3	1		1				10		
Wrentham	179	24	Felt	Jonathan		2			1	1	1		1				6		
Wrentham	179	25	Blake	Jason				1		3			2				6		
Wrentham	179	26	Blake	Eliab	2	1		1		2	1		1				8		
Wrentham	179	27	Dupee	Charles				1						1			2		
Wrentham	179	28	Blake	Daniel	2			1		2			1				6		
Wrentham	179	29	Rockwood	Elisha		1	1	1		2		1		1			7		
Wrentham	179	30	Blake	John Junr			1	1		1	2	1		1			7		

TOWN	PG#	LN#	HEADS OF HOUSEHOLD		FREE WHITE MALES					FREE WHITE FEMALES					TOTAL ALL OTHER	TOTAL SLAVES	TOTALS	DISTRICT/ TOWNSHIP	NOTES
			LAST NAME	FIRST NAME	under 10	10 to 16	16 to 26	26 to 45	45 and over	under 10	10 to 16	16 to 26	26 to 45	45 and over					
Wrentham	179	31	Adams	Joseph	1				1					1			3		
Wrentham	179	32	Richardson	Amos	1			1		3			1				6		
Wrentham	179	33	Ware	Ezra		1	1	1			1	2					6		
Wrentham	180	1	Farrington	Lewis	1			1		4			1				7		
Wrentham	180	2	Fuller	Thomas				1									1		
Wrentham	180	3	Cobb	Joseph				1				1	1				3		
Wrentham	180	4	Cobb	Herman		1				1		1					3		
Wrentham	180	5	Farrington	Elijah	1		1	1		1	1		1				6		
Wrentham	180	6	Whiting	Thaddeus	4	2		1			1		1				9		
Wrentham	180	7	Messenger	Daniel	1		1	1				1	1				5		
Wrentham	180	8	Ware	Elias	2	2	2	1		2		1	2				12		
Wrentham	180	9	Fisher	Richard Junr	2		1	1		1		1					6		
Wrentham	180	10	Sensapauh	John S.	1		1			1		1					4		
Wrentham	180	11	Fisher	Richard				2		1		1					4		
Wrentham	180	12	Fisher	Pliny	1		1				1						3		
Wrentham	180	13	Grant	Ebenezer			1	1		1	2	1	1				7		
Wrentham	180	14	Fisher	Calvin	2	1		1				1					5		
Wrentham	180	15	Guild	William	1		1			1	1						4		
Wrentham	180	16	Craige	John			1	1					1				3		
Wrentham	180	17	Craige	Elijah			1			1		2	1				5		
Wrentham	180	18	Belcher	John	4	1		1		1		1					8		
Wrentham	180	19	Fisher	Cyrus	1	1		1		3		1					7		
Wrentham	180	20	Fisher	Jacob	2			1		1		1					5		
Wrentham	180	21	Bennett	Isaac		1	3	1		2			2				9		
Wrentham	180	22	Haven	Elias				1		3	2	1	1				8		
Wrentham	180	23	Davis	Jonathan			2	1		4		1					8		
Wrentham	180	24	Jilson	Nathaniel		1		1		1			1				4		
Wrentham	180	25	Brown	Lemuel	1	1	1	1	1	1	2		1				9		
Wrentham	180	26	Shaw	Noah	1			1				1					3		
Wrentham	180	27	Brown	Lemuel Junr		1	2	2		3	1	1					10		
Wrentham	180	28	Archer	Amos	2	1		1				1	1				6		
Wrentham	180	29	Pratt	Isaac		1	1					1					3		
Wrentham	180	30	Bacon	Daniel	2			1				1	1				5		
Wrentham	180	31	Fisher	David				1		1	1		1				4		
Wrentham	180	32	Fisher	Luther	2	1		1		2		1	1				8		
Wrentham	180	33	Fisher	Ebenezer Junr	2	1		1		2		1					7		
Wrentham	180	34	Cubleau	Charles Maride											1		1		
Wrentham	181	1	Cowell	Samuel		1	3	1		2		1	1				9		
Wrentham	181	2	Hall	John			1	2		1		1	2				7		
Wrentham	181	3	Hall	John Junr	1	1	1	1				2					6		
Wrentham	181	4	Bean	Cyrus			3						3	1			7		
Wrentham	181	5	Maddy	John	1					3	4	2	2				12		
Wrentham	181	6	Hawes	James	4		1			1		1	1				8		
Wrentham	181	7	Ware	Molly							1	2	1				4		
Wrentham	182	1	Fairbanks	Joshua	1		1			1		1					4		
Wrentham	182	2	Gillmore	John	1	1	1			1		1					5		
Wrentham	182	3	Ware	Oliver 2d		1	1						2				4		

TOWN	PG#	LN#	LAST NAME	FIRST NAME	FREE WHITE MALES under 10	10 to 16	16 to 26	26 to 45	45 and over	FREE WHITE FEMALES under 10	10 to 16	16 to 26	26 to 45	45 and over	TOTAL ALL OTHER	TOTAL SLAVES	TOTALS	DISTRICT/TOWNSHIP	NOTES
Needham	147	51	*	Elab	1			1						2			4		
Medway East Parish	91	1	Abbee	Joseph	1	1		1		2			1				6		
Medway West Parish	95	6	Adams	Aaron	1		1	1				1	1				5		
Bellingham	159	18	Adams	Amos	3	1						1	1	1			8		
Bellingham	159	23	Adams	Caleb		1	1			2			1	1			6		
Medfield	85	6	Adams	Darius	1			1		1			1				4		
Quincy	39	12	Adams	Ebenz				1			2		1	1			5		
Medway West Parish	95	1	Adams	Eliakim	1	1	2	1		1	2	1					9		
Medfield	85	2	Adams	Elijah		2			1	1	1		1				7		
Quincy	39	8	Adams	Eliz Wid.				1						1			2		
Medway West Parish	95	8	Adams	Ezra		1						1					2		
Medfield	85	5	Adams	George W.			1			1			1	1			4		
Medfield	85	4	Adams	Gershom	1			1			1		1	1	1		5		
Medway West Parish	95	3	Adams	Hezekiah			1			2			1				4		
Franklin	165	8	Adams	James	1		1	1		1		1	1				6		
Medway East Parish	91	5	Adams	Jasper	2			1		1		1	1				6		
Quincy	39	5	Adams	Jedediah	2	1		1		1			1	1			7		
Milton	44	5	Adams	Jno		1	1	1	1	1	1			1			7		
Franklin	166	34	Adams	John	1	2	2		1	3	1	1		1			12		
Medway West Parish	95	2	Adams	John				1					1				2		
Quincy	39	1	Adams	John			5	3	1	1	1	3	1	2			17		President of the United States
Randolph	123	4	Adams	John	1	1		1		2			1				6		
Medway East Parish	91	9	Adams	Jonathan				1					1				2		
Medway East Parish	91	4	Adams	Jonathan 3rd		1	1	1					1				4		
Medway East Parish	91	6	Adams	Jonathan Jun				1					1				2		
Wrentham	179	31	Adams	Joseph	1			1					1				3		
Quincy	39	13	Adams	Josiah	1			1		1	2		1				6		
Bellingham	159	20	Adams	Levi			2			1			1				4		
Medway West Parish	95	7	Adams	Mary							2		1				3		
Medway East Parish	91	8	Adams	Micah	2			1		2			2				7		
Quincy	39	7	Adams	Micajah	2		2	1		2			1				8		
Franklin	165	12	Adams	Moses	1	2			1				1				7		
Medway West Parish	95	5	Adams	Moses				1					1				2		
Milton	44	3	Adams	Moses				1					1				2		
Franklin	163	30	Adams	Nathaniel		1			1	1		2					5		
Franklin	163	28	Adams	Nehemiah	2	2		2		1	2						9		
Bellingham	159	19	Adams	Obadiah				1					1				2		
Medway West Parish	95	4	Adams	Obadiah		2		1		1		2	1	1			8		
Medway East Parish	91	2	Adams	Oliver		1		1			1		1				4		
Franklin	165	7	Adams	Peter					1			1	1				3		
Stoughton	117	1	Adams	Peter			2	2	1			1		1			7		
Quincy	39	2	Adams	Peter B. Esq	1		2	1	1	1	2						8		
Milton	44	4	Adams	Saml	1	1	1		1	1	1		1				7		
Bellingham	159	17	Adams	Samuel	3	1	3	1			1	1	1				11		
Dorchester	51	1	Adams	Seth	3	1		2		1		2	1	1			11		
Medway East Parish	91	7	Adams	Silas	2			1					1				4		
Medway East Parish	91	3	Adams	Silvanus	1			1					1		1		4		
Franklin	163	18	Adams	Thaddeus	1	1	1		1			1	1				7		
Medfield	85	1	Adams	Thomas				2	1	1		1	1				6		
Medway West Parish	95	9	Adams	Thomas	3	1			1	2	1	1		1			10		
Quincy	39	10	Adams	Thomas		1		1		1		1	1				5		
Franklin	169	31	Adams	Timothy			1				1	1					3		
Franklin	163	32	Adams	Wiliiam	1	2			1			1	2	1			8		
Quincy	39	9	Adams	Willm					1				1				2		
Roxbury	106	28	Adams	Zabdiel	2		4	2		2			1	1			12		
Medfield	85	3	Admas	Elijah Jun	1			1		1			1				4		
Weymouth	78	10	Agar	Benjm					1								1	South Parish	
Weymouth	78	11	Agar	Jonan	2	1		1		2		1					7	South Parish	
Stoughton	118	2	Agher	Jedidiah	1			1		1		1					4		
Roxbury	115	9	Akers	William	1	1	1	1		1	1	1	1	1			9	3rd Parish	
Bellingham	161	6	Albee	Alpheus				1		1		1					3		
Medway West Parish	95	13	Albee	Amos	1	1		1		1			1				5		
Medway West Parish	95	10	Albee	John	1		1	1		1				2			6		
Medfield	85	16	Alby	Asa			1	1					1				3		
Randolph	123	1	Alden	Ebenezer	1	1		1	1				2				7		
Bellingham	159	4	Alden	Elijah			1			1		1					3		
Roxbury	106	24	Alden	Hannah	1					1			1				3		
Needham	145	2	Alden	Henry				1					1				2		
Bellingham	161	8	Alden	Noah			1		1	1	3		1				7		
Randolph	123	2	Alden	Silas	4	2	1	1		1		2	1				12		
Needham	145	1	Alden	Silas Col.	1		1	1		2			1				6		
Needham	145	4	Alden	Silas Junr	3			1					1				5		
Randolph	123	3	Alden	Simeon	1	2		1		2			1				7		
Needham	145	3	Alden	William	3		1			1		1	1				7		
Roxbury	114	12	Aldin	Solomon	1		4	1		2	1		1				10	3rd Parish	
Franklin	169	7	Aldis	Ebenezer					1		2		1				4		
Wrentham	171	34	Aldrich	Asa		2	1		1	1			1				6		
Bellingham	161	30	Aldrich	Laban	1	1	1		1	2	2	1					9		
Wrentham	172	1	Aldrich	Nathaniel	2			1					1				4		
Milton	44	6	Alexander	Best											2		2		
Walpole	26	2	Allen	Abel		1			2				1				4		

TOWN	PG#	LN#	LAST NAME	FIRST NAME	FREE WHITE MALES under 10	10 to 16	16 to 26	26 to 45	45 and over	FREE WHITE FEMALES under 10	10 to 16	16 to 26	26 to 45	45 and over	TOTAL ALL OTHER	TOTAL SLAVES	TOTALS	DISTRICT/ TOWNSHIP	NOTES
Braintree	66	7	Allen	Abigail Wid.	1					2			1	1			5		
Franklin	163	12	Allen	Abijah	2	1	3		1		1	1		1			10		
Walpole	31	27	Allen	Amos	1			1		1				1			4		
Randolph	123	6	Allen	Benja				1									1		
Canton	129	2	Allen	Beth*			1			1		1					3		
Walpole	26	4	Allen	Daniel	1		1						1				3		
Walpole	26	5	Allen	David	1		1			2	1	1					6		
Dover	149	2	Allen	Eleazer		1	1										2		
Medfield	85	13	Allen	Eliakim							1			1			2		
Dover	149	6	Allen	Fisher		1	1		1			1		1			5		
Braintree	66	2	Allen	Jacob		2	1		1				1				5		
Medfield	85	12	Allen	James		1		1		1		2	2				7		
Sharon	31	2	Allen	James	4	1		1		1			1				8		
Franklin	168	19	Allen	John		2	5		1	1		2		1			12		
Medfield	85	8	Allen	Jonathan					1			1		1			3		
Braintree	66	1	Allen	Joseph	2	1	1		1	2	2	3		1			13		
Walpole	26	1	Allen	Joshua			1					1					2		
Braintree	66	3	Allen	Lemuel			1			2	1		1	1			6		
Medway West Parish	95	11	Allen	Mary	2		1						1	1			5		
Dover	149	4	Allen	Mary Wid.									1	1			2		
Medfield	85	10	Allen	Nathan			2		1			1		1			5		
Walpole	26	3	Allen	Nathan	1		1			1		1					4		
Medway West Parish	95	12	Allen	Nathaniel			1	1		2			1				5		
Medfield	85	7	Allen	Noah					1				1				2		
Dover	149	3	Allen	Perez	1			1		2			1				5		
Medfield	85	9	Allen	Phinehas	4			1		1		2	1				9		
Randolph	123	5	Allen	Samuel				1		2			1	1			5		
Medfield	85	11	Allen	Sarah									1				1		
Medfield	85	14	Allen	Sarah Jun	1								1				2		
Sharon	31	1	Allen	Seth	1			1			1		1				4		
Canton	129	1	Allen	Thomas	2			1		1		1					5		
Dover	149	1	Allen	Timothy		2	3		2			1		1	1		10		
Stoughton	118	3	Allen	Tural			1	1			1	1	1				5		
Medfield	85	15	Allen	William	3	1		1		1			1				7		
Milton	44	2	Alleyne	Abel	3		1	1		2	1	2	1	1			12		
Quincy	39	6	Alleyne	Josiah				1					1				2		
Dedham	140	35	Alonso	House	2			2	2			2	4		4		16		
Wrentham	175	6	Alverson	David					1				1				2		
Wrentham	177	27	Ambler	John	2			1		1			1				5		
Dedham	136	1	Ames	Luther Esq	2		4	1		2	2		1				12		
Dedham	136	2	Ames	Nathaniel Esq		1		1				1		1			4		
Milton	44	1	Amory	Jno	1			1		1	1	2					6		
Dorchester	51	2	Anderson	James	1			1				1					3		
Sharon	31	3	Andrews	Darrius	3			1			1						5		
Dedham	141	1	Andrews	David				1				1					2	1st Parish	
Dorchester	51	3	Andrews	Jno				1		2			1				4		
Quincy	39	11	Apthorp	P.H.	1	1	1			2		3	1	2			11		
Medfield	85	18	Archelus	James											2		2		
Wrentham	180	28	Archer	Amos	2	1		1					1	1			6		
Medfield	85	17	Armsby	Ader										2			2		
Wrentham	173	10	Armsby	Unity	2	1	1				2		1				7		
Weymouth	74	2	Arnold	Alexander	1			1		1							3	North Parish	
Bellingham	160	13	Arnold	Daniel			1			1		1					3		
Quincy	39	4	Arnold	Daniel	2			1		1			1				5		
Braintree	66	4	Arnold	John V.	1		1	1		2			1				6		
Quincy	39	3	Arnold	Jos N	2	1		1		2	1		1				8		
Braintree	66	5	Arnold	Moses			1										1		
Braintree	66	6	Arnold	Ruth Wid.		1					1	2					4		
Weymouth	74	3	Arnold	Saml Junior	1		4			1	1	1					8	North Parish	
Weymouth	74	1	Arnold	Samuel			2		1		1	1					5	North Parish	
Roxbury	103	22	As Overseer of the Poor		1				8	1				11			21		
Brookline	115	5	Aspenwall	John	3	1	4	2				1	1				12		
Brookline	115	6	Aspenwall	Lucy								1	1				2		
Brookline	115	8	Aspenwall	William Doc		3	4		1	1	1	1	2		4		17		
Dedham	136	5	Atherton	Abner			3					1					4		
Stoughton	117	2	Atherton	Consider				1				1		1			3		
Dorchester	51	4	Atherton	Jemima						2				2			4		
Needham	145	5	Atherton	Jesse		1					1						2		
Stoughton	117	3	Atherton	John		2	1		1		1	1		1			7		
Stoughton	118	1	Atherton	John Junr	1			1		1		1					4		
Dedham	136	3	Avery	Jonathan			1		1			2		1			5		
Brookline	114	1	Ayers	Ebenezer	2		1	2		1			1				7		
Dover	149	7	Ayers	Eleazer	2			1					1				4		
Dover	149	5	Ayers	Jesse	3			1		1			1				6		
Brookline	114	4	Ayers	Jonathan	2			1				1					4		
Dedham	136	10	Babcock	Jason	1		3	1			1						6		
Dover	149	24	Bacon	Aaron				1		3		1					5		
Franklin	163	24	Bacon	Charlotte									3				3		
Walpole	27	19	Bacon	Daniel	1			1		1			1				4		
Wrentham	180	30	Bacon	Daniel	2				1				1				5		

TOWN	PG#	LN#	LAST NAME	FIRST NAME	M under 10	M 10-16	M 16-26	M 26-45	M 45 over	F under 10	F 10-16	F 16-26	F 26-45	F 45 over	TOTAL ALL OTHER	TOTAL SLAVES	TOTALS	DISTRICT/ TOWNSHIP	NOTES
Wrentham	172	14	Bacon	Elias				1			1	2		1			5		
Needham	145	8	Bacon	Ephriam				1		3			1				5		
Roxbury	113	12	Bacon	Henry		1		1		1		1		1			5	3rd Parish	
Franklin	166	29	Bacon	Joseph			1	1		1			1				4		
Roxbury	107	4	Bacon	Joseph	1			1		2			1				5		
Dover	149	18	Bacon	Josiah				1						2			3		
Dover	149	23	Bacon	Josiah Jr	3	2		1				1	1				8		
Needham	145	9	Bacon	Moses	2			1			1	1	1				6		
Franklin	166	30	Bacon	ruth				1					2				3		
Franklin	166	31	Bacon	Seth		1		1					1				3		
Dover	149	15	Bacon	Silas	3	1		1		1		1		1			8		
Dover	149	14	Bacon	William		1		1					1				3		
Walpole	27	7	Bacon	William				1			1		1				3		
Walpole	27	20	Bacon	William Jr	2	1		1		1			1				6		
Milton	45	5	Badcock	Leml			1			2		1	1	1			6		
Milton	44	17	Badcock	Thomas	1			1			1	1	1				5		
Milton	44	10	Badcock	Wm	1		1	1					1				4		
Milton	44	11	Badcock	Wm Jun	1		1	1		1	1						5		
Dorchester	53	5	Badlam	Ezra		2				1		1					4		
Weymouth	74	8	Badlam	Saml		2	1			1	2		1				7	North Parish	
Dorchester	51	6	Badlam	Steph		1	5	1	1			2		1	1		12		
Weymouth	74	9	Badlam	Unity									2				2	North Parish	
Milton	45	7	Baggs	Seth	3		1	1			1	1	1				8		
Weymouth	78	38	Bailey	Abraham			1				1						2	South Parish	
Canton	129	6	Bailey	Dudley		1	1	1					1				4		
Canton	129	7	Bailey	Eunice									1				1		
Canton	129	3	Bailey	Henry				1				2		1			4		
Canton	129	4	Bailey	Israel		1	1	1					2				5		
Weymouth	78	12	Bailey	Nathl			1						1				2	South Parish	
Franklin	166	5	Bailey	Prince											2		2		
Weymouth	78	13	Bailey	Saml		2		1		2			1				6	South Parish	
Canton	129	5	Bailey	Samuel		1						1					2		
Weymouth	78	22	Baily	Edward			1						1				2	South Parish	
Dorchester	52	25	Baker	Abigail						1			1	1			3		
Franklin	163	20	Baker	Abijah	1		1	1		1	1						5		
Dedham	136	12	Baker	Daniel				1				2	4				7		
Roxbury	111	8	Baker	David	2		1	1					1				5	2nd Parish	
Sharon	32	8	Baker	Ebenezer		1						1					2		
Walpole	27	16	Baker	Ebenezer		1						1	1				3		
Dorchester	52	24	Baker	Edmund	3		1						2				6		
Roxbury	101	5	Baker	Eleazer	1		1						1				3		
Sharon	31	7	Baker	Elijah	2		1	1					1	1			6		
Sharon	32	4	Baker	Elijah Jr		2		1		2		2	1				8		
Dedham	143	5	Baker	Eliphalet				1					1	1			3	2nd Parish	
Dedham	136	11	Baker	Eliphalet 3d	1		3	1					1	1			7		
Dedham	143	7	Baker	Eliphalet Jun	1			1	1	1			1				5	2nd Parish	
Dorchester	52	27	Baker	George				3	1	1			1				6		
Dover	149	16	Baker	Jabez	1	1	1	1	1	1		1	2	2			11		
Dover	149	17	Baker	Jabez Jr	2			1					1				4		
Dorchester	51	7	Baker	James				1				2		1			4		
Dorchester	52	16	Baker	James		1		1					2				4		
Dorchester	52	19	Baker	James Jr	2			1		1			1				5		
Dedham	143	3	Baker	Jeremiah		1	1	1		2	1		2				8	2nd Parish	
Dorchester	51	8	Baker	Jno		1	1	1				1	1				5		
Dedham	143	6	Baker	John	2		1	1		1			1				6	2nd Parish	
Roxbury	111	7	Baker	John			1	1	1	1	1		1				6	2nd Parish	
Roxbury	111	21	Baker	John Junr	1			1					1				3	2nd Parish	
Dedham	143	4	Baker	Joseph		1	1	1		1		2	1				8	2nd Parish	
Roxbury	106	23	Baker	Mary								1	1				2		
Dedham	143	2	Baker	Mary Wid									1				1	2nd Parish	
Roxbury	115	1	Baker	Preserved		1	2	1	1				1				6	3rd Parish	
Dorchester	52	17	Baker	Saml		1	1	1		1				1			5		
Dorchester	51	15	Baker	Saml 3d	1			1					1				3		
Foxborough	23	3	Baker	Samuel				1					1				2		
Dorchester	52	28	Baker	Susan		1				1		1	1	1	1		5		
Milton	45	6	Baker	Thomas			1						1				2		
Dedham	143	8	Baker	Timothy		2		1	1	1		1	1	1			7	2nd Parish	
Walpole	26	7	Baker	Ziba		1		1		1	1		1				5		
Roxbury	105	32	Balaney	William	1	2	1	1		1		2	1				9		
Foxborough	23	4	Bales	John		1		1			1		1				4		
Wrentham	171	18	Ballou	Darius	1			1		4	2		1				9		
Wrentham	171	7	Ballou	Elizabeth	1		1					1	1				4		
Wrentham	171	9	Ballou	Flavius	1		1					1					3		
Wrentham	171	10	Ballou	Mary						1		1					2		
Wrentham	170	17	Ballou	Pelatiah	1		1						1				3		
Medway East Parish	91	10	Ballou	Thomas	2			1		1			1				5		
Medway East Parish	91	19	Barber	George				1		3	1		1				6		
Wrentham	172	20	Barber	George			1						1				2		
Medway West Parish	95	14	Barber	Joseph				1					1				2		
Medway West Parish	95	15	Barber	Joseph Jun	3			1		1			1				6		
Medway East Parish	91	20	Barber	Seneca	1			1		1							4		

82

TOWN	PG#	LN#	LAST NAME	FIRST NAME	FREE WHITE MALES under 10	10 to 16	16 to 26	26 to 45	45 and over	FREE WHITE FEMALES under 10	10 to 16	16 to 26	26 to 45	45 and over	TOTAL ALL OTHER	TOTAL SLAVES	TOTALS	DISTRICT/ TOWNSHIP	NOTES
Walpole	27	17	Barden	Phillip				1						1			2		
Roxbury	107	19	Barns	William	2		3	2			1	1	1				10		
Braintree	68	5	Barrett	John	2	1		1		1		1	1	1			8		
Dover	149	20	Barridge	Abigail Wid.			1	1				1	1	1			5		
Wrentham	172	29	Barrons	William	2			1		2			1				6		
Walpole	27	14	Barrows	David	3			1		2		1	1	1			9		
Roxbury	101	2	Barry	Samuel			8	1				1	1	1			12		
Cohasset	153	24	Bartles	James	1	1	1	1		1		1	1				8		
Roxbury	104	18	Bartlett	John Doc	1			1		2	2	1	1				8		
Quincy	40	34	Bass	Benj Esq		1			3				2	1			7		
Bellingham	159	7	Bass	Benjamin		1		1	1				1	1			5		
Quincy	40	24	Bass	David			2	1					1	1			5		
Quincy	40	33	Bass	Hezekiah		1	1	1						1			4		
Quincy	40	31	Bass	Jona Deac	3		2	1		2			1	1			10		
Quincy	40	25	Bass	Josiah	1	1		2	1	1			1	1			8		
Quincy	40	2	Bass	Saml				1						1			2		
Randolph	123	7	Bass	Samuel	2	2	2	1		1		1	1	1			11		
Quincy	40	5	Bass	Seth				1		1			1				3		
Braintree	68	6	Bates	*	1			1					1	1			4		
Weymouth	74	18	Bates	Alpheus	1	2	1	1		3			1				9	North Parish	
Cohasset	153	3	Bates	Ambrose	1			1		3	1	2	1				9		
Cohasset	154	4	Bates	Anna		1	1		1	2	1	1		1			8		
Cohasset	154	15	Bates	Bella	2			1		1			1				5		
Cohasset	153	36	Bates	Daniel	2		1						1				4		
Bellingham	161	29	Bates	Eli	1		2	1		2			1				7		
Weymouth	74	23	Bates	Elisha	3			1		2	1		1				8	North Parish	
Weymouth	74	12	Bates	Elnathan		1	1	1	1			2		1			7	North Parish	
Weymouth	74	24	Bates	Eunice								1		1			2	North Parish	
Bellingham	160	9	Bates	Ezekiel		1	1		1	2			1	1			7		
Bellingham	160	10	Bates	Ezekiel Jun		2							1				3		
Weymouth	74	17	Bates	Jesse	2		1		1	3		2	1				10	North Parish	
Bellingham	159	11	Bates	John			1			2		1					4		
Weymouth	78	34	Bates	John Ward	4			1		1	2	1	1	1			11	South Parish	
Cohasset	154	5	Bates	Jonathan	2	1	1	1		1			1				7		
Cohasset	152	5	Bates	Joseph				1				2		1			4		
Cohasset	153	10	Bates	Joshua	1	1	1		1		1			1			6		
Weymouth	74	14	Bates	Joshua		1		2	1	2	1	1					8	North Parish	
Bellingham	161	27	Bates	Laban	1	1	3		1	1	1	3		1			12		
Weymouth	74	6	Bates	Levi	4	1	1	1		3	2		1				13	North Parish	
Cohasset	154	25	Bates	Robert	1			1		2			1				5		
Weymouth	78	28	Bates	Robert	1	1		1		1	1	1	1	1			8	South Parish	
Weymouth	78	35	Bates	Saml		2	2		1	2	2			2			11	South Parish	
Weymouth	78	33	Bates	Saml 2d	2	2	1	2		2			1	1			11	South Parish	
Cohasset	152	3	Bates	Samuel			2	1	1	1		1	2		1		9		
Dedham	136	13	Bates	Samuel	1	2					1	1	1				6		
Weymouth	74	13	Bates	Silvanus	2	1		1		1			1				6	North Parish	
Weymouth	78	23	Bates	Thaddeus	1	1		1		3			1				7	South Parish	
Cohasset	152	42	Bates	Theodore		2		1		2	1		2				8		
Weymouth	74	21	Bates	Urban		1	2	1	1			2		1			8	North Parish	
Weymouth	74	29	Bates	William				1		1			1	1			3	North Parish	
Stoughton	118	5	Battle	Curtis	2			1		3			1	1			8		
Dover	149	10	Battle	Ebenezer Jr	3	1		1		2		1					8		
Dover	149	8	Battle	Ebenzer			1		1			1		1			4		
Stoughton	118	6	Battle	Edward	1		2	1		2			1				7		
Dover	149	12	Battle	Hezekiah	1	1		1		1	1	1					6		
Dover	149	9	Battle	John				2						2			4		
Dover	149	13	Battle	Jonathan	1	2		1		2	1		1				8		
Stoughton	118	4	Battle	Jonathan	2	3		1		1	2		1				10		
Dover	149	11	Battle	Josiah	3	1		1		1	1	1					8		
Dover	149	22	Battle	Nathaniel	1	1		1		2			1				6		
Quincy	40	14	Baxter	Ed W	3		1	1		1	3		1				10		
Dorchester	52	29	Baxter	Edw. W.	3	1	2	1		1			1				9		
Medfield	86	1	Baxter	John	1		2		1		1	1		2			8		
Quincy	40	17	Baxter	Jona		1	2	2		2			1				8		
Quincy	40	18	Baxter	Jona Jun			2	1		1			1				5		
Quincy	40	4	Baxter	Joseph		1		1				2		1			5		
Quincy	40	19	Baxter	Saml	1			1					1				3		
Quincy	40	20	Baxter	Thompson		1			3					1	2		7		
Quincy	40	30	Baxter	Wm	2		2	2		1			2				9		
Cohasset	154	44	Beal	Abel	1			1				1		1			4		
Cohasset	154	47	Beal	Andrew	1		1					1					3		
Weymouth	74	28	Beal	Azariah				1						1			2	North Parish	
Cohasset	154	46	Beal	Daniel		2	1						1				4		
Cohasset	153	41	Beal	David		1	1	1		3		2					8		
Cohasset	153	42	Beal	Hezekiah			1			5			1				7		
Cohasset	152	12	Beal	Jacob				1						2			3		
Cohasset	152	13	Beal	John	3		2	1		2			1				9		
Cohasset	154	3	Beal	Joseph				1			1			1			3		
Cohasset	154	32	Beal	Joshua		1	1							1			3		
Cohasset	154	14	Beal	Lewis Alias	1			1					1				3		
Cohasset	154	45	Beal	Seth	3			1		1			1				6		
Cohasset	153	40	Beal	Thomas		1			1		1			1			4		

TOWN	PG#	LN#	LAST NAME	FIRST NAME	FREE WHITE MALES					FREE WHITE FEMALES					TOTAL ALL OTHER	TOTAL SLAVES	TOTALS	DISTRICT/ TOWNSHIP	NOTES
					under 10	10 to 16	16 to 26	26 to 45	45 and over	under 10	10 to 16	16 to 26	26 to 45	45 and over					
Quincy	40	9	Beale	Hannah										1			1		
Quincy	40	6	Beale	Jona	2	1		1			1		1		1		7		
Quincy	40	11	Beale	Richard			1			2		2	1				6		
Dorchester	52	3	Beales	Jacob	3		2			1	1		1				8		
Weymouth	74	25	Beales	Nathl				1					1				2	North Parish	
Weymouth	78	36	Beales	Sarah									3				3	South Parish	
Weymouth	78	24	Beales	Uriah	1			1		1		1	1	1			6	South Parish	
Dorchester	52	21	Beales	Zebulon	1		1						1				3		
Randolph	124	1	Beals	Eleazar	2	1	2	1		3	1	1	1				12		
Weymouth	74	4	Beals	Hannah									1				1	North Parish	
Randolph	124	2	Beals	Iseael				1				1	1				3		
Randolph	123	18	Beals	John	1	1	1			1			1				5		
Weymouth	74	19	Beals	Lazarus A.	1			1				1		1			4	North Parish	
Wrentham	181	4	Bean	Cyrus			3					3	1				7		
Roxbury	103	35	Bedge	John			1							1			2		
Dedham	136	16	Bedlam	Lemuel			1				1	3	1				6		
Dedham	136	9	Bedlam	William		1		1		1			1				4		
Roxbury	105	31	Beduna	Benjamin			1										1		
Cohasset	152	11	Beers	Mary									1				1		
Stoughton	118	7	Belcher	Atherton			1			2	1		1				5		
Randolph	123	10	Belcher	Billy	2		1			3			1				7		
Randolph	123	17	Belcher	Ebenezer				1									1		
Stoughton	118	8	Belcher	Edward			1			1			1				3		
Foxborough	22	2	Belcher	Eleazer		1	2	1					1				5		
Foxborough	22	3	Belcher	Eleazer Jr			1			1			1				3		
Canton	129	9	Belcher	Elisha		1				2		1					4		
Randolph	123	13	Belcher	Epgraim	2	1		1		1			1				6		
Randolph	123	16	Belcher	John	1			1				1					3		
Wrentham	180	18	Belcher	John	4	1		1			1		1				8		
Randolph	123	15	Belcher	Jonathan	1		1	1					1	1			5		
Sharon	32	10	Belcher	Jonathan			1	1					1				3		
Canton	129	8	Belcher	Joseph	2	1		1		2		1	1				9		
Randolph	123	11	Belcher	Joseph	2		2	1				1	2	1			10		
Stoughton	118	11	Belcher	Joseph			1	1					1	1			4		
Milton	44		Belcher	Moses		1		1		1	2		1				6		
Randolph	123	8	Belcher	Nathaniel	2		1	1		2	3		1				10		
Stoughton	118	10	Belcher	Oliver	1		1	1		1	1						5		
Randolph	123	9	Belcher	Richard	1	1	1	1						2			6		
Quincy	40	29	Belcher	Sam Jun	3	1		2		1			1				8		
Dorchester	51	11	Belcher	Saml	1		3	1		2	2	2					11		
Foxborough	23	7	Belcher	Samuel	1			1		2			1				5		
Randolph	123	12	Belcher	Samuel		2	1	1		3	1		1				9		
Randolph	123	14	Belcher	Thomas		1		1				3	1	1			7		
Braintree	68	1	Belcher	Uriah		1		1		1	2		1				6		
Roxbury	108	5	Belknap	Charles			1						2				3		
Stoughton	118	19	Belknap	Isaac	1			1		1	1	1					5		
Canton	129	11	Bemis	Joseph		1	1						1				3		
Wrentham	180	21	Bennett	Isaac		1	3	1		2			2				9		
Cohasset	154	26	Bent	Abel			1	1			1		1				4		
Milton	44	12	Bent	Jno		1	1			1	1		1				5		
Milton	45	11	Bent	Joseph		1	1			1	2		1				6		
Milton	45	1	Bent	Josiah	1	1	2	1	1	2		2					10		
Quincy	40	16	Bent	Lemuel			1			2			1				4		
Quincy	40	15	Bent	Nedebiah	1	1	1			1	1	2		1			9		
Milton	44	13	Bent	Shepherd	2		1						1				4		
Canton	129	10	Bent	William		1	1			1	1			1			6		
Cohasset	152	30	Beorker	Maria									2				2		
Dedham	136	6	Berry	James	1		1			1			1				4		
Cohasset	155	2	Berter	Thomas	1	1		1		2	2		1				8		
Dedham	136	4	Betile	Betsey						1			1				2		
Quincy	40	1	Beule	Benj Esq			1				2	1			1		5		
Quincy	40	28	Beule	Lillie						3	2	2	1				8		
Cohasset	152	17	Bevins	Peter	1		1					1					3		
Roxbury	104	19	Bicknall	Humphrey	3	1	3	1		1	1		1				11		
Weymouth	74	22	Bicknell	Bathsheba	1					2		1	2				6	North Parish	
Weymouth	74	10	Bicknell	Benjm		1	1	1				1	1				5	North Parish	
Weymouth	74	15	Bicknell	Zachariah				1				1	1				3	North Parish	
Quincy	40	22	Bicknelll	Peter	1	2	2	1		5		2	1				14		
Milton	44	9	Bidge	Joseph	1			2		1	1	2					7		
Sharon	32	12	Billing	Anna W		1	1						1	1			4		
Canton	130	1	Billing	Beulah Wid.									2				2		
Canton	129	14	Billing	Isaac			1	1					1	1			4		
Canton	129	18	Billing	Jacob			1	1					1				3		
Sharon	32	5	Billing	James J	3		1			2			1				7		
Canton	129	17	Billing	John	1	1	1			1			1				5		
Canton	129	13	Billing	Jonathan	1		1	1		3	1		1				8		
Sharon	32	7	Billing	Joseph		1	1			2		1	1				6		
Sharon	32	6	Billing	Lewis		1				1		1					3		
Canton	129	21	Billing	Mary Wid.		1							1	1			3		
Canton	129	20	Billing	Nathl	1									1			3		
Canton	129	19	Billing	Peter			1			4	2		1				8		
Canton	129	22	Billing	Rebecca Wid.	1	1	2			1		1	1				7		
Canton	129	12	Billing	Roger			1				1		1				3		

TOWN	PG#	LN#	LAST NAME	FIRST NAME	FREE WHITE MALES					FREE WHITE FEMALES					TOTAL ALL OTHER	TOTAL SLAVES	TOTALS	DISTRICT/ TOWNSHIP	NOTES
					under 10	10 to 16	16 to 26	26 to 45	45 and over	under 10	10 to 16	16 to 26	26 to 45	45 and over					
Canton	129	15	Billing	Samuel					1	1				1			3		
Canton	129	16	Billing	Stephen	1		2	1	1	1			1	1			8		
Sharon	32	3	Billing	James	3			1		2			1				7		
Roxbury	110	23	Billing	Benjamin		1	3	1		4		2	1				12	2nd Parish	
Quincy	40	26	Billings	Edmd	1		1	1				3	1		2		9		
Sharon	31	10	Billings	Elijah		1			1			1		1			4		
Dedham	141	4	Billings	Elkanah	1	1		1					1				4	1st Parish	
Sharon	31	8	Billings	Hath*	2			1		2	1		1				7		
Foxborough	23	6	Billings	Jacob				1		3	1		1				6		
Quincy	40	27	Billings	Jno	2	2		1		2	1	1	1				10		
Sharon	31	4	Billings	Jonathn	1		1	1	1	1	1		1	1			8		
Milton	45	2	Billings	Joseph	2		2	1			1	2	1				9		
Roxbury	110	25	Billings	Lemuel	1	2	3	1			2	1	1				11	2nd Parish	
Sharon	31	6	Billings	Leonard	3		3	1		1		1	1				10		
Walpole	27	13	Billings	Richard		1	1		1	1		1	1				6		
Foxborough	22	1	Billings	Samuel		1		1	1	1	1	1					6		
Sharon	31	5	Billings	William	1	1		1			1		1				5		
Dorchester	51	14	Billings	Moses				1		1		2					4		
Dorchester	51	12	Billings	Oliver		1	1				1		1				5		
Dorchester	51	13	Billings	Oliver Jr	1			1				2					4		
Weymouth	74	27	Binney	Elkanah		1			1					1			3	North Parish	
Weymouth	74	26	Binney	Joshua	2			1		1		1					5	North Parish	
Dorchester	52	15	Bird	Aaron		1	1	1						2			6		
Dorchester	52	12	Bird	Aaron Jr	3		1	1		1	2		1				9		
Stoughton	118	16	Bird	Abner	1			1		2			1				5		
Stoughton	118	15	Bird	Asa				1		5			1				7		
Dorchester	51	17	Bird	Benjamin	1		1			1			1				4		
Needham	145	15	Bird	Benjamin	1		1	1		3		1	1				8		
Dorchester	52	30	Bird	Calvin			1			1			1				3		
Needham	145	14	Bird	Ebenezer	1		1	1				1	1				5		
Dorchester	52	8	Bird	Edward	2	1		1		1	2	1	1				9		
Dorchester	52	5	Bird	Elizabeth									1	1			2		
Stoughton	118	17	Bird	Elizabeth	1					1	1		1				4		
Dorchester	53	6	Bird	George	1		1	1					1				4		
Dorchester	53	7	Bird	Henry		1	1		3	1		2		1			9		
Stoughton	118	13	Bird	Isaac	1		1	1	1	2	1	4		1			12		
Roxbury	107	8	Bird	James		2		1		4			1				8		
Dorchester	53	2	Bird	Jona		1	1		1			1	1	1			6		
Dorchester	52	9	Bird	Jona Jr		1	1	2					1	2			7		
Dorchester	53	3	Bird	Jona Jr	1			1					1				3		
Stoughton	118	12	Bird	Lemuel	2		1		1	1	2	1		1			9		
Dorchester	52	2	Bird	Mary									1				1		
Dorchester	51	18	Bird	Oliver			4						1				5		
Dorchester	53	8	Bird	Saml	4	1		1		1	1	1					9		
Dorchester	52	4	Bird	Samuel		2		2			2	1					7		
Roxbury	104	28	Bird	Samuel		1	1			1							3		
Stoughton	118	14	Bird	Samuel		1	1		1	2		1	1				7		
Dorchester	52	6	Bird	Sarah	1		1			1		1	2	1			7		
Dorchester	52	14	Bird	Wm	2		1	1					1				5		
Stoughton	118	18	Bisbee	Benjamin	2		1	1	1	2		1	1	1			10		
Dorchester	52	1	Bisbee	Jona			1			1			1				3		
Wrentham	176	18	Bishop	Seth	1		1						1				3		
Quincy	40	3	Black	Moses		3		1		1		3	1		2		11		
Quincy	40	10	Black	Rachel								2	1				3		
Wrentham	175	31	Blackington	George		1		1		1	1		1				5		
Needham	145	12	Blackinton	Othniel		1	1					2					4		
Canton	130	2	Blackman	Adam				1			2	1	1		1		6		
Dorchester	52	33	Blackman	James	1		3					1	1				6		
Canton	130	4	Blackman	John	1			1		2			1				5		
Dorchester	52	13	Blackman	Jona	2			1		1			1				5		
Dorchester	51	16	Blackman	Leml	2	1		1		1		1	1				7		
Canton	130	5	Blackman	Ruth Wid.		1						1		1			3		
Canton	130	3	Blackman	Saml		1		1		2	1		1				6		
Dorchester	53	1	Blackman	Saml	2			1						3			6		
Dorchester	52	34	Blackman	Saml Jr	1	1		1		1			1				5		
Roxbury	112	10	Blackman	Sarah		2	1				1			1			5	3rd Parish	
Dorchester	52	31	Blackman	Unite	4		1			1	1		1				8		
Milton	44	16	Blade	James				1				1		2			4		
Dorchester	52	26	Blagge	Saml		1	1	1		3	1		1		1		9		
Wrentham	174	7	Blake	Abijah				1					1				2		
Franklin	166	4	Blake	Abraham Jr	3			1	1	1		1	1				8		
Wrentham	178	23	Blake	Alpheus		1				1			1				3		
Wrentham	175	4	Blake	Andrew		1	1				1		1				4		
Wrentham	172	27	Blake	Asa				2					1				3		
Franklin	167	3	Blake	Calvin		1		1		2	1	1					6		
Wrentham	179	22	Blake	Daniel	1			1		2		1	1				6		
Wrentham	179	28	Blake	Daniel	2			1		2			1				6		
Wrentham	173	5	Blake	Darius	1			1		1			1				4		
Walpole	26	13	Blake	Ebenezer			1	1				1		1			4		
Walpole	27	15	Blake	Ebenezer			1					1					2		

TOWN	PG#	LN#	LAST NAME	FIRST NAME	FREE WHITE MALES under 10	10 to 16	16 to 26	26 to 45	45 and over	FREE WHITE FEMALES under 10	10 to 16	16 to 26	26 to 45	45 and over	TOTAL ALL OTHER	TOTAL SLAVES	TOTALS	DISTRICT/ TOWNSHIP	NOTES
Wrentham	172	28	Blake	Ebenezer	2	1		1				1		1			6		
Wrentham	177	29	Blake	Ebenezer			1				1			1			3		
Wrentham	179	26	Blake	Eliab	2	1		1		2	1		1				8		
Walpole	27	18	Blake	Elizabeth						1	2		1				4		
Wrentham	174	10	Blake	Enoch			1					1					2		
Dorchester	52	20	Blake	Enos	1		1	1		1	1			1			6		
Wrentham	178	5	Blake	Ezra	2	1	2		1	1	2	1		1			11		
Wrentham	177	25	Blake	Jacob	1			1		3		2	1				8		
Wrentham	179	21	Blake	Jacob			1	1					1				3		
Dorchester	52	11	Blake	James				1			1		1				3		
Wrentham	179	25	Blake	Jason			1			3		2					6		
Wrentham	174	4	Blake	Jeremiah		1		1	1		1	1	3				8		
Wrentham	173	13	Blake	John				1					1				2		
Wrentham	179	30	Blake	John Junr		1	1			1	2	1		1			7		
Milton	45	9	Blake	Liba			1						1				2		
Wrentham	177	30	Blake	Luther		1					1						2		
Wrentham	179	18	Blake	Nathan	1			1		2	2		1				7		
Dorchester	51	9	Blake	Nathl	2	2	1	1		2		1					9		
Franklin	163	4	Blake	Phillip	1			1		1		1	1				6		
Dorchester	52	7	Blake	Rachel									2				2		
Wrentham	178	4	Blake	Robert		3	2		1		1	1		2			10		
Franklin	167	4	Blake	Robert Jun	1		1				1		1				5		
Wrentham	174	8	Blake	Samuel	2			1		1	1		1				6		
Wrentham	175	15	Blake	Samuel	4		1	1		1			1				8		
Dorchester	52	22	Blake	Seth	3			1		1			1				6		
Franklin	166	19	Blake	Solomon			1	1				1	1				4		
Wrentham	174	9	Blake	Solomon			1	1			1		1				4		
Canton	130	6	Blake	Stephen		1		1			1		1				4		
Weymouth	78	29	Blanchard	Abner				1				1					2	South Parish	
Weymouth	74	7	Blanchard	Ann		1	2				1	1		1			6	North Parish	
Weymouth	78	16	Blanchard	Bela			2					1					3	South Parish	
Weymouth	78	17	Blanchard	Daniel		2	1	1		1			1				6	South Parish	
Weymouth	78	14	Blanchard	Danl Wid			3	1			1	1	1				7	South Parish	
Weymouth	74	20	Blanchard	David	2		1	1		4	3	1	1				13	North Parish	
Braintree	66	8	Blanchard	Ephraim				1		1		1					3		
Dorchester	52	32	Blanchard	Fran.		1		1		3			1				6		
Weymouth	78	32	Blanchard	John	1	1	1	1		1	1		1				7	South Parish	
Stoughton	118	21	Blanchard	Jonathan	6			1					1				8		
Weymouth	78	31	Blanchard	Josiah	1			1		1			1				4	South Parish	
Weymouth	78	15	Blanchard	Nathl	3	1		1		4			1				10	South Parish	
Weymouth	78	20	Blanchard	Nicholas				1		1			1				3	South Parish	
Weymouth	78	21	Blanchard	Nichos Junior	2	1		1		3			1				8	South Parish	
Weymouth	78	18	Blanchard	Saml			1	1					1				3	South Parish	
Weymouth	78	10	Blanchard	Saml 2d			1	1				1					3	South Parish	
Braintree	68	4	Blanchard	Samuel	2		1						1				4		
Weymouth	78	30	Blanchard	Thomas		1		1		1	3	1					7	South Parish	
Stoughton	118	20	Blanchard	William	2	1	2	1		1		1	1				9		
Roxbury	102	35	Blaney	Samuel		1		2		1			1				5		
Stoughton	118	9	Bleker	John			1				1		1				3		
Wrentham	173	17	Blinn	George		1		1		2	1		1				6		
Wrentham	172	16	Bliss	Isaac	2			1		1			1				5		
Needham	145	22	Blodgett	Simon				1				1	1				3		
Wrentham	175	5	Blose	Samuel	1		1			1		2		1			7		
Needham	145	21	Bodridge	Galen		1	1			1		2		1			6		
Braintree	68	3	Booth	William				1			1		1				3		
Cohasset	152	4	Bordman	Micajah	2			1			1		2				6		
Dorchester	51	10	Bordman	Wm				1		1		1	2				5		
Milton	45	8	Boris	L.L.		2		3	1		1	1	2		1		11		
Roxbury	106	12	Bosson	William	3	1	1		1	2		4	1				13		
Bellingham	161	26	Bosworth	Ichabod	2			1		2			1				6		
Cohasset	154	16	Bourne	Thomas			1			3	1	1	1				8		
Wrentham	170	15	Bowdella	M.	1			1		1	1				3		7		
Wrentham	176	28	Bowdich	Samuel	2		2	1		2			1	1			10		
Braintree	66	11	Bowditch	John		2		1				1	1				5		
Braintree	66	10	Bowditch	Jona	1	1	1	1		3							7		
Braintree	66	9	Bowditch	William	1			1		1			1				5		
Dorchester	51	5	Bowdoin	James		2	2	3	1		2	1	3				14		
Roxbury	105	7	Bowen	John	2			1		1		1	1				6		
Roxbury	105	6	Bowen	Samuel				1									1		
Wrentham	177	16	Bowers	Isaac											3		3		
Milton	44	18	Bowman	James	2	1		1		2	1		1				8		
Roxbury	107	28	Bowman	Lucy			4				1		1		1		7		
Wrentham	173	20	Boyaden	James		1	1		1		1		1				5		
Wrentham	173	21	Boyaden	James Junr	1	1		1		1		1					5		
Wrentham	173	18	Boyaden	Richard	1	1	2		1		2		1				8		
Wrentham	177	9	Boyd	Bethuel	1			1		2			1				5		
Franklin	167	24	Boyd	John				1					1				2		
Franklin	167	20	Boyd	Willard		1		2			2				1		6		
Foxborough	23	1	Boyden	Amos	1	1		1		1			1				5		
Medfield	86	4	Boyden	Amos	3			1					1				5		
Medfield	86	2	Boyden	Asa		1			1		1	1					5		
Walpole	27	12	Boyden	Asa	1			1		3			1				6		

86

TOWN	PG#	LN#	LAST NAME	FIRST NAME	FREE WHITE MALES					FREE WHITE FEMALES					TOTAL ALL OTHER	TOTAL SLAVES	TOTALS	DISTRICT/ TOWNSHIP	NOTES
					under 10	10 to 16	16 to 26	26 to 45	45 and over	under 10	10 to 16	16 to 26	26 to 45	45 and over					
Dedham	143	9	Boyden	Benjamin		1			1		1		1	1			5	2nd Parish	
Walpole	27	5	Boyden	Benjamin			1	1	1					1			4		
Dedham	143	10	Boyden	Benjamin Junr	1		2						1				4	2nd Parish	
Walpole	31	28	Boyden	Daniel	1		1				1	1	1				5		
Foxborough	23	5	Boyden	Elijah	3		1	1		1			1				7		
Walpole	27	4	Boyden	Elijah	4		2	1		1	1	1	1				11		
Walpole	26	9	Boyden	Ezekiel				1					1				2		
Walpole	27	3	Boyden	Jacob	2	2		1					1				6		
Medway East Parish	91	21	Boyden	Jairus	1		1	1		1		1	1				6		
Walpole	26	6	Boyden	Joel								1	1				3		
Walpole	27	9	Boyden	John				1					1				2		
Walpole	26	8	Boyden	John 3d			1		1	2	1		1				6		
Walpole	27	21	Boyden	John Jr			1		1			1		1			4		
Walpole	27	1	Boyden	Jonathan	1			1					1				3		
Walpole	27	8	Boyden	Joshua			1		1			1	1				4		
Walpole	27	6	Boyden	Phinas	3	2		1				1	1				8		
Walpole	26	10	Boyden	Samuel			2		1					2			5		
Walpole	27	11	Boyden	Sarah W		1				1		1		2			4		
Foxborough	23	2	Boyden	Seth	2	1		1		3			1	1			9		
Medfield	86	3	Boyden	Silas	1			1		2			1				5		
Brookline	114	16	Boylston	Joshua				1				1		2			4		
Quincy	40	12	Bracket	James J	1			2		1		2			1		7		
Quincy	40	21	Bracket	James J		2		1				1	1				5		
Quincy	40	32	Bracket	Joseph		2		1				1		2			6		
Needham	145	20	Bracket	Lemuel	1		1		1	3	1	1	1				9		
Quincy	40	13	Bracket	Peter		2			3	2			1				8		
Stoughton	118	22	Bracket	Samuel			1	1	1		2		1				6		
Roxbury	111	25	Bradford	John Revd	1	1	1	1			3	2					9	2nd Parish	
Medfield	86	8	Bradford	Walter	1	1		1		2			1				6		
Roxbury	101	4	Bradley	Lemual	1		1			1			1				4		
Milton	45	4	Bradley	Stephen	2	1		1				1		1			6		
Sharon	32	9	Bradshaw	Nathl				1					1				2		
Sharon	32	11	Bradshaw	Nathl 2	2	1		1	1	2			1				8		
Roxbury	108	15	Braid	John			1					1					2		
Franklin	169	15	Braly	Silence									1				1		
Medfield	86	13	Bran	Lucy											1		1		
Wrentham	170	4	Brastow	Beriah	1	2	1		1	2		2		1			10		
Medfield	86	7	Breck	Edward	2			1		1			1				5		
Medfield	86	6	Breck	Jonathan	4	1		1		1			1				8		
Medfield	86	5	Breck	Joseph		1	1		1	1		2	1				7		
Roxbury	106	33	Brewer	Ebenezer	2			1		1	1		1				6		
Wrentham	170	5	Brewer	Edward	1			1			1	1	1				4		
Roxbury	112	13	Brewer	Joseph				1					1				2	3rd Parish	
Roxbury	103	18	Brewer	Nathaniel	1			1		3	1		1				7		
Roxbury	112	15	Brewer	Sarah	2						1	3	1				7	3rd Parish	
Milton	45	10	Brewer	Wid.									1				2		
Roxbury	101	7	Brewer	William		1	1	3		1	2	1	1	1			11		
Medway East Parish	91	23	Bridges	Elijah	1		1					1					3		
Roxbury	113	18	Bridgun	Petre											3		3	3rd Parish	
Quincy	40	8	Briesler	Jno	1			1		1		1					4		
Dorchester	53	4	Brigden	Zachr	2		1			1	1		1				6		
Canton	130	7	Briggs	Betty									3				3		
Milton	44	8	Briggs	Daniel	3	2	6	6	3		1	4	1				26		
Cohasset	153	33	Briggs	Ichabod	1			1	1	1			1				5		
Stoughton	118	23	Briggs	Joel Revd	2	2		1		2		1	1				9		
Cohasset	154	20	Briggs	Joseph	2			1	1	2			1				7		
Dedham	141	2	Briggs	Sarah									1				1	1st Parish	
Cohasset	154	19	Briggs	Seth			1		1			1	1				4		
Dedham	136	17	Briggs	Solomon			1		1	1	1	1					4		
Stoughton	118	24	Briggs	Stephen		1			1	3	1	1	1	1			9		
Needham	145	11	Bright	Michel		1		1					1				3		
Roxbury	113	23	Brimmer	Martin	1			1	1			6		1	2		12	3rd Parish	
Medway East Parish	91	22	Broad	Ephraim				1					1				2		
Roxbury	110	11	Broad	John			2										2	2nd Parish	
Milton	44	7	Bronsden	Benj	2	1		1		2		1					7		
Milton	45	3	Bronsden	Jno B.	2	2		1	1	1		1		2			9		
Brookline	115	4	Brooks	Samuel	4		1	1					1				7		
Dedham	136	7	Brooks	Timothy			1										1		
Needham	145	18	Browd	Thodore				1	1				1				3		
Needham	145	6	Browd	Timothy		1	1					1		1			5		
Wrentham	175	16	Brown	Asa	1		1	2	1			1		1			7		
Needham	145	23	Brown	Jacob	1	1		1					1				4		
Brookline	114	5	Brown	Jeremiah	1			1		3	1		1				7		
Dover	149	21	Brown	John	2	1		1		2	1		1				8		
Franklin	168	27	Brown	Joseph	3	1		1		1	1	1	1				9		
Roxbury	107	18	Brown	Joseph	2			1		2	1	1	1				8		
Needham	145	7	Brown	Joshua					1	2	2			1			6		
Wrentham	180	25	Brown	Lemuel	1	1	1	1	1		1	2		1			9		
Wrentham	180	27	Brown	Lemuel Junr		1	2	2		3	1	1					10		
Quincy	40	23	Brown	Saml	1	1	1		1			2		1			7		
Cohasset	152	32	Brown	Samuel			1					2					3		

TOWN	PG#	LN#	HEADS OF HOUSEHOLD		FREE WHITE MALES					FREE WHITE FEMALES					TOTAL ALL OTHER	TOTAL SLAVES	TOTALS	DISTRICT/ TOWNSHIP	NOTES
			LAST NAME	FIRST NAME	under 10	10 to 16	16 to 26	26 to 45	45 and over	under 10	10 to 16	16 to 26	26 to 45	45 and over					
Needham	145	19	Brown	Samuel		1			1			1		1			4		
Needham	145	10	Brown	William					1					1			2		
Walpole	27	10	Bruce	David			1			1			1				3		
Roxbury	108	33	Bruce	Stephen	1	2	1		1	1	2	1	1		1		12		
Dedham	143	11	Buckmaster	Edward	2			1		1			1				5	2nd Parish	
Dorchester	52	23	Budge	David		1				1			1				3		
Roxbury	102	30	Bugbee	Ebenezer	3			1		1	1	2		1			9		
Roxbury	102	20	Bugbee	Edward	2			1		1	1		1				6		
Wrentham	177	26	Bugbee	Samuel		1		1									2		
Dedham	141	3	Bullard	Abigail									1				1	1st Parish	
Medway East Parish	91	14	Bullard	Abigail		1						1		1			3		
Medway East Parish	91	17	Bullard	Adam		1		1			1	2		1			6		
Sharon	32	1	Bullard	Benj	2			1		2	2	1	1				9		
Bellingham	160	16	Bullard	Daniel	1		1		1	1	1	1					6		
Bellingham	160	27	Bullard	Elisha	1	3			1	2		1	1				9		
Needham	145	16	Bullard	Epheriam		1			1			1		2			5		
Dedham	136	15	Bullard	Isaac				1		1	1	1	1				5		
Medway West Parish	95	16	Bullard	Isaac		1	2	1			1	3	1				9		
Walpole	26	12	Bullard	Joel	1			1		2			1				5		
Dedham	136	14	Bullard	John	2	2		1		2	2	2	1	1			13		
Medfield	86	12	Bullard	John			1						2				3		
Sharon	32	2	Bullard	Judith W								1	1				2		
Medway East Parish	91	18	Bullard	Liberty	1		1					1					3		
Medway West Parish	95	17	Bullard	Malichi	1		1	1		1	1						5		
Needham	145	17	Bullard	Nathaniel	2	1	1	1		2	1	1	1				10		
Medway East Parish	91	16	Bullard	Ralph	1		1					1					3		
Walpole	26	11	Bullard	Seth Esq		1		1				1		1			4		
Medfield	86	11	Bullard	Silas	1			1		1	1	1					5		
Sharon	31	9	Bullard	Silas			1	1		2		1		1			6		
Medway East Parish	91	15	Bullard	Timothy			1					1					2		
Dedham	136	8	Bullard	William	3		2	2				1	1				9		
Walpole	27	2	Bullard	William			1	1				1		1			4		
Needham	145	13	Bullen	Amaziah	1	1			1	1	1	2	1				8		
Medway East Parish	91	11	Bullen	Daniel				1		1	1		1				4		
Medway West Parish	95	18	Bullen	Elizabeth			1			1	1	2		1			6		
Medfield	86	10	Bullen	Ichabod			1						1				2		
Medway East Parish	91	13	Bullen	Jeduthun	2	1		1		1			1				6		
Medway East Parish	91	12	Bullen	Jonathan	1	1	1			2			2				7		
Medfield	86	9	Bullen	Moses		2	1					1	1				5		
Cohasset	152	21	Burbanks	John	1		1	1		1		2		1			7		
Cohasset	152	22	Burbanks	Timothy	2	1		1		1			1	1			7		
Roxbury	107	31	Burditt	Nathan		6	1	1		4			1	1			14		
Braintree	69	?	Burnell	Ephraim			1					1					2		
Bellingham	160	23	Burr	Asa			1				1		1				3		
Bellingham	159	24	Burr	Elisha	1	2	1	1		1			1				7		
Canton	130	10	Burr	Seymour											1		1		
Roxbury	99	8	Burrel	James			1	1		2	1	1	1				7		
Weymouth	74	16	Burrell	Asa	1		1					1		1			4	North Parish	
Weymouth	78	39	Burrell	Daniel				1					1				2	South Parish	
Canton	134	53	Burrell	David			1					1		1			3		
Roxbury	105	15	Burrell	Jerusha	1	1	1	2		2	3	2		1			13		
Weymouth	74	11	Burrell	Joseph	1	1		1		2			1				6	North Parish	
Weymouth	78	25	Burrell	Reuben Wid	1					2			1				4	South Parish	
Weymouth	78	37	Burrell	Robert	2			1		3			1				7	South Parish	
Weymouth	78	26	Burrell	Saml				1		1				1			3	South Parish	
Weymouth	78	27	Burrell	Saml Junr	1			1		1		1		1			5	South Parish	
Canton	134	54	Burrell	Samuel	1			1		1		1					4		
Quincy	40	7	Burrell	Seth			1	1					1	1			4		
Roxbury	103	12	Burrell	Silvanus	1	1		1		2	1		1				7		
Randolph	124	3	Burres	David	3		1						1				5		
Dover	149	19	Burridge	John	1			1		2			1				5		
Dorchester	52	10	Burrill	Benj	1			1		3			1				6		
Braintree	66	12	Burrill	Peter	1	1		1		3	1		1				8		
Weymouth	74	5	Burrill	Peter Widw of	*	*	*	*	*	*	*	*	*	*			*	North Parish	
Canton	130	9	Bussey	Basheba Wid.								1	1				2		
Canton	130	8	Bussey	Benjamin				1					1				2		
Dorchester	52	18	Bussey	Jno	2	1	1	1		1		1	1		2		10		
Quincy	40	35	Butch	Jno	2		1			1			1				5		
Franklin	169	30	Butterworth	Noah	1		1	1		3	2		1				9		
Bellingham	159	6	Butterworth	Otis	1	1		1		1		1					5		
Brookline	114	14	Cabett	George Esq			3		1		2	2	1				9		
Milton	45	12	Cabot	Samuel	2	3		2		2	2		3				14		
Needham	145	24	Caffree	John				1	1				1				3		
Dedham	136	24	Cain	Paul	1		1		1	3	1		1				8		
Sharon	32	32	Callaft	W John			1	1				1	1				4		
Milton	45	17	Canady	Benj	1		2		1	3	1		1				9		
Randolph	124	4	Canady		1							1		1			3		First name left blank
Weymouth	74	37	Canterbury	John	2		1	2		2			1				8	North Parish	
Canton	130	15	Canterbury	Samuel	2			1					1				4		
Canton	130	11	Capen	Andrew	2	1		1		1			1	1			7		
Stoughton	119	11	Capen	Benja & Abraham		1	1	2				1	1				6		

TOWN	PG#	LN#	LAST NAME	FIRST NAME	FREE WHITE MALES under 10	10 to 16	16 to 26	26 to 45	45 and over	FREE WHITE FEMALES under 10	10 to 16	16 to 26	26 to 45	45 and over	TOTAL ALL OTHER	TOTAL SLAVES	TOTALS	DISTRICT/ TOWNSHIP	NOTES
Canton	130	12	Capen	Christopher		1			1				1	1			4		
Dorchester	54	3	Capen	Ebenz	2	1			2			2		1			8		
Stoughton	119	7	Capen	Edward			1		1		1			1			4		
Stoughton	119	9	Capen	Edward Junr	3	1		1		1	1		1				8		
Stoughton	119	6	Capen	Elisha	1		1			2			1				5		
Stoughton	119	8	Capen	James	3	1	1	1		2	1		1				10		
Dorchester	54	8	Capen	Jno		1		1	1				1				4		
Dorchester	54	6	Capen	Jno Jr	2	1	4		1	2	2	1		2			15		
Canton	130	14	Capen	John		1	2	1		1		2					7		
Stoughton	119	3	Capen	John	3			1						1			7		
Stoughton	119	1	Capen	Jonathan				1				1	1				3		
Stoughton	119	2	Capen	Jonathan Jr	1			1		2	3		1				8		
Dedham	136	23	Capen	Nathaniel	1			1		2	1		1				6		
Braintree	68	11	Capen	Nathl				1		1		1					3		
Braintree	68	12	Capen	Saml	1		2	1		2		1					8		
Dorchester	53	13	Capen	Saml		1	2	2		3	1		1	1			11		
Dorchester	53	35	Capen	Saml Jr	1		1	1				1	1	1			6		
Canton	130	13	Capen	Samuel		2		1						2			5		
Stoughton	119	4	Capen	Samuel				1		1		1					3		
Stoughton	119	10	Capen	Uriah			1			1			1				3		
Stoughton	119	5	Capen	William			2			1	1		1				5		
Sharon	32	16	Capin	Elijah				1						1			2		
Sharon	32	22	Capin	Ezekiel		1	1	1	1		1		1				6		
Sharon	32	23	Capin	Jerusha Wd			1	1	1		1		1				5		
Sharon	32	19	Capin	Lemuel	1	2		1			1		1				6		
Sharon	32	27	Capin	Oliver			3						2				5		
Sharon	32	33	Capin	Samuel		1		1		3			1				6		
Braintree	68	19	Capron	Thomas				1					1	1			3		
Dedham	143	12	Carby	Carolina									1	1			2	2nd Parish	
Quincy	41	9	Carey	Alpheus	3	1	2	1		1	2	1	1				12		
Roxbury	114	9	Carey	John		1	1			2	2	2	1				9	3rd Parish	
Foxborough	23	16	Carpenter	Ezra	2	1			1	1	1	2	1				9		
Foxborough	23	15	Carpenter	John	1	1		1		1			1				5		
Foxborough	23	14	Carpenter	Peter	3		1	1					1				6		
Foxborough	23	13	Carpenter	Sarah Wd									1	1			2		
Stoughton	119	13	Carr	William	2			1			1						4		
Canton	130	16	Carrel	Samuel				1		1			1				3		
Walpole	27	25	Carrol	Jonathan		2	2		1			2		1			8		
Dover	150	5	Carryl	George Doc	1			1	1	1		1	1	1			7		Rev. Benjamin Carryl included
Dorchester	53	12	Carter	Josiah		1				1	1						3		
Quincy	41	16	Catin	Peter	1		1			2			1				5		
Walpole	27	28	Ceaveland	John			1	1	1					1			5		
Roxbury	109	11	Chamberlain	Nehemiah	1	1		1		1	1		1				6	2nd Parish	
Roxbury	109	10	Chamberlain	Sarah		1							1	1			3	2nd Parish	
Roxbury	109	12	Chamberlain	Stephen			1							1			2	2nd Parish	
Dedham	141	9	Chamberland	Isaac	2		1					1	1				5	1st Parish	
Roxbury	113	5	Chamberlin	Stephen Junr	2			1		1			1				5	3rd Parish	
Dorchester	54	11	Champney	Caleb				1						1			2		
Roxbury	108	25	Champney	Elizabeth							1			1			2		
Dorchester	54	10	Champney	James		1		1		2			1				5		
Dorchester	54	12	Champney	Jno			1		1		1			2			5		
Roxbury	103	21	Champney	Jonathan				1						1			2		
Quincy	41	19	Chandler	Elipht	2			1		1	1		1				6		
Canton	130	17	Chandler	Joseph		1	1	1		2	1		1				7		
Quincy	41	7	Chandler	Wm	2	2		1		2			1				8		
Bellingham	161	4	Chase	Allen	1			1		1			1				4		
Randolph	124	11	Cheeseman	Silas	1			1		3			1	1			7		
Weymouth	79	2	Cheesman	Hosea	1	1			1	2	1	1					7	South Parish	
Braintree	68	18	Cheesman	M Wid.		1				2		1	1				5		
Braintree	68	22	Cheesman	Mary Wid							1	1	1				3		
Braintree	68	17	Cheesman	Saml	1			1					1	1			4		
Braintree	68	14	Cheesman	Stephen	1			1		1	1	1	1	1			7		
Medway East Parish	91	31	Chenery	Benjamin	1		1	1		3			1				7		
Medfield	86	31	Chenery	Elisha		1					1						2		
Medfield	86	29	Chenery	Ephraim			2	1	1		1	1					7		
Roxbury	109	3	Chenery	Ephraim		1						1					2	2nd Parish	
Medfield	86	28	Chenery	Oliver	3		1	1		1	1		1				8		
Medfield	86	30	Chenery	Simeon	1	1		1		2	1			2			8		
Dover	150	6	Cheney	John	2			1		3			1				7		
Dover	150	1	Cheney	Joseph	2	1		1			1		1	1			7		
Dover	149	27	Cheney	Simon		1		1				1		1			4		
Roxbury	106	2	Cheney	Thomas		1		1	1	1	1		1	1			6		
Medfield	86	26	Cheney	Timothy	1	2		1		1	1		1				7		
Medfield	86	27	Cheny	Levi			1	1		1	1		1	1			4		
Wrentham	175	1	Chever	Amos				1				1	2	1			5		
Wrentham	175	2	Chever	Amos Junr			1						1				2		
Wrentham	175	12	Chever	Cyrus		1				3		1					5		
Wrentham	174	35	Chever	Daniel				1			3		1				5		
Wrentham	175	10	Chever	Ebenezer				1					1	2			4		
Wrentham	178	3	Chever	Elias	1			1		1			1				4		
Wrentham	175	11	Chever	James				1					1				2		

TOWN	PG#	LN#	LAST NAME	FIRST NAME	FREE WHITE MALES under 10	10 to 16	16 to 26	26 to 45	45 and over	FREE WHITE FEMALES under 10	10 to 16	16 to 26	26 to 45	45 and over	TOTAL ALL OTHER	TOTAL SLAVES	TOTALS	DISTRICT/ TOWNSHIP	NOTES
Wrentham	175	17	Chever	James 2nd			2							2			4		
Wrentham	176	21	Chever	John				1					1	1			3		
Wrentham	176	22	Chever	John Junr	1		1	1		1		1					5		
Wrentham	174	34	Chever	Royal			1					2					3		
Wrentham	177	20	Chever	Timothy			1	1					1				3		
Dover	150	8	Chickering	David	1			1		2			1				5		
Dedham	141	7	Chickering	Jabez Rev		1		1		1			2				5		1st Parish
Dover	149	28	Chickering	Jesse	4			1		1			1				7		
Dover	150	2	Chickering	John		1				1			1				3		
Dover	150	3	Chickering	John Jr	1			1					1				3		
Dover	149	26	Chickering	Nathaniel	5	2	1		2	1			1				12		
Roxbury	108	6	Child	Aaron	1			1		1			1				4		
Roxbury	111	24	Child	Abner			1	1		1			1				4		2nd Parish
Brookline	114	10	Child	Elijah		1		1					1				3		
Dedham	136	21	Child	Francis		3	1						1				5		
Roxbury	112	17	Child	Phinehas		2	1	1		2	1	1		1			9		3rd Parish
Brookline	114	6	Child	Solomon		1	1	1		1		1	1				7		
Roxbury	113	19	Child	Stephen	1	2	2	3		3		1	1				13		3rd Parish
Milton	45	22	Childs	Wm	1		1			2			1				5		
Bellingham	162	2	Chilson	John	3	1	1		2	1	1	1					10		
Bellingham	161	1	Chilson	Joseph	2			1		1	1	1					6		
Bellingham	161	2	Chilson	Joshua	4	1		1		1	1		2				10		
Wrentham	177	18	Clafflin	Noah		1	1	1					1				5		
Dedham	136	19	Clail	Joseph	2		1			1			1				5		
Dorchester	53	22	Clap	Ann								1		1			2		
Braintree	68	16	Clap	Barnard	1		1			1			1				4		
Roxbury	104	31	Clap	Caleb	1	1	5	1		2		1		1	1		12		
Dorchester	53	18	Clap	Charles		1	1	1					1				4		
Walpole	27	26	Clap	Daniel	1		1						1				3		
Dorchester	53	26	Clap	David			1						1				2		
Dorchester	53	9	Clap	Eben Esq.	4	1	1		4	1	1	2	1				15		
Walpole	27	35	Clap	Ebenezer			1			1			1				3		
Walpole	27	36	Clap	Ebenezer Jr		1	1	1		1			1				5		
Walpole	27	43	Clap	Eleazer	2	1	1		1	2	1	1	1				10		
Walpole	27	32	Clap	Elijah			1						1				2		
Walpole	27	44	Clap	Elipha		1	1			2		1					5		
Walpole	27	34	Clap	Eliphalet	1			1					1				3		
Walpole	27	24	Clap	Eliphalet Jr			1			3			1				5		
Walpole	27	39	Clap	Elizabeth		1							1				2		
Dorchester	53	20	Clap	Ezekiel	3		1	1				1	1				7		
Walpole	27	37	Clap	Ichabod		1	1	1					1				4		
Walpole	27	38	Clap	Jacob		2	1	1					1	2			7		
Dorchester	54	1	Clap	James	2		1		1		1						5		
Dedham	136	18	Clap	Jesse		1	3		1	1	1						7		
Roxbury	106	5	Clap	John		3	1		3	1	1	1					10		
Stoughton	119	12	Clap	John	2	1		2					1	1			7		
Dorchester	53	25	Clap	Jona	1								1	2			5		
Dorchester	53	31	Clap	Joseph	2	1	2		1	2	1			4			13		
Dorchester	54	1	Clap	Joseph Jr		1				2		1					4		
Walpole	27	22	Clap	Joshua Esq			1						1				2		
Walpole	27	31	Clap	Joshua Jr				1			1			1	1		4		
Dorchester	53	10	Clap	Lemuel		1	3	1				2		1			8		
Walpole	27	27	Clap	Levi	3	1	1		1			1					7		
Dorchester	53	21	Clap	Nathl	2	1		1	1	2	1		2				10		
Walpole	27	23	Clap	Oliver		2	1				1	1					5		
Walpole	27	40	Clap	Oliver Jr	2			1					1				5		
Dorchester	53	24	Clap	Pen 3d			1			3			1				5		
Dorchester	53	23	Clap	Pen Jr	2		1			1			1				5		
Dorchester	53	19	Clap	Roger	2		1	1					1	1			6		
Walpole	28	2	Clap	Rufus		2		1		1	1	1					6		
Dorchester	53	14	Clap	Saml	1	1	8		1				2	1			14		
Dorchester	53	15	Clap	Saml 3rd	1	1	1						1				4		
Dorchester	53	27	Clap	Saml Jr			1						1				2		
Dorchester	53	28	Clap	Seth			1		1				1				3		
Walpole	27	41	Clap	Th*n*			1						1				2		
Walpole	27	42	Clap	Thadeus	2		1	1					1	1			6		
Dorchester	54	5	Clap	Thomas				2						2			4		
Foxborough	24	2	Clap	Thomas	2		1	1	1	3			1	1			10		
Walpole	28	1	Clap	Thomas			1			1			1				3		
Sharon	33	2	Clap	Timothy	3			1	1				1	1			7		
Foxborough	24	6	Clap	William	1	1	1	2				1	1	1			10		
Medfield	86	23	Clark	Aaron	2			1					1				4		
Medfield	86	24	Clark	Abigail		1								1			2		
Randolph	124	8	Clark	Amasa		1				1		1					3		
Sharon	32	30	Clark	Appallus	1			1		2		1					5		
Franklin	167	6	Clark	Asa					1					1			2		
Medway West Parish	95	21	Clark	Asa			1							1			2		
Sharon	32	26	Clark	Asa		1		1				2		1			5		
Randolph	124	7	Clark	Atkins	2	1	1		1	1	1	2	1				10		
Randolph	124	5	Clark	Barnabas			2			2	1	1	1				6		

TOWN	PG#	LN#	LAST NAME	FIRST NAME	FREE WHITE MALES					FREE WHITE FEMALES					TOTAL ALL OTHER	TOTAL SLAVES	TOTALS	DISTRICT/ TOWNSHIP	NOTES
					under 10	10 to 16	16 to 26	26 to 45	45 and over	under 10	10 to 16	16 to 26	26 to 45	45 and over					
Medfield	86	22	Clark	David		1			1			1	1	1			5		
Franklin	167	32	Clark	Dyer		1	2		1					1			5		
Franklin	167	33	Clark	Dyer Jun			1			2			1				4		
Medfield	86	17	Clark	Ebenezer	1	1	1		1	1	1		1	1	1		9		
Needham	146	1	Clark	Ebenezer		1			1	1			1	1			5		
Braintree	68	13	Clark	Ebenz	2				1	2	2	1	1		1		10		
Medfield	86	14	Clark	Edward				1			1		1				3		
Foxborough	23	11	Clark	Elbridge	1			1				1					3		
Medfield	86	19	Clark	Elias				1			1		1				3		
Medway East Parish	91	24	Clark	Elijah			1	1					1				3		
Medfield	86	21	Clark	Elisha	1			1		1			1				4		
Randolph	124	10	Clark	Eliza Wid							1		1				2		
Foxborough	24	3	Clark	Elkanah	3			1		1				1			6		
Wrentham	171	22	Clark	Frederick	1			1					1				3		
Braintree	68	23	Clark	Hannah Wid						1	2	1	1				5		
Braintree	68	7	Clark	Hobart				1									1		
Sharon	32	15	Clark	Hosea	1			1		1			1				4		
Dedham	136	20	Clark	Jacob		1	2				1						4		
Foxborough	24	4	Clark	Jacob				1					1				2		
Medfield	86	20	Clark	Jacob				1					1				2		
Randolph	124	6	Clark	Jacob	3			1		2			1				7		
Braintree	68	21	Clark	John				1					1				2		
Medway West Parish	95	22	Clark	John	3		1	1				1	1				7		
Medway East Parish	91	29	Clark	John 3rd	2		1	1				1					5		
Medway East Parish	91	28	Clark	John Jun			1			1			1				3		
Medfield	86	15	Clark	Joseph				1					1				2		
Medfield	86	18	Clark	Joseph Jun			1	1					1				3		
Randolph	124	9	Clark	Joshua	1	2		1					1	1			6		
Medway West Parish	95	20	Clark	Martha									1				1		
Quincy	41	11	Clark	Mary Wid.			2				1		1				4		
Foxborough	23	8	Clark	Nathaniel			2	1	1	1			1				6		
Foxborough	23	9	Clark	Nathaniel				1					1				2		
Foxborough	23	12	Clark	Nathaniel Jr	2			1		1	1	1					6		
Medway East Parish	91	30	Clark	Oliver	1			1		1		1					4		
Walpole	27	29	Clark	Oliver		1		1					1				3		
Wrentham	171	31	Clark	Onismus			1					1					2		
Quincy	41	3	Clark	Saml								1		1	1		2		
Brookline	114	18	Clark	Samuel		1	2	1	1	2	1	1	2	1			11		
Franklin	168	29	Clark	Samuel	1		2	1		1	1	1	1				8		
Medway West Parish	95	19	Clark	Samuel	2		1	1					2				6		
Medfield	86	16	Clark	Seth		1	1						1				3		
Walpole	27	30	Clark	Seth Esq	1		1	1				1					4		
Sharon	32	17	Clark	Silvanus	1	1				1			1				5		
Medway East Parish	91	27	Clark	Stephen		1	1		1	2	1	1	1	2			10		
Wrentham	171	30	Clark	Stephen		1	1		1	2				1			6		
Foxborough	24	5	Clark	Thacher	4			1		1	1		1				8		
Medway East Parish	91	25	Clark	Theodire		1			1			1	1		1		5		
Sharon	32	14	Clark	Thomas	2			1		3	1	1					9		
Medway East Parish	91	26	Clark	Timothy		1	1	1					1				4		
Foxborough	23	10	Clark	William		1		1		1		3		1			7		
Medfield	86	25	Clark	William	1	1		1	1	1	1	2		1			9		
Needham	146	2	Clark	William	1	2		1		1	1	1					8		
Quincy	40	36	Clark	Wm. Rev.			1			1			1		1		4		
Milton	45	26	Clarke	George	1			1					1				3		
Wrentham	172	33	Cleavland	John		1		1		1		1					4		
Franklin	167	7	Cleavland	Samuel	1		1					1					3		
Dover	150	4	Cleveland	David			2	1		1	3		1				8		
Medfield	87	1	Cleveland	Edward		1		1				1		1			4		
Medway West Parish	95	28	Cleveland	Samuel	1		1	1		1		1	1				6		
Medfield	87	2	Cleveland	Zimri	4	1		1		2	1	1					10		
Quincy	41	6	Cleverly	Benj 2d	2			1		2		1					6		
Quincy	41	5	Cleverly	Jno	1			1	1	2			1				6		
Weymouth	74	31	Cleverly	Jona		1	1					1					3	North Parish	
Quincy	41	13	Cleverly	Joseph	2			1		1			3	1			8		
Quincy	41	4	Cleverly	Thom		1		1		1					1		4		
Needham	146	3	Clough	John				1				1		1			3		
Milton	45	14	Coats	Ezra	1			1		2	4		2				10		
Wrentham	177	34	Cobb	Ebenezer			3	1	1	1	2						8		
Wrentham	180	4	Cobb	Herman		1				1		1					3		
Wrentham	176	11	Cobb	Jeremiah	1	1	1		1	1		1		1			7		
Wrentham	177	8	Cobb	John		1			1	1	1	1					5		
Wrentham	176	26	Cobb	John Junr	2			1					1				4		
Sharon	32	20	Cobb	Jonathan	1	1							1				4		
Wrentham	180	3	Cobb	Joseph				1				1	1				3		
Wrentham	170	13	Cobb	Joseph Junr			1			2		1					4		
Franklin	168	35	Cobb	Luther	1			1		1			1				4		
Wrentham	176	27	Cobb	Otis				1		5			1				7		
Bellingham	159	22	Cobb	Samuel				1					1				2		
Dedham	141	10	Cobbett	Daniel	2			1	1		1		1		1		7	1st Parish	
Dedham	141	6	Cobbett	Phillip	1	1	1		1		1	1		1			7	1st Parish	

TOWN	PG#	LN#	LAST NAME	FIRST NAME	FREE WHITE MALES					FREE WHITE FEMALES					TOTAL ALL OTHER	TOTAL SLAVES	TOTALS	DISTRICT/ TOWNSHIP	NOTES
					under 10	10 to 16	16 to 26	26 to 45	45 and over	under 10	10 to 16	16 to 26	26 to 45	45 and over					
Medway East Parish	91	32	Coffee	Ishmael											5		5		
Braintree	73	29	Coffen	Robert											3		3		
Roxbury	113	6	Colburn	Levi			1						1				2	3rd Parish	
Roxbury	108	34	Colbourn	Thomas				1					1				2		
Dedham	143	21	Colburn	Benjamin	1		2						2				5	2nd Parish	
Dedham	143	26	Colburn	Comforth									1				1	2nd Parish	
Dover	150	7	Colburn	Danforth				1					1				2		
Dedham	143	13	Colburn	Eliphalet	2			1					1	1			5	2nd Parish	
Dedham	143	19	Colburn	Ichabod		1	1		1	1		1	1	1			7	2nd Parish	
Dedham	143	14	Colburn	Isaac				1									1	2nd Parish	
Dedham	143	15	Colburn	Isaac Junr	1			1		5	1		1				9	2nd Parish	
Dedham	143	18	Colburn	Jonathan	2			1					1				4	2nd Parish	
Needham	146	4	Colburn	Joseph			1			1			1				3		
Dedham	141	8	Colburn	Lemuel	1			1		3			1				6	1st Parish	
Dedham	143	23	Colburn	Lewis	1			1		2		1	1				6	2nd Parish	
Dedham	143	20	Colburn	Nathan				1									1	2nd Parish	
Dedham	136	25	Colburn	Nathan Junr				1									1		
Dedham	143	17	Colburn	Phinehas		1		1		1			1				4	2nd Parish	
Dedham	143	24	Colburn	Richard	1		1	2	1	3			1	1			10	2nd Parish	
Dedham	143	22	Colburn	Seth	1			1			1	1					4	2nd Parish	
Dedham	143	25	Colburn	Thomas	1			1		3		1	1				7	2nd Parish	
Dedham	143	16	Colburn	Timothy		1		1	1				1	1			5	2nd Parish	
Medfield	87	3	Cole	Asa	2			1		1			1	1			6		
Wrentham	171	17	Cole	Noah	1	1		1		2			1				6		
Dorchester	53	32	Cole	Wm				1		1				1			3		
Wrentham	178	18	Coleman	Job		1	1	1		1			1	1			6		
Braintree	73	30	Coleman	William											2		2		
Dorchester	53	17	Collier	Saml	3						1		1	1			6		
Roxbury	106	18	Collins	Hannah		1		1		1				1			4		
Milton	44	15	Collum	Baker				1		3			1				5		
Braintree	68	15	Colson	Bolter	1	1			1	3			1				7		
Weymouth	78	40	Colson	Josiah			1	1					1	1			4	South Parish	
Weymouth	78	41	Colson	Thomas 3d		1		1						1			3	South Parish	
Weymouth	75	1	Colson	Thomas Junr		1		1				1					3	North Parish	
Dedham	136	26	Columbia	Leuia	2			1		2			1				6		
Bellingham	159	12	Combs	Jesse	2			1		1			1				5		
Bellingham	158	4	Combs	John	1			1				1	1	1			5		
Foxborough	24	1	Comee	Benjamin			1	1		2	1	1					6		
Foxborough	23	17	Comee	John				1						1			2		
Foxborough	23	18	Comee	John Jr	1	2		1		3	1	1		1			10		
Foxborough	23	19	Comee	Oliver	2	2		1		2			1				8		
Wrentham	171	16	Comstock	Nathan		1	3	1		4		1	1	1			12		
Sharon	32	31	Coney	Ichabod	2	2		1		1		2	1				9		
Roxbury	101	25	Coney	John	2		1	1					1				6		
Sharon	32	29	Coney	Joseph				1						1			2		
Sharon	33	1	Coney	Nathaniel		1		1				1	1	1			5		
Sharon	32	25	Coney	Thomas				1						1			2		
Dedham	141	5	Coney	William		1	2	1						1			5	1st Parish	
Wrentham	171	2	Cook	Aaron	1	1	2	1		1	2	1		1			10		
Bellingham	160	3	Cook	Abner	1			1					1				3		
Wrentham	171	6	Cook	Abner Junr	2			1		2			1				6		
Wrentham	171	8	Cook	Abner Junr			2	1				1	2	1			7		
Bellingham	162	9	Cook	Benjamin	2	1		1		1	2		1				8		
Bellingham	160	7	Cook	Daniel	2			1		1		2	1				7		
Wrentham	174	14	Cook	Daniel			2					1	1				4		
Bellingham	160	6	Cook	David	1	2		1					1				5		
Bellingham	160	2	Cook	Elias	2			1				1	1				5		
Needham	145	26	Cook	Elikiam Junr		1		1					1				3		
Needham	145	25	Cook	Elikim				1					1		1		3		
Bellingham	161	18	Cook	Elisha			1						1				2		
Bellingham	161	10	Cook	Ezekiel				1					1	1			3		
Franklin	169	3	Cook	Jaire	3			1		1	1	1	1				8		
Bellingham	160	8	Cook	John		1		1		1			1				4		
Bellingham	161	5	Cook	Noah				1					1	1			3		
Wrentham	171	1	Cook	Ruben				1		2		1					4		
Dorchester	53	34	Cook	Russell	1	2		1		1	3		1				10		
Quincy	41	8	Cook	Thomas	3	1		1		3			1				9		
Franklin	169	13	Cook	Whipple	2			1		1			1				5'		
Bellingham	162	11	Cook	Zi*	1		1	1		3			1				7		
Bellingham	161	9	Cook	Ziba	2		1	1		1			1				6		
Roxbury	107	10	Cooke	Jonathan	1			1		1			1				4		
Roxbury	109	1	Cookson	Samuel				1	1			1	1	1	1		5	2nd Parish	
Dorchester	53	16	Coolidge	Eliz		1				1			1				3		
Roxbury	102	8	Cooper	Isaac			41			1		1					3		
Braintree	68	9	Copeland	Asa				1		2		1					4		
Milton	45	21	Copeland	Ephrm			1						1				2		
Weymouth	74	36	Copeland	Gershom	1		1	1					1	1			5	North Parish	
Weymouth	74	38	Copeland	Gershom Junr	1	1		1		2			1				6	North Parish	
Milton	45	29	Copeland	Isaac	4			1	1	1	1						9		
Weymouth	75	4	Copeland	John				1					1				2	North Parish	
Weymouth	79	3	Copeland	John				1					1				2	South Parish	

TOWN	PG#	LN#	LAST NAME	FIRST NAME	FREE WHITE MALES					FREE WHITE FEMALES					TOTAL ALL OTHER	TOTAL SLAVES	TOTALS	DISTRICT/ TOWNSHIP	NOTES
					under 10	10 to 16	16 to 26	26 to 45	45 and over	under 10	10 to 16	16 to 26	26 to 45	45 and over					
Quincy	40	37	Copeland	Saml		2		1		3	1		2				9		
Quincy	41	1	Copeland	Sarah							1		1				2		
Braintree	68	8	Copeland	Seth			1		1					1			3		
Walpole	27	33	Copp	Samuel			1	1				1		2			5		
Roxbury	110	4	Corey	Anna						1	2		1				4	2nd Parish	
Roxbury	110	7	Corey	Benjamin			5	2				1	1				9	2nd Parish	
Brookline	114	30	Corey	Elijah	2	1	2	1				2					8		
Roxbury	110	5	Corey	Hannah										1			1	2nd Parish	
Brookline	114	31	Corey	Timothy			3		1	2	2		1				9		
Milton	45	20	Cotton	Joseph											5		5		
Wrentham	177	22	Cowden	John				1					1				2		
Wrentham	181	1	Cowell	Samuel		1	3	1		2		1	1				9		
Weymouth	74	35	Cowen	Howland	3	1		1				2	1				8	North Parish	
Dorchester	54	7	Cox	Capt. Henry	2	2	4	1			1	1					11		
Quincy	41	10	Cox	Saml	2	2		1		1		1	1				8		
Dorchester	53	33	Cox	Samuel		1		1					1				3		
Dorchester	53	11	Coxil	Jno		1	4	1		1		1					8		
Roxbury	101	29	Craft	Abigail	1	1	5				3		1				11		
Roxbury	114	5	Craft	Caleb		1	6		2	1	1		1	1	1		13	3rd Parish	
Roxbury	108	18	Craft	Mary			1						4	1			6		
Roxbury	115	16	Craft	Samuel			2		1			1		1	1		6	3rd Parish	
Wrentham	180	17	Craige	Elijah				1		1			2	1			5		
Wrentham	180	16	Craige	John				1	1					1			3		
Wrentham	172	17	Craige	Moses		1	1			3		1					7		
Quincy	41	12	Cranch	Richa Esq		1			1	2	1	1	1				7		
Canton	130	18	Crane	Abner		1			1					1			3		
Canton	130	28	Crane	Amariah				1			2	1	1				5		
Canton	130	26	Crane	Calvin		1	1	1		1			1				5		
Stoughton	119	14	Crane	Ebenezer			1	1		3			1				6		
Quincy	41	17	Crane	Ebenz	2			1		2			1	1			7		
Canton	130	27	Crane	Elijah	1	2	3	1		2			1	1			11		
Quincy	41	15	Crane	Elisha L.	1		1			1			1				4		
Canton	130	21	Crane	Friend	1		1						1				3		
Canton	130	23	Crane	Henry	1				2			1		1			5		
Dorchester	53	29	Crane	Isaac	1		1	1	1	1			1				6		
Milton	45	24	Crane	Jerem	1			1	1	2		1	2				8		
Dorchester	54	9	Crane	Leml	3		1	1		1			2				8		
Canton	130	22	Crane	Nathan	1	1	2		1	2	2	1		3			13		
Roxbury	105	11	Crane	Nathaniel	1			1					1	1			4		
Canton	130	25	Crane	Peter			1		1	2	1	1	1				7		
Milton	45	18	Crane	Seth			2		1				1	1			5		
Canton	130	19	Crane	Silas				1		2			1				4		
Milton	45	13	Crane	Thom Esq		1	1		1				1	1			5		
Quincy	41	2	Crane	Thomas	1			1			1		1				4		
Milton	45	23	Crane	Vose				1					3	1			5		
Canton	130	24	Crane	William			7	1	1	2		1	2		1		15		
Canton	130	20	Crane	Year*				1					1				2		
Roxbury	111	2	Crawley	Abraham	3			1					2	1			7	2nd Parish	
Cohasset	155	3	Creed	Olive	1								1				2		
Milton	45	16	Crehore	Benj		1	1	1		1				1			5		
Dedham	136	22	Crehore	Elisha	1			1		2		1	1	1			7		
Milton	45	15	Crehore	Jno			2	1		2	1		1				7		
Milton	45	28	Crehore	Jno S.	3		1	1		1			1				7		
Roxbury	101	10	Crehore	Joseph	2	1	1	1		1	1		1				8		
Dorchester	53	30	Crehore	Saml	2	2	3	1		1			1	1			11		
Milton	45	25	Crehore	Thomas	4		5	1		1	1	3	1				16		
Milton	45	27	Crehore	Wm			1		1				3				5		
Milton	45	19	Crehore	Wm B.	1		4		1	2			2				10		
Canton	130	29	Crosman	George	1		1		1	1	1	1	1				7		
Wrentham	171	33	Crowning	Clifford Junior	2			1		2		1					6		
Wrentham	180	34	Cubleau	Charles Maride											1		1		
Wrentham	176	7	Cummings	Benoni	2	1				3			1	1			9		
Roxbury	105	34	Cummins	Cezar											6		6		
Roxbury	107	33	Cummins	Jacob				1			3						4		
Sharon	32	24	Cummins	Joseph	2	2		1	1	1			1	1			9		
Roxbury	107	30	Cummins	William	1	1		1		2			1				6		
Roxbury	107	11	Cuningham	Lois	3						1		1				5		
Roxbury	101	26	Cunningham	William				1	1								2		
Dorchester	54	2	Curen	Jno 3d		1		1	1			2		1			6		
Sharon	32	21	Curtis	Calvin	2			1					1				4		
Quincy	41	18	Curtis	Edwd	3			1		1	1		1	1			8		
Sharon	32	28	Curtis	Francis		1	1	1				1					4		
Roxbury	107	24	Curtis	Hannah		1				3	1	1					6		
Roxbury	102	34	Curtis	Isaac		1		2				1	2				6		
Medway East Parish	92	1	Curtis	Jeremiah	2	1	1	1		2			1				8		
Braintree	68	20	Curtis	Job	1		1		1				1	1			5		
Randolph	124	12	Curtis	Jonathan		1		1						2			4		
Randolph	124	13	Curtis	Jonathan		1		1						2			4		
Roxbury	100	4	Curtis	Joseph			4	1			1	1	1	1			9		
Stoughton	119	17	Curtis	Moses	1		1	1		2	1		1				7		
Quincy	41	14	Curtis	Noah	3		3	1	1				2	1			11		
Sharon	32	18	Curtis	Oliver	3												5		

93

TOWN	PG#	LN#	LAST NAME	FIRST NAME	M under 10	M 10–16	M 16–26	M 26–45	M 45+	F under 10	F 10–16	F 16–26	F 26–45	F 45+	TOTAL ALL OTHER	TOTAL SLAVES	TOTALS	DISTRICT/TOWNSHIP	NOTES
Sharon	32	13	Curtis	Phillip	2	2		1		1			1	1			8		
Medway East Parish	92	2	Curtis	Rachel										1			1		
Braintree	68	10	Curtis	Saml			1	1		1		1	1				5		
Randolph	124	14	Curtis	Samuel		1		1		1			1				4		
Stoughton	119	15	Curtis	Thomas	1	2	1	1				1		1			7		
Stoughton	119	16	Curtis	William Jnr	1	1	2		2	3	1		1				11		
Weymouth	79	1	Cushing	Adam	1	3	1	1		1			1				8	South Parish	
Weymouth	79	4	Cushing	Beale			1			3		1					5	South Parish	
Weymouth	74	39	Cushing	Bela			1			3		1					5	North Parish	
Cohasset	154	34	Cushing	Benjamin			1	1		1			1				4		
Weymouth	74	30	Cushing	Er	2	1	1		1	1		2		1			9	North Parish	
Weymouth	75	3	Cushing	Grace										2			2	North Parish	
Cohasset	152	40	Cushing	Job	1			2		1	1		1	1			7		
Weymouth	74	40	Cushing	John	3			1		1		1					6	North Parish	
Weymouth	75	2	Cushing	Reg* Junr	2		1			1		1					5	North Parish	
Weymouth	74	32	Cushing	Saml	1			1					1				3	North Parish	
Weymouth	74	33	Cushing	Thomas	1	1		1		2			1	1			7	North Parish	
Weymouth	74	34	Cushing	Thomas Junr	3		1	1					1				6	North Parish	
Cohasset	152	14	Cushing	Timothy				1				2		2			5		
Weymouth	74	41	Cushing	Zenas			1										1	North Parish	
Bellingham	162	19	Cushman	Martha	1	1	1			1	1		1				6		
Roxbury	112	19	Cutler	Benjamin Clark	1	1		1		2	1		1	1	1		9	3rd Parish	
Medway West Parish	95	23	Cutler	Calvin	2		1	1		2		1	1				8		
Medway West Parish	95	26	Cutler	Elisha				1		1	1		1				4		
Medway West Parish	95	27	Cutler	Nathaniel	2		1	1		1		1		1			7		
Medfield	87	5	Cutler	Oliver	1			1		1	1		1				5		
Medfield	87	4	Cutler	Simeon				2	1	1		2		1			6		
Medway West Parish	95	24	Cutler	Simon		1		1				2	2				6		
Medway West Parish	95	25	Cutler	Simon Jun			1			1			1				3		
Roxbury	108	24	Cutting	Ephraim		3	2					1					6		
Needham	146	17	Daggett	Asa		1		1					1				3		
Wrentham	179	3	Daggett	Ebenezer	1	1		1		1			1				5		
Roxbury	107	9	Daggett	Jesse	3	2	2	3	1	1	1	1	2				16		
Roxbury	101	18	Dale	John			1		2				1				4		
Dedham	137	5	Damon	David	2		1	1		2			1	1			8		
Dedham	137	4	Damon	Jonathan	1	2	1	1		2	1		2				10		
Weymouth	75	13	Damon	Jonathan	2			1		2	1	1	1				8	North Parish	
Brookline	114	28	Dana	Daniel			2					2					4		
Dedham	137	10	Dana	David	2		2	1	1	1	1	1	1	1			11		
Brookline	114	25	Dana	Jonathan	1		3	1		1	1	1					8		
Needham	146	16	Dana	Luther	1			1					1				3		
Needham	146	14	Daniells	Timothy				1									1		
Medway East Parish	92	5	Daniels	Abigail		1	1					1		1			4		
Franklin	168	5	Daniels	Adams		1	1					1		1			4		
Franklin	167	5	Daniels	Amariah		1		1				1		1			4		
Medway East Parish	92	7	Daniels	Amos			1					1					2		
Medway East Parish	92	10	Daniels	Asa		1		1					1				3		
Medway East Parish	92	11	Daniels	Asa Jun		1		1		1			1				4		
Franklin	168	31	Daniels	David	4		1	1					1	1			8		
Franklin	168	32	Daniels	Eleazer	1		1	1	2				1	1			8		
Foxborough	24	7	Daniels	Francis			1		1	1		2					5		
Franklin	168	30	Daniels	Henry			1					1	1				3		
Medway East Parish	92	13	Daniels	Henry			1						1				2		
Medway East Parish	92	14	Daniels	Henry Jr		1		1		1			1				4		
Foxborough	24	9	Daniels	James	1			1		1			1				4		
Medway East Parish	92	3	Daniels	Jeremiah				1					1				2		
Needham	146	13	Daniels	Jeremiah		1	1			2		1	1				6		
Medway East Parish	92	4	Daniels	Jeremiah Jun	3		1						1				5		
Medway East Parish	92	12	Daniels	Jesse			1			1	2		1				5		
Franklin	166	11	Daniels	Joel		1		1		1			1				4		
Franklin	166	17	Daniels	Joseph	2			2		1		1					6		
Medway East Parish	92	8	Daniels	Joseph				1					1				2		
Needham	146	12	Daniels	Joseph		1	1	1				1	1				5		
Medway East Parish	92	9	Daniels	Lemuel	1	1	1				1	1					5		
Medway East Parish	92	6	Daniels	Moses		2	1			2		1					6		
Franklin	168	4	Daniels	Nathan	1	2		2				1	1	1			8		
Medfield	87	6	Daniels	Noah	1		2	1		1	1		1				7		
Roxbury	109	15	Daniels	Richard	1		1		3				1				6	2nd Parish	
Medway East Parish	92	15	Daniels	Sabin	1		1						1				3		
Franklin	166	18	Daniels	Unity								1	1	1			3		
Franklin	169	14	Darling	Benjamin	1			1		1			1				4		
Bellingham	162	5	Darling	Cornelius			1				1		1				3		
Wrentham	175	7	Darling	Elias	2		1			1			1				5		
Bellingham	161	24	Darling	Jacob			3						1				4		
Bellingham	162	4	Darling	Jerusha	1			1					1				3		
Bellingham	162	7	Darling	Joshua		1	1	1		1	1		1				6		
Bellingham	161	23	Darling	Rachael	1							1					2		
Bellingham	162	8	Darling	Samuel				1					1				2		
Bellingham	160	22	Darling	Samuel 2d	1	1	1	1		2	1		1				8		
Bellingham	162	10	Darling	Seth		2							1				3		
Bellingham	159	21	Darling	Simon	2		1						1				4		
Medway West Parish	95	29	Darling	Abel	2		1			3			1				7		

TOWN	PG#	LN#	LAST NAME	FIRST NAME	FWM under 10	FWM 10 to 16	FWM 16 to 26	FWM 26 to 45	FWM 45 and over	FWF under 10	FWF 10 to 16	FWF 16 to 26	FWF 26 to 45	FWF 45 and over	TOTAL ALL OTHER	TOTAL SLAVES	TOTALS	DISTRICT/ TOWNSHIP	NOTES
Brookline	114	17	Dascom	Daniel		2	1			3			1				7		
Roxbury	111	3	Dascom	John			1			1		1					3	2nd Parish	
Foxborough	24	8	Daufance	Martin		2			1	1			1				5		
Milton	46	8	Davenport	Adam		1	1	1				3					6		
Roxbury	101	6	Davenport	Benjamin		1							1				2		
Dorchester	54	27	Davenport	Dan	2			1		2			1	1			7		
Dorchester	54	18	Davenport	Eben Jr		2						1					3		
Dorchester	54	14	Davenport	Ebenz		1	2	1	1	1			2				8		
Dorchester	54	15	Davenport	Elisha	1	1		1	1	1		3		1			8		
Dorchester	54	26	Davenport	Ephm	4		1			1			1				7		
Dorchester	54	23	Davenport	Isaac	2	1		1		1	1		1				7		
Milton	45	30	Davenport	Isaac		1	3		1	1	1	1	2				10		
Canton	130	30	Davenport	Jesse	2	1		1		1	2		1				8		
Dorchester	54	25	Davenport	Jno			1			1			1				3		
Roxbury	101	1	Davenport	Joseph	1	1		2	1			1	1		1		8		
Milton	45	31	Davenport	Nath		1	2	1	1		1	1		1	1		9		
Dorchester	54	22	Davenport	Saml			1	1		5	2		1				10		
Canton	130	31	Davenport	Samuel		2	1		1	1	1	2	1				9		
Milton	46	3	Davenport	Wm		2			1	1		1		1			6		
Roxbury	110	26	Davis	Aaron		1	1	1	3	2	3		1	1			13	2nd Parish	
Roxbury	106	34	Davis	Aaron Junr		1	2	1		2		1	2	1	1		11		
Roxbury	110	22	Davis	Amasa	1		1	1		1	1		1	1			7	2nd Parish	
Milton	45	32	Davis	Amos			1			1			1				3		
Roxbury	115	15	Davis	Benjamin	2		2	2				1	1				8	3rd Parish	
Roxbury	107	27	Davis	Charles	1		1	1			1	3		1			8		
Brookline	114	23	Davis	Ebenezer	3		3	1		1		1	1		1		11		
Roxbury	113	4	Davis	Ezra	2	1	1	1	1	1	1		1				9	3rd Parish	
Roxbury	114	3	Davis	Increase		1		1		1			1				4	3rd Parish	
Roxbury	101	30	Davis	Isaac			5	1			1	1	1				9		
Roxbury	102	37	Davis	Jacob		1			1				1				3		
Roxbury	109	6	Davis	John		1	2		2	1	1						7	2nd Parish	
Roxbury	102	36	Davis	John 3d	2			1	1	1			1				6		
Roxbury	109	16	Davis	John Junr			1	1				1	1				4	2nd Parish	
Wrentham	180	23	Davis	Jonathan			2	1		4			1				8		
Roxbury	103	34	Davis	Jonathan Doc		1			1	1		1	1				5		
Dedham	137	12	Davis	Joshua G.	1			1				1	1				4		
Milton	46	4	Davis	Lemuel		3			1			1					5		
Roxbury	105	5	Davis	Lemuel	1			1		1		1					4		
Roxbury	107	2	Davis	Moses	1			1		2		1	1		1		7		
Roxbury	111	20	Davis	Nathaniel			1	1		4			1	1			8	2nd Parish	
Roxbury	109	13	Davis	Noah		1	2	2	1		1	3		1			11	2nd Parish	
Quincy	41	21	Davis	Rufus	1			1					1				3		
Roxbury	110	27	Davis	Samuel	1		1	1		1			1				5	2nd Parish	
Roxbury	111	28	Davis	Sarah										2			2	2nd Parish	
Roxbury	105	1	Davis	Stephen	3			1		2			2				8		
Roxbury	107	3	Davis	Susannah		1	1				1	3	1				7		
Roxbury	107	1	Davis	William			1			1							2		
Wrentham	172	25	Day	Benjamin					1				1				2		
Walpole	28	5	Day	Ebenezer			1			3	1		1				6		
Walpole	28	3	Day	Jeremiah		1	1		1		1	1		2			7		
Wrentham	170	11	Day	Jeremiah			2	2				2	2	1			9		
Wrentham	178	8	Day	Jesse			1		1	2	3		1				8		
Needham	146	8	Day	John		1			1	1	1		1	1			6		
Dedham	137	11	Day	Jonathan					1					1			2		
Walpole	28	4	Day	Joseph			1		1		1	1		1			5		
Dover	150	13	Day	Ralph	1			1		3	1		1				7		
Wrentham	173	8	Day	Robert	1	1		1			2		2				7		
Wrentham	172	8	Day	Samuel	3	1	2		1	2	1	1	3				14		
Canton	131	29	de la Goix	Cloude				1					1		1		3		
Dedham	141	12	Dean	Benjamin				1					1				2	1st Parish	
Franklin	165	9	Dean	Ebenezer				1					1				2		
Dedham	141	15	Dean	Francis		1		1				2					4	1st Parish	
Franklin	165	10	Dean	Ichabod		1	2		1			2		1			7		
Dedham	136	27	Dean	John		1	1	1					1				4		
Dedham	141	16	Dean	John	1		1	1		2		1		1			7	1st Parish	
Dedham	137	7	Dean	Joseph		1	1	1			2	1	1				7		
Dedham	143	27	Dean	Joseph	1			1		1			1				4	2nd Parish	
Dover	150	14	Dean	Luke	2	1		1		2			1				7		
Dedham	141	13	Dean	Phinehas E.			1				2		1				4	1st Parish	
Dedham	141	14	Dean	Samuel W.	1			1		1	1		1				5	1st Parish	
Franklin	168	16	Dean	Seth		1	1	1			1		1				5		
Dedham	141	11	Dean	William		1		1					1				3	1st Parish	
Dorchester	54	19	Deluce	Francis				1					1				2		
Dorchester	54	17	Deluce	Jno	2			1		2		1					6		
Needham	146	15	Deming	Charles	2		1			2		1					6		
Needham	146	18	Deming	Rebaca Wid.								1	1				2		
Roxbury	108	11	Dennison	James	1		1	1		1		1					5		
Braintree	68	26	Denton	Ebenezer	3			1		2	1	2	1				10		
Braintree	68	27	Denton	Jacob	2	2		1		1	1		1	2			10		
Weymouth	79	7	Derby	Abner	3			1		1			1				6	South Parish	
Weymouth	79	6	Derby	Jona					1					1			2	South Parish	
Braintree	68	28	Derby	Jonathan			1	1		3	1		1				7		
Dorchester	54	16	Deune	Ebenz		1	4		1			1		1			8		

TOWN	PG#	LN#	LAST NAME	FIRST NAME	FREE WHITE MALES					FREE WHITE FEMALES					TOTAL ALL OTHER	TOTAL SLAVES	TOTALS	DISTRICT/ TOWNSHIP	NOTES
					under 10	10 to 16	16 to 26	26 to 45	45 and over	under 10	10 to 16	16 to 26	26 to 45	45 and over					
Needham	146	5	Devenport	Benjamin		1		1		1			2	1			6		
Needham	146	6	Devenport	Enoch	1			1		1				2			5		
Bellingham	159	5	Dewing	Elijah	2			1		3	1		1				8		
Needham	146	7	Dewing	Henry	1			1	1	1		1	1	1			7		
Needham	146	11	Dewing	Martha									1				1		
Needham	146	10	Dewing	Nathan	1	2	1	1		1	1		1				8		
Needham	146	9	Dewing	Timothy	1	1			1	1	1			1			6		
Walpole	28	7	Dexter	Mary W			2						1	1			4		
Roxbury	101	16	Dexter	Willibar	2			1		1			1	1			6		
Canton	130	32	Dickerman	Enoch	1	1	1	1					2	1			7		
Canton	130	33	Dickerman	Ezra			1			1	2	1	1				6		
Stoughton	119	18	Dickerman	John	3		1		1	2	1		1				9		
Stoughton	119	19	Dickerman	John Junr	1			1		1			2				5		
Roxbury	112	30	Dickerman	Lemuel				1		2	1		1				5	3rd Parish	
Stoughton	119	20	Dickerman	Peter	2			1		2	1		1				7		
Dorchester	54	24	Dickerman	Rebe									2				2		
Roxbury	104	17	Dillaway	Samuel	2		1			1		2					6		
Roxbury	108	31	Dimsdell	Charles	2		1				2		1				6		
Milton	46	2	Dingley	Jno	1		1	1					1				4		
Milton	46	5	Dixon	Robert	3		1			2		1					7		
Cohasset	152	2	Doane	Elisha Esq	1	3	1	2		2		1	3				13		
Dorchester	54	28	Dodge	Richard											5		5		
Dedham	137	6	Doggett	Isaac			1					1					2		
Dedham	137	8	Doggett	Samiel	1		1		1		1			1			5		
Dorchester	54	20	Dolbear	Jno				1	1				1	1			4		
Roxbury	102	25	Domineque				1	1					1				3		First name left blank
Dorchester	54	21	Dorrine	James	1		1			1			1				4		
Roxbury	105	22	Dove	John	1	2		1		1		1		1			7		
Dedham	137	9	Dowes	Edward		1		1		1			1	2			6		
Roxbury	101	8	Downer	Eliphalet Decn		5		1		1			1				8		
Canton	130	34	Downs	Jesse	2	1		1		3	1		1				9		
Canton	130	35	Downs	Oliver	1	1		1		3			1				7		
Roxbury	105	2	Dowse	James	2			1		1			1				5		
Sharon	33	9	Drake	*	1	1	2		1	1		1	1				8		
Sharon	33	6	Drake	Abial	1	1	1		1			2		1			7		
Stoughton	119	26	Drake	David	2	1		1		1	1		1				7		
Stoughton	119	23	Drake	Enoch	2	1		1		3			1				8		
Sharon	33	10	Drake	George	1	1	1					2		1			6		
Sharon	33	13	Drake	Hannah	2		1			2			1	1			7		
Canton	130	36	Drake	John	3		1			2			1				8		
Sharon	33	3	Drake	John			1	1				2		1			5		
Sharon	33	11	Drake	John V		1		1			1			1			4		
Sharon	33	5	Drake	Joseph			1										1		
Stoughton	119	22	Drake	Lemuel		1		1				1	2				5		
Sharon	33	12	Drake	Moses	2	2		1					1				6		
Stoughton	119	21	Drake	Nathan			1		1			1	2				5		
Sharon	33	7	Drake	Nathan	2	1		1		2	1		1				8		
Sharon	33	4	Drake	Nathaniel	1			1		1		1					4		
Sharon	33	8	Drake	Spencer	1			1		1		1					4		
Stoughton	119	24	Drake	William	2	2	1		1	2				2			10		
Stoughton	119	25	Drake	Ziba	2	1		1				2	1				8		
Dedham	143	28	Draper	Daniel	2	1		1					1				5	2nd Parish	
Dedham	137	3	Draper	Desire									1				1		
Roxbury	110	30	Draper	Grace			1						1	1			3	2nd Parish	
Dedham	137	2	Draper	Ira	2	2		1		1		1	2				9		
Dover	150	9	Draper	John & Nolten	1			2	1	1			2	1			8		
Bellingham	162	18	Draper	Jonathan		1	1		1	1			2	1			7		
Dedham	143	29	Draper	Joseph	1	1	2		1	1	1	3	1	1			12	2nd Parish	
Dover	150	12	Draper	Josiah	1			1			1		1	1			5		
Dover	150	15	Draper	Lidia Wid.									1	1			2		
Roxbury	111	12	Draper	Mary									1				1	2nd Parish	
Dover	150	11	Draper	Michel		1	1	1		2			1				6		
Roxbury	111	29	Draper	Moses	1			1		1		1	1				5	2nd Parish	
Roxbury	109	17	Draper	Nathan	1		1	1		3	1	1		1			9	2nd Parish	
Dorchester	54	13	Draper	Phillip	2			1					1	1			5		
Dedham	137	1	Draper	William	2			1		1	1	1	2				8		
Roxbury	110	18	Draper	William		1	2	2		1	1		1				8	2nd Parish	
Dover	150	10	Draper	Jesse	1		1	1		1	1	1					6		
Wrentham	170	8	Druce	Samuel	1	2		4		1		1	1		2		12		
Milton	46	6	Drue	Jno										2			2		
Milton	46	7	Drue	Wm										4			4		
Roxbury	113	25	Duballet	John				1			1				1		3	3rd Parish	
Roxbury	110	19	Dudley	Ebenezer	1		3	1		1			1				7	2nd Parish	
Roxbury	105	14	Dudley	Elijah	1		1			3	1		1				7		
Roxbury	101	32	Dudley	Sarah		1								1			2		
Roxbury	102	7	Duich	Benjamin		1		1			1	2					5		
Canton	130	37	Dunbar	Elijah		1	1		1		2	1		1			7		
Stoughton	119	27	Dunbar	Peter	1	1	3		1				1	1			8		
Stoughton	119	28	Dunbar	Rebecca Wid									1	1			2		
Wrentham	173	27	Dunbar	Simeon	1								1				3		
Canton	130	38	Dunlap	John		1								1			3		

TOWN	PG#	LN#	LAST NAME	FIRST NAME	FREE WHITE MALES under 10	10 to 16	16 to 26	26 to 45	45 and over	FREE WHITE FEMALES under 10	10 to 16	16 to 26	26 to 45	45 and over	TOTAL ALL OTHER	TOTAL SLAVES	TOTALS	DISTRICT/TOWNSHIP	NOTES
Milton	46	1	Dunmore	Arch.	3			1					1				5		
Roxbury	109	7	Dunster	Isaiah		2	2	1					2	1			8	2nd Parish	
Wrentham	172	26	Dunton	Ambrose			1						1				2		
Wrentham	179	27	Dupee	Charles					1					1			2		
Wrentham	179	23	Dupee	Charles Junr	1	1	2	1		3	1		1				10		
Walpole	28	6	Dupee	James	1	1	1	1		1			1	1			7		
Quincy	41	20	Dwelly	Jno		1	3	2			1	2					9		
Quincy	41	22	Dwelly	Leml	2			1					1				4		
Weymouth	75	5	Dyer	Asa		1			1				1	1			4	North Parish	
Weymouth	75	9	Dyer	Asa Junior	1			1		2			1				5	North Parish	
Weymouth	75	6	Dyer	Benjamin				1		2			1	1			5	North Parish	
Weymouth	75	16	Dyer	Jacob	3		1	1		1		1	1		1		9	North Parish	
Weymouth	79	5	Dyer	John	1	1	1	1		1		1	1				7	South Parish	
Weymouth	75	10	Dyer	Joseph				1		1			1	2			5	North Parish	
Braintree	68	24	Dyer	Peter	3	1	2	1		2			1	2			12		
Braintree	68	25	Dyer	Peter 2d			1						2				3		
Weymouth	75	15	Dyer	Releaf			1					1		1			3	North Parish	
Weymouth	75	8	Dyer	Ruth						1			1				2	North Parish	
Weymouth	75	7	Dyer	Samuel	1			1		3	1		1				7	North Parish	
Weymouth	75	11	Dyer	Solomon	1	1		1		1		1	1				6	North Parish	
Weymouth	75	14	Dyer	Susanna								1		1			2	North Parish	
Weymouth	75	12	Dyer	William	2			1					1				4	North Parish	
Dedham	137	23	Eagens	James	2			1		1			1				5		
Dedham	137	17	Eaton	Desire				1									1		
Dedham	137	14	Eaton	Isaac		1	1		1	1		1		1	1		7		
Dedham	137	15	Eaton	John		1		1				1	1				4		
Dedham	137	19	Eaton	Luther	1			1		2	1		1				6		
Dorchester	54	33	Eaton	Pearson		2			2	1	1	1					7		
Dedham	137	18	Eaton	Thomas		1	1	1			1						4		
Needham	146	21	Eaton	William	1			1		2			1	1			6		
Needham	146	20	Edes	Amos		1	1		1	2	1	1	1				8		
Needham	146	19	Edes	John			1		1			1	1	1			5		
Canton	131	1	El*nes	Benjamin			1						1				2		
Walpole	28	14	Ellis	Aaron	1			1		1			1				4		
Dedham	143	38	Ellis	Aaron	1				1					1			3	2nd Parish	
Dorchester	55	1	Ellis	Abel			1	1	1	1	1			1			6		
Medfield	87	14	Ellis	Abigail									1				1		
Medway West Parish	96	1	Ellis	Abijah	2					2		1	1				7		
Dedham	137	16	Ellis	Abner			1	1		2			1				5		
Dedham	143	31	Ellis	Abner		1	2	2		1			1	1			8	2nd Parish	
Medfield	87	7	Ellis	Abner	2			1					1				4		
Medway East Parish	92	22	Ellis	Abner		1		1	1	1		2		1			6		
Brookline	114	7	Ellis	Amasa		1	1	1			1	1	1				5		
Bellingham	160	4	Ellis	Amos		1		1				2		1			5		
Franklin	167	13	Ellis	Daniel	1			1		2			1				5		
Dedham	143	34	Ellis	David			1	1				2		1			5	2nd Parish	
Medway East Parish	92	19	Ellis	Ebenezer			1		1				2	1			5		
Walpole	28	8	Ellis	Eliphalet		1	1	1		2			1				6		
Dedham	143	35	Ellis	George	1			1			1	1	1				5	2nd Parish	
Medfield	87	12	Ellis	George	1	1		1		1	1		1				6		
Medway East Parish	92	16	Ellis	Henry				1				1	1				3		
Medway East Parish	92	17	Ellis	Henry Jun				1		1		1					3		
Dedham	143	33	Ellis	Ichabod			2		1	1	1			1			6	2nd Parish	
Medfield	87	8	Ellis	Jemima			1							1			2		
Dedham	141	22	Ellis	John	1	1	2		1			2	1	1	1		10	1st Parish	
Medway East Parish	92	20	Ellis	John				1				1	1				3		
Walpole	28	9	Ellis	John	1		1		1	2	3	1	1				10		
Walpole	28	11	Ellis	John Jr	1		1						1				3		
Medway East Parish	92	21	Ellis	John Jun		1	1		1	1	1		1				6		
Dedham	141	24	Ellis	John Junr			1			3			1				5	1st Parish	
Dover	150	16	Ellis	Jonathan		2	2			3	3	1					11		
Dedham	137	20	Ellis	Joseph	2			1					1				6		
Franklin	168	17	Ellis	Joseph				1						1			2		
Walpole	28	12	Ellis	Joseph		1		1				1	1	1			5		
Dedham	141	23	Ellis	Lemuel	1			1		1			1				4	1st Parish	
Medway East Parish	92	25	Ellis	Luther				1		2							3		
Walpole	28	10	Ellis	Moses		1	2	1				1					5		
Dedham	143	36	Ellis	Nathan				1		2				1			4	2nd Parish	
Medfield	87	9	Ellis	Nathan				1						1			2		
Medfield	87	10	Ellis	Obed		1							1				2		
Dedham	143	30	Ellis	Oliver	1	1	1		1	1	1		1	1			8	2nd Parish	
Medfield	87	11	Ellis	Oliver			1	1					1	1			4		
Medway West Parish	96	2	Ellis	Oliver		1		1		1			1				4		
Walpole	28	13	Ellis	Oliver	2	1		1		2			1				7		
Dover	150	17	Ellis	Rebecca										3			3		
Franklin	166	27	Ellis	Royal	1			1				1					3		
Medway East Parish	92	18	Ellis	Samuel	1			1		1			1				4		
Medfield	87	13	Ellis	Sarah								2	1				3		
Medway East Parish	92	23	Ellis	Seth					1				1				2		
Medway East Parish	92	24	Ellis	Simeon	1			1		1		1	1				5		
Franklin	168	18	Ellis	Timothy	1	1	2		1	1	1	1	1	1			10		

TOWN	PG#	LN#	LAST NAME	FIRST NAME	FREE WHITE MALES					FREE WHITE FEMALES					TOTAL ALL OTHER	TOTAL SLAVES	TOTALS	DISTRICT/ TOWNSHIP	NOTES
					under 10	10 to 16	16 to 26	26 to 45	45 and over	under 10	10 to 16	16 to 26	26 to 45	45 and over					
Dedham	143	37	Ellis	William		1	2	1	1			1	2	1			9	2nd Parish	
Franklin	163	6	Emmons	Nathaniel		1	2		1	1	1	2		1	1		10		
Canton	131	2	Endicott	Abigail Wid.			2						1	1			4		
Dedham	137	22	Endicut	John			1			1		1	1				4		
Canton	131	3	Estey	John	2		1			1		1	1				6		
Sharon	33	18	Estey	John				1					1				2		
Sharon	33	16	Estey	Lemuel				1		3	1		1				6		
Roxbury	113	26	Estey	Lucy	3					1	1		1	1			7	3rd Parish	
Sharon	33	17	Estey	Samuel	1			2					1	1			5		
Dorchester	54	32	Evans	Jeremh			1	1						1			3		
Canton	131	5	Everenden	Benja	2	1			1	3			1				8		
Canton	131	4	Everenden	Mary Wid.	1								2	1			4		
Roxbury	102	39	Everet	Nathaniel					1	1	1			1			4		
Foxborough	24	10	Everett	Aaron		1	2		1		2	1		1			8		
Dedham	141	20	Everett	Abel				1	1	3	2	1	1				9	1st Parish	
Dedham	141	17	Everett	Asa	1	1			1	1	1		1				6	1st Parish	
Wrentham	177	12	Everett	Daniel	1	1	1	2		3	3	1	1	1			14		
Dedham	141	18	Everett	Ebenezer		2			1			1		2			6	1st Parish	
Dedham	141	19	Everett	Ebenezer Jun	3			1					1				5	1st Parish	
Sharon	33	15	Everett	Edward		1	1		1	1	2	1		1			8		
Dedham	143	32	Everett	Isaac		1			1					2			4	2nd Parish	
Milton	46	9	Everett	Isachar			1					2					3		
Dedham	137	13	Everett	Israel Junr				1				2	2				5		
Dedham	137	21	Everett	Isreal & son Wm	1	2				2	1						6		
Foxborough	24	14	Everett	Jesee			1			2			1				4		
Wrentham	179	2	Everett	John			1				1			1			3		
Foxborough	24	12	Everett	Joseph	2	1		1	1	1			1				7		
Dedham	141	25	Everett	Josiah				1						1			2	1st Parish	
Wrentham	179	19	Everett	Marcus			1			1			1				3		
Foxborough	24	11	Everett	Millie		1	2						1	1			5		
Dorchester	54	30	Everett	Moses	3	2	3	1		1		1	2	1			14		
Dorchester	54	29	Everett	Oliver	2	2	1		1	2			1	1			10		
Sharon	33	14	Everett	Oliver			1		1		2			1			5		
Foxborough	24	13	Everett	Richard		1		1				1	1	1			5		
Dorchester	54	31	Everett	Sam H			1	1				2					4		
Wrentham	177	13	Everett	Timothy		1		1		1	1		1				5		
Dedham	141	21	Everett	William	3	1		1		2	1		1	1			10	1st Parish	
Quincy	41	23	Everson	Wm P.	1			1		1			1				4		
Braintree	69	13	Fagg	Daniel	2	1		1		2	1		2				9		
Dedham	141	34	Fairbank	William	1	1			1		1		1				5	1st Parish	
Dedham	141	31	Fairbanks	Abner	2			1					1				4	1st Parish	
Franklin	165	14	Fairbanks	Asa				1					1	1			3		
Franklin	165	15	Fairbanks	Asa Jun	1	1	1	1		2	2		1				9		
Sharon	33	22	Fairbanks	Benj				1					1				2		
Sharon	33	23	Fairbanks	Benj Jr	1		1			1			1				4		
Dedham	143	40	Fairbanks	Benjamin		1		1		1	2						5	2nd Parish	
Dedham	143	41	Fairbanks	Benjamin Junr	1	1	1			1		1	1				6	2nd Parish	
Dedham	141	32	Fairbanks	David	1	1		1					1				5	1st Parish	
Needham	146	45	Fairbanks	David	1		1			2	1		1				6		
Dedham	137	26	Fairbanks	Ebenezer Jun	1	1	2	1	1	2	1	2	1	1			13		
Wrentham	173	31	Fairbanks	George				1		1	1		1				4		
Dedham	137	29	Fairbanks	Isreal				1									1		
Dedham	137	30	Fairbanks	Isreal Junr	1	1		1		1	1						6		
Wrentham	176	23	Fairbanks	James	1	1		2		1		2	1				8		
Sharon	33	27	Fairbanks	Jerh	1		1			2			1				5		
Bellingham	158	1	Fairbanks	Joseph	2	1	1			1		1	1	1			9		
Wrentham	182	1	Fairbanks	Joshua	1		1					1	1				4		
Wrentham	172	9	Fairbanks	Molly	1					2	1		1				5		
Dedham	137	25	Fairbanks	Oliver				1		2		1	1	1			6		
Dedham	137	38	Fairbanks	Samuel				1						1			2		
Roxbury	111	13	Fairbanks	Samuel	1		1			1			1				4	2nd Parish	
Medway East Parish	92	26	Fairbanks	Silas	1	1		1		3		1	1				8		
Franklin	167	34	Fairbanks	Willard		1	1				1		1				3		
Walpole	28	35	Fales	Aaron	1		1		1	1				1			5		
Walpole	28	26	Fales	Abiather	2	2		1		2	1	1	1				10		
Walpole	28	20	Fales	C Aaron	2	1		1		2	1		1				8		
Needham	146	48	Fales	Daniel	1			1				1					3		
Wrentham	178	33	Fales	David				1						1			2		
Wrentham	178	34	Fales	David Junr	4			2		5	1		2				14		
Walpole	28	24	Fales	Ebenezer	1		1	2	1	1		1	1	2			11		
Dedham	141	33	Fales	Eliphilet	1	1	1	1		1				1			7	1st Parish	
Walpole	28	34	Fales	Jabez	1		1						1				3		
Medway West Parish	96	3	Fales	James	1		1	1					1				4		
Wrentham	179	17	Fales	John				1			1			1			3		
Walpole	28	23	Fales	Joseph		1	1		1	2		1	1	1			8		
Dedham	137	31	Fales	Joshua G.	1	2		1				1	1				6		
Dedham	137	32	Fales	Margrett										1			1		
Walpole	28	17	Fales	Moses				1						1			2		
Walpole	28	18	Fales	Moses Jr	1	1		1		2	1		1				7		
Wrentham	173	28	Fales	Nathan	1		1	1		2		1	1	1			8		

TOWN	PG#	LN#	HEADS OF HOUSEHOLD		FREE WHITE MALES					FREE WHITE FEMALES					TOTAL ALL OTHER	TOTAL SLAVES	TOTALS	DISTRICT/ TOWNSHIP	NOTES
			LAST NAME	FIRST NAME	under 10	10 to 16	16 to 26	26 to 45	45 and over	under 10	10 to 16	16 to 26	26 to 45	45 and over					
Dedham	137	41	Fales	Nehemiah	1	2			1	1	1	2		1			9		
Dedham	137	40	Fales	Samuel		1			1	1	1		2				6		
Walpole	28	28	Fales	Samuel			1	1				1	1				4		
Wrentham	178	22	Fales	Samuel	3	1		1		3			1				9		
Walpole	28	31	Fales	Sarah Wd						1		1	1				3		
Walpole	28	32	Fales	Sewel			1			1		1					3		
Dorchester	55	2	Fales	Stephen	1	1	1		1		1		3				8		
Walpole	28	33	Fales	Stephen		1	1					1	1				4		
Braintree	69	10	Fanon	Asaph		1	1	1		1	1	1	1				7		
Braintree	69	9	Fanon	Azariah				1					1				2		
Braintree	69	7	Fanon	Caleb			1			3			1	1			6		
Braintree	69	8	Fanon	James	2	1	1		1	1			1				7		
Roxbury	115	13	Farewell	Abraham			4					1					5	3rd Parish	
Needham	146	31	Farria	Alexander				1				1	1				3		
Canton	131	7	Farrington	Abel	1		1					1					3		
Wrentham	174	20	Farrington	Daniel				1					1				2		
Wrentham	180	5	Farrington	Elijah	1		1		1	1	1		1				6		
Foxborough	24	20	Farrington	Eliph	3		1	1		1		1					7		
Stoughton	119	29	Farrington	George L.	1	2		1		1		1					6		
Dorchester	55	6	Farrington	Jno	1			1				1					3		
Dorchester	55	7	Farrington	Jno				1					1				2		
Walpole	28	30	Farrington	John			1	1						1			3		
Milton	46	13	Farrington	Jona	2			1		1			1				5		
Canton	131	6	Farrington	Jonathan				1						1			2		
Wrentham	173	14	Farrington	Josiah	2			1		1			1				5		
Wrentham	180	1	Farrington	Lewis	1			1		4			1				7		
Wrentham	174	17	Farrington	Oliver	1		2	1		2		1	1	1			9		
Roxbury	111	14	Farrington	Stephen	1		1	1			1	2	1				7	2nd Parish	
Quincy	41	27	Faxon	Benj	3		1					1					5		
Randolph	124	25	Faxon	Daniel		1				1	1						3		
Randolph	124	24	Faxon	Edward	1		3		1					1			8		
Roxbury	102	5	Faxon	Eleb	2	2	2	1		1		1	1				10		
Roxbury	101	12	Faxon	Nathaniel		2		1					1				4		
Roxbury	104	29	Fedder	James	1			1		2			1				5		
Sharon	33	25	Felch	Isaac	4	1		1		1	2		1				10		
Roxbury	102	1	Fellows	John M.	1			1		2			1				5		
Milton	46	16	Felt	Benjamin	2	2	1		1	1	1	1		1			10		
Wrentham	179	24	Felt	Jonathan		2			1	1	1			1			6		
Needham	146	46	Felton	Daniel		1	1	1					1	1			5		
Roxbury	106	25	Felton	Joshua				1					2	1			4		
Roxbury	106	26	Felton	Nathaniel				1					1	1			3		
Medway West Parish	96	5	Feltt	Moses	1							1					2		
Medway West Parish	96	4	Feltt	William		1		1					2				4		
Milton	46	12	Fenne	Mary	1					1		1					3		
Quincy	41	29	Fenno	Jesse	1			1		2			2				6		
Weymouth	75	18	Fenno	Saml	1			1		1			1				4	North Parish	
Canton	131	9	Fenns	Charles				1		1				1			3		
Canton	131	8	Fenns	Elijah		1	2	1		1	1		1	1			8		
Canton	131	10	Fenns	Sarah Wid.										1			1		
Wrentham	172	30	Ferrigo	James			1	1				2		2			6		
Quincy	41	33	Field	Gilbert		1		1		3			1				6		
Dorchester	55	11	Field	Issac H.	3	2	1	1	1	2		1	1	1			13		
Quincy	41	25	Field	Jackson	2	1	1		1	3	1		1				10		
Quincy	41	28	Field	James incd the P	2		1		1	1			1				6		
Quincy	41	31	Field	Joseph		1			1	2		1	1	1			7		
Quincy	41	24	Field	Lydia Wid.	1	1			1	1			1				5		
Dorchester	55	5	Field	Thomas	1			1		2			1				5		
Dorchester	55	8	Field	Timothy	2	1		1		2	1		1				8		
Needham	146	29	Fisher	Aaron	3	2		1					1				7		
Sharon	33	21	Fisher	Aaron	2	1		2				1	1	1			8		
Canton	131	16	Fisher	Abel	1	1		1		2	1		1				7		
Wrentham	174	23	Fisher	Abijah		1		1			1			1			4		
Franklin	168	10	Fisher	Amos	1		1	1		1			1				5		
Dedham	143	39	Fisher	Asa		1		1				1		1			4	2nd Parish	
Franklin	163	7	Fisher	Asa	1	2		1		1			1				6		
Dedham	144	5	Fisher	Benjamin			3						1				4	2nd Parish	
Franklin	168	8	Fisher	Caleb	2		2	1		1		2	1				9		
Wrentham	180	14	Fisher	Calvin	2	1		1				1					5		
Wrentham	180	19	Fisher	Cyrus	1	1		1		3			1				7		
Walpole	28	19	Fisher	Daniel		2		1						1			4		
Franklin	163	13	Fisher	Daniel C.	1			1		2			1				5		
Walpole	28	21	Fisher	Daniel Jr	2			1		1	1						5		
Sharon	33	24	Fisher	David		1		1				1	1	1			5		
Wrentham	180	31	Fisher	David			1				1	1		1			4		
Wrentham	174	19	Fisher	David Junr	2		4	2			1	1	1				11		
Medfield	87	19	Fisher	Dorcas										1			1		
Dorchester	55	13	Fisher	Ebene			1	1				1	1				4		
Dedham	143	42	Fisher	Ebenezer		1		1					1				3	2nd Parish	
Wrentham	180	33	Fisher	Ebenezer Junr	2	1		1		2			1				7		
Franklin	167	8	Fisher	Eleazer Jun	2		1	1	1	1	1		1				8		
Medway East Parish	92	27	Fisher	Elihu		2				2		2					6		
Canton	131	15	Fisher	Elijah	2		1	1		2		2					8		

TOWN	PG#	LN#	LAST NAME	FIRST NAME	FREE WHITE MALES					FREE WHITE FEMALES					TOTAL ALL OTHER	TOTAL SLAVES	TOTALS	DISTRICT/ TOWNSHIP	NOTES
					under 10	10 to 16	16 to 26	26 to 45	45 and over	under 10	10 to 16	16 to 26	26 to 45	45 and over					
Dedham	141	30	Fisher	Eliphilet				1				1		1			3	1st Parish	
Canton	131	13	Fisher	Experience Wid.								1	1				2		
Canton	131	11	Fisher	Ezekiel			1	1	2		1	1	1				7		
Needham	146	25	Fisher	George	1	1	5	2		1		2	1				13		
Franklin	168	9	Fisher	Hezekiah			1						1				2		
Wrentham	176	9	Fisher	Isaac	1		1	1					1				4		
Franklin	163	11	Fisher	Jabez				3			1		1				5		
Canton	131	14	Fisher	Jabin	3			2		2			1				8		
Sharon	33	26	Fisher	Jacob		1		1					1				3		
Wrentham	180	20	Fisher	Jacob	2		1			1			1				5		
Franklin	166	32	Fisher	Jason	2	2	1			1	1	1	1				9		
Dover	150	18	Fisher	Jesse			1	2			1	3	1				8		
Medway West Parish	96	8	Fisher	Joel		1		2		1		1	1				6		
Dedham	144	1	Fisher	John		1		2			1		1				5	2nd Parish	
Medfield	87	15	Fisher	John			1	1					1	1			4		
Medway West Parish	96	7	Fisher	John	1		1			2			1				5		
Franklin	163	10	Fisher	Joseph	1		1	1		1		1	1				6		
Needham	146	24	Fisher	Joseph			1	1		2	1		1				6		
Dedham	137	33	Fisher	Josiah		1		1					1				3		
Canton	131	12	Fisher	Lemuel		1	2	1		3	1	1	1				10		
Wrentham	173	16	Fisher	Leonard	4		1			1			1				7		
Roxbury	102	28	Fisher	Lever	1		1			1			1				4		
Franklin	165	5	Fisher	Levi		1	1			2	3		1				8		
Franklin	167	15	Fisher	Lewis	2	1	1	1		1		1	1		1		9		
Wrentham	171	24	Fisher	Lewis	4		1			1			1				7		
Medfield	87	17	Fisher	Luther	1		1			2	1		1				6		
Wrentham	180	32	Fisher	Luther	2	1	1			2		1	1				8		
Medfield	87	23	Fisher	Mary		1	1							1			3		
Dover	150	23	Fisher	Mary Wid.										1			1		
Dover	150	24	Fisher	Moses	1		1			1		1					4		
Franklin	168	15	Fisher	Moses	1			1		3		1					6		
Franklin	168	11	Fisher	Nathan				1					1				2		
Dedham	143	43	Fisher	Nathaniel				1				1	1				3	2nd Parish	
Needham	146	26	Fisher	Nathaniel		1		1				2	1				5		
Medfield	87	16	Fisher	Obed		1		1		1	1		1				5		
Dedham	141	29	Fisher	Oliver	1		1	1					1				4	1st Parish	
Dedham	141	26	Fisher	Oliver Junr	3		1					1					5	1st Parish	
Medfield	87	18	Fisher	Paul	1	1	1			2	1		1				7		
Franklin	169	29	Fisher	Peter		1	3	1		1	1	1	1				10		
Wrentham	180	12	Fisher	Pliny	1		1						1				3		
Wrentham	180	11	Fisher	Richard				2			1		1				4		
Wrentham	180	9	Fisher	Richard Junr	2		1	1		1			1				6		
Foxborough	24	19	Fisher	Ruth W							1	2	1				4		
Canton	131	17	Fisher	Samuel		1	1	1				1	1				5		
Dover	150	19	Fisher	Samuel	2	2	1	1				1	1				8		
Needham	146	27	Fisher	Samuel			1	1		1	2		2				7		
Wrentham	176	15	Fisher	Samuel	1	1		1				1	1	1			6		
Walpole	28	27	Fisher	Sarah Wd		1								1			2		
Dedham	137	34	Fisher	Sarah Wid	1		2	1		1	1		2	1			9		
Wrentham	174	13	Fisher	Seth	3								1				4		
Medway West Parish	96	6	Fisher	Simon				1					1				2		
Dedham	137	42	Fisher	Timothy	3		1	2		1	1		2	1			11		
Franklin	164	22	Fisher	Timothy		1		1					2	1			5		
Wrentham	179	14	Fisher	Timothy	2		1			1	1	1					6		
Franklin	164	23	Fisher	Timothy Junr	3	1	1			1	1		1				8		
Wrentham	170	3	Fisher	William	2		1			1	1	1					7		
Needham	146	28	Fisher	Zubia Wid									1				1		
Needham	146	38	Fisk	Enoch	3		1		1	1	3	2	1				12		
Medfield	87	20	Fisk	Jonathan		1	1			1			1				4		
Dover	150	20	Fisk	Nathaniel	1		1					1					3		
Needham	146	39	Fisk	Peter Doct			1										1		
Needham	146	36	Flagg	Elishua	1	1	1			1		2					6		
Needham	146	22	Flagg	Solomon			1										1		
Needham	146	37	Floyd	Phillip	1	1	1	1	1	3	1		1				10		
Foxborough	26	28	Foalhing		7		4	1	3	3	2	2	2				24		First name blank
Walpole	28	16	Foley	Jonathan	2		1	2		1							6		
Wrentham	175	24	Follett	Luther			1			1			1				3		
Roxbury	103	2	Forbes	Elisha		1	2					2	1				6		
Bellingham	159	13	Force	Amariah	2		2						1	1			7		
Wrentham	170	14	Force	Elijah				1			1		1				4		
Weymouth	75	17	Ford	David	1		1			4			1				7	North Parish	
Milton	46	10	Ford	James	1	2	1	4				1	1				10		
Milton	46	15	Ford	Jessaniah	2		1	1		1		2	1		1		9		
Milton	46	11	Ford	Waitstill			1					2	2	1			6		
Bellingham	159	1	Forrester	Ezra		1	1	1		1	1	1	1	2			9		
Foxborough	24	17	Forrist	Amos			1						1				2		
Foxborough	24	16	Forrist	Ebenezer			1			2	1		1				5		
Foxborough	24	15	Forrist	Samuel			1					1					2		
Sharon	33	31	Forrist	Samuel	2	1				2			1				7		
Dorchester	55	4	Foster	Edward	2	2		1		2		2	1				10		
Dorchester	55	9	Foster	Jacob		1	1			2			1				5		

TOWN	PG#	LN#	HEADS OF HOUSEHOLD		FREE WHITE MALES					FREE WHITE FEMALES					TOTAL ALL OTHER	TOTAL SLAVES	TOTALS	DISTRICT/ TOWNSHIP	NOTES
			LAST NAME	FIRST NAME	under 10	10 to 16	16 to 26	26 to 45	45 and over	under 10	10 to 16	16 to 26	26 to 45	45 and over					
Walpole	28	15	Foster	Lois										1			1		
Roxbury	107	34	Foster	Rufus	1			1				1					3		
Dorchester	55	3	Foster	Timothy		1		1					1	1			4		
Quincy	41	32	Fowle	Jacob	3	1	1	1		1		1	1				9		
Roxbury	102	38	Fowle	Jonathan	2			1		3	1		1				8		
Dorchester	55	10	Fowler	Saml	2			1		3	1	2	2	1			12		
Roxbury	106	27	Fox	Ebenezer	1	2		1					1	1			6		
Wrentham	170	10	Francour	John				1		2	1		1		3		8		
Wrentham	175	32	Franklin	John		1	1	1					1				4		
Wrentham	175	33	Franklin	Solomon	3			1		1			1				6		
Foxborough	24	18	Freeman	James			2		1	2	4			1			10		
Bellingham	161	25	Freeman	Nathan					1					1			2		
Franklin	169	9	Freeman	Otis	3	1								1			5		
Roxbury	104	24	Freeman	Phillip	2			1		2		1	1				7		
Roxbury	102	6	Freeman	Samuel				1		4			1				6		
Randolph	124	22	French	Adonijah	1			1		1			1				4		
Braintree	69	4	French	Ahaz	1	1		1		3	1		1				8		
Braintree	68	32	French	Asa			1			1		1					3		
Dedham	144	3	French	Benjamin					1	2	1		1				5	2nd Parish	
Dedham	144	4	French	Benjamin Junr			1			1			1				3	2nd Parish	
Braintree	68	30	French	Caleb		1	1					1	2				5		
Milton	46	14	French	David		2	1						1				4		
Sharon	33	29	French	Edward		1		1		3		2	1				7		
Braintree	69	1	French	Elisha			1				1			1			3		
Braintree	69	2	French	Elisha Junr	3		2	1					1				7		
Randolph	124	23	French	Esther			1						1				2		
Weymouth	79	8	French	Jacob	1	1		1		2			1				6	South Parish	
Braintree	69	6	French	James		1				1		1					3		
Canton	131	20	French	Jason	3			1				1					5		
Stoughton	119	30	French	John				1					1	1			3		
Stoughton	119	32	French	John 2d				1						1			2		
Stoughton	119	31	French	John Junr	1			1		1				1			4		
Randolph	124	15	French	Joshua	2	1	1	1		2			1	1			9		
Braintree	69	5	French	Josiah	1				1			1	1	1			5		
Randolph	124	17	French	Jotham	1	1	2	1		1		1	1	1			9		
Quincy	41	26	French	Lucy Wid.		2								1			3		
Randolph	124	19	French	Luther	2	1	1	1					1	1			7		
Braintree	68	29	French	Moses		1			1	2		1		1			6		
Quincy	41	30	French	Moses	4		1							1			6		
Canton	131	21	French	Nathl				1		1				1			3		
Randolph	124	21	French	Nehemiah		1		1					1	1			4		
Braintree	69	11	French	Saml 2d	1		1	1		1				1			5		
Braintree	69	12	French	Samuel	3		1	1		1				1			7		
Canton	131	19	French	Samuel	1		2	1		3				1			8		
Dedham	144	2	French	Samuel	1	1			1	1	1			1			6	2nd Parish	
Braintree	69	3	French	Silence Wid		1	1			1				1			4		
Braintree	68	31	French	Silvanus				1		1			1				3		
Canton	131	18	French	Thomas	1	1		1	1	1				1			6		
Randolph	124	18	French	Thomas	1	1	4		1	2	1	2		1	1		14		
Needham	146	30	French	Timothy	3			2		1		1	1				8		
Randolph	124	20	French	William	1	2	1	1		1	1			1			8		
Stoughton	119	33	French	William		1	3		2		2	2		2			12		
Randolph	124	16	French	Zenas	2		1	1		2		1	1	1			9		
Cohasset	155	5	Frent	Abel Jr	3			1						1			5		
Walpole	28	29	Frizel	A John		1		1		3			1				6		
Walpole	28	22	Frizel	John				1						1			2		
Wrentham	174	5	Frost	Jonathan		1	1			1		1					4		
Wrentham	174	15	Frost	Moses		1								1			2		
Sharon	33	28	Frost	Peter	1	1	2		1	1			1				7		
Wrentham	178	20	Frost	Samuel	1			1		1	2	3	1				9		
Brookline	114	20	Fryman	Hannah						1		1		1			3		
Dedham	137	35	Fuller	Aaron		1	1		1			1		1			5		
Needham	146	43	Fuller	Abigail Wid									1				1		
Dorchester	55	12	Fuller	Amasa	2	1	1	2				1	1				8		
Needham	146	33	Fuller	Amos		2		1	1				1	1			6		
Medway West Parish	96	9	Fuller	Asa					1					1			2		
Franklin	167	16	Fuller	Augustine	1		1					1		1			4		
Dover	150	21	Fuller	David				1						1			2		
Dover	150	22	Fuller	David Jr	2	1		1		1	1		1				7		
Roxbury	103	6	Fuller	Ebenezer				1		2			1				4		
Sharon	33	19	Fuller	Ebenezer	2			1				1					6		
Needham	146	34	Fuller	Eleazer		1			1				1	2			5		
Dedham	141	27	Fuller	Eliphilet	2	1		1				1	1				6	1st Parish	
Needham	146	47	Fuller	Elishua	2	1		1		1	1		1				7		
Medfield	87	21	Fuller	Elizabeth									1	1			2		
Needham	146	23	Fuller	Enoch			3					1					4		
Needham	147	25	Fuller	Hannah Wid.		1								1			2		
Sharon	33	30	Fuller	Jeremiah	2			1					1	1			5		
Needham	146	44	Fuller	Jerusha Wid		1	1			1				1			4		
Medfield	87	22	Fuller	John	1	1			1	1		2		1			7		
Dedham	141	28	Fuller	Jonathan			1		1	2			2	1			8	1st Parish	
Needham	146	40	Fuller	Jonathan			1			2			1				4		

TOWN	PG#	LN#	LAST NAME	FIRST NAME	FREE WHITE MALES under 10	10 to 16	16 to 26	26 to 45	45 and over	FREE WHITE FEMALES under 10	10 to 16	16 to 26	26 to 45	45 and over	TOTAL ALL OTHER	TOTAL SLAVES	TOTALS	DISTRICT/ TOWNSHIP	NOTES
Canton	131	22	Fuller	Lemuel			1						1				2		
Sharon	33	20	Fuller	Lemuel			1		1				1	1			4		
Dedham	137	36	Fuller	Lidia Wid	1							1	1				3		
Needham	146	35	Fuller	Robert	1			1					1				3		
Walpole	28	25	Fuller	Samuel		1		1					1				3		
Needham	146	32	Fuller	Solomon		1	2	1					1	2			7		
Wrentham	180	2	Fuller	Thomas				1									1		
Needham	146	41	Fuller	William Esq			2	1		2	1		1	1			8		
Needham	146	42	Fuller	William Junr		1		1			1		1				4		
Dedham	137	37	Furrington	Benjamin	1		1		1		1	1		2			7		
Dedham	141	35	Furrington	David	2		1			1		1	1				6	1st Parish	
Dedham	137	39	Furrington	Ebenezer	2			1		1		1	1				6		
Dedham	137	27	Furrington	Ebenezer	1	2		1			1	1	2				8		
Dedham	137	24	Furrington	Nathaniel								1		1			2		
Dedham	137	28	Furrington	Stephen	1		3	1		1			1		1		8		
Roxbury	107	14	Gale	Calven	3			3		1			1				8		
Walpole	29	9	Gallett	Augustin			1	1	2	4	1		2				11		
Roxbury	107	7	Gallope	Richard		1		1		1		1					4		
Sharon	33	32	Gannet	Benjamin			1	2	1				1	1			6		
Sharon	34	3	Gannet	Benjamin J	1			1		1	1	1	1				6		
Sharon	34	1	Gannet	Joseph	1	1		1		5	2	1	1				12		
Roxbury	114	15	Gardner	Caleb		1	2	1		3		2	1	1			11	3rd Parish	
Roxbury	115	5	Gardner	Isaac S. Esq	1	1	2	2			2			2			10	3rd Parish	
Milton	46	19	Gardner	Jno	1			1				2					4		
Needham	146	53	Garfield	Moses		1	2	1	1		1	1	1				8		
Dedham	140	36	Garish	Jack											5		5		
Dorchester	56	3	Garvin	Patrick	1			1				1					3		
Stoughton	119	34	Gay	Aaron		1		1	1				1				4		
Quincy	42	7	Gay	Abigail						2		1	1				4		
Roxbury	110	13	Gay	Amasa	1		1			2		1	1				6	2nd Parish	
Milton	46	26	Gay	Asa	1		1			1	2	1					6		
Dedham	141	44	Gay	Charles	1		1					2					4	1st Parish	
Dedham	144	20	Gay	Colburn		1	1				1						3	2nd Parish	
Dedham	138	7	Gay	Daniel	1			1	1			1	1				5		
Dedham	138	10	Gay	David & Ichabod	1	1		1	1			1	1				6		
Dedham	142	5	Gay	Ebenezer		1		1	1	1			1				5	1st Parish	
Dedham	144	11	Gay	Hannah Wid									2				2	2nd Parish	
Quincy	42	6	Gay	Henry L.	2			1		2	1		1				7		
Stoughton	120	1	Gay	Hezekiah		1	3		1		1	1		2			9		
Dedham	142	1	Gay	Ichabod				1									1	1st Parish	
Dedham	144	6	Gay	Ichabod Dr	1							1	1	2			6	2nd Parish	
Dedham	142	4	Gay	Ichabod Junr	1			1		2			1				5	1st Parish	
Medfield	87	24	Gay	Jason	1			1		1			2				5		
Dedham	141	43	Gay	Jesse	1	1		1			1	1		1			6	1st Parish	
Milton	46	24	Gay	Jno	2			1					1				4		
Roxbury	105	3	Gay	Joel	3		3	2	1	3		3	1				15		
Needham	146	51	Gay	Jonathan		2	1		2			2		2			9		
Needham	146	52	Gay	Jonathan Junr			1			1	1	1					4		
Dedham	144	8	Gay	Joseph	1			2	1		1	2					7	2nd Parish	
Wrentham	178	9	Gay	Joseph	2			1	1	1			1				6		
Dedham	144	9	Gay	Josiah				1					2				3	2nd Parish	
Dedham	144	19	Gay	Lemuel	1		1	1		1		1	1				6	2nd Parish	
Stoughton	120	2	Gay	Lemuel	1	2	1		2				1	3			10		
Dedham	144	16	Gay	Luther	4		2	1					2				9	2nd Parish	
Stoughton	120	4	Gay	Mary Wid		1	1					2	3	1			8		
Dedham	144	10	Gay	Moses		1	1		1					2			5	2nd Parish	
Dedham	142	6	Gay	Nathaniel				1	1		1		1				4	1st Parish	
Stoughton	119	35	Gay	Nathaniel		2	1			1			1				5		
Dedham	142	2	Gay	Oliver	1	1	1						1				4	1st Parish	
Roxbury	111	17	Gay	Samuel			1										1	2nd Parish	
Dedham	144	15	Gay	Seth			1	1				1	1	1			5	2nd Parish	
Sharon	33	35	Gay	Solomon		1	1		1				2	1			6		
Dover	150	27	Gay	Stephen	1			1	4			1					7		
Dedham	144	17	Gay	Thadues	2			1		1	1		1				6	2nd Parish	
Franklin	163	25	Gay	Thomas		2		1					1				4		
Dedham	138	2	Gay	Timothy		3	3	1		2			1				10		
Franklin	163	21	Gay	Timothy	4		1					1					6		
Stoughton	120	3	Gay	Timothy	1	2	1	1		2	1	1					9		
Dedham	142	3	Gay	Wilks	1	1						2					4	1st Parish	
Dedham	144	18	Gay	Willard	1	2	3	1		1		1	2				10	2nd Parish	
Dedham	144	7	Gay	William	1	3	1		1			1	2				9	2nd Parish	
Walpole	29	2	Gay	Benjamin	1			1	1	1	3		1				8		
Walpole	29	4	Gay	Calvin	1			2	1	2		1	1				8		
Walpole	29	11	Gay	Jacob	3	1		1				1					6		
Walpole	29	7	Gay	Joel	1	1	1		2			1					6		
Walpole	29	3	Gay	Joseph		1		1				1					3		
Wrentham	177	6	George	John	1	1			1	1	1		1				6		
Wrentham	177	4	George	Thomas	1	2		1	1	2	2		1				10		
Wrentham	176	4	George	Thomas Junr			1		1		1						3		
Milton	46	23	Gibbins	Jno	3		1		1		1						6		
Roxbury	115	7	Gibbs	Daniel		2			1								3	3rd Parish	
Medway West Parish	96	10	Gibbs	James		1				1							2		

TOWN	PG#	LN#	HEADS OF HOUSEHOLD		FREE WHITE MALES					FREE WHITE FEMALES					TOTAL ALL OTHER	TOTAL SLAVES	TOTALS	DISTRICT/ TOWNSHIP	NOTES
			LAST NAME	FIRST NAME	under 10	10 to 16	16 to 26	26 to 45	45 and over	under 10	10 to 16	16 to 26	26 to 45	45 and over					
Needham	147	3	Gibson	James			1			1		1					3		
Dorchester	55	20	Gibson	Saml	2			1					1				4		
Sharon	34	6	Gilbert	Samuel	1		1						1				3		
Sharon	33	34	Gilbert	Solomon	3	1			1	2			1				8		
Canton	131	23	Gill	Benjamin			2		1		1		1	1			6		
Canton	131	25	Gill	Benjamin Jr	2	1	1	1		1			1				7		
Canton	131	24	Gill	Elijah	1	2	1		1	2		2		1			10		
Milton	46	17	Gill	Jacob	1		1		1	1	1	1		1			7		
Canton	131	27	Gill	John	1		1	1				1					4		
Canton	131	26	Gill	Nathan			1			1			1				3		
Needham	147	2	Gill	William	2			4		1			1				8		
Wrentham	179	7	Gillmore	Andrew			1	1						1			3		
Wrentham	179	10	Gillmore	Andrew Junr	4	2		1		1			1				9		
Wrentham	179	9	Gillmore	Daniel	2			1		4			1				8		
Franklin	164	19	Gillmore	David				1						1			2		
Franklin	164	15	Gillmore	James				1				1		1			3		
Wrentham	176	12	Gillmore	James	3	1		1		1	1		1				8		
Franklin	164	18	Gillmore	James 2nd		1				1		1					3		
Wrentham	182	2	Gillmore	John	1	1		1				1	1				5		
Franklin	164	20	Gillmore	Joseph	1			1					1	1			4		
Wrentham	179	8	Gillmore	Lemuel		1	1	1		2	2	2	1				10		
Franklin	164	16	Gillmore	Robert		2		1		1			1				5		
Franklin	164	12	Gillmore	William	5			1					1				7		
Brookline	114	33	Gilman	Lucy				1					2	1	1		5		
Franklin	164	11	Gilmore	Mary							1			1			2		
Dorchester	55	19	Gleason	James	1			1		2			1				5		
Dorchester	55	15	Glover	Alex 3d	1		1	1		1			1				5		
Dorchester	55	16	Glover	Alex Jr	2			1		1	1			1			6		
Dorchester	55	14	Glover	Alexand	3	1		1				1		1			7		
Quincy	42	4	Glover	Benj W.			1					1					2		
Dedham	144	12	Glover	David			1			1		1					3	2nd Parish	
Quincy	42	3	Glover	Ebenr				1		1				1			3		
Dorchester	55	24	Glover	Ebenz				1		1	1		1	1			5		
Dorchester	55	23	Glover	Edward		1		2		2			1	1			7		
Quincy	42	1	Glover	Elisha	1		3	1	1				2	1			9		
Dorchester	56	1	Glover	Enoch			1	1	1					1			4		
Dorchester	56	2	Glover	Enoch Jr			1	1						1			3		
Dedham	144	13	Glover	Henry									1	2			3	2nd Parish	
Needham	147	1	Glover	Henry	1	1		1		4			1				8		
Dorchester	55	22	Glover	Josh				1		2		1					4		
Quincy	42	2	Glover	Josiah				1						1			2		
Quincy	41	35	Glover	Nathl		1		1		1		1					4		
Dorchester	55	26	Glover	Saml	1	1		1					1				4		
Dorchester	55	25	Glover	Saml Jr				2		1			1				4		
Sharon	34	4	Glover	Samuel	2			1		2	1	1	1				8		
Stoughton	120	6	Glover	Samuel	1			1				1	1				4		
Stoughton	120	5	Glover	Thomas		1	1		1					1			4		
Quincy	42	5	Glover	Wm			4		1	1			1				7		
Dorchester	55	18	Glover	Edw	4			1	5	1	1		2	4			18		including the poor of the town
Roxbury	107	35	Goddard	Ebenezer	1				1	2	1		1	1			7		
Roxbury	108	19	Goddard	Ebenezer Junr			1			1		1					3		
Roxbury	115	12	Goddard	John				1					1	1			3	3rd Parish	
Roxbury	115	14	Goddard	Joseph	2	1	2	2		3	2	1	1				16	3rd Parish	
Stoughton	120	7	Goldthwait	Jacob	1			1						1			3		
Stoughton	120	8	Goldthwait	Jacob Jr	1			1					1				3		
Stoughton	120	10	Goldthwait	Lot				1		1				1			3		
Stoughton	120	9	Goldthwait	Timothy	4	1		1		1				1			8		
Canton	131	28	Gooch	Samuel	3			1		2	1		1				8		
Roxbury	110	29	Goodnough	Ephraim	2		2			1		2					7	2nd Parish	
Dover	150	25	Gooking	Daniel	1	1		1						1			4		
Roxbury	111	9	Gookins	Edmund				1						1			2	2nd Parish	
Roxbury	107	16	Gore	Joseph	2			1		1	1	1		1			7		
Roxbury	106	17	Gore	Joshua				1		1		2	1				5		
Roxbury	100	3	Gore	Paul	2		4	1				1	1				11		
Roxbury	105	25	Gore	Samuel		1		1	1					1			4		
Roxbury	105	26	Gore	Samuel Junr				1		1		2					4		
Dedham	140	34	Gorham	David				1									1		
Dedham	138	1	Gorthorp	William						1							1		
Dorchester	55	21	Gould	Alzah	3		1	1	2		3	1	1	1			13		
Wrentham	174	16	Gould	Cyrus	1	1	3	1		1		2	1	1			11		
Wrentham	174	2	Gould	Daniel				1					1	1			3		
Medway East Parish	92	29	Gould	Esther										1			1		
Sharon	34	2	Gould	Ezra	1	1			1		1			1			5		
Dedham	138	8	Gould	George Maj		1	1	1						2			5		
Roxbury	101	31	Gould	Jacob			3	1		2			1	1			8		
Roxbury	112	8	Gould	John	2		1			1		1					5	3rd Parish	
Dedham	144	21	Gould	John Doc		1		1			1	2	1	1			7	2nd Parish	
Medway East Parish	92	28	Gould	Joshua				1				2		1			4		
Sharon	34	5	Gould	Kezia									1	2			3		
Walpole	29	16	Gould	Lincon		1		1					1				3		
Sharon	34	7	Gould	Nathaniel	1	1	1	2		1			1				7		
Roxbury	103	19	Gould	Otis		1	2	1		1	1		2				8		

TOWN	PG#	LN#	HEADS OF HOUSEHOLD LAST NAME	FIRST NAME	FREE WHITE MALES under 10	10 to 16	16 to 26	26 to 45	45 and over	FREE WHITE FEMALES under 10	10 to 16	16 to 26	26 to 45	45 and over	TOTAL ALL OTHER	TOTAL SLAVES	TOTALS	DISTRICT/ TOWNSHIP	NOTES
Franklin	169	23	Gould	Peter A.	2			1					1		1		5		
Milton	46	30	Gould	Sarah										1			1		
Sharon	33	33	Gould	Simon	1			1		2		1					5		
Wrentham	176	17	Gould	Whiting			1			2			1	1			5		
Dedham	144	14	Graham	William				1					1				2	2nd Parish	
Wrentham	172	6	Grant	Benjamin				1					1	1			3		
Wrentham	171	11	Grant	Beriah	1			1		2			1				5		
Wrentham	172	7	Grant	David	2	1		1					1				5		
Wrentham	180	13	Grant	Ebenezer				1	1	1	2	1		1			7		
Wrentham	172	5	Grant	Joseph			1	1		1			1				4		
Medway West Parish	96	13	Grant	Joshua	2			1		1	1	1					6		
Wrentham	172	2	Grant	Joshua	3		2	2		1	1		2				11		
Wrentham	174	28	Grant	Justus	1		1						1				3		
Wrentham	172	4	Grant	Luther	1		1						1				3		
Wrentham	172	3	Grant	Moses		1	2		2			2		2			9		
Wrentham	171	12	Grant	Rhodes			1							2			3		
Dover	150	26	Gray	Benjamin		2	1		1	1		1		1			7		
Roxbury	113	10	Gray	Thomas Revd	1	1		1		1		1	2	1			8	3rd Parish	
Walpole	29	15	Grayham	William	1		1	1		1		1					5		
Medway West Parish	96	11	Green	John	1		1			1			1	1			5		
Roxbury	102	29	Green	John	2	1		1		1	1		1				7		
Medway West Parish	96	12	Green	Luther	2			1		1			1				5		
Medfield	87	25	Green	Warwick											7		7		
Dorchester	55	17	Greenleaf	Benj				1					1				2		
Quincy	41	34	Greenleaf	Danl			2					1	1				4		
Roxbury	112	33	Greenough	David	1		2	1	2		2	1		1	1		11	3rd Parish	
Dedham	138	3	Greenwood	Isaac				1			1	1	1				4		
Needham	146	50	Greenwood	Samuel	4	1		1		1		1	1				9		
Roxbury	110	6	Griggs	James	2	1		2				1		3			9	2nd Parish	
Brookline	115	2	Griggs	Joshua	1	1	1	2		3		2	1				11		
Brookline	114	37	Griggs	Samuel	3	2	1	1		2		2	1				11		
Roxbury	111	6	Griggs	Thomas		1		1			1		1				4	2nd Parish	
Roxbury	110	21	Griggs	William	1	1		1		2			1	1			7	2nd Parish	
Walpole	29	13	Griggs	William	1			1					1				3		
Medway East Parish	92	30	Grout	Nathan	1	1		1		1	1		1				6		
Foxborough	24	23	Grover	Amasa	2	2		1					1	1			8		
Dedham	142	7	Grover	George W.	1			1		1			1				4	1st Parish	
Foxborough	24	22	Grover	Jabez		1		1		1			1				4		
Milton	46	20	Grover	Nathl	1			1					1				3		
Milton	46	18	Grover	Sam K		2	3	1	1	1		1	2	1			11		
Milton	46	21	Grover	Thomas				1					1				2		
Walpole	29	10	Guild	Aaron				1					1				2		
Dedham	141	37	Guild	Aaron Junr	1	1		1					1				4	1st Parish	
Dedham	141	36	Guild	Aaron Majr	1			1					1				3	1st Parish	
Dedham	141	40	Guild	Abner	2	1	1	1		2	1	1	1				10	1st Parish	
Dedham	138	5	Guild	Amasa	2		2	1		1			1				7		
Wrentham	178	16	Guild	Benjamin				1						2			3		
Dedham	138	6	Guild	Calvin			3			1	1						5		
Franklin	164	25	Guild	Ebenezer	1		2	1		2		2	1				9		
Wrentham	176	10	Guild	Ebenezer	1	1		1		2		2	1				8		
Foxborough	24	21	Guild	Elias	1	2	1	1		1		1	1				8		
Stoughton	120	11	Guild	Elmer				1		2	1		1				5		
Walpole	29	6	Guild	Hathannah	1			1			1	1					4		
Walpole	29	8	Guild	Herman				1									1		
Stoughton	120	12	Guild	Israel	2	1		1					1				5		
Dedham	141	38	Guild	Jacob		1		1			1		1				4	1st Parish	
Walpole	29	14	Guild	Jacob	2			1					1				4		
Dedham	141	42	Guild	Joel	4		1	1		1			1				8	1st Parish	
Dedham	138	9	Guild	John		1	1	1		1			1				5		
Wrentham	178	17	Guild	John	1			1		1	1	1	1				7		
Walpole	29	12	Guild	Joseph	1		1	1			1		1				5		
Wrentham	178	2	Guild	Joseph		1		1				3		1			6		
Walpole	28	37	Guild	Joseph Jr	2			1					1				4		
Wrentham	178	11	Guild	Lansen	1			1					1				3		
Dedham	141	41	Guild	Moses	3	1	1	1		2		1	1				10	1st Parish	
Dedham	141	39	Guild	Oliver		1		1		1		1					4	1st Parish	
Walpole	29	5	Guild	Rebeckah	1						1	1		1			4		
Wrentham	178	10	Guild	Richard				1					1				2		
Wrentham	178	12	Guild	Richard Junr	1			1		1			1				4		
Dedham	138	4	Guild	Ruben			4	1		2		1	1	1			10		
Franklin	164	24	Guild	Samuel	1	1	1	1		2	2		1	1			10		
Walpole	28	36	Guild	Samuel				1					1				2		
Wrentham	175	30	Guild	Samuel	2	1	1	1			1		1	1			8		
Walpole	29	1	Guild	Samuel Jr	3			1		1			1				6		
Dedham	138	11	Guild	Sarah Wid		1						1		2			4		
Wrentham	180	15	Guild	William	1			1		1		1					4		
Milton	46	29	Gulliver	Cornelius			2	1			2			1			6		
Milton	46	27	Gulliver	Jno				1									1		
Milton	46	28	Gulliver	Leml			1					1					2		
Milton	46	22	Gulliver	Nathl								1		1			2		

TOWN	PG#	LN#	LAST NAME	FIRST NAME	FREE WHITE MALES					FREE WHITE FEMALES					TOTAL ALL OTHER	TOTAL SLAVES	TOTALS	DISTRICT/ TOWNSHIP	NOTES
					under 10	10 to 16	16 to 26	26 to 45	45 and over	under 10	10 to 16	16 to 26	26 to 45	45 and over					
Milton	46	25	Gulliver	Rufus	2			1		2			1				6		
Dorchester	55	27	Gurley	Jno	2		1			1		1	2				7		
Needham	146	49	Gurnet	Susana	1							1	2				4		
Randolph	124	26	Gurney	Giles			1					1					2		
Dover	149	25	Guy	Bethsheba									1				1		
Dover	150	28	Guy	Jonathan				1		1							2		
Dedham	138	23	Hadley	Simon	1			1		1			1				4		
Wrentham	177	24	Hall	Abijah	1			1		1		1					4		
Wrentham	171	28	Hall	Amariah	1	2		1		3		1					8		
Bellingham	161	14	Hall	Asa	1			1					1				3		
Quincy	42	8	Hall	Edward	2			1		1		1					5		
Dorchester	57	13	Hall	Hopestill				1				1	1				3		
Cohasset	154	8	Hall	James	3	3		1		1		1	1				10		
Dorchester	57	14	Hall	Jno	2	1		1		1		1	1				7		
Dorchester	57	15	Hall	Jno			1					1					2		
Quincy	42	10	Hall	Jno		1	2	1				2	1				7		
Walpole	29	24	Hall	John	1	1		1		1		1	1				6		
Wrentham	181	2	Hall	John			1	2		1		1	2				7		
Wrentham	181	3	Hall	John Junr	1	1	1	1				2					6		
Walpole	29	25	Hall	Josiah	3	2		1		1			1				8		
Dorchester	57	12	Hall	Richard		1	1	1				2	2				7		
Dorchester	56	17	Hall	Solomon	4		1			2			1				8		
Medfield	87	26	Hamant	Asa				1	1								3		
Medfield	87	27	Hamant	Asa Jun				1									1		
Medfield	87	28	Hamant	Francis		2		1						1			4		
Medfield	87	29	Hamant	Timothy				1				1					2		
Medway East Parish	93	9	Hamant	Timothy				1	1					1			3		
Roxbury	114	17	Hammon	Jonathan	1	2	1	1		2	1		1				9	3rd Parish	
Roxbury	113	13	Hammond	Mary						2			1				3	3rd Parish	
Needham	147	6	Hamond	Peter			1										1		
Roxbury	101	3	Hancock	Belcher	3	1	1		1	1		1	2				10		
Wrentham	174	32	Hancock	Dolly		1	1	1				1	1				5		
Wrentham	177	11	Hancock	Henry		1		1	1	1		1	1				6		
Wrentham	177	10	Hancock	Mathew								1	1				2		
Walpole	29	17	Hanes	Benjamin		2	2	1		1	1		1				8		
Dorchester	57	3	Hanes	Edward				1		2			1				4		
Roxbury	114	14	Harbach	Thomas	2	1	1	1		1			1				7	3rd Parish	
Dover	150	32	Harden	Elias		1	1		1	1	2		1				7		
Medfield	88	3	Harding	Abraham	2			1			1		2				6		
Medway East Parish	93	7	Harding	Abraham		1	2	1		1	1		1				7		
Franklin	164	6	Harding	Asa	1		1	1		1		1					5		
Medway East Parish	93	8	Harding	Asa	2	1		1		2		1					7		
Franklin	164	5	Harding	Elisha		1			1	1			1				4		
Franklin	166	1	Harding	James	1			1		2		1					5		
Weymouth	75	25	Harding	James	3			1		1		1	1				7	North Parish	
Medway West Parish	96	14	Harding	Job	3	1		1		1			1				7		
Medfield	88	1	Harding	Keziah								1		1			2		
Medfield	88	2	Harding	Moses B.		1		1		1		1	1				5		
Medfield	88	4	Harding	Nathan		1	1	1				1	1				5		
Medway East Parish	93	1	Harding	Stephen	3	1	1	1		1		1					8		
Medway East Parish	93	2	Harding	Theodore			1	1				1		1			4		
Medway East Parish	93	3	Harding	Theophilus	1		1					1					3		
Medway East Parish	93	6	Harding	Thomas	2	2		1		2	1		2				10		
Medway East Parish	93	5	Harding	Timothy	1	1		1		2		1					6		
Medway East Parish	93	4	Harding	Uriah		1		1		1	1		1				5		
Milton	47	1	Harling	Thomas		1		1					2				4		
Sharon	34	20	Harlon	Ebenezer	2	2		1		1			1				7		
Sharon	34	12	Harlon	N Mathew	1		1	1		2	2		2				9		
Sharon	34	14	Harlon	Ruth Wd								1	1				2		
Sharon	34	24	Harlow	Elizabeth Wd								1	1				2		
Braintree	70	15	Harmon	Ebenz	1			1					1				3		
Dedham	142	8	Harmon	Michel				1		1			1				3	1st Parish	
Braintree	70	14	Harmon	William				1					1				2		
Roxbury	101	34	Harriman	Moses	1		2	1		1	1	1					7		
Stoughton	120	13	Harris	Eliza Wid	1			1		2		1	1	1			7		
Brookline	114	9	Harris	Elizabeth								1		1			2		
Dedham	138	15	Harris	Enoch	1	1	4	1		2			2				11		
Roxbury	110	32	Harris	Jamima									1				1	2nd Parish	
Brookline	114	8	Harris	John		2	2	1		1		2	2	1			11		
Walpole	29	26	Harris	Nicholas				1									1		
Roxbury	102	2	Harris	Noah				1		1			1				3		
Dorchester	56	4	Harris	Thad. M	2	2	1	1		1	1	1	1				10		
Needham	147	10	Harris	Michel		1	1		1	3		2		1			9		
Needham	147	5	Harrison	Joseph	1	1	1			2	1	1	1				9		
Brookline	115	1	Hart	Jacob			3						1				4		
Medfield	88	5	Harthorn	Moses	4		1	1		2	1		1				10		
Wrentham	172	10	Hartshom	Silas	1			1			1		1				4		
Walpole	29	20	Hartshorn	Asa	1	1		1		1			3				7		
Franklin	163	9	Hartshorn	David	1		2	1		1		1	1				7		
Walpole	29	22	Hartshorn	Ebenezer	1			1		2		2					6		
Walpole	29	30	Hartshorn	Fisher	1		1		1	2		1	1				8		

TOWN	PG#	LN#	HEADS OF HOUSEHOLD		FREE WHITE MALES					FREE WHITE FEMALES					TOTAL ALL OTHER	TOTAL SLAVES	TOTALS	DISTRICT/ TOWNSHIP	NOTES
			LAST NAME	FIRST NAME	under 10	10 to 16	16 to 26	26 to 45	45 and over	under 10	10 to 16	16 to 26	26 to 45	45 and over					
Foxborough	24	27	Hartshorn	Jeremiah	1	2			1	1	1	1	1				8		
Foxborough	24	28	Hartshorn	Jesee	1			1		1		2	1				6		
Walpole	29	28	Hartshorn	John				1			1		1				3		
Walpole	29	23	Hartshorn	Lewis	3			1		1			1				6		
Dover	150	30	Hartshorn	Obed	1	1		1									3		
Walpole	29	19	Hartshorn	Richard		1	1		1			2		1			6		
Walpole	29	21	Hartshorn	Samuel	1	3			1	1		1	1				8		
Walpole	29	18	Hartshorn	Timothy				1				1		1			3		
Canton	131	31	Hartwell	David	2			1	1			1	1	1			7		
Canton	131	30	Hartwell	John				1						1			2		
Quincy	42	9	Hartwich	Adam			1			2		1					4		
Quincy	42	17	Hartwich	Fred	2		2	1		1	1	1					8		
Quincy	42	11	Hartwich	Peter	2		2	1		3		1					9		
Quincy	42	20	Hartwick	Charles	1			1		2		1					5		
Brookline	114	2	Harvey	Jacob				1					1				2		
Roxbury	112	18	Hatch	Crowell	1		2		1	3	1			1			9		3rd Parish
Wrentham	175	8	Hathaway	Peleg			1			1			1				3		
Wrentham	180	22	Haven	Elias				1			3	2	1	1			8		
Dedham	138	12	Haven	Jason Rev			1						1	1			4		
Dover	150	29	Haven	Joseph & Noah		1		1	1		1		1				5		
Dedham	138	13	Haven	Samuel Esq			1			1	1	1	1				5		
Franklin	165	3	Hawes	Amos	1	1	1	1			1		2				7		
Roxbury	102	19	Hawes	Benjamin			1	2					1				4		
Wrentham	174	22	Hawes	Benjamin		1		1	1			1		1	1		6		
Wrentham	171	19	Hawes	David	1			1	1	1	1	1		1			7		
Wrentham	178	7	Hawes	Ebenezer	1			1	1	1		1	1	1			7		
Wrentham	171	20	Hawes	Elisha	2			1		3		1	1				8		
Needham	147	4	Hawes	Esther									1				1		
Wrentham	178	15	Hawes	George	1		2	1		1		1					7		
Wrentham	181	6	Hawes	James	4			1		1		1	1				8		
Dorchester	57	7	Hawes	Jesse	1		1					1					3		
Dorchester	56	29	Hawes	Jno				1					1				2		
Medway West Parish	96	15	Hawes	Joel	2	1	1	1		2	1	1	1				10		
Weymouth	79	21	Hawes	John	1			1	1	1	1			1			5		South Parish
Wrentham	177	28	Hawes	John	1	2	1	1					1				6		
Weymouth	79	22	Hawes	John Junior	1	1	1	1		1		1					6		South Parish
Dorchester	57	17	Hawes	Joseph		1		1			1	1	2	1			7		
Franklin	165	2	Hawes	Joseph				1			1		1				3		
Needham	147	8	Hawes	Joseph		1		1		1			1				4		
Weymouth	79	23	Hawes	Joseph			1			2		1					4		South Parish
Franklin	164	29	Hawes	Josiah				1				1					2		
Franklin	164	30	Hawes	Levi		1		1		2		1	1				6		
Roxbury	106	9	Hawes	Mary	2	1				1	1	1					6		
Wrentham	178	13	Hawes	Nathan		1	1	2	1	1	1	1					8		
Dorchester	57	6	Hawes	Saml		1						1					2		
Needham	147	12	Hawes	Samuel	1		1			2		1					5		
Dedham	138	20	Hawes	Shuba Wid								1		2			3		
Wrentham	174	6	Hawes	William	1		1	1		3		4	1				11		
Franklin	164	4	Hawkins	Sarah						1				1			2		
Canton	131	33	Hawse	Jonathan	1	3			1	2				1			8		
Stoughton	120	14	Hawse	Levi				1		2	1	2		1			9		
Canton	131	32	Hawse	Sarah Wid.	4	1					1	1	1	1			9		
Quincy	42	13	Hayden	Abel	1			1		2			1				5		
Quincy	42	14	Hayden	Abel	1			1		2			1				5		
Roxbury	104	26	Hayden	Abner		1		1		1			1				4		
Braintree	70	21	Hayden	Amin*					1	4	1		1				7		
Braintree	69	35	Hayden	Benj Junr	2		1	1		2			1	1			8		
Quincy	42	21	Hayden	Caleb	2		1	2		1			2				8		
Quincy	42	23	Hayden	Caleb Jr	2	1		1		1			1				6		
Braintree	70	17	Hayden	Clement	1				1	1				1			4		
Stoughton	120	15	Hayden	Ebenezer	1	1		1	1	1	2		1	1			9		
Braintree	70	30	Hayden	Ebenz	2			1						1			4		
Braintree	69	34	Hayden	Eli	4		1	1		1		1	1				9		
Quincy	42	22	Hayden	Elisha	2	1							1				4		
Cohasset	153	37	Hayden	Ezra		1		1		1			1				4		
Wrentham	175	14	Hayden	Isaac	1			1		1		1					4		
Wrentham	175	13	Hayden	Jerusha			2						1				3		
Braintree	70	22	Hayden	Job			1			2		1					4		
Braintree	70	19	Hayden	Levi	1	2		1		2				1			7		
Stoughton	120	16	Hayden	Moses		1			1			1	1				4		
Braintree	70	26	Hayden	Nathl	1			1		2			1				5		
Quincy	42	24	Hayden	Nathl	4	1		1					1				7		
Braintree	70	16	Hayden	Nehe		2		1	1				1				5		
Braintree	70	24	Hayden	Nehel	2			1		1	2		1				7		
Braintree	70	20	Hayden	Oliver	2			1		1			1				5		
Braintree	70	2	Hayden	Robert		1	4	1	1			1	1	1			10		
Braintree	70	27	Hayden	Stephen	1			1				1					3		
Randolph	124	27	Hayden	Stephen	1		1					1					3		
Braintree	69	36	Hayden	Thomas			1			4	1	1					7		
Randolph	124	28	Hayden	Ziba			1			2		2	1				6		
Dover	150	31	Hayns	Aaron	1	4		4		2			1	1			13		

TOWN	PG#	LN#	LAST NAME	FIRST NAME	FREE WHITE MALES under 10	10 to 16	16 to 26	26 to 45	45 and over	FREE WHITE FEMALES under 10	10 to 16	16 to 26	26 to 45	45 and over	TOTAL ALL OTHER	TOTAL SLAVES	TOTALS	DISTRICT/ TOWNSHIP	NOTES
Braintree	69	14	Hayward	Daniel		1			1		1			1			4		
Braintree	69	17	Hayward	David P	1	1		1	1	1		1		1			7		
Braintree	69	18	Hayward	Debh Wid	2		1						1	1			5		
Braintree	69	15	Hayward	John	3	2		1		1	1	1	1				10		
Braintree	69	16	Hayward	Nathl	2			1	1	1			1				6		
Canton	131	34	Hayward	Rachel			1							1			2		
Medway West Parish	96	16	Haywood	Nahum	1		1	1					1				4		
Roxbury	105	33	Healey	Sarah	2		2			2	1		1				8		
Dorchester	57	16	Hearsy	Amos	1			1					2	1			5		
Dorchester	57	8	Hearsy	Bela	2			1		1			1				5		
Dorchester	56	11	Hearsy	Stephen	1			1		1			1				4		
Dorchester	56	18	Hearsy	Zerub			1						1				2		
Bellingham	158	9	Heath	Daniel	1			1					1	1			4		
Roxbury	115	4	Heath	Ebenezer	1		2	1		3	1	1	1				10	3rd Parish	
Roxbury	115	3	Heath	John		1			1				2	3	1		8	3rd Parish	
Roxbury	101	23	Heath	Joseph	1	1		1					1	1			5		
Roxbury	101	27	Heath	Peleg			2	1		1	2		1				7		
Quincy	42	18	Heath	Saml W.		1				2	1		1				5		
Roxbury	103	13	Heath	Samuel		1	2	1					1				5		
Roxbury	113	22	Heath	Samuel		1	2			1	1	2	1				8	3rd Parish	
Roxbury	103	7	Heath	William Esq Honble	1	2		1					1	1	1		7		
Roxbury	103	8	Heath	William Junr	2			1		1			1				5		
Wrentham	178	1	Heaton	Nathaniel			1	1					1	1			4		
Franklin	169	17	Heaton	Samuel	2			1	2	2	2		1	1			9		
Roxbury	102	16	Hendrake	David	1			1		1			1				4		
Dorchester	57	11	Henly	Wm			1	1		2	1		1				6		
Canton	131	36	Henry	Joseph				1		2	1			1			5		
Foxborough	24	24	Henry	Joseph		1	2	1		1				1			6		
Foxborough	24	29	Henry	Joseph V			1			2				1			4		
Stoughton	120	17	Henry	Michael		1		1		1				1			4		
Canton	131	35	Henry	William		1		1				1	1	1			5		
Dedham	138	14	Hensey	Elijah		1				1	1	1	1				5		
Milton	47	14	Henshaw	Han	1			1				1	1	1			5		
Roxbury	111	16	Henshaw	John	2			1		3			1				7	2nd Parish	
Cohasset	153	23	Herd	George	2			1	1				1				5		
Brookline	114	11	Herren	Jesse		1		1		1			1				4		
Dedham	144	22	Herring	Peletiah	1			1		1				1			4	2nd Parish	
Franklin	169	16	Herrington	James	2			1		2	2		1				8		
Dorchester	57	1	Herrington	Rus.	3		1	1					1	1			7		
Roxbury	108	21	Hersey	Zerubable		1				1		1					3		
Sharon	34	8	Hervins	Amasa	4			1		1			1				7		
Sharon	34	11	Hervins	Elijah	1		1	1				1		2			6		
Sharon	34	16	Hervins	Enock	1	1	1	1		1			1	1			7		
Sharon	34	10	Hervins	Samuel		1	1					1		1			3		
Sharon	34	9	Hervins	William	1			1						1			3		
Wrentham	174	18	Hewes	George R.T	1	1			1		1			1			5		
Foxborough	24	25	Hewes	John	1	1		1		1	4		1				9		
Franklin	168	28	Hewes	Solomon	1		2	1					1				5		
Sharon	34	32	Hewins	Benjamin		1				1		1	2	1			7		
Sharon	34	33	Hewins	David	1			1		1			1				4		
Sharon	34	28	Hewins	Ebenezer		1		1	1	1		1		1			6		
Sharon	34	35	Hewins	Enock Jr		1		1		3		1	1				7		
Sharon	34	27	Hewins	F*			1			2			1				4		
Sharon	34	21	Hewins	Jacob		1	1		1	1				1			7		
Sharon	34	26	Hewins	Jacob Jr	1	1			1	3			1				7		
Sharon	34	25	Hewins	John			1			1			1	1			4		
Sharon	34	31	Hewins	Joseph Esq		1		1		1	1		1				5		
Roxbury	101	24	Hide	Huldah	2						1			1			4		
Roxbury	114	16	Hide	Thaddeus		1		1		1				1			4	3rd Parish	
Roxbury	114	11	Higginson	Stephen	1		1		1		1	3	1	1			9	3rd Parish	
Bellingham	158	7	Hill	David	1	1		1					1	1			5		
Weymouth	75	32	Hill	Ebenezer				1						1			2	North Parish	
Walpole	29	27	Hill	George	1			1		1			2				6		
Bellingham	162	21	Hill	Jesse			1						1				2		
Canton	132	1	Hill	John				1				1		1			3		
Bellingham	159	16	Hill	Jonathan				1					1				2		
Medway East Parish	93	17	Hill	Jonathan				1		1				1			3		
Canton	132	2	Hill	Joses	1			1		2		1	1	1			7		
Walpole	29	29	Hill	Josiah			1			1			1				3		
Medfield	88	6	Hill	Mary	1									1			2		
Medway East Parish	93	15	Hill	Moses			1	1	1	1			1				6		
Medway East Parish	93	16	Hill	Moses Jun			1						1				2		
Canton	132	4	Hill	Nathaniel	1			1		2			1				5		
Medway East Parish	93	14	Hill	Reuben	1		1						1				3		
Medway East Parish	93	13	Hill	Samuel		1			1					1			3		
Bellingham	159	14	Hill	Sarah	1	1				2			1				5		
Medway East Parish	93	11	Hill	Simon				1					1	1			3		
Medway East Parish	93	12	Hill	Simon Jun	1			1		2			1				5		
Medway East Parish	93	10	Hill	Timothy			1			1			1				3		
Canton	132	3	Hill	Washington			1			1			1	1			4		
Franklin	164	9	Hills	Jason	3			1		2							7		

TOWN	PG#	LN#	LAST NAME	FIRST NAME	FREE WHITE MALES under 10	10 to 16	16 to 26	26 to 45	45 and over	FREE WHITE FEMALES under 10	10 to 16	16 to 26	26 to 45	45 and over	TOTAL ALL OTHER	TOTAL SLAVES	TOTALS	DISTRICT/ TOWNSHIP	NOTES
Franklin	164	8	Hills	Joseph					1					1			2		
Franklin	164	10	Hills	Joseph Jun	2			1					1				4		
Medfield	88	7	Hinsdale	Abigail									1				1		
Dorchester	56	5	Hitchborn	Benj			1	1	1			3	1		3		10		
Dorchester	57	4	Hitchings	Wm		1	1	1		2		2	1				8		
Stoughton	120	18	Hixon	Jeremiah	2	1		1		1			2				7		
Sharon	34	17	Hixon	Richard	1			1		1		1	1				5		
Medway West Parish	96	21	Hixson	Asa	3			1		1		1					6		
Medway West Parish	96	18	Hixson	Isaac	3	1		1				1	1				7		
Medway West Parish	96	19	Hixson	Reuben	1			1		2			1				6		
Medway West Parish	96	17	Hixson	Seth				1					2				3		
Braintree	69	30	Hobart	Abraham	1		1					1					3		
Braintree	69	28	Hobart	Adam		1		1				1		1			4		
Braintree	69	29	Hobart	Adam Junr			1					1					2		
Braintree	69	27	Hobart	John	1		1		1	3	1	1	1	1			10		
Quincy	42	19	Hobart	Saml	2	1		1		2	2		1				9		
Braintree	70	1	Hobart	William		1	2	1		1			1				6		
Sharon	34	15	Hodgers	Benjamin		2	1	1	1	1		2		1			9		
Foxborough	24	26	Hodgers	Spencer	1	1	2			1		1	1				7		
Bellingham	158	14	Holbrook	Aaron			1	1				1	1	1			5		
Braintree	70	8	Holbrook	Abel	3			1		2			1	1			8		
Bellingham	158	12	Holbrook	Abigail									1				1		
Wrentham	173	4	Holbrook	Abigail	1						1		1				3		
Weymouth	76	1	Holbrook	Abizer				1					1				2	North Parish	
Weymouth	79	15	Holbrook	Abner	1			1				1					3	South Parish	
Bellingham	160	5	Holbrook	Amasa	2		1	1		2			1				7		
Milton	46	31	Holbrook	Amos	1				1	2	1	1	1		1		8		
Bellingham	158	15	Holbrook	Amzi	1			1		3		1	1				7		
Weymouth	79	16	Holbrook	Benja				1					1				2	South Parish	
Braintree	70	12	Holbrook	Caleb		1		1					1				3		
Roxbury	103	27	Holbrook	Daniel				1									1		
Wrentham	173	12	Holbrook	Daniel				2	1	1		1		1			5		
Bellingham	158	11	Holbrook	Darius	1		1			1			1				4		
Weymouth	79	17	Holbrook	David			1	1									2	South Parish	
Wrentham	173	1	Holbrook	David	1	2	1		1		1		1				7		
Braintree	70	4	Holbrook	David	2		1	1	1	2	1	2					10		
Braintree	70	9	Holbrook	Eben	2	1	1	1		2	1	1					10		
Braintree	69	25	Holbrook	Elisha	1		1			2		1					5		
Weymouth	75	30	Holbrook	Elisha		1		1				2		1			5	North Parish	
Braintree	70	23	Holbrook	Esther Wid.						1		1					2		
Bellingham	160	1	Holbrook	Henry		1	1	1			1		2				6		
Wrentham	174	1	Holbrook	Henry	1	1		1						1			4		
Randolph	125	1	Holbrook	Ichabod	2	2	1	1	1	1	1		2				11		
Braintree	70	5	Holbrook	James	2	2	2	1	3		1	1	1	1			14		
Wrentham	173	22	Holbrook	James	1	1		1				1	1				5		
Stoughton	120	19	Holbrook	Jason	1			1		2			1				5		
Weymouth	79	11	Holbrook	Jerusa Wid		1	2	1			1		1	1			7	South Parish	
Bellingham	159	25	Holbrook	Jesse				1					2				3		
Braintree	69	24	Holbrook	John	1		2		1	2	1	1	1				9		
Weymouth	76	4	Holbrook	John	2		1	1		2			1				7	North Parish	
Weymouth	79	14	Holbrook	John	2			1		1		1		3			8	South Parish	
Braintree	70	29	Holbrook	John 2d	1		1					1					3		
Braintree	69	26	Holbrook	Joseph	1		1	1				1					4		
Braintree	70	13	Holbrook	Joshua	1			1		1		1					4		
Weymouth	75	22	Holbrook	Josiah			1	1				1		2			8	North Parish	
Wrentham	173	11	Holbrook	Mary	2		1	1				2			1		7		
Bellingham	159	26	Holbrook	Molly	3	1	1					2	1				8		
Bellingham	158	13	Holbrook	Nathan	1			1					1				3		
Braintree	70	6	Holbrook	Nathl	1	1	2	1		1	2	1	1				10		
Weymouth	79	12	Holbrook	Nathl		1	2	1		1			1				6	South Parish	
Weymouth	79	18	Holbrook	Nathl Junr	2	1	2	1		1	1		1				9	South Parish	
Braintree	70	10	Holbrook	Nehel						1	1		1				4		
Braintree	70	11	Holbrook	Nehel Junr	2			1					1				4		
Medway West Parish	96	20	Holbrook	Partridge	1		1	2		1			1				6		
Bellingham	160	18	Holbrook	Peter	3	1		1		1	1		1				8		
Braintree	70	28	Holbrook	Peter	1		1			1	1						4		
Wrentham	173	23	Holbrook	Samuel				1		1			1				3		
Bellingham	158	6	Holbrook	Seth		2	1		1	1	4	1					10		
Weymouth	76	5	Holbrook	Silvanus	3			1		1			1				6	North Parish	
Weymouth	79	20	Holbrook	Silvanus	2			1		1			1				5	South Parish	
Bellingham	158	10	Holbrook	Stephen			1	1					1				3		
Braintree	70	7	Holbrook	Thomas	1		3		1	2	1	2		1			11		
Randolph	125	2	Holbrook	Thomas	2	2			1	1		1					7		
Dorchester	57	5	Holden	Ezekiel			1					1					2		
Brookline	114	26	Holden	James	2		1	1		1			1				6		
Dorchester	56	28	Holden	Jno	2			1		2		1	1				7		
Canton	132	10	Holden	Joel												2	2		
Dorchester	56	20	Holden	Justin	2	1		1				1	1				6		
Dorchester	56	22	Holden	Phin			1		1	1		2		1			6		
Dorchester	56	21	Holden	Saml				1				1		1			3		
Dorchester	56	19	Holden	Steph			1					1					2		

TOWN	PG#	LN#	LAST NAME	FIRST NAME	FREE WHITE MALES under 10	10 to 16	16 to 26	26 to 45	45 and over	FREE WHITE FEMALES under 10	10 to 16	16 to 26	26 to 45	45 and over	TOTAL ALL OTHER	TOTAL SLAVES	TOTALS	DISTRICT/ TOWNSHIP	NOTES
Dorchester	56	23	Holden	Wm				1						1			2		
Randolph	125	3	Hollis	Adam	1		1	1		2			1	1			7		
Randolph	125	5	Hollis	Ambrose	5			1						1			7		
Weymouth	79	24	Hollis	Betty Wid			1					1	1				3	South Parish	
Braintree	70	25	Hollis	Daniel			1						1				2		
Weymouth	79	19	Hollis	Hosea	1			1					1				3	South Parish	
Braintree	69	23	Hollis	James		2	1		2			2		3			10		
Weymouth	79	9	Hollis	Jesse			1			2		1					4	South Parish	
Braintree	69	19	Hollis	John		1		1					2	1			5		
Randolph	125	4	Hollis	John				1	1					1			3		
Braintree	69	22	Hollis	John Junr	1			1		3		1	1	1			8		
Braintree	69	21	Hollis	Joseph	2			1		2	1		1				7		
Braintree	69	20	Hollis	Nathl	1		1	2	1				1	1			7		
Braintree	69	33	Hollis	Silas	3	2	2	1				1	1	1			11		
Braintree	69	31	Hollis	Thomas	1		1	1		1	2			1			7		
Braintree	69	32	Hollis	Thomas Jun				1		3	1	1					6		
Sharon	34	30	Holmes	Benjamin	1			1					2				4		
Dedham	138	24	Holmes	Ebenezer	1		3	1		2	1	1		1			10		
Sharon	34	19	Holmes	Ebenezer	3			1		1	1			1			7		
Dorchester	57	2	Holmes	Ilsach	2			1		1				1			5		
Dedham	144	23	Holmes	John				1			1	1	1				4	2nd Parish	
Sharon	34	36	Holmes	John				1				1		1			3		
Stoughton	120	20	Holmes	John				1						1			2		
Stoughton	120	25	Holmes	John 2d	3	1		1		1	1	1	1				9		
Canton	132	5	Holmes	Joseph	1	1		1		1			1				5		
Stoughton	120	26	Holmes	Joseph				1					2	1			4		
Sharon	34	34	Holmes	Luther			1					1		1			3		
Stoughton	120	23	Holmes	Luther			1	1					1	1			4		
Stoughton	120	22	Holmes	Mather	1		1	1		2	2	1	1				9		
Stoughton	120	21	Holmes	Philip		1			1			1	1	1			5		
Sharon	34	22	Holmes	Samuel			1	1						1			3		
Stoughton	120	24	Holmes	Samuel	1		1	1		1	1			1			6		
Sharon	34	23	Holmes	Samuel Jr	3			1		3			1				8		
Canton	132	6	Holmes	Unity Wid.		1	1					1		1			4		
Sharon	34	18	Holmes	William		1		1		1		1					4		
Sharon	34	29	Holmes	Zebulon				1						1			2		
Sharon	34	13	Homer	Zebulon V	3	1	1	1		2	1		1				10		
Milton	47	9	Hooker	Wm	2			1		2			1	1			7		
Roxbury	112	32	Hopkins	Michael	2	1		1		1	1		2				8	3rd Parish	
Milton	47	6	Horten	Patience				1					1	1			3		
Milton	47	5	Horten	Steph			1			1	1	1		1			5		
Quincy	42	26	Horton	Enoch				1	1					1			3		
Milton	47	19	Horton	Samuel		2		1				1		1			5		
Medfield	88	8	Hosker	William				1						1			2		
Milton	47	11	Houghton	Jason	5	1		1		1			1				9		
Milton	47	8	Houghton	Jno		1		2					1				4		
Milton	47	18	Houghton	Oliver				1					2				3		
Milton	47	12	Houghton	Ralph				1						1			2		
Milton	47	17	Houghton	Silas		1		1						1			3		
Dorchester	56	7	How	Abraham	2		3	4	1	1		1	2		1		15		
Dorchester	56	9	How	Elizabeth				1						1			2		
Dorchester	56	10	How	Isaac		2	4	1		1	1	1	1				11		
Dorchester	56	12	How	Isaac Jr		1	1					1					3		
Dorchester	57	9	How	Jno Jun	1	1		1		1	1		1				6		
Dorchester	56	8	How	Joseph	1		1					1					3		
Milton	47	15	How	Margaret	1	1				1	1		1				5		
Dorchester	56	6	How	Relief										2			2		
Randolph	124	30	Howard	Aaron	1	1		1					1	1			5		
Randolph	124	34	Howard	Asa	1		1			1		1					4		
Randolph	124	35	Howard	Ebenezer				1						1			2		
Bellingham	158	17	Howard	Elisha				1						1			2		
Randolph	124	33	Howard	Eliza Wid										1			1		
Cohasset	154	6	Howard	Gideon			1	1			1						3		
Quincy	42	25	Howard	James				1	1	1				2			5		
Dorchester	56	26	Howard	Jno C.			1				1	1			2		5		
Wrentham	171	26	Howard	John	2		1	1					1				5		
Randolph	124	29	Howard	Joshua		1		1			1	1					4		
Roxbury	108	17	Howard	Samuel		1		1		2	1	1	1				7		
Randolph	124	31	Howard	Simeon		1		1			1			1			4		
Randolph	124	32	Howard	Zebulon Jr		1			1	2	2			1			6		
Canton	132	7	Howard	Zechariah Rev.	1		1	1					1				4		
Roxbury	112	22	Howe	David	3			1				1	1	1			7	3rd Parish	
Roxbury	101	28	Howe	George	2		1	1		1	1		1				7		
Dorchester	56	14	Howe	James B.	1	1	3	2					2				9		
Dorchester	56	16	Howe	Jno		1	2		1			1	1	1			7		
Brookline	114	24	Howe	John	1			1		1				1			4		
Dedham	138	19	Howe	Joseph	2		1					1					4		
Dedham	138	21	Howe	Joseph & Hemon Bostick		2	2										4		
Dorchester	56	15	Howe	Moses		1				2	1						4		
Roxbury	106	30	Howe	Susannah			4		1	1	1	2		2			11		
Dedham	138	17	Howe	Thomas				1				1		1			3		
Dedham	138	16	Howe	Thomas Junr	2			1		2			2				7		

TOWN	PG#	LN#	HEADS OF HOUSEHOLD		FREE WHITE MALES					FREE WHITE FEMALES					TOTAL ALL OTHER	TOTAL SLAVES	TOTALS	DISTRICT/ TOWNSHIP	NOTES
			LAST NAME	FIRST NAME	under 10	10 to 16	16 to 26	26 to 45	45 and over	under 10	10 to 16	16 to 26	26 to 45	45 and over					
Dedham	138	18	Howe	William	1		6	2	1	2		2	2				16		
Foxborough	26	29	Howe	Zadack		1		1				2		1					
Roxbury	113	27	Hoyt	Elna	3	1		1				1	1	2			9	3rd Parish	
Roxbury	103	4	Hoyt	Lewis	2			1			2		1				6		
Quincy	42	15	Hubart	Josh		1		2	1	1	1		1				7		
Quincy	42	16	Hubart	Peter	1	1		1		4			1				8		
Randolph	125	6	Hubbard	Enoch		1		1		1			1				4		
Randolph	125	7	Hubbard	Nathl				1					1	1			3		
Milton	47	16	Hubbert	Caleb	2		2	1		1		1	1				8		
Braintree	70	31	Hudson	Adonian	1	1		1		1		2	1				7		
Cohasset	154	12	Hudson	Ebenezer			1			1		1					3		
Randolph	125	8	Hudson	Eli	1		1						1				3		
Cohasset	154	48	Hudson	Ezra				1									1		
Cohasset	154	42	Hudson	Ford	3			1		1			1				6		
Cohasset	153	39	Hudson	Ibroke			1			3			1				5		
Dorchester	57	10	Humphrey	Abij				1		1		1	1				4		
Dorchester	56	24	Humphrey	James	2		5	1		3	3		1	2			17		
Weymouth	75	19	Humphrey	James			1	1						1			3	North Parish	
Weymouth	75	31	Humphrey	James 2d	1		3	1		2	2			1			10	North Parish	
Weymouth	75	28	Humphrey	James 3d			1			3			1				5	North Parish	
Cohasset	152	9	Humphrey	Jonathan	3	2		1		2			1				9		
Weymouth	75	29	Humphrey	Joseph	3			1		2			1				7	North Parish	
Weymouth	75	33	Humphrey	Josiah				1			1		1				3	North Parish	
Milton	47	2	Humphrey	Nath	1	1		1					1				4		
Weymouth	75	27	Humphrey	Saml				1		1			1				3	North Parish	
Weymouth	75	34	Humphrey	Saml	2			1		1			1				5	North Parish	
Weymouth	75	26	Humphrey	Silence Wid	1		1	1					3	1			7	North Parish	
Dorchester	56	27	Humphrey	Sus.			2	1				2		1			6		
Weymouth	76	2	Humphrey	William	2			1		1			1				5	North Parish	
Dorchester	56	25	Humphrey	Wm		1		1				1	1	1			5		
Cohasset	154	24	Hunphrey	Sally	1						1						3		
Milton	47	7	Hunt	Abner				1									1		
Weymouth	75	20	Hunt	Asa	3			1		1	2		1				9	North Parish	
Weymouth	75	23	Hunt	Ebenz	1		1		1	1		1		1			6	North Parish	
Weymouth	75	24	Hunt	Ebenz Jun	1	1	1	1					1				5	North Parish	
Braintree	70	3	Hunt	Elihu				1					1				3		
Canton	132	8	Hunt	Ephraim			1			2	1		1				5		
Wrentham	176	3	Hunt	Ephraim	2	1	1			1	4	1		1			11		
Milton	47	13	Hunt	Gideon			2						1				3		
Milton	47	10	Hunt	Isaac			1				1		1				3		
Dorchester	56	13	Hunt	Jeremiah	1		1							1			3		
Canton	132	9	Hunt	John	2		1			2			1				6		
Quincy	42	27	Hunt	Joseph	1		1			2		1					5		
Milton	47	3	Hunt	Lemuel	3	1		1		3			1				9		
Quincy	42	12	Hunt	Mary			1			3		1		1			6		
Weymouth	79	10	Hunt	Nancy Wid						2			1				3	South Parish	
Weymouth	79	13	Hunt	Robert	2	1	2			2	1	2		2			13	South Parish	
Weymouth	76	3	Hunt	Saml	1		1			1	1		1				5	North Parish	
Milton	47	4	Hunt	Samuel	3		2	1		1			1	3			11		
Braintree	70	18	Hunt	Thomas			1					1	1				3		
Weymouth	75	21	Hunt	Zachariah	1	1	1						1				4	North Parish	
Roxbury	105	18	Hunting	Asa		1		1		1			2	1			6		
Needham	147	7	Hunting	Daniel			1		1	2	1		1				6		
Randolph	125	9	Hunting	Daniel	2			1						2			5		
Randolph	125	12	Hunting	Hannah Wid	2					1	1		1				5		
Needham	147	11	Hunting	Hezekiah		1						1					2		
Needham	147	9	Hunting	Israel	3		1	1		1	1	1	1				9		
Roxbury	113	17	Hunting	Jabez	1	1	2	2		1		1	1		1		11	3rd Parish	
Randolph	125	10	Hunting	Joseph			2	1		1	1	2	1				9		
Randolph	125	11	Hunting	Nathl		1		1				1		1			4		
Roxbury	107	32	Hurd	Precilla									1				1		
Roxbury	115	10	Hyslop	David			2	1	1	1		2	1				8	3rd Parish	
Medway West Parish	96	22	Ide	Daniel	2		1	1					1				6		
Wrentham	177	5	Ide	James			1			1		1	1				4		
Sharon	35	8	Ingraham	Benjm	1	1						2		1			6		
Brookline	114	3	Jackson	Abraham				1				1					2		
Roxbury	106	14	Jackson	Antipas	2			1		1			1				5		
Needham	147	15	Jackson	Epheraim		1	2	1			1	2	1				8		
Roxbury	114	19	Jackson	Jonathan	1		2		1	2			2				8	3rd Parish	
Randolph	125	16	Jackson	Peter				1					1				2		
Needham	147	13	Jackson	Phinehas			1			2	2		1				6		
Roxbury	114	4	Jackson	Thaddeus	3		2	1	1	1	3	3		1			15	3rd Parish	
Franklin	166	33	Jackson	William			1						2				3		
Dorchester	57	18	Jacobs	Benj	1	1	1	1		1		1	1		1		8		
Roxbury	108	23	James	Charles			2			1		1					4		
Cohasset	152	35	James	Christopher	2	1			1		1		1				6		
Cohasset	152	18	James	Galen	2	3			1			2	1				9		
Roxbury	107	21	James	Joseph	1	1	8	1		1		2					14		
Weymouth	79	32	Jeff	James	1		1						1				3	South Parish	
Weymouth	76	10	Jeffs	John				1			1		1				3	North Parish	
Wrentham	171	5	Jenks	Job	2		1	1		1		1					6		
Wrentham	170	16	Jenks	Luke	1		1			1		1					5		
Wrentham	171	4	Jenks	William				1				2		1			4		
Dover	150	34	Jepson	John	2			1		1	2			1			7		

TOWN	PG#	LN#	LAST NAME	FIRST NAME	FREE WHITE MALES under 10	10 to 16	16 to 26	26 to 45	45 and over	FREE WHITE FEMALES under 10	10 to 16	16 to 26	26 to 45	45 and over	TOTAL ALL OTHER	TOTAL SLAVES	TOTALS	DISTRICT/ TOWNSHIP	NOTES
Medfield	88	9	Jerauld	James		1		1	1			1					4		
Wrentham	176	8	Jerauld	Mary										1			1		
Wrentham	180	24	Jilson	Nathaniel			1		1		1			1			4		
Dorchester	57	19	Johnson	David	2			1		1	1	1	1				7		
Canton	132	11	Johnson	Ezekiel	1	2		1		1	1		1				7		
Medfield	88	10	Johnson	Joseph		2		1	1	1		1		1			7		
Roxbury	101	20	Johnson	Joseph				1		1			1				3		
Stoughton	120	28	Johnson	Lewis				1				1					2		
Stoughton	120	27	Johnson	Nathaniel	2			1		1			1				5		
Quincy	42	28	Johnson	Thomas											3		3		
Braintree	70	33	Jones	Abraham	1	3		1		3		1	1				10		
Randolph	125	13	Jones	Abraham	1	3		1		3	1		1				10		
Roxbury	111	19	Jones	Alden	2		1					1	1				5	2nd Parish	
Cohasset	153	38	Jones	Catherine						1			2	3			6		
Bellingham	160	26	Jones	Daniel		1		1					1				3		
Bellingham	160	25	Jones	David				1		1		2					4		
Dorchester	57	22	Jones	Delivernc										2			2		
Dorchester	57	21	Jones	Eben				1						2			3		
Dorchester	57	23	Jones	Elijah	2	1		1				1		1			6		
Weymouth	76	6	Jones	Elisha		1		1					1	1			4	North Parish	
Weymouth	76	8	Jones	Elisha Junior	1			1		2			1				5	North Parish	
Canton	132	12	Jones	Ephraim				1						1			2		
Foxborough	24	30	Jones	Frances	3		1	1		1	1		1				8		
Canton	132	14	Jones	Hannah Wid.									1	1			2		
Dedham	138	22	Jones	Henry				1						1			2		
Weymouth	76	7	Jones	James		1		1					1				3	North Parish	
Roxbury	110	3	Jones	John		1		1						1			3	2nd Parish	
Dover	150	33	Jones	John Col & son A	1		1	1		1	2		1	1			8		
Milton	47	22	Jones	Joseph				1						1			2		
Roxbury	101	21	Jones	Lewis			1	1		3			1				6		
Randolph	125	15	Jones	Mary										1			1		
Medway East Parish	93	20	Jones	Nathan		1		2	1	1		2	1				8		
Milton	47	21	Jones	Nathan	1			1		1	1		1				5		
Randolph	125	14	Jones	Ransel	3			1		1	1		1				7		
Quincy	42	29	Jones	Saml				1									1		
Medway East Parish	93	19	Jones	Simson		1	1	1		2			1	1			7		
Medway East Parish	93	18	Jones	Thomas				2						1			3		
Dedham	140	32	Jones	Walter				1									1		
Sharon	35	4	Jonson	Benjamin	2	1		1				1	1	2			8		
Sharon	35	2	Jonson	Caleb	1	1		1		2			1				6		
Sharon	35	7	Jonson	Isaac		2	1	1	1	4	1		1				11		
Sharon	35	1	Jonson	John		1		1		2			1				5		
Sharon	35	5	Jonson	Joshua	3	3		1				1	1				9		
Sharon	35	3	Jonson	Obadiah		2		1		2			1				6		
Stoughton	120	29	Jordan	Abraham				1					1	1			3		
Canton	132	13	Jordan	George	1	1		1		3			1				7		
Sharon	35	6	Jordan	Jacob			1	1		2				1			5		
Stoughton	120	30	Jordan	Joseph				1									1		
Canton	132	16	Jordan	Mary Wid.						1			1	1			3		
Canton	132	15	Jordan	Nathl	1			1		1			1				4		
Dorchester	57	20	Jordan	Oliver	2		2					1	1	1			6		
Braintree	70	32	Jordan	Peleg		1	1	1				1	1				5		
Roxbury	103	1	Jordon	John			1					1					2		
Brookline	114	22	Jordon	Josiah	2	2		1		1	1	1	1				9		
Dedham	138	25	Jourdan	Richard		1	3							1			5		
Needham	147	14	Jourden	Jesse	2			1		2	1		1				7		
Weymouth	79	31	Joy	Benjm	1	1		1			1		1				5	South Parish	
Roxbury	108	22	Joy	Charles	2		1						1				4		
Weymouth	79	28	Joy	David				1				2	1	1			5	South Parish	
Weymouth	79	30	Joy	David Junr	1			1		3			1				6	South Parish	
Weymouth	79	27	Joy	Ebenezer						1		1	1				3	South Parish	
Milton	47	20	Joy	Elizabeth		1						2		1			4		
Weymouth	79	26	Joy	Nehemiah				1				2	1				4	South Parish	
Weymouth	79	29	Joy	Turner	1			1					1				3	South Parish	
Weymouth	79	25	Joy	William		2		1					1	1			5	South Parish	
Weymouth	76	9	Joyce	Thomas			2	1		1		1					5	North Parish	
Cohasset	153	6	Joze	Amos				1						1			2		
Cohasset	154	33	Joze	Asa	1		1			1		1					4		
Cohasset	153	7	Joze	Olive		1	1					2		1			5		
Cohasset	154	43	Joze	Susannah	1							1		1			3		
Roxbury	100	1	Juro	French Consul				1						1			2		
Wrentham	174	21	Kallock	Cornelius		1		1				1	1				4		
Sharon	35	11	Kallock	Thomas	2			1	1	1		2	1				8		
Franklin	164	26	Keaton	Thankful	1		1	1			1	1		1			6		
Stoughton	120	31	Keith	Barnabas		1		1					1				3		
Walpole	30	4	Keith	John	1			1		3			1				6		
Bellingham	161	17	Kelly	Elisha	1		2	1				1		2			7		
Walpole	29	38	Kendal	Jonathan		1			1		1			1	1		5		
Canton	132	20	Kenney	David				1						1			2		
Stoughton	120	32	Kenney	Elijah	4			1					1				6		
Canton	132	18	Kenney	John				1					1	1			3		
Canton	132	19	Kenney	Nathan			1					1					2		

TOWN	PG#	LN#	HEADS OF HOUSEHOLD LAST NAME	FIRST NAME	FREE WHITE MALES under 10	10 to 16	16 to 26	26 to 45	45 and over	FREE WHITE FEMALES under 10	10 to 16	16 to 26	26 to 45	45 and over	TOTAL ALL OTHER	TOTAL SLAVES	TOTALS	DISTRICT/ TOWNSHIP	NOTES
Canton	132	17	Kenney	Nathl				1						1			2		
Dorchester	57	26	Kent	Eliz	1								4				5		
Milton	47	24	Keyes	Nathanl				1						1			2		
Medway West Parish	96	23	Kibbee	Isaac	1	1	1			1	1			1			7		
Bellingham	159	15	Kilburne	Henry			1			1			1				3		
Bellingham	160	17	Kilburne	Simeon	1		1			3			1				6		
Dorchester	57	28	Kilton	Eben Jr	4		1			2			1				8		
Dorchester	57	27	Kilton	Ebenz	2			2					1	1			6		
Dorchester	57	29	Kilton	Edward	2		1			1				1			5		
Dorchester	57	24	Kilton	James				1		1		1		1			4		
Dorchester	57	30	Kilton	Thankfull						2		1		1			4		
Randolph	125	17	Kimbal	William	2		1				1		1				5		
Medway West Parish	96	24	Kimbel	Nathaniel	2		1						1				4		
Bellingham	161	19	King	John			1	1					1				3		
Dover	150	35	King	Solomon			1			1		1					3		
Brookline	114	27	King	William		1	1	1		2			1				6		
Dorchester	57	25	King	William	1		1			1		1					4		
Sharon	35	10	Kingman	Benjam	1		1	1						1			4		
Weymouth	76	11	Kingman	Ebenz	4		1	1	1			1	1				9	North Parish	
Randolph	125	19	Kingman	James				1						1			2		
Weymouth	79	34	Kingman	John	1			1						1			3	South Parish	
Weymouth	79	35	Kingman	John 2nd				1				1		1			4	South Parish	
Weymouth	79	33	Kingman	Zachariah		1	1						1				3	South Parish	
Franklin	167	26	Kingsbury	Aaron			1			1	1	1					4		
Medfield	88	11	Kingsbury	Amos			1	1					1	1			4		
Needham	147	29	Kingsbury	Asa			1						1				2		
Walpole	30	3	Kingsbury	Asa	1			1					1	3			6		
Franklin	167	28	Kingsbury	Benjamin	2		1	1			2		1				7		
Needham	147	26	Kingsbury	Daniel		1		1		2	1		1				6		
Walpole	29	33	Kingsbury	Daniel	1		1	1	1	2			1				7		
Needham	147	28	Kingsbury	David		1		1		1	1			1			5		
Franklin	167	27	Kingsbury	Elizabeth			1			1				1			3		
Dedham	144	24	Kingsbury	Enoch			1	2						1			4	2nd Parish	
Dedham	138	29	Kingsbury	Ezekeil	2	1		1		1		2					7		
Canton	132	23	Kingsbury	Fisher		2		1						1			4		
Needham	147	27	Kingsbury	Iasiah	2			1		2	1		1				7		
Walpole	30	1	Kingsbury	Jacob			1			1							2		
Dedham	142	9	Kingsbury	James			1	1			2		1				5	1st Parish	
Franklin	167	19	Kingsbury	James	2			1					1				4		
Needham	147	23	Kingsbury	Jonathan		2		1		1		1	1				6		
Needham	147	16	Kingsbury	Jonathan Col.		2	1	1				2		1			7		
Canton	132	24	Kingsbury	Joseph	2		1							1			4		
Needham	147	18	Kingsbury	Joseph		2	2	1		1	1			1			8		
Walpole	29	37	Kingsbury	Joseph	2		1			1			1	1			6		
Needham	147	24	Kingsbury	Joseph Junr	1	1	1			1				1			5		
Randolph	125	18	Kingsbury	Joshua		1		1		1				1			4		
Dedham	138	27	Kingsbury	Joshua G.				1						1			2		
Dedham	138	26	Kingsbury	Keziah Wid	1		1			1		1		1			5		
Dedham	138	28	Kingsbury	Moses		1	1			1		2					5		
Needham	147	22	Kingsbury	Moses		2		2				1		1			6		
Needham	147	17	Kingsbury	Moses Junr	1	1		1		1				1			5		
Foxborough	24	33	Kingsbury	Nathan				1			2		1				4		
Walpole	29	35	Kingsbury	Nathan				1						1			2		
Dedham	144	25	Kingsbury	Nathaniel	1		1	1					1	1			5	2nd Parish	
Sharon	35	9	Kingsbury	Nathaniel				1						1			2		
Dedham	144	26	Kingsbury	Nathaniel Junr	1		1						1	1			4	2nd Parish	
Dedham	139	30	Kingsbury	Noah	1		1	3					1				6		
Needham	147	19	Kingsbury	Samuel	1		1	2					1				5		
Walpole	30	2	Kingsbury	Samuel	1		1	2			1						5		
Needham	147	20	Kingsbury	Sarah									1				1		
Walpole	29	32	Kingsbury	Seth				1					1				2		
Walpole	29	34	Kingsbury	Seth Jr	1			1					1				3		
Walpole	29	36	Kingsbury	Solomen	1	1		1		3		1	1				8		
Franklin	167	31	Kingsbury	Stephen	1		2	1		1		1					6		
Franklin	167	18	Kingsbury	Timothy	1		1	1					1	1			5		
Needham	147	21	Kingsbury	Timothy		1		2	1				1	1			6		
Walpole	29	31	Kingsbury	William			1	2				1					4		
Medway East Parish	93	21	Kingsbury	Zibina			1						1				2		
Canton	132	25	Kinsley	Adam	1	1	4	2		1	1	1	2				13		
Canton	132	26	Kinsley	Silas	2		1			1			1	1			6		
Medfield	88	12	Kitterage	Peter											4		4		
Roxbury	108	26	Kittle	Samuel	3		1	1					1				6		
Franklin	169	1	Knapp	Moses	3	1	5	3	1	1	1	1	1				17		
Milton	47	23	Kneeland	Susan			1						1	1			3		
Roxbury	108	7	Knower	Benjamin	1			1		1	2	5	1				11		
Wrentham	175	3	Knowlton	Benjamin				1			1	1	2				5		
Milton	47	26	Lamb	Moses	1	2	2	1		1			1	1			9		
Cohasset	152	10	Lambert	Henry		1		1					1	1			4		
Roxbury	104	9	Lambert	William				1		3	1		2			2	9		
Braintree	70	38	Lane	John	1		1	1					2				5		
Roxbury	104	1	Langdon	Mary							2	1		1			4		

TOWN	PG#	LN#	LAST NAME	FIRST NAME	FWM under 10	FWM 10 to 16	FWM 16 to 26	FWM 26 to 45	FWM 45 and over	FWF under 10	FWF 10 to 16	FWF 16 to 26	FWF 26 to 45	FWF 45 and over	TOTAL ALL OTHER	TOTAL SLAVES	TOTALS	DISTRICT/ TOWNSHIP	NOTES
Roxbury	102	3	Langley	Ester		1	4			1	1		1				8		
Dorchester	58	19	Lapham	Elisha	2			1		2			2				7		
Weymouth	76	15	Larabee	Asa				1		2			1				4	North Parish	
Roxbury	106	19	Larvley	Daniel	3	1		1					3				8		
Franklin	166	36	Lathbridge	James				1		1			1				3		
Franklin	166	35	Lathbridge	Samuel			1		1	1	1		2				6		
Franklin	167	17	Lathbridge	Samuel Junr		2	1		1	1	1		1				7		
Cohasset	152	8	Lathrop	Anselam	1			1		1	1		1				5		
Cohasset	152	1	Lathrop Esq	Thomas				1						1			2		
Sharon	35	16	Laurance	David		2		1		5		1	1				10		
Roxbury	107	12	Lawrance	Seth			4						1				5		
Franklin	166	16	Lawrence	Cephas	4	1		1		3			1				10		
Franklin	167	14	Lawrence	Daniel	2			1		1			1				5		
Medway West Parish	96	25	Lawrence	David	1			1		1			1				4		
Medfield	88	17	Lawrence	Elihu	1				1	3	2	1	1				9		
Franklin	164	7	Lawrence	Ozias	1			1		1			1				4		
Stoughton	120	33	Leach	Lot	1		1	1		2		1	1				7		
Dedham	138	32	Lealand	Isaac		1			1	3		1	2				8		
Brookline	115	3	Learnard	Daniel	2		2		1	1	3	1	1				11		
Dover	150	36	Leatherbee	Thomas		1		1					1				3		
Roxbury	104	10	Lee	William		1	1			2		1	1				6		
Dorchester	58	10	Leeds	Benj. B.	2		1	1	1	1		1					7		
Dorchester	58	11	Leeds	Jno					1				1				2		
Dorchester	58	6	Leeds	Josiah	2	1		1					1				5		
Dorchester	58	7	Leeds	Mary							1		2				3		
Dorchester	58	2	Leeds	Miguel			4	1				2	1		1		9		
Dorchester	58	8	Leeds	Nathan		1							1				3		
Stoughton	120	34	Leeds	Nathaniel	1			1		2	1		1				6		
Dorchester	57	33	Leeds	Saml					1					1			2		
Dorchester	58	1	Leeds	Saml 3rd	2			1		2			1				6		
Dorchester	57	32	Leeds	Saml Jr	1			1		3		1	1	1			6		
Dorchester	58	12	Leeds	Susan			1					1		1			3		
Dorchester	58	5	Leeds	Thomas	2	1		1	1	3			1				9		
Roxbury	107	25	Leland	Ebenezer	2	1	1	1		1	1		1	1			9		
Dorchester	58	16	Lemish	Jno	2	1		1		2	1		1				8		
Dedham	144	29	Lenley	Levi	1				1	1		1	1				5	2nd Parish	
Dorchester	58	14	Leonard	*			3						1				4		
Canton	132	27	Leonard	Enoch		1	2		1				1	2			7		
Roxbury	107	29	Leonard	Grant				1		1		1					3		
Foxborough	24	32	Leonard	Jacob	2		1	1		2			1				7		
Foxborough	24	31	Leonard	Mehitible W	1	1	1				1			1			5		
Sharon	35	14	Leonard	Nathl		2	1	2					1				6		
Canton	132	28	Leonard	Uriah	3			1		1		2	1	1			9		
Sharon	35	15	Leonard	Walley	3				1	1			1				6		
Roxbury	99	10	Leprelete	Deborah		1	1							1			3		
Roxbury	99	9	Lethbridge	Fisher		1		1						1			3		
Roxbury	103	15	Lethbridge	Mary									2				2		
Roxbury	105	8	Levens	Joel			1	2		1			1				5		
Brookline	114	38	Leverett	William	1		1	1				1					4		
Roxbury	102	26	Lewes	James	2		1	1		2	1		1				8		
Roxbury	102	27	Lewes	John		1	1			1		1		1			5		
Dedham	138	34	Lewis	Abner		1		1					1				3		
Dedham	144	28	Lewis	Andrew	1				1	1	1			1			5	2nd Parish	
Canton	132	31	Lewis	Benjamin	2			1		1			1				5		
Walpole	30	6	Lewis	David	1			1		2			1	1			6		
Dedham	142	10	Lewis	Hannah Wid		1								2			3	1st Parish	
Walpole	30	5	Lewis	Isaac		1	1	1		1			1				5		
Dedham	142	12	Lewis	Jabez	1			1					1				3	1st Parish	
Dorchester	58	9	Lewis	Jacob	1	1	1	1		1	1	1			5		12		
Dorchester	58	17	Lewis	James	1			1		2	2		1				7		
Canton	132	29	Lewis	James H.				1		1		1	2				5		
Sharon	35	13	Lewis	Job											4		4		
Weymouth	76	17	Lewis	Jonathan				1		2			1	1			5	North Parish	
Dedham	138	35	Lewis	Joseph	2		2	1				2	1		1		9		
Dedham	142	11	Lewis	Joseph		1							1				2	1st Parish	
Dedham	138	31	Lewis	Joseph Junr	1		3	3		1		1	2				11		
Needham	147	31	Lewis	Joshua		2		1		1	2	1		1			8		
Dedham	144	27	Lewis	Meletia									1				1	2nd Parish	
Dedham	142	13	Lewis	Nathaniel				1					1	1			3	1st Parish	
Dedham	138	33	Lewis	Paul		1		1				1					3		
Dedham	142	14	Lewis	Rachel Wid		1				4			2				7	1st Parish	
Canton	132	30	Lewis	Saban		1		1					1	1			4		
Dedham	138	37	Lewis	Samuel		1		1		1		1		1			5		
Cohasset	154	18	Lewis	Susannah		1					2	1	1				5		
Medway West Parish	96	26	Lewitt	Peter		2		1		2			1				6		
Cohasset	153	16	Lichfield	Job	1	1		1		3			1				7		
Cohasset	153	17	Lichfield	Noah	1	1		1		2	1		1				7		
Milton	47	25	Lillie	Jno May	3			1		1		3		1	1		10		
Cohasset	152	47	Lincoln	Abraham	2	2	2	1					1	1			9		
Cohasset	154	39	Lincoln	Abraham	1			1		1		1	1				5		
Cohasset	152	29	Lincoln	Christopher	1			1		2		1	1	1			7		

TOWN	PG#	LN#	LAST NAME	FIRST NAME	FREE WHITE MALES under 10	10 to 16	16 to 26	26 to 45	45 and over	FREE WHITE FEMALES under 10	10 to 16	16 to 26	26 to 45	45 and over	TOTAL ALL OTHER	TOTAL SLAVES	TOTALS	DISTRICT/ TOWNSHIP	NOTES
Cohasset	152	25	Lincoln	Elisha	2	1		1		1			1				6		
Cohasset	154	40	Lincoln	Ephraim	1	1			1	2	1		1	1			8		
Cohasset	153	35	Lincoln	Fanny	1							1	1				3		
Weymouth	76	14	Lincoln	Frederick	1	1		1		3			1				7	North Parish	
Cohasset	153	43	Lincoln	Hezekiah		1		1		2			1				5		
Cohasset	153	28	Lincoln	James	1			1		2	1		1				6		
Cohasset	152	43	Lincoln	Jerom	2	2	1	1		2			1				9		
Cohasset	155	1	Lincoln	John			1						1				2		
Cohasset	153	25	Lincoln	Mordiecia			1						2	3			6		
Cohasset	153	22	Lincoln	Obediah			1						1				2		
Cohasset	153	26	Lincoln	Sarah			1				1		1				3		
Cohasset	153	27	Lincoln	Uriah		1	1	1			1	2	1				7		
Franklin	167	1	Lincoln	William	1		1						3	1			6		
Cohasset	153	44	Lincoln	Zenas	2	1		1		2	1		1				8		
Randolph	125	25	Lindfield	Benjamin	2		1	1					1				5		
Randolph	125	23	Lindfield	David		1		1				1	1				4		
Randolph	125	24	Lindfield	Saml	1	1	1	1			1	1	1				7		
Randolph	125	20	Lindfield	William			1						1				2		
Randolph	125	21	Lindfield	Wm 2d		1		1			1	2	1				6		
Randolph	125	22	Lindfield	Wm 3d	2	1	1	1		1	1		1				8		
Dorchester	58	3	Litchfield	Josiah				1									1		
Randolph	125	26	Littlefield	Aaron	2	1		1		1	1		1				7		
Randolph	125	27	Littlefield	Hannah Wid							1		1				2		
Stoughton	120	35	Littlefield	Nathl				1					1	1			3		
Stoughton	120	36	Littlefield	Nathl Jr	4			1		1			1				7		
Stoughton	120	37	Littlefield	Samuel	3	1		1		1	1		1				8		
Roxbury	111	18	Loewes	Timothy			1							1			2	2nd Parish	
Braintree	70	34	Loring	Daniel	1	2		3		2			1	1			10		
Roxbury	113	16	Loring	Elijah			4		1				1	1			8	3rd Parish	
Cohasset	154	28	Lothrop	John	3	1		1		1			1				7		
Needham	149	13	Lott	David			1			1	1		1				4		
Weymouth	80	5	Loud	Benjamin	1		1	2		3			1				8	South Parish	
Weymouth	80	6	Loud	Daniel	3			1		2			1				7	South Parish	
Weymouth	79	36	Loud	David	2	1	3	1				1	1				9	South Parish	
Weymouth	76	18	Loud	Eliot			3	1		2			1				7	North Parish	
Weymouth	80	4	Loud	Eliphalet	3			1		2	3	1	1				11	South Parish	
Weymouth	80	3	Loud	Hulda Wid	2	1						1	1				5	South Parish	
Weymouth	80	2	Loud	Jacob			1						1				2	South Parish	
Weymouth	76	19	Loud	Joseph			1						1				2	North Parish	
Weymouth	76	16	Loud	Silvanus	3	2		1		3	1	1	1				12	North Parish	
Weymouth	80	1	Loud	William			1						1	1			3	South Parish	
Weymouth	80	9	Loud	Wm Junr			1			1	1		1				4	South Parish	
Needham	147	32	Lovel	Joseph	2	1	1						1				5		
Sharon	35	12	Lovel	Samuel				1						2			3		
Stoughton	120	30	Lovel	Susanna		1						1	1	1			4		
Medfield	88	13	Lovell	David			1										1		
Weymouth	76	20	Lovell	David	2			1					1	2			6	North Parish	
Weymouth	76	22	Lovell	David	1	1		1					1	1			5	North Parish	
Medfield	88	14	Lovell	David Jun			1						1	1			3		
Medfield	88	15	Lovell	Dyer		1		1					3	1			6		
Braintree	70	36	Lovell	Eben			1										1		
Braintree	70	40	Lovell	Jacob			1		1			1					3		
Weymouth	76	13	Lovell	James		1		2			1	1	1				6	North Parish	
Weymouth	80	7	Lovell	John			1						1				2	South Parish	
Medway East Parish	93	22	Lovell	Joseph			1						1				2		
Weymouth	80	8	Lovell	Lemuel	2	1	1						1				5	South Parish	
Medfield	88	16	Lovell	Moses	1	2		2				2	1	1			9		
Medway East Parish	93	23	Lovell	Nathaniel		1	3	1					1		1		7		
Braintree	70	41	Lovell	Silas			1						2				3		
Weymouth	76	12	Lovell	Solomon			1										1	North Parish	
Braintree	70	39	Lovell	Stephen	1			1		2			1				5		
Weymouth	76	21	Lovell	Yardly		1		1					1	1			4	North Parish	
Medway West Parish	96	27	Loverain	Thaddeus	3		1	1					1	1			7		
Roxbury	112	12	Lovering	Joseph		1		1					1	1			4	3rd Parish	
Dorchester	58	15	Low	Catharine		1				2			1	1			5		
Roxbury	113	8	Lowder	Henry		2							1				3	3rd Parish	
Roxbury	113	9	Lowder	John			1							2			3	3rd Parish	
Dedham	138	36	Lowder	Samuel	1	1	1		1				1	1	3		9		
Roxbury	108	32	Lowell	John Esq Honble		1	2		1			2	2	1	2		11		
Roxbury	115	6	Lucas	John	1	1		1				2	1				6	3rd Parish	
Randolph	125	28	Ludden	Hezekiah		1		1					2	2			6		
Randolph	125	29	Ludden	Samuel	1		1			3		1	1				8		
Braintree	70	35	Ludden	Silvanus			1		1			2					4		
Braintree	70	37	Lufkin	Jacob	2			2		1			1				6		
Dorchester	58	4	Lunders	Wm	1		1						1				3		
Roxbury	103	14	Lynch	Dennis	5			1		1			1				8		
Dorchester	58	18	Lyon	Benj	4		1			1			1				7		
Roxbury	110	16	Lyon	Benjamin			1			2			1	1			5	2nd Parish	
Milton	47	27	Lyon	Jacob	1			1		1			1				4		
Roxbury	107	13	Lyon	Jason	2	1		1					1	1			6		
Needham	147	30	Lyon	Peter		3	2			3			1	1			10		
Canton	132	32	Lyon	Ruth Wid.										1			1		
Dorchester	57	31	Lyon	Saml B.	4	3	1	1		1			1	1			12		
Dorchester	58	13	Lyon	Thomas	1		1	1		1				1			5		

TOWN	PG#	LN#	LAST NAME	FIRST NAME	FREE WHITE MALES					FREE WHITE FEMALES					TOTAL ALL OTHER	TOTAL SLAVES	TOTALS	DISTRICT/ TOWNSHIP	NOTES
					under 10	10 to 16	16 to 26	26 to 45	45 and over	under 10	10 to 16	16 to 26	26 to 45	45 and over					
Roxbury	110	15	Lyon	Thomas			1	1	1				1	4			8	2nd Parish	
Sharon	35	25	Mackintosh	Andrew	1			1		1			1				4		
Canton	132	33	Madden	John			1	1		2			1	1			6		
Randolph	126	1	Madden	John Jr	2			1		2	1		1				7		
Wrentham	181	5	Maddy	John	1					3	4	2	2				12		
Roxbury	103	24	Magee	James		2	1		1	5	1	1	2	1	3		17		
Franklin	168	33	Makepiece	William	1			1		1			1				4		
Wrentham	172	24	Mann	Amherst	1		2			1			1	1			6		
Randolph	125	31	Mann	Benjamin			2		1	2	1	2		1			9		
Walpole	30	12	Mann	Benjamin	3	1			1			1	1				7		
Franklin	169	18	Mann	Elias	1			1		2	1			1			6		
Medfield	88	18	Mann	Elias		1				1				1			3		
Dorchester	58	26	Mann	Ephrm				1		1				1			3		
Cohasset	154	22	Mann	George			1			1	1		1	1			5		
Wrentham	172	22	Mann	George		1	1		1					1			4		
Dedham	138	46	Mann	Harmon	3		1	2		1	1			1			9		
Wrentham	178	28	Mann	jacob		2			1				1		1		5		
Dover	150	38	Mann	James		1	2		1			1		1			6		
Wrentham	170	9	Mann	James			3	2		2			2	1	1		11		
Wrentham	176	25	Mann	Jason	1			1		2			1	1			6		
Wrentham	178	25	Mann	Jeremiah			1						1				2		
Randolph	125	32	Mann	Joseph	1	1	1	1		2			1				7		
Wrentham	173	34	Mann	Moses		1	1		1		1	2		1			7		
Needham	147	45	Mann	Moses Col.		2	1		2	2	1		1				9		
Franklin	169	20	Mann	Nathan		1			1	1	1	2		1			7		
Medway West Parish	97	1	Mann	Ralph	2	1	1		1	1			1				7		
Dedham	138	41	Mann	Robert		1			1	1							3		
Medfield	88	19	Mann	Rufus	2		1	1		1	1	1					7		
Randolph	125	30	Mann	Seth		1	1	1	1	1		2		1			8		
Walpole	30	20	Mann	Seth		1				1					1		3		
Franklin	164	21	Mann	Susannah			1					2		1			4		
Franklin	169	19	Mann	Thomas	2	1	1	1		1	1	1	1				9		
Wrentham	178	27	Mann	Thomas				1						2			3		
Walpole	30	11	Mann	Timothy			1	1		1			1	1			5		
Dorchester	58	29	Mann	Wm		1	1		1	2	1	1	1	1			9		
Dorchester	59	14	Mann	Wm	2			1		1	1		1				6		
Dorchester	59	4	Manning	George	1	1				2			1				6		
Needham	147	36	Mansfield	Epes	1			1		3	1		1				7		
Dorchester	59	9	Mansfield	Shu	2		2	1		2		1	1				9		
Roxbury	105	4	Mansfield	Stephen	3	1		1		2			1				8		
Braintree	71	2	Mansfield	Zenas	2			1				1					4		
Cohasset	153	2	Marble	Ephraim	2			1		1			1				5		
Cohasset	154	23	Marble	Noah					1					1			2		
Roxbury	108	28	Marean	Samuel	2			1		1			1				5		
Randolph	126	2	Mark	Josiah	2			1		1			1				5		
Quincy	42	35	Marsh	Jona	2				1	1	1		1				6		
Quincy	42	34	Marsh	Wilson	1	1	1		1	3	3			1			11		
Walpole	30	18	Marsh	Caleb	3			1					1				5		
Needham	147	35	Marshal	Jacob	1				1	1				1			4		
Milton	47	32	Marshal	Jno		1			1	1				1			4		
Walpole	30	17	Marshal	John	2	1	2		1	2	1		1				10		
Dorchester	59	2	Marshal	Joseph					1	1			1				3		
Stoughton	121	1	Marshall	Benja			2		1	1	1		1				6		
Roxbury	108	13	Marshall	Benjamin		1	1					1	1				4		
Dorchester	58	27	Marshall	Moses				1		2			1				4		
Roxbury	108	30	Marvel	Jonathan				1				1		1			3		
Dedham	138	38	Mash	Martin	1		3						2				6		
Medway East Parish	93	24	Mason	Abner			1	1						2			4		
Medfield	88	23	Mason	Alpheus	1	1	2	1		1	1	1	1		1		10		
Medfield	88	21	Mason	Amos		1	1			1		2		1			6		
Medfield	88	20	Mason	Asa			1	1					1	1			4		
Foxborough	25	10	Mason	Elias	2			1		1			1	1			6		
Medway East Parish	93	25	Mason	Harding	2			1					1				4		
Dover	150	37	Mason	John			1	1					1	1			4		
Medfield	88	22	Mason	Johnson	3			1		1			1	1			7		
Roxbury	115	2	Mason	Jonathan Esq	2		1	2		2	2	3	2	2			16	3rd Parish	
Dedham	138	39	Mason	Thadues	2		1	1		1		1	1				7		
Dedham	138	40	Mason	William		1			1				1	2			5		
Dedham	144	30	Mason	William Junr	1	1				1	2	1		1			7	2nd Parish	
Roxbury	104	30	Mathews	Gardner			1			1			1				3		
Canton	133	1	Maxwell	Thompson	1			1		2	1			1			6		
Milton	48	1	May	Joseph	1				1	4				1			7		
Roxbury	113	24	May	Lemuel		1	2		1			2		1			7	3rd Parish	
Canton	132	34	May	Luther	2	1		2		1		2					8		
Canton	132	35	May	Rebecca Wid.										1			1		
Roxbury	112	16	May	Solomon	1		2	1				1		1			6	3rd Parish	
Roxbury	111	11	May	John					1	2				1			4	2nd Parish	
Roxbury	110	9	Mayo	John	1			1	1				1	1			5	2nd Parish	
Roxbury	109	8	Mayo	Thomas		1		1				1	1	1			5	2nd Parish	
Roxbury	100	2	Mayo	Thomas 3d	3			1		2			1				7		
Roxbury	103	31	Mayo	Thomas Junr	1		1	1		2		1	1				7		
Roxbury	102	17	Mayo	William	2			1		1				3			7		

TOWN	PG#	LN#	LAST NAME	FIRST NAME	M<10	M10-16	M16-26	M26-45	M45+	F<10	F10-16	F16-26	F26-45	F45+	TOTAL ALL OTHER	TOTAL SLAVES	TOTALS	DISTRICT/TOWNSHIP	NOTES
Roxbury	112	1	McCarthy	Anna			1				1		1	2	1		6	3rd Parish	
Roxbury	102	12	McCarthy	Sarah								1		1			2		
Roxbury	102	11	McCarthy	William			1	1				1		1			4		
Dorchester	58	31	McCurney	Mic.				1		1				1			3		
Needham	147	49	McIntire	Jemima									1	1			2		
Roxbury	108	8	McIntire	Mary									1				1		
Needham	147	48	McIntire	Sarah Wid.	2		1						1	1			5		
Needham	148	1	McIntosh	Ebenezer	3	1	2	1					1				8		
Needham	147	47	McIntosh	Gideon		1		1		1			1				4		
Dorchester	59	3	McIntosh	James	2		1			1		1					5		
Dorchester	59	13	McIntosh	Jerem	1	1	1		1	3	1	1		1			10		
Needham	147	46	McIntosh	Royal	1	1		1		4			1	1			9		
Dorchester	59	12	McIntosh	Steph.	3		1					1	1				6		
Needham	147	44	McIntosh	William Col.		1		1					1				3		
Milton	47	28	McKean	Joseph		1						3					4		
Canton	132	21	McKendry	Archibald	2		1			2	1		1				7		
Canton	132	22	McKendry	Ruth Wid.								1	1				2		
Milton	47	29	McLean	Agnes								1		2	1		4		
Cohasset	152	24	Mcorble	Priscilla										1			1		
Quincy	42	32	Meads	Wm P.	1	1		1		2			1				6		
Canton	133	2	Means	John	1			1		2	1		1				6		
Quincy	42	30	Mears	George				1					1				2		
Roxbury	108	14	Mears	James		1		1		1			1				4		
Roxbury	104	13	Mears	James Junr			1				1		1				3		
Dorchester	59	6	Melish	Saml	1		1			1	1		1	1			6		
Roxbury	106	16	Mellish	Betsey								3		1			4		
Dorchester	59	7	Mellish	Jno		1		1		5	1	2		1			11		
Brookline	114	13	Meriam	Abel	1		3				1						5		
Stoughton	121	2	Merion	Wid Lidia	1	1	1			1	1		1				6		
Quincy	42	36	Merrick	Richd											2		2		
Dorchester	59	11	Merrifield	Abij.			1							2			3		
Dorchester	59	10	Merrifield	Sam		1		1					1				3		
Wrentham	180	7	Messenger	Daniel	1		1	1			1		1				5		
Wrentham	170	6	Messenger	Ebenezer	1		1	1		2			1				6		
Wrentham	177	19	Messenger	George W.	1			1		1	1		1				5		
Wrentham	170	1	Messenger	John				1						1			2		
Wrentham	170	2	Messenger	John Junr	5			1					1				7		
Wrentham	177	17	Messenger	Swicher		1		1					1				3		
Walpole	30	21	Messinger	James				1									1		
Franklin	164	3	Metcalf	Abijah	1		1	1		1	1		1				6		
Franklin	166	15	Metcalf	Asa		1		1		1	1		1				5		
Franklin	166	21	Metcalf	Billy		1	2	1		2		1		1			8		
Franklin	165	6	Metcalf	Calvin	2		1	1		2		1	1				8		
Foxborough	25	3	Metcalf	Cornelius			1			1		1					3		
Wrentham	179	1	Metcalf	David	1	1		1		2	1	1	1				9		
Franklin	163	15	Metcalf	Ebenezer								1					1		
Franklin	163	8	Metcalf	Hanan		1		1			1		1				4		
Franklin	165	4	Metcalf	Hannah									1				1		
Bellingham	162	20	Metcalf	Hepzibah								1	1				2		
Franklin	164	2	Metcalf	James				1						1	1		3		
Franklin	167	30	Metcalf	James Junr		1	1	1		2		2	1				8		
Franklin	167	12	Metcalf	John		1	2	1				1	1				6		
Franklin	168	21	Metcalf	Jonathan	1		2	1		4		1	1				10		
Dedham	138	43	Metcalf	Joseph	1	1		1		1			1				5		
Wrentham	171	15	Metcalf	Lewis	1			1					1				3		
Medway West Parish	97	2	Metcalf	Luther	1	1	6					1	2				12		
Franklin	166	14	Metcalf	Nathan	2	1	1	1		2			1				8		
Medway East Parish	93	26	Metcalf	Philip	2			1		1			1				5		
Franklin	168	20	Metcalf	Samuel		1	1	1		1	1	2	1				8		
Wrentham	171	14	Metcalf	Silas		1	1	1		1			1				5		
Franklin	168	25	Metcalf	Silence	1							1	1				3		
Bellingham	162	22	Metcalf	Stephen	1	1	2	1				1	1				7		
Wrentham	171	13	Metcalf	Thomas	2	1	3		1	2	2	1	1				13		
Franklin	163	14	Metcalf	Timothy	2	1		1		1			1				6		
Franklin	164	1	Metcalf	Titus	1			1						1			3		
Dedham	138	42	Metcalf	Wid Ruth									1				1		
Roxbury	105	29	Milet	Samuel		4	1		1			2	2	1			11		
Quincy	42	31	Miller	Eben Esq			2						1	1			4		
Dorchester	58	30	Miller	H.K.	3	1		2		1		1	1				9		
Foxborough	25	2	Miller	Helfon	1			1		1	2	2	1				8		
Needham	147	33	Miller	James	1		1					1					3		
Franklin	164	14	Miller	Jesse	2		1		1			1					5		
Quincy	42	33	Miller	Jno				2		2		1					5		
Franklin	164	13	Miller	Joseph								1	1	1			3		
Franklin	167	23	Miller	Nathaniel	1		1	1				1					4		
Needham	147	42	Mills	Benjamin		1							1				2		
Needham	147	38	Mills	David	1			1				1		2			5		
Needham	147	50	Mills	Enoch		1		1					1				3		
Needham	147	39	Mills	Ezra	3			1	3				1				8		
Milton	48	3	Mills	Fuller	2			1				1	2				6		

TOWN	PG#	LN#	LAST NAME	FIRST NAME	M <10	M 10-16	M 16-26	M 26-45	M 45+	F <10	F 10-16	F 16-26	F 26-45	F 45+	TOTAL ALL OTHER	TOTAL SLAVES	TOTALS	DISTRICT/ TOWNSHIP	NOTES
Needham	147	43	Mills	Lemuel	2		1		1	1	2		1				8		
Needham	147	40	Mills	Oliver	1	2		1	1	1		1	1	1			9		
Needham	147	41	Mills	William				1					1				2		
Braintree	71	1	Milton	Robert			1	1		1							4		
Roxbury	102	22	Minot	Drever											8		8		
Dorchester	59	8	Minott	G.R.	1			1		1		1	1				5		
Dorchester	58	21	Minott	George	1		2	1		1	1	1	1	2			10		
Dorchester	58	22	Minott	Jno		1	1	1	1	2	1	2					9		
Walpole	30	19	Miriam	Ebenezer					1	1				1			3		
Milton	47	30	Mitchel	Andrew	2	1	1	1				2					7		
Stoughton	121	10	Monk	Christopher	2			1		1	1		1				6		
Stoughton	121	7	Monk	Elijah		1	1		1		2	2	1				8		
Stoughton	121	3	Monk	Eliphelet				1						1			2		
Stoughton	121	4	Monk	Eliphelet Jr	2			1		1			1				5		
Stoughton	121	6	Monk	George				1			1		1				3		
Stoughton	121	5	Monk	Jacob	2	1		1				1	1				6		
Stoughton	121	9	Monk	Lemuel	2			1				1					4		
Stoughton	121	8	Monk	William					1		1			1			3		
Dedham	138	44	Montague	Rev William					1								1		
Canton	133	8	Montgomery	John	1	1		1		2			1				6		
Walpole	30	13	Morey	George Revd	2	1			1	2	1		1				8		
Needham	147	37	Morrall	Isaac Doct	1	2	1		2	1		1	1	2			11		
Dedham	138	45	Morrell	Elikim	1	1		1		1	1			2			7		
Foxborough	25	1	Morse	*	1	2		1		1		2	1				8		
Walpole	30	14	Morse	Aaron			1						1				2		
Medway West Parish	97	3	Morse	Abner	1	1	1	1		2	1	1	1	1			10		
Foxborough	24	43	Morse	Adam			2	1	1					1			5		
Walpole	30	16	Morse	Agnes Wd			1		1					1			4		
Foxborough	24	42	Morse	Amos		1	1		1	1	2		1				7		
Needham	147	34	Morse	Amos	1			1					1				3		
Canton	133	6	Morse	Asa	3	1		1		1			1				7		
Foxborough	25	7	Morse	Asa			1	1						1			3		
Medway West Parish	97	5	Morse	Benoni				1				1		1			3		
Medway East Parish	93	28	Morse	Benoni Jun		1		1	1	3	1	1	1				9		
Foxborough	24	35	Morse	Daniel				1						1			2		
Franklin	163	22	Morse	Darius	3		1	1					1	1			7		
Dedham	142	22	Morse	David	1	1		1		1	1	1					6	1st Parish	
Medfield	88	24	Morse	Eliakim		1		1					2				4		
Medfield	88	25	Morse	Eliakim Jun	1	1	1			1	1		1				6		
Sharon	35	26	Morse	Elijah	1			1		2			1				5		
Sharon	35	20	Morse	Eliphalet		1		1		3	1		1				7		
Foxborough	24	36	Morse	Elisha		1		1						2			4		
Walpole	30	7	Morse	Ezekiel	1			1		2		1					5		
Sharon	35	17	Morse	Ezra		1		1				1		1			4		
Dedham	142	20	Morse	George		1		1		1	1	1					5	1st Parish	
Sharon	35	21	Morse	Gillead		1		1		1		1		1			5		
Foxborough	25	8	Morse	Head	3			1		1			1				6		
Canton	133	7	Morse	Henry		1		1		2	3		1				8		
Medway West Parish	97	4	Morse	Henry				1				1		1			3		
Foxborough	24	39	Morse	Jacob		1		1				1		1			4		
Bellingham	160	24	Morse	James		1						1					2		
Medfield	88	27	Morse	James		1		1	1					1			4		
Foxborough	25	4	Morse	Jarvis				1		1		1					3		
Franklin	169	28	Morse	Jason	3		1	1		1	1		1				8		
Foxborough	24	40	Morse	Jedediah				1			1			1			3		
Dorchester	59	5	Morse	Jno			1			2		1					4		
Canton	133	5	Morse	John			1	1						1			3		
Dedham	142	18	Morse	John				1						1	1		3	1st Parish	
Foxborough	25	5	Morse	John			1					1	1				3		
Sharon	35	22	Morse	John	1	1		1		2			1				6		
Dedham	142	19	Morse	John Junr	2	1			1			1		1			6	1st Parish	
Sharon	35	19	Morse	Joseph		1		1	1				1	1			5		
Stoughton	121	11	Morse	Joseph	1	2	1		1	2	1		1				9		
Sharon	35	24	Morse	Joseph Jr	2	1		1					1				5		
Walpole	30	9	Morse	Joshua			1	1						1			3		
Walpole	30	8	Morse	Jotham			1		1		1			2			5		
Wrentham	171	25	Morse	Keturah	1					2			1				4		
Sharon	35	23	Morse	Levi	1		1	1	1	1		2	1	1			9		
Foxborough	24	34	Morse	Margaret										1			1		
Dedham	142	15	Morse	Mehitable	1	1		1				1	1	1			6	1st Parish	
Sharon	35	18	Morse	Nathaniel		2		1					1	1			5		
Walpole	30	15	Morse	Obadiah		1		1		1			1				5		
Dedham	142	23	Morse	Oliver			1	1				1		1			4	1st Parish	
Foxborough	25	9	Morse	Oliver	2			1					1				4		
Wrentham	173	6	Morse	Otis	1			1		2			1				5		
Walpole	30	10	Morse	Richard	1	1		1					1				4		
Canton	133	3	Morse	Saml	1	1			1	1		1	1				6		
Foxborough	25	6	Morse	Samuel		1			1		1			1			4		
Canton	133	4	Morse	Samuel Junr	1			1						1			3		
Franklin	168	1	Morse	Sarah			1			1		1		1			4		

TOWN	PG#	LN#	LAST NAME	FIRST NAME	FWM <10	FWM 10-16	FWM 16-26	FWM 26-45	FWM 45+	FWF <10	FWF 10-16	FWF 16-26	FWF 26-45	FWF 45+	TOTAL ALL OTHER	TOTAL SLAVES	TOTALS	DISTRICT/TOWNSHIP	NOTES
Dedham	142	16	Morse	Sarah Wid										2			2	1st Parish	
Dedham	142	21	Morse	Seth	1	2	2		1		1		1				8	1st Parish	
Foxborough	24	41	Morse	Simon				1				1		1			3		
Foxborough	24	37	Morse	Solomon				1					1	1			3		
Medfield	88	26	Morse	Thaddeus			1			3			1				5		
Medway East Parish	93	27	Morse	Thomas	1			1		1	1	1		3			8		
Foxborough	24	38	Morse	Timothy				1				1		1			3		
Stoughton	121	17	Morton	Abigail Wid									2	1			3		
Stoughton	121	12	Morton	Ambrose	2	3		1				1	1				8		
Stoughton	121	15	Morton	Eleazar				1		4			1				6		
Dorchester	59	1	Morton	Henry				1		1			1				3		
Stoughton	121	13	Morton	Isaac	1		1	1		1			1				5		
Stoughton	121	16	Morton	Nathl		2	1						1				4		
Dorchester	58	20	Morton	Perez				3		3	1	1	1		3		12		
Stoughton	121	14	Morton	Seth			1	1		2			1				5		
Milton	47	31	Morton	Thad	2	1		1				1					5		
Dorchester	58	32	Mosely	P.M.			1										1		
Dorchester	58	28	Mosely	Thom.	2	1	1	1		1	2	1	1	1			11		
Dorchester	58	24	Munro	Saml				1						1			2		
Dorchester	58	25	Munro	Thom.			1	1		1		1	1				5		
Dorchester	58	23	Munro	Wm			1						1				2		
Roxbury	112	5	Munroe	Daniel	1	1		1						1			4	3rd Parish	
Roxbury	106	1	Munroe	Jedediah			1	2			2		1				6		
Roxbury	106	4	Munroe	Nehemiah		1	5	1		1			1	1			10		
Roxbury	111	27	Murdock	Ebenezer	1	1	1	1					1	1			6	2nd Parish	
Roxbury	111	26	Murdock	Ephraim				1		2	1		1				5	2nd Parish	
Brookline	114	15	Murdock	Nathaniel	1		3	1		2		1	1				9		
Milton	48	2	Murray	Jno				1					1				2		
Roxbury	104	32	Murreil	Joseph	1		1	1		3			1				7		
Needham	149	17	Muze	Benoi	1		1			2		1					5		
Braintree	71	11	Nash	Asa	1			1		2		1					5		
Braintree	71	10	Nash	Benjm		2		1		4			1				8		
Weymouth	76	33	Nash	Charles	1			1		2			1				5	North Parish	
Weymouth	76	34	Nash	Ebenezer	1		1						1				3	North Parish	
Weymouth	76	26	Nash	Elisha					1								1	North Parish	
Weymouth	76	27	Nash	Ezra	1	1		1		3	1			1			8	North Parish	
Weymouth	76	25	Nash	Job	2	2			1	1	1		1	1			9	North Parish	
Weymouth	80	11	Nash	John				1									1	South Parish	
Weymouth	76	29	Nash	Joseph				1				1		1			3	North Parish	
Weymouth	76	30	Nash	Joseph Junr	4	1		1	1	1	2		1				11	North Parish	
Weymouth	80	10	Nash	Joshua	1	1	1	1		1			1				6	South Parish	
Braintree	71	12	Nash	Marcy Wid			1							1			2		
Braintree	71	13	Nash	Miriam Wid		1						1					2		
Weymouth	76	24	Nash	Moses	1	1	1		1	2	1	1		1			9	North Parish	
Weymouth	76	31	Nash	Timothy	1		1	1		1			2	1			7	North Parish	
Weymouth	76	32	Nash	Zadoc	1	2		1						1			5	North Parish	
Weymouth	76	28	Nash	Zichri	3	1	1	1						2			8	North Parish	
Walpole	30	24	Nason	Jesse			1	1				1					3		
Walpole	30	25	Nason	Nathanael	1			1						1			3		
Walpole	30	23	Nason	Willaby	2			1		1		1		1			6		
Walpole	30	22	Needham	John			1	1	2		1	1	2				8		
Dorchester	59	16	Neuman	Henry	3			1		2			1	1			8		
Braintree	71	7	Newcomb	Abraham	1			1					1				3		
Braintree	71	5	Newcomb	Bryant	4	2		1		2	1		1				11		
Quincy	42	40	Newcomb	Charles	3			1		2	2		1	1			10		
Quincy	42	39	Newcomb	Eben Jr.	1			1		1		1	1				5		
Braintree	71	3	Newcomb	Ebenz			1	1	1					1			4		
Quincy	42	48	Newcomb	Jno	5	2	3			1	1	2	1	2			17		
Quincy	42	38	Newcomb	Jno R.	3			1		1			1				6		
Braintree	71	8	Newcomb	Jona	1		3			2		1					7		
Braintree	71	9	Newcomb	Micah			1	1						2			4		
Braintree	71	6	Newcomb	Remember	3			1		2			1	1			8		
Quincy	42	37	Newcomb	Richd			1		1				1	1			4		
Braintree	71	4	Newcomb	Saml		1	1		1	1	1		1				6		
Roxbury	99	2	Newell	Abigail									1	1			2		
Needham	148	3	Newell	Elizabeth Wid.										1			1		
Needham	148	5	Newell	George	1			1		1			1				4		
Dover	150	39	Newell	Jesse	2			1		3			1				7		
Dover	150	40	Newell	Jonathan			2						1				3		
Needham	148	4	Newell	Josiah		1	1	2		2		1	1				8		
Dedham	138	47	Newell	Ruben Maj	1			1			1						3		
Wrentham	175	18	Newell	Silas	1			1		1			1				4		
Roxbury	108	1	Newman	Andrew		1	1		1		1			1			5		
Cohasset	152	7	Newrich	Hezekiah								1		1			2		
Cohasset	154	27	Nichols	Aaron	3	1		1		1			1	1			8		
Cohasset	154	27	Nichols	Ambrose	1			1		1	1	1	1				5		
Cohasset	152	41	Nichols	Caleb	2		1		1		1	1	1				7		
Cohasset	154	30	Nichols	Daniel	1			1				1	1	1			5		
Cohasset	154	35	Nichols	David	3	1		1		1		1	1				8		
Cohasset	154	29	Nichols	Doc Israel		1				1			2	1			5		
Cohasset	153	47	Nichols	Enoch	2			1		1			1	1			6		
Cohasset	152	6	Nichols	John	1	1		1		2		1	1				7		

TOWN	PG#	LN#	LAST NAME	FIRST NAME	M under 10	M 10 to 16	M 16 to 26	M 26 to 45	M 45 and over	F under 10	F 10 to 16	F 16 to 26	F 26 to 45	F 45 and over	TOTAL ALL OTHER	TOTAL SLAVES	TOTALS	DISTRICT/ TOWNSHIP	NOTES
Cohasset	154	36	Nichols	Lott	1		1		1	2	2	1		1			9		
Cohasset	152	16	Nichols	Maria									1	1			2		
Cohasset	154	38	Nichols	Nathaniel		1		1		1	1	1	1				6		
Cohasset	154	41	Nichols	Nathaniel Junr				1			2		1				4		
Cohasset	154	17	Nichols	Percie Jones	2		1			1			1				5		
Cohasset	154	10	Nichols	Peter		1		1		2	2	1		1			8		
Cohasset	154	13	Nichols	Thomas	2			1		1			1				5		
Dorchester	59	15	Nicholson	Jno			2	1		3		1	2				9		
Wrentham	176	32	Nicholson	John		1		1					1				3		
Quincy	42	44	Nightingale	Dan	1		1			1		1					4		
Quincy	42	46	Nightingale	Eben	2	3	1			1			1				8		
Braintree	71	14	Nightingale	Elisha	2		1					1					4		
Quincy	42	45	Nightingale	Jno	1	2	1			2		1					7		
Quincy	42	42	Nightingale	Jos.			2	1		3			1				7		
Quincy	42	41	Nightingale	Reg	1	3				1	1						6		
Quincy	42	47	Nightingale	Saml	1		1	1				1	1				5		
Quincy	42	43	Nightingale	Saml Jr	3			1		1			1				6		
Randolph	126	7	Niles	Ebenezer				1				1		1			3		
Dorchester	59	17	Niles	Ebenz	3	2	2	1		2			2				12		
Randolph	126	4	Niles	Isaac	1			1		1	1			2			6		
Randolph	126	5	Niles	Jacob	1			1		2			2				6		
Randolph	126	6	Niles	Joshua				1		3			1				5		
Randolph	126	3	Niles	Nathaniel		1		1			1			1			4		
Roxbury	106	11	Nolen	Thomas				1		1			1				3		
Roxbury	103	20	Nolin	George	1			1		2			1				5		
Franklin	168	24	Norcrose	Asa	1			1					2				4		
Weymouth	76	23	Norton	Jacob Revd	4	1							2				8	North Parish	
Wrentham	178	19	Norton	Jerusha	1		1			2			1				5		
Weymouth	80	12	Norton	John				1			1		1				3	South Parish	
Randolph	126	8	Noyes	David	1	2	1	1		1		1	1				8		
Dedham	139	1	Noyes	James				1		1							2		
Dedham	139	2	Noyes	Nathaniel				1		1		1					3		
Needham	148	2	Noyes	Thomas Revd.			1										1		
Randolph	126	9	Nucumb	Samuel			1						1	1			3		
Cohasset	153	34	Oakes	Jonah				1		3	1	2	1				8		
Cohasset	152	34	Oaks	Josiah Widow		1	1					1			1		4		
Needham	148	7	Obrine	Richard				1		3			1				5		
Needham	148	6	Ockinton	David		1		1				1		1			4		
Cohasset	152	15	Oliver	Timothy		1		1		1	1	1	1				6		
Medfield	88	28	Onion	David	1	2	1						1	1			6		
Weymouth	80	13	Orcutt	Andrew				1						1			2	South Parish	
Cohasset	152	45	Orcutt	Ignatious		1	1	1					1				4		
Weymouth	80	14	Orcutt	Moses	2		1	1		2	2		1				9	South Parish	
Dedham	139	3	Orion	Anna Wid		2	2					1	1	1			7		
Dedham	144	31	Orion	Elihu	3			1		1		1	1	1			8	2nd Parish	
Roxbury	104	20	Orr	Mary		1							1	1			3		
Stoughton	121	18	Osgood	Samuel		1		1	1	1			1	2			7		
Cohasset	153	29	Osier	Martha									1	1			2		
Stoughton	121	22	Packard	Abiezer			3		1				1	2			7		
Stoughton	121	21	Packard	Benja	3			1		1	1		1	1			8		
Randolph	126	10	Packard	Samuel		1	1					1					3		
Roxbury	108	16	Packard	Seth		5	1	1		2				1			10		
Walpole	30	35	Page	Asa				1			4	1	1				7		
Stoughton	121	19	Page	Charles	2	1	1		1	1	1	3	1	1			12		
Walpole	30	34	Page	Joseph		1		1		1	2		1	1			7		
Walpole	30	37	Page	Oliver	1		1					1					3		
Foxborough	25	30	Paine	Abial	3	1			1		1	2	1				9		
Foxborough	25	13	Paine	Anna Wd	1	2							1				4		
Foxborough	25	12	Paine	Asa	3			1		1			1	1			7		
Randolph	126	12	Paine	Benjamin	4	1		1					1	1			8		
Bellingham	161	21	Paine	Dan	1			1		1	1	1	1				6		
Foxborough	25	31	Paine	Enoch		1	1		1	1	1		1				6		
Needham	148	10	Paine	Epheriam	1			1		1	1			1			5		
Bellingham	160	20	Paine	Gideon				1				1		1			3		
Foxborough	25	32	Paine	Jacob	3	2	2		1	1			1	1			11		
Randolph	126	14	Paine	Nathl				1		1			2				4		
Randolph	126	13	Paine	Silas	4			1		1			1	1			8		
Foxborough	25	28	Paine	Stephen	1		1						1				3		
Bellingham	160	21	Paine	Thomas			1	1		1	2			1			6		
Foxborough	25	11	Paine	William		1	1						2	1			5		
Randolph	126	11	Paine	Zeba	3			1					2				6		
Dorchester	60	6	Palfrey	Jno	3			1			1	1	1				7		
Walpole	30	36	Palley	Nathael		1	2		1	2	1		2	1			10		
Dedham	142	26	Palmer	Anna								1					1	1st Parish	
Needham	148	8	Palmer	Stephen Revd.	1		2	1		2	1	1	1				9		
Roxbury	109	14	Pane	Samuel				1						1			2	2nd Parish	
Roxbury	114	6	Parker	Caleb	1			1					1	1			4	3rd Parish	
Needham	148	13	Parker	Jacob				2						1			3		
Roxbury	112	2	Parker	John	2		2	1			3		2	2			12	3rd Parish	
Dedham	140	30	Parker	Jonathan	1		1	1		1		1	1				6		
Needham	148	9	Parker	Nathaniel				1					1				2		
Needham	148	16	Parker	Olive Wid.		1				4		1	1				7		

TOWN	PG#	LN#	HEADS OF HOUSEHOLD LAST NAME	FIRST NAME	FWM under 10	FWM 10 to 16	FWM 16 to 26	FWM 26 to 45	FWM 45 and over	FWF under 10	FWF 10 to 16	FWF 16 to 26	FWF 26 to 45	FWF 45 and over	TOTAL ALL OTHER	TOTAL SLAVES	TOTALS	DISTRICT/ TOWNSHIP	NOTES
Roxbury	105	21	Parker	Ruben	1	1	1	3					1				7		
Dorchester	60	3	Parker	Sally				1					1				2		
Needham	148	14	Parker	Samuel	2			1					1				4		
Milton	48	7	Parker	Solom			1	1		1			1				4		
Needham	148	15	Parker	William	3			1		3			1				8		
Roxbury	102	33	Parker	William	1			1					1				3		
Franklin	165	11	Parkhurst	Moses	1			1		2			1				5		
Medway East Parish	94	4	Parnel	Benjamin		1		1		2			2				6		
Medway East Parish	94	3	Partridge	Darius		1		1					1				3		
Franklin	166	28	Partridge	Eleazer		1		1	1	1	1	1		1			6		
Medway West Parish	97	7	Partridge	Elijah	1			1				1	1	1			5		
Medway West Parish	97	10	Partridge	Ezekiel			2						1				3		
Walpole	30	29	Partridge	Henry				1					1				2		
Walpole	30	31	Partridge	Henry Jr	1	1	1			2	1	1		1			8		
Bellingham	158	2	Partridge	Job		1	1	1	1	1	2	2		1			10		
Medway West Parish	97	6	Partridge	Joel	1		1		1	2	1		1				7		
Bellingham	158	3	Partridge	Joseph	1	2	1		2	1		2		2			11		
Medway East Parish	93	30	Partridge	Joshua				1				1		1	2		5		
Medfield	89	1	Partridge	Nathan				1					2				3		
Medway West Parish	97	9	Partridge	Nathaniel				1				1	1				3		
Medfield	89	2	Partridge	Oliver	2			1					1				4		
Walpole	30	30	Partridge	Otis	4	2		1	1	2	1		1				12		
Medway East Parish	93	29	Partridge	Samuel	1	1		1		2	2	2		1			10		
Medway East Parish	94	1	Partridge	Seth				1					1				2		
Medway West Parish	97	8	Partridge	Simeon		2		1					1				4		
Roxbury	108	2	Partridge	Thaddeus				1		1			1				3		
Wrentham	176	24	Partridge	Timothy	1			1		3			1				6		
Medway East Parish	94	2	Partridge	Ziba	1		1	1		1			1				5		
Canton	133	9	Patrick	Deborah Wid.									1				1		
Roxbury	108	20	Patrick	Phinehas	2			1				1					4		
Walpole	30	32	Pattee	Benjamin		1		1		2	1		1				6		
Foxborough	25	29	Patten	David		1		1		3		1	1				7		
Roxbury	106	32	Patten	Nathaniel	1	1	2	1		2			1				8		
Roxbury	106	35	Patten	William		3	1			1			1				6		
Dedham	139	4	Paul	Ebenezer		1	3	1		1			1				7		
Stoughton	121	20	Paul	Samuel	2		1	1		1	1		1				7		
Dorchester	60	10	Paul	Wm	1			1		2			1				5		
Roxbury	106	15	Payson	Abigail								1		1			2		
Dorchester	59	24	Payson	George	1	1		1		4			1				8		
Foxborough	25	22	Payson	Phillips	1	1				2		1					5		
Dorchester	59	23	Payson	Saml			1						1				2		
Dorchester	59	29	Payson	Saml	2		2	1		1	1	1		1	1		10		
Roxbury	113	7	Payson	Stephen	2	1	4		1			1	1	1			11	3rd Parish	
Foxborough	25	21	Payson	Swift		1		1		1	1		1				5		
Walpole	30	33	Payton	Kezia Wd		1							1				2		
Weymouth	77	4	Peakes	Joseph	1		1		1	1	1		1				7	North Parish	
Franklin	164	17	Pearce	John	3			1		1		1					6		
Braintree	71	26	Peck	Elijah			1					1					2		
Wrentham	175	27	Peck	Jesse	1		1				1						3		
Wrentham	175	26	Peck	Solomon		1		1					1				3		
Roxbury	101	19	Peirce	Eli			1		1			1					3		
Needham	148	12	Peirce	Elikem	3	1		1		1			1				7		
Roxbury	101	9	Peirce	James	1			1		1			1				4		
Brookline	114	19	Peirce	John Rev		1	1			1			1				4		
Roxbury	104	27	Peirce	Lemuel	1		1	2		1			1				6		
Roxbury	106	6	Peirce	Martin	1	1		1		2	1	1	1				8		
Roxbury	101	33	Peirpont	Robert	2	1	2	5		1			1	2			14		
Stoughton	121	24	Pendergrass	John	1			1		2			1				5		
Dedham	142	24	Peniman	Jacob				1					1				2	1st Parish	
Braintree	71	21	Penniman	Asa	1		2					1					4		
Braintree	71	18	Penniman	Barzilla	3		1	1				1					6		
Bellingham	159	8	Penniman	Daniel		1		1		1	1		1				5		
Braintree	71	22	Penniman	Ebenz	1			1				1	1				4		
Braintree	71	23	Penniman	Ebenz Junr			1			1			1				3		
Randolph	126	15	Penniman	Enoch			1			2		1		1			5		
Braintree	71	19	Penniman	Ezra			1						1				2		
Medway East Parish	94	5	Penniman	James			1						1	1			3		
Bellingham	159	9	Penniman	Nathan			1			1			1				3		
Braintree	71	20	Penniman	Samuel	3		1			2			1				7		
Braintree	71	15	Penniman	Stephen			1			3			1				5		
Braintree	71	16	Penniman	Stephen Junior	3		1			1			1				6		
Braintree	71	17	Penniman	William		3	1	1				1	1				7		
Franklin	167	22	Perrigo	James Junr	2			1					1				4		
Roxbury	112	6	Perry	Benjamin		1	1			1			1				4	3rd Parish	
Medfield	89	6	Perry	Daniel		1	1		1				2	2			7		
Medfield	89	7	Perry	Eleazer				1		2	1		1				5		
Bellingham	162	3	Perry	Lot		1		1		1			1				4		
Milton	48	8	Perry	Nehemh	3		1						1				5		
Dover	150	42	Perry	Samuel	4		1	1		2		1	1				10		
Franklin	167	2	Perry	Simeon		1	1			1			1				4		
Dorchester	60	7	Perry	Thom.	2			1		1			1				5		

TOWN	PG#	LN#	LAST NAME	FIRST NAME	FWM under 10	FWM 10 to 16	FWM 16 to 26	FWM 26 to 45	FWM 45 and over	FWF under 10	FWF 10 to 16	FWF 16 to 26	FWF 26 to 45	FWF 45 and over	TOTAL ALL OTHER	TOTAL SLAVES	TOTALS	DISTRICT/TOWNSHIP	NOTES
Dedham	139	8	Persons	Eli		2	5	1					1				9		
Roxbury	114	10	Peter	John	2			1		2	2		1				8	3rd Parish	
Medfield	89	3	Peters	Adam				1				1		1			3		
Medfield	89	5	Peters	Jethro				1				1					2		
Medfield	89	4	Peters	William		1	2	1		1		1					6		
Foxborough	25	16	Pettee	Benjamin		1	1	1					1	1			5		
Foxborough	25	18	Pettee	David	1			1		1			1				4		
Foxborough	25	17	Pettee	Hezekiah	3			1		2	1		1				8		
Foxborough	25	33	Pettee	Oliver	1	1	1	1		1	1		1				7		
Dedham	144	32	Pettee	Samuel		1		1						1			3	2nd Parish	
Foxborough	25	20	Pettee	Simon	1	1	2	1		2				1			8		
Foxborough	25	19	Pettee	William				1						1			2		
Dedham	140	31	Pettengill	John	1			1						1			3		
Dover	150	41	Petterlow	Eve									1	1			2		
Canton	133	13	Pettingill	Elkhanah				1				1		1			3		
Medway East Parish	94	6	Philips	Jedidiah	1	1		1		1		2		1			7		
Bellingham	162	1	Phillips	Joshua	1		1	1		2	2	1	1				9		
Weymouth	77	1	Phillips	William				1									1	North Parish	
Weymouth	77	15	Phillips	William Junr			1			2			1				4	North Parish	
Quincy	42	54	Phipps	Thom	2	1		1		2	1	1	1				9		
Dedham	142	27	Phipps	William		1		1					1				3	1st Parish	
Bellingham	161	20	Pickering	Samuel			1	1				2	1	1			6		
Bellingham	161	13	Pickering	Simon	1			1		3			1				6		
Dorchester	60	4	Pierce	Abrahm			1	1		3			1				6		
Dorchester	59	30	Pierce	Benj		1	2		1				2	1			7		
Milton	48	9	Pierce	Charles	3	2		1	1	1			1	1			10		
Dorchester	59	19	Pierce	Edward	2	2	1	1	1	1		3	2				13		
Dorchester	60	1	Pierce	Heph	1		1	1					2				5		
Canton	133	10	Pierce	Jesse	1			1			1		1				4		
Dorchester	60	8	Pierce	Jno		1	2	1	1	2		4		1			12		
Dorchester	60	11	Pierce	Jno	1	1	4		1			1	1	1			10		
Milton	48	13	Pierce	Jno				1					2				3		
Quincy	42	50	Pierce	Jonas		1	1					1	1				5		
Dorchester	59	20	Pierce	Joseph			2	1		1			1	1			6		
Milton	48	10	Pierce	Lettrice							1		1				2		
Quincy	42	53	Pierce	Richd	1			1		2			1				5		
Dorchester	59	21	Pierce	Robert				1				1	1				3		
Milton	48	11	Pierce	Rufus	2		1		1	1	2	3	1				11		
Dorchester	59	18	Pierce	Saml		1	2	1	1	1	1		1				8		
Stoughton	121	23	Pierce	Seth		1		1		2			1				5		
Dorchester	59	22	Pierce	Thom.	2	1		1		2	3		1				10		
Randolph	126	16	Pierce	William	1			1				1					3		
Milton	48	12	Pierce	Wm	3	1		1		1	1		1				8		
Roxbury	108	29	Pierpont	Ebenezer				1				1	1				3		
Medway West Parish	97	11	Pike	Elijah	2			1		1			1				5		
Milton	48	6	Pinchbeck	Wm F.	1			1		1	1		1				5		
Canton	133	12	Pitcher	Abijah			1			1		1					3		
Canton	133	11	Pitcher	Eliakim		1		1						1			3		
Canton	133	14	Pitter	Nathl	2			1						1			4		
Medfield	89	11	Plimpton	Abigail			1							1			2		
Medfield	89	10	Plimpton	Amos				1				1					2		
Foxborough	25	14	Plimpton	Asa	1	2	1	1				1	1	2			9		
Medfield	89	13	Plimpton	Augustus		1	1						1	1			4		
Medfield	89	14	Plimpton	David				2		2			1	1	1		7		
Medfield	89	15	Plimpton	David Jun	2			1		2	1		1				7		
Foxborough	25	15	Plimpton	Elijah	1	2		1					1				5		
Medway East Parish	94	7	Plimpton	Ezekiel	1	1		1		1		1	1				7		
Medway West Parish	97	12	Plimpton	Job			1	1		1				1			4		
Medfield	89	16	Plimpton	Joseph			1			1			1				3		
Medfield	89	8	Plimpton	Ruth										1			1		
Medfield	89	12	Plimpton	Sarah			1							2			3		
Medfield	89	9	Plimpton	Silas			2		1				2				5		
Sharon	35	28	Plimpton	Zeba			2		1	1	1		1				6		
Weymouth	77	3	Plumber	Joseph				1					1				2	North Parish	
Roxbury	104	16	Poignard	David	1			1			2	1	1				6		
Milton	48	15	Pollock	Susan							1	2		1			4		
Wrentham	178	30	Pond	Abijah		1	2		2	2		3	3		1		14		
Wrentham	174	24	Pond	Abner Junr	2			1					1				4		
Wrentham	179	5	Pond	Barnard	2			1		1	1		1				6		
Franklin	169	25	Pond	Barzilla	1	1		1		2	1	1	2				9		
Franklin	166	26	Pond	Bejamin			3	1									4		
Franklin	166	23	Pond	Benajah	2			1		2			1				6		
Wrentham	173	2	Pond	David		1	1	1						3			6		
Walpole	30	28	Pond	Eli	1			1		1			1				4		
Franklin	166	20	Pond	Elihu	2		1	1		1		1	1	2			9		
Wrentham	178	32	Pond	Elijah	4			1		1			1				7		
Dedham	139	7	Pond	Eliphalet Capt	1	1	1		1	1	1			1	2		9		
Franklin	166	10	Pond	Goldsbury	1	1		1					1				4		
Franklin	166	24	Pond	Hezekiah			1		1		1		1	2			6		
Franklin	166	25	Pond	Ichabod	1			1					1				3		

TOWN	PG#	LN#	LAST NAME	FIRST NAME	Free White Males under 10	10 to 16	16 to 26	26 to 45	45 and over	Free White Females under 10	10 to 16	16 to 26	26 to 45	45 and over	TOTAL ALL OTHER	TOTAL SLAVES	TOTALS	DISTRICT/ TOWNSHIP	NOTES
Wrentham	179	16	Pond	Increase	1	1		1					1	1			5		
Wrentham	177	32	Pond	Jabez	1			1		1		1					4		
Wrentham	178	31	Pond	Jacob				1						1			2		
Franklin	163	3	Pond	Jamotis	2			1				1		2			6		
Wrentham	179	13	Pond	Jeremiah				1						2			3		
Roxbury	111	15	Pond	John		2		1				1		1			5	2nd Parish	
Dedham	139	5	Pond	Jonas		1		1	2		1		1				6		
Wrentham	179	4	Pond	Joseph				1						2			3		
Franklin	168	12	Pond	Malkiah		1	1	1						1			5		
Dedham	139	21	Pond	Moses	1			1		3	1	1	1	1			9		
Medway East Parish	94	8	Pond	Moses			1	1	1	1			1	1			6		
Walpole	30	26	Pond	Nathan				1					1				2		
Walpole	30	27	Pond	Nathan Jn	3	2		1		2			1				9		
Franklin	166	9	Pond	Oliver				1				1	1				3		
Wrentham	179	15	Pond	Oliver			1	2	1		1	2	1				8		
Franklin	166	6	Pond	Oliver Junr	1			1		2			2				6		
Franklin	163	5	Pond	Oliver N.	1		1	1		2			1				6		
Wrentham	173	3	Pond	Pellue	1		1	1		1	2		1				7		
Wrentham	172	13	Pond	Reuben			1		1		1			1			4		
Franklin	168	2	Pond	Robert				1				1	1				3		
Franklin	168	3	Pond	Robert Junr	3		1	1		1		1	2	1			10		
Dedham	139	22	Pond	Samuel	1			1		2		1					5		
Franklin	168	13	Pond	Samuel		2		2					1				5		
Franklin	167	10	Pond	Solomon	1		1	1		1			2				6		
Franklin	166	22	Pond	Timothy	2		1			2			1				6		
Wrentham	177	31	Pond	Timothy				1			1		1				3		
Franklin	168	14	Pond	William	2			1		1	1		1				6		
Wrentham	177	7	Pond	William				1		4			1				6		
Wrentham	177	33	Pond	William				1		3	1		1				6		
Weymouth	80	24	Pool	Gardner		1				1							2	South Parish	
Braintree	71	27	Pool	Thomas	1			1		2			1				5		
Weymouth	80	19	Pool	Thomas			1		1			1		1			4	South Parish	
Dedham	139	9	Poor	Daniel	1	1	2	1		1	1		1				8		
Quincy	42	52	Pope	Asa	1	1		1		1		1					6		
Dorchester	59	27	Pope	Elijah				1			2	1	1				5		
Dorchester	59	28	Pope	Fred & Wm	2		3	1		1		2					9		
Stoughton	121	25	Pope	Frederick		1	1		1	1			1				5		
Quincy	42	55	Pope	Jno			1		2			1					4		
Dorchester	59	26	Pope	John		1		1	1	1			1	2			7		
Milton	48	4	Pope	Joseph		1		1		2		1					5		
Stoughton	121	28	Pope	Lazarus	2	1	1		1		1	3		1			10		
Stoughton	121	27	Pope	Ralph				1		1			1				3		
Stoughton	121	26	Pope	Sarah Wid		1	?				2	1		1			7		
Stoughton	121	32	Porter	Abigail Wid									1				1		
Randolph	126	17	Porter	Abijah			1			1			1				3		
Weymouth	77	7	Porter	Abner				1					1				2	North Parish	
Stoughton	121	31	Porter	Cyrus		1						1					2		
Quincy	42	49	Porter	David			1					1					2		
Weymouth	80	16	Porter	Isaac Wid of							2	1	1				4	South Parish	
Wrentham	176	29	Porter	John	2			1		1	1		1				6		
Weymouth	77	6	Porter	Jonathan		1		1			2		2				6	North Parish	
Randolph	126	18	Porter	Joseph	2	2		1		2			1				8		
Stoughton	121	29	Porter	Joseph				2		1	1		1				5		
Weymouth	80	22	Porter	Joseph				1				2	1				4	South Parish	
Weymouth	77	18	Porter	Joseph Junr	1		1						1				3	North Parish	
Wrentham	178	29	Porter	Libbeus	1		1			2	1		1	1			7		
Stoughton	121	30	Porter	Robert	1	1		1					1				4		
Weymouth	77	8	Porter	William				1					1				2	North Parish	
Roxbury	111	4	Posthill	Robert			1	1		1			1	1			5	2nd Parish	
Bellingham	159	2	Potter	Olney	2		1			1			1				5		
Cohasset	152	20	Power	Jesse	1	1		1		3	1	1	1				9		
Cohasset	153	31	Pratt	Aaron		1	1	3	1		1	2					9		
Cohasset	153	9	Pratt	Aaron Junr	1		1	1		3	1		1				8		
Weymouth	77	5	Pratt	Abiah	1	1		1		2	1		1				7	North Parish	
Foxborough	25	26	Pratt	Abijah	2	1		1		1	1		1				7		
Weymouth	77	17	Pratt	Abner		2		1					1	1			5	North Parish	
Weymouth	77	16	Pratt	Asa	3			1		2			1				7	North Parish	
Weymouth	76	40	Pratt	Benjamin 2d		1		1		2	1		1				6	North Parish	
Weymouth	77	12	Pratt	Benjamin Junr		1	1	1		1	1	1	1				7	North Parish	
Weymouth	77	14	Pratt	Benjm	1			1					1	1			4	North Parish	
Medfield	89	18	Pratt	Dan	2	1	1						1				5		
Cohasset	153	46	Pratt	Ephraim	3			1		1			1				6		
Weymouth	80	15	Pratt	Ezra			3		1		1	1	2	1			9	South Parish	
Weymouth	76	37	Pratt	Ichabod	1	1		1		1			1	1			6	North Parish	
Foxborough	25	23	Pratt	Isaac		1		1		1	1	1	1				6		
Weymouth	80	18	Pratt	Isaac	1	1		1		3		1					7	South Parish	
Wrentham	180	29	Pratt	Isaac		1	1						1				3		
Quincy	42	56	Pratt	James	1		1					1					3		
Weymouth	76	36	Pratt	James	1		1	1		1		1		1			6	North Parish	
Braintree	71	24	Pratt	Jesse		1		1						2			4		
Foxborough	25	25	Pratt	Jessee				1			1	3	1				6		
Milton	48	14	Pratt	Joel	1		1				1						3		

TOWN	PG#	LN#	LAST NAME	FIRST NAME	FREE WHITE MALES under 10	10 to 16	16 to 26	26 to 45	45 and over	FREE WHITE FEMALES under 10	10 to 16	16 to 26	26 to 45	45 and over	TOTAL ALL OTHER	TOTAL SLAVES	TOTALS	DISTRICT/ TOWNSHIP	NOTES
Cohasset	153	13	Pratt	John		1	1							1			3		
Weymouth	76	42	Pratt	Jona Junior	2			1		1				1			5	North Parish	
Weymouth	76	35	Pratt	Jonathan		1			1	1	1	1		1			6	North Parish	
Bellingham	161	7	Pratt	Joseph	3	1		1		1			1				7		
Cohasset	153	12	Pratt	Joseph	2		1	1		1		2	3	1			11		
Weymouth	80	23	Pratt	Joseph	3			1		1	2			1			8	South Parish	
Weymouth	77	2	Pratt	Joshua		2	1	1		1			1	1			7	North Parish	
Weymouth	77	19	Pratt	Laban	3	1					1		1				7	North Parish	
Foxborough	25	27	Pratt	Levi	1			1		1				1			4		
Weymouth	80	25	Pratt	Mary Wid		1							1	1			3	South Parish	
Weymouth	80	20	Pratt	Matthew	2	1	1		1	2		2		1			10	South Parish	
Weymouth	80	21	Pratt	Matthew Junr		1							1				2	South Parish	
Weymouth	76	41	Pratt	Peter		1		1				1	1				4	North Parish	
Dorchester	60	9	Pratt	Phebe			7	2					1				10		
Weymouth	77	11	Pratt	Robert	2			1		1				1			5	North Parish	
Braintree	71	25	Pratt	Saml	2			1						1			4		
Cohasset	153	32	Pratt	Samuel		1		1		5				1			8		
Needham	148	11	Pratt	Samuel		1	2		1			1		1			6		
Weymouth	77	9	Pratt	Samuel	3	1	2			1	2			1			10	North Parish	
Weymouth	77	10	Pratt	Samuel Junr	1		1						1				3	North Parish	
Foxborough	25	24	Pratt	Sarah Wd	1		1					3		1			6		
Weymouth	76	39	Pratt	Silvanus			1					1		1			3	North Parish	
Roxbury	104	8	Pratt	Simeon		2	1	1		1	1			1			8		
Weymouth	76	38	Pratt	Stephen		1	1	1					1	2			6	North Parish	
Weymouth	77	13	Pratt	Stephen		1	1	1						2			5	North Parish	
Cohasset	152	39	Pratt	Thomas	1		2	2	1			1	2	1			10		
Dedham	139	6	Pratt	William	1			1		2			2	1			7		
Roxbury	104	22	Pratt	William	1		1						1				3		
Weymouth	80	17	Pratt	Zenas	2	1	1	1		2		1		1			9	South Parish	
Quincy	42	58	Pray	Benj	3	1		1		2		1	1	1			10		
Quincy	42	51	Pray	Jno	2	2	3	1		1		1	1				13		
Quincy	42	57	Pray	Samuel				1			1			1			3		
Medfield	89	17	Prentiss	Thomas Rev	3	1	2	1	1	4	1	1	1	2			17		
Cohasset	152	48	Prescott	Caleb	1			1		1		1		1			5		
Dorchester	59	25	Preston	Edwd	1	1	2	2		2	1	1	1				11		
Dorchester	60	2	Preston	Jno		3		1		3			1				8		
Dorchester	60	5	Preston	Sarah			1							3			4		
Roxbury	102	21	Prince	Darbee											5		5		
Roxbury	111	1	Prince												2		2	2nd Parish	First name left blank
Cohasset	152	27	Pritchit	Theodore			1				1			1			3		
Milton	48	5	Proctor	Waren	1			1		1			1				4		
Medway East Parish	94	10	Puffer	Job	4			1			1		1				7		
Canton	133	15	Puffer	John		1		1	2					1			5		
Sharon	35	27	Puffer	Mattathias				1						1			2		
Medway East Parish	94	9	Puffer	William				1						1			2		
Quincy	42	60	Quincy	Josiah Esq			1	1		1			2				5		
Quincy	42	59	Quincy	Morton Esq			1		1				1	1	1		5		
Sharon	35	29	Quinzey	Marquis			1			1		1					3		
Roxbury	106	36	R*ll	Thomas	3	2		1	1	2	1		1				11		
Roxbury	106	10	Ramsdell	Masheck				1					1						
Milton	48	17	Ramsen	Dyar		2		1		2		1	1	1			8		
Sharon	35	30	Randal	Benjm Esq		1		1		1		1	3	1	1		9		
Sharon	35	33	Randal	Joseph			3	1		1							5		
Dorchester	60	22	Randal	Saml			1	1		3	2	1		1			9		
Roxbury	112	20	Randall	Abraham		1		1				1	1				4	3rd Parish	
Dorchester	60	12	Randall	Robt			1			2			1				4		
Sharon	35	41	Rapakeel	John				1		2	1			1			5		
Milton	48	20	Raven	James				1						1			2		
Quincy	42	61	Rawson	Jona	2	2		1		3			1				9		
Wrentham	171	32	Ray	Enos		1		1		2		1	1				6		
Wrentham	171	21	Ray	Mary	2	2						1	1				6		
Wrentham	176	20	Read	Jesse				1		1							2		
Roxbury	103	28	Read	John Esq			1	1						1	1		4		
Roxbury	103	29	Read	John Junr	2	1	1		1	1		1	1				8		
Wrentham	179	12	Read	Jonathan			1	1		1	1			1			5		
Wrentham	177	2	Read	Zachariah		1	2	1				1	1				6		
Randolph	126	20	Reed	Asa	1		1					2					4		
Weymouth	80	32	Reed	Ezra	2	1	2	1		2		1	1	1			11	South Parish	
Randolph	126	19	Reed	Frederick		1	1			2			1	1			5		
Weymouth	80	31	Reed	Frederick	1			1		1				1			4	South Parish	
Milton	48	22	Reed	James			1	1		1				1			4		
Canton	133	16	Reed	James	3	1		1						1			6		
Randolph	126	21	Reed	Jesse			1										1		
Dover	150	48	Reed	John	2			2		1				1			6		
Milton	48	18	Reed	Josiah	1			1		2			1				5		
Milton	48	21	Reed	Noah	1			1		1		1	1				5		
Weymouth	77	20	Reed	Samuel			1	1				2		1			5	North Parish	
Weymouth	77	27	Reed	Thomas			1			4			1				6	North Parish	
Braintree	71	28	Reed	William		1		1		2	2			1			7		
Canton	133	17	Reed	William	1			1						1			3		
Braintree	71	29	Reed	William Junr			1			1			1				3		
Stoughton	121	33	Reynolds	Philip			1	1		1			1				4		
Walpole	31	1	Rhoade	Eleazer			1	1		3				1			5		

TOWN	PG#	LN#	LAST NAME	FIRST NAME	FREE WHITE MALES					FREE WHITE FEMALES					TOTAL ALL OTHER	TOTAL SLAVES	TOTALS	DISTRICT/ TOWNSHIP	NOTES
					under 10	10 to 16	16 to 26	26 to 45	45 and over	under 10	10 to 16	16 to 26	26 to 45	45 and over					
Walpole	30	40	Rhoade	Eliphalet		1	1		1	3	1	1	1				9		
Sharon	35	32	Rhoades	Daniel	3		1	1		2	2	3	1	1			14		
Sharon	35	40	Rhoades	Simeon				1					1				2		
Dedham	142	25	Rhoads	Eleazer	1		1		1			1		1			5	1st Parish	
Dedham	142	17	Rhoads	Wid										2			2	1st Parish	
Wrentham	176	1	Rhodes	Simeon			1	1				1		1			4		
Wrentham	174	27	Rhodes	Timothy	2	2	1	1		1		1	2	1			11		
Foxborough	25	36	Rhods	Stephen	1			1		2		1		1			6		
Weymouth	77	21	Rice	David				1			1		1				3	North Parish	
Weymouth	77	25	Rice	David Junr	3			1		2		1		1			8	North Parish	
Weymouth	77	22	Rice	John		1		1		3				1			6	North Parish	
Weymouth	77	23	Rice	Jonah		1	1		1	2		1	2	2			10	North Parish	
Sharon	35	38	Richard	Benjam Jr	1			1		1		1					4		
Sharon	35	37	Richard	Benjamin			1		1		1			1			4		
Sharon	35	34	Richard	Daniel	1	1	1	1	1				3	1			9		
Sharon	35	36	Richard	Ebenezer		1	1	2	2				2	1			9		
Sharon	35	35	Richard	Jeremiah	2								2	1			6		
Quincy	42	62	Richard	Jno P.	1		3	1		1			1	1			8		
Walpole	30	38	Richard	John		1		1					1				3		
Sharon	35	31	Richard	William		1	1	1		1							4		
Dedham	144	34	Richards	Abel	1		2		1	1		1		1			7	2nd Parish	
Dedham	139	17	Richards	Abiather				1						1			2		
Dedham	139	18	Richards	Abiather Junr	2	1	2		1	3		1	1	1			12		
Roxbury	110	14	Richards	Abigail	1					2			1	1			5	2nd Parish	
Dedham	139	19	Richards	Abigail Wid							1	1		1			3		
Roxbury	114	18	Richards	Ebenezer	1		2	1		1			1	1			7	3rd Parish	
Roxbury	110	10	Richards	Edward				1				1					2	2nd Parish	
Roxbury	110	1	Richards	Elizabeth									1				1	2nd Parish	
Dedham	144	35	Richards	Fredrick		1		1						1			3	2nd Parish	
Dedham	139	10	Richards	Jabez		1	1			2		2					6		
Weymouth	80	29	Richards	Jacob	2			1		3	1		1				8	South Parish	
Weymouth	80	28	Richards	James	1		1	1	1				1	1			6	South Parish	
Weymouth	80	30	Richards	James 2d	1			1		2		1					5	South Parish	
Dedham	139	11	Richards	Jesse	3			1		2			1				7		
Dedham	144	33	Richards	John				1					2		1		4	2nd Parish	
Dedham	139	16	Richards	Jonathan	1	1		2		2	1	1	1				9		
Dedham	139	20	Richards	Joseph	2			1		1				1			5		
Dover	150	49	Richards	Joseph	4	1		1						1			7		
Roxbury	110	2	Richards	Joseph			2		1			1		1			5	2nd Parish	
Stoughton	121	34	Richards	Joseph			2		1		1	1		1			6		
Roxbury	110	12	Richards	Joshua	1		3	1		1		1	1				8	2nd Parish	
Dover	150	50	Richards	Josiah		1		1									2		
Dover	150	43	Richards	Lemuel				1			1	1		1			4		
Roxbury	110	17	Richards	Levi			1	1		1			1				4	2nd Parish	
Dedham	139	12	Richards	Luther	1			1			1	1					6		
Weymouth	80	27	Richards	Nath				1				1		1			3	South Parish	
Weymouth	77	24	Richards	Nathl Junr			1	1		1	2		1				6	North Parish	
Weymouth	80	35	Richards	Phebe Wid	1						1		1				3	South Parish	
Roxbury	110	34	Richards	Rebecca	1									1			2	2nd Parish	
Dover	150	46	Richards	Richard		1	1	1	1	1			1	1			7		
Weymouth	80	36	Richards	Robert				1		2			1				4	South Parish	
Dedham	139	15	Richards	Ruben	1	1	2	1					1	1			7		
Dorchester	60	20	Richards	Saml	1			1		1	1		1				5		
Dedham	139	13	Richards	Samuel	1	3		1		2	1	1	1				10		
Dover	150	45	Richards	Solomon	1	1		1		1	1		1				6		
Weymouth	80	34	Richards	Thomas	1			1		1	1	1					5	South Parish	
Dedham	139	14	Richards	Timothy	1	1		1					1	1			5		
Dover	150	44	Richards	William			1	1				1		1			4		
Dorchester	60	21	Richards	Wm		1	1	1		1	1		1				6		
Franklin	168	6	Richardson	Abigail		1					3	1	1				6		
Medway West Parish	97	14	Richardson	Abigail				1					1	2			4		
Medway East Parish	94	11	Richardson	Abijah	1		2		1	2	2	1	1				10		
Franklin	163	16	Richardson	Amasa	2	1		1					1				5		
Medway West Parish	97	15	Richardson	Amos			2			1		2		1			6		
Wrentham	179	32	Richardson	Amos	1			1		3		1					6		
Medway East Parish	94	19	Richardson	Asa	1			1		3		1					6		
Medway East Parish	94	18	Richardson	Asa P		1		1				1		1			4		
Wrentham	177	3	Richardson	Daniel	1			1				1	1				4		
Franklin	163	19	Richardson	Daniel	2	1	2		1			3		1			10		
Needham	148	19	Richardson	Ebenezer				1						1			2		
Franklin	163	31	Richardson	Eli		1	2		1			1		1			6		
Medway East Parish	94	17	Richardson	Elisha	1		2		1	3				1			8		
Franklin	163	26	Richardson	Ezekiel	1			1			1	2					5		
Medway East Parish	94	20	Richardson	Ezra	2	1	1	1		2	1	2	1				11		
Medway West Parish	97	13	Richardson	James	2			1		3	1		1	1			9		
Wrentham	173	25	Richardson	Jason		1		1		2		1	1	1			7		
Franklin	169	4	Richardson	John				1				1		1			3		
Franklin	169	5	Richardson	John W.	1		1		1			1					4		
Medway East Parish	94	12	Richardson	Joseph	1		1			2		1					5		
Franklin	163	27	Richardson	Leva				1		3	2		1				7		
Medway East Parish	94	15	Richardson	Moses			1		1			1	1				4		
Medway East Parish	94	16	Richardson	Moses Jun			1			1		1					3		

124

TOWN	PG#	LN#	HEADS OF HOUSEHOLD LAST NAME	FIRST NAME	FREE WHITE MALES under 10	10 to 16	16 to 26	26 to 45	45 and over	FREE WHITE FEMALES under 10	10 to 16	16 to 26	26 to 45	45 and over	TOTAL ALL OTHER	TOTAL SLAVES	TOTALS	DISTRICT/ TOWNSHIP	NOTES
Medway East Parish	94	13	Richardson	Oliver				1		1				1			3		
Wrentham	173	24	Richardson	Samuel				1			1		1	1			4		
Medway East Parish	94	14	Richardson	Simeon	1	1	1		1	3	1	1		2			11		
Needham	148	18	Richardson	Timothy	1	1		1		1			1	1			6		
Stoughton	121	35	Richmond	Edward Revd		1		1		1		1	1				5		
Dorchester	60	23	Rine	Dennis	1			1					1				3		
Weymouth	80	33	Ripley	Eliphalet				1		4	2		1				8	South Parish	
Quincy	42	63	Ripley	Spencer		1		1		1	1						4		
Weymouth	77	26	Ripley	William				1						2			3	North Parish	
Roxbury	104	11	Roads	Moses		1	1						1				3		
Wrentham	176	30	Robbins	Comfort		1		1					1	1			4		
Milton	48	16	Robbins	Ed H.	2			1		2	3		1		2		11		
Wrentham	176	31	Robbins	Experience									1	1			2		
Needham	148	17	Robbins	Jeremiah		1				1		1					3		
Dover	150	51	Robbins	Nathaniel	1			1		1			1				4		
Walpole	30	39	Robbins	William		1		1		1	1		1				5		
Dorchester	60	18	Robertson	Jno		1		1				1	1		3		7		
Foxborough	25	34	Robins	Eleazer				1						1			2		
Roxbury	105	28	Robins	William		1				1		2					4		
Wrentham	176	16	Robinson	Benjamin				1						1			2		
Dorchester	60	15	Robinson	Edwd	1	1	6	3				1	1				13		
Dorchester	60	16	Robinson	James	1		2	1	1				1				6		
Dorchester	60	13	Robinson	Jas. Maj.		1	7	2		1	1		3	1			16		
Dorchester	60	17	Robinson	Jerus.	1			1					3	1	1		7		
Brookline	114	34	Robinson	John		2		1		2		1	1				7		
Foxborough	25	35	Robinson	Seth		1	1	1		2		1	1				7		
Dorchester	60	24	Robinson	Sukey								1	2				3		
Dorchester	60	19	Robinson	Thom		1		1				1					3		
Roxbury	107	21	Robinson	Thomas T.		1		1		1		2					5		
Medway East Parish	94	21	Rockwood	Amos	1		1	1	1		1			1			6		
Franklin	168	7	Rockwood	Benjamin	1			1		1				1			4		
Wrentham	179	29	Rockwood	Elisha		1	1	1		2		1		1			7		
Bellingham	160	19	Rockwood	Levi		2		1				1		1			5		
Medway West Parish	97	16	Rockwood	Moses Jun	1	1		1	1			1					5		
Franklin	166	8	Rockwood	Samuel		1		1		1	1		2				6		
Franklin	163	2	Rockwood	Seth	1			1				1	2				4		
Franklin	166	7	Rockwood	Timothy	1	1		1				1	1	1			6		
Roxbury	106	13	Roe	James			1			1		1					3		
Weymouth	80	26	Rogers	John			1			1		2		2			6	South Parish	
Sharon	35	39	Ronald	Benjamin	1	1		1		1			1	2			7		
Medway West Parish	97	17	Rose	Samuel											2		2		
Medway East Parish	94	22	Royall	Prince	1								1		1		3		
Medfield	89	19	Ruggels	Josiah	1			1		3			1				6		
Milton	48	19	Ruggles	Jno			1	1	1	1		1	1				6		
Wrentham	179	6	Ruggles	Joel	4	3	1	1		2	1		1	1			14		
Dover	150	47	Ruggles	John			1	1		1			1				4		
Roxbury	104	7	Ruggles	Joseph Esq		1	3	1		1			1	2			9		
Roxbury	104	5	Ruggles	Joseph Junr	2		1	1	1	3			1	1			10		
Roxbury	104	6	Ruggles	Martha			1	3					2	2	1		10		
Roxbury	103	23	Ruggles	Nathaniel Esq	1	1	1	1				1	2	1	2		10		
Roxbury	107	15	Rumrill	Aaron	1			1		2		1		1			6		
Dorchester	60	14	Russel	Jno	1	1	3						1				6		
Needham	148	20	Russell	Thomas	1	2		1		1			1	1			7		
Stoughton	121	36	Ryne	Dennis				1		2			1				4		
Braintree	71	30	Salisbury	Ambrose	1			1		2	2	1		1			8		
Braintree	71	31	Sampson	Joshua	2			1		1			2				6		
Braintree	71	32	Sampson	Joshua Junior	1		1			1		1					4		
Roxbury	107	6	Samson	Stephen	6	1	1	1		1			2				12		
Medway West Parish	97	18	Sanford	David Rev				1				1	1	1			4		
Medway West Parish	97	19	Sanford	Philo	2	2	1	1		3	1		1				11		
Stoughton	121	37	Sargant	Wm B.	3	1		1		2			1				8		
Quincy	43	7	Saunders	Jno				1			1	2		1			5		
Quincy	43	12	Saunders	Wm				1			3			1			5		
Roxbury	103	11	Saunderson	Daniel				1			1			1			3		
Sharon	36	4	Savage	William						2		1					3		
Sharon	35	42	Savel	Benjamin			1	1					2	1			5		
Quincy	43	5	Savel	Edward	1	1				2	1		1				7		
Sharon	36	3	Savel	John	1	1	3	1		1		1	1				9		
Sharon	36	6	Savel	Mary Wd			2						2	1			5		
Dedham	142	35	Savel	William			4	1			1	1		1			8	1st Parish	
Dorchester	61	8	Savil	Jno		1				1		1					3		
Quincy	43	13	Savil	Nathl	3			1						1			5		
Quincy	43	14	Savil	Saml				1						1			2		
Quincy	43	11	Savil	Saml Jr	1	1	3	1		2	2	2					12		
Roxbury	108	3	Sawen	John	1		3	2		1		2					9		
Randolph	126	22	Sawin	Eliphelet		2		1						2			5		
Randolph	126	23	Sawin	Eunice Wid	1								1				2		
Needham	148	44	Sawing	Levi	1		1	1		4	1		1				9		
Franklin	169	12	Sayles	Daniel	2	2	1	1		1	1	2	1				11		
Wrentham	173	19	Sayles	Elisha	1		2	1			1			1			6		
Bellingham	158	8	Schamels	John	1	1	1	2	1	1	1	3	2	1	1		15		

TOWN	PG#	LN#	LAST NAME	FIRST NAME	FREE WHITE MALES					FREE WHITE FEMALES					TOTAL ALL OTHER	TOTAL SLAVES	TOTALS	DISTRICT/ TOWNSHIP	NOTES
					under 10	10 to 16	16 to 26	26 to 45	45 and over	under 10	10 to 16	16 to 26	26 to 45	45 and over					
Franklin	169	11	Scott	David					1					1			2		
Roxbury	113	28	Scott	Ebenezer	1	1			1	3	2		1				9	3rd Parish	
Franklin	169	2	Scott	Ichabod	1			1		1			1				4		
Bellingham	162	12	Scott	John		1	1		1			2	1	1			7		
Bellingham	161	16	Scott	Jonathan	1		1	1			1	1	1				6		
Roxbury	109	9	Scott	Judith	1							1	2	1	2		7	2nd Parish	
Bellingham	161	12	Scott	Samuel		1	4		1			2	1	1			10		
Bellingham	161	15	Scott	Saul	2		1	1		3	3	1	1				12		
Bellingham	162	13	Scott	Sylvanus		2		1				1	1				5		
Medfield	89	21	Seabry	Elijah	1		1					1		1			4		
Roxbury	104	14	Seaver	Benjamin	3	1	2	1				1	1	1	1		11		
Roxbury	102	31	Seaver	Ebenezer Esq	2	1	5	2	1	3		1	2	1			18		
Franklin	168	34	Seaver	Ichabod		1		1		1	1	1	1				6		
Roxbury	105	10	Seaver	John	1	1		1		1			1				5		
Roxbury	104	21	Seaver	Joseph			1					2					3		
Medfield	89	20	Seaver	Joshua		1		1						1			3		
Roxbury	104	23	Seaver	Nathaniel			1				1		1				3		
Roxbury	101	22	Seaver	Susannah									1	1			2		
Roxbury	102	32	Seaver	Tabatha			1						1	1			3		
Roxbury	102	10	Seaver	William	1		4	1		1		1	1				9		
Roxbury	106	20	Seaver	William	2			1				1	1				5		
Wrentham	180	10	Sensapauh	John S.	1		1			1			1				4		
Canton	133	21	Shales	Elizabeth Wid.									1	1			2		
Canton	133	18	Shaller	Ebenezer				1						1			2		
Canton	133	20	Shaller	Isaac	1		1			1		1					4		
Canton	133	19	Shaller	Michael	2		1	2		2			2				9		
Brookline	114	36	Sharp	Sarah									1	1			2		
Brookline	114	35	Sharp	Stephen		1	4	1	1			1	1	1	1		11		
Foxborough	26	4	Shaw	Asa	1		1			3		1	1				7		
Weymouth	80	37	Shaw	David	2		1			1			1				5	South Parish	
Foxborough	26	5	Shaw	George			1			1			1				3		
Weymouth	80	39	Shaw	Jeremiah	2		1			2			1				6	South Parish	
Weymouth	80	38	Shaw	John & Jesse	1	1	1	1		2	1		3				11	South Parish	
Wrentham	170	7	Shaw	Mason	1		1				1	1					4		
Weymouth	81	1	Shaw	Nathaniel	2		2	1		2		2					9	South Parish	
Wrentham	180	26	Shaw	Noah	1		1						1				3		
Foxborough	26	8	Shaw	Thomas					1			1		1			3		
Quincy	43	1	Shaw	Wm Esq	1	2		3			2	1	2		3		14		
Braintree	71	34	Shear	Stephen	1		1						1				3		
Foxborough	26	1	Shearman	Job		2		1		1		1	1				6		
Foxborough	26	10	Shearman	John	1		1			1			1				4		
Bellingham	162	15	Shearman	Nathan		1							1				2		
Bellingham	162	14	Shearman	Nehemiah			1							1			2		
Foxborough	26	9	Shearman	Obed	1		1			2			1	1			6		
Bellingham	162	16	Shearman	Seth			2	1	1	3	1		1				9		
Roxbury	105	27	Shed	Grace	2		1					1	1				5		
Roxbury	101	17	Shed	Mary										1			1		
Bellingham	161	28	Sheepee	Hoppin			1						1				2		
Sharon	36	9	Shelley	Abner	4	2		1		1				1			9		
Foxborough	26	7	Shelley	Jonathan			1	1				1	1				4		
Foxborough	26	6	Shelley	Jonathan Jr	2		1	1				1	1				6		
Canton	133	24	Shepard	Basheba Wid.		1	1					1		1			4		
Wrentham	177	21	Shepard	Benjamin		1	2		2			6		1			12		
Wrentham	177	23	Shepard	Benjamin Junr	1		1					2					4		
Canton	133	23	Shepard	Jesse	1		1			3			1				6		
Canton	133	27	Shepard	Nathaniel	2		1				1		1				5		
Canton	133	26	Shepard	Oliver	1		1			1			1				4		
Dorchester	60	27	Shepard	Ralph	2	4	1						1				8		
Stoughton	122	1	Shepard	Samuel	1		1	1			2		1				6		
Canton	133	25	Shepard	Thomas	2		1			1			1				5		
Canton	133	22	Shepard	William E		1	1	1				1		1			5		
Wrentham	177	15	Shepard	Jonathan			2	1		1	2		1				7		
Wrentham	175	25	Shepardson	Isaac	3	2		1		1	1		1				9		
Wrentham	175	28	Shepardson	Nathaniel		1		1					1				3		
Needham	148	38	Sheperd	Isaac		1	2		1	2	1		1				8		
Foxborough	25	47	Shephard	Ephraim	2	2		1		1	1		1				8		
Foxborough	25	44	Shephard	Jacob		2	2	1		1	2	2	1				11		
Dedham	142	34	Shephard	John	3		4	1		3	3		1				15	1st Parish	
Foxborough	25	43	Shephard	John		2		2		2			1				7		
Foxborough	25	45	Shephard	Joseph		1	1			1	2		1				6		
Foxborough	25	46	Shephard	Joseph Jr			1					1	1				3		
Roxbury	105	9	Shepherd	James				1				1	1	1			4		
Roxbury	112	3	Shepherd	William	1		1	1		1			1				5	3rd Parish	
Milton	49	2	Sherman	Jno	1	2		1		2	1		1				8		
Medway West Parish	97	20	Shumway	Jabez		1					2	1	1	1			6		
Dedham	142	28	Shuttleworth	Ebenezer				1						2			3	1st Parish	
Dedham	139	30	Shuttleworth	Jeremiah		1	1	1			2						5		
Milton	49	4	Silvester	Benj	2		1						1				4		
Canton	133	28	Silvester	Benjamin	1		1					1	1	1			5		
Randolph	126	30	Silvester	Philip	1		1						1				3		
Dorchester	60	30	Simmons	Benj	2		1			1			1				5		
Needham	149	10	Simon	Edward			1			1			1				3		

TOWN	PG#	LN#	LAST NAME	FIRST NAME	FWM under 10	FWM 10 to 16	FWM 16 to 26	FWM 26 to 45	FWM 45 and over	FWF under 10	FWF 10 to 16	FWF 16 to 26	FWF 26 to 45	FWF 45 and over	TOTAL ALL OTHER	TOTAL SLAVES	TOTALS	DISTRICT/ TOWNSHIP	NOTES
Dedham	139	32	Sisk	Edward				1							1		2		
Roxbury	102	23	Skillings	Pollidore											5		5		
Needham	149	11	Skiner	Job	1		1			1		1					4		
Dorchester	60	25	Skinner	Jno	1	1		1	2		1	2	1				9		
Needham	148	47	Slack	Benjamin	1		1	1		2	1		1				7		
Needham	148	46	Slack	Elizabeth										1			1		
Wrentham	176	19	Slack	Joel	2		1	1		2			1	1			8		
Brookline	114	21	Slack	Samuel	1	1	1	2		1		1	1				8		
Canton	134	1	Slade	Phillis											4		4		
Roxbury	103	26	Sloan	David	1	1		1			2		1				6		
Milton	48	26	Sloane	Peter				1					1				2		
Bellingham	160	30	Slocum	Simon	1	1	1		1	2	1		1				8		
Medfield	90	2	Smith	Aaron			1			2			1				4		
Needham	148	34	Smith	Aaron				1		3	1	1					7		
Dedham	143	1	Smith	Abigail							1			1			2	1st Parish	
Walpole	31	15	Smith	Abigail Wd							1		1				2		
Dedham	139	43	Smith	Abner	1		1	1			1		1				5		
Medfield	90	3	Smith	Amos			1	1		1	1	2	1				7		
Roxbury	106	22	Smith	Amos			3	2		1				1			7		
Dover	150	53	Smith	Asa		1		1		1			1				4		
Walpole	31	7	Smith	Asa				1		1	1		1				4		
Dedham	139	44	Smith	Barach	1			1		2	1		1				6		
Needham	148	35	Smith	Benjamin			1			4			1				6		
Wrentham	173	26	Smith	Christopher			1	1		2			1				5		
Needham	148	22	Smith	Cristopher				1		1			1	1			4		
Needham	149	12	Smith	Cristopher Junr		1		1		1			1				4		
Needham	148	37	Smith	Daniel		1		1				1		1			4		
Needham	148	30	Smith	David		1		1						1			3		
Needham	148	31	Smith	David Junr	1	1	1	1		1	1		1				7		
Medfield	89	24	Smith	Drucilla	2					2		2		1			7		
Roxbury	105	13	Smith	Ebenezer	1	1	1		1	1		2	2	1			10		
Dover	150	52	Smith	Ebenezer		1	2		1	1		2		1			8		
Walpole	31	13	Smith	Eleazer	3			1		1			1				6		
Stoughton	122	3	Smith	Elijah		1		1					1				3		
Medfield	90	1	Smith	Enos	1	1		1				1	1				5		
Canton	133	29	Smith	Ephraim				1						1			2		
Medfield	89	28	Smith	Ephraim	1			1		1	1		1				5		
Canton	133	32	Smith	Ephraim Jr	1			1		2	1		1	1			7		
Franklin	167	9	Smith	G*	1	1		1					1				4		
Needham	148	24	Smith	George	1			1	1	1		1					5		
Dedham	139	26	Smith	Henry			1		1					1			3		
Milton	48	28	Smith	Henry				1									1		
Walpole	31	5	Smith	Henry				1		1		1					3		
Sharon	36	8	Smith	Huel Jr	2			1		5			1				9		
Milton	48	27	Smith	Isaac	3			1		2		1	1				8		
Randolph	127	7	Smith	Isaac	1	1	2		1		1		2	2			10		
Sharon	35	43	Smith	Isaac		1	1		1			1		1			5		
Walpole	31	9	Smith	Isaac	1	1	1		1			2		1			7		
Medfield	89	22	Smith	Isaiah	2			1		3			1				7		
Dedham	142	36	Smith	Jacob	2				1	1	1		1				6	1st Parish	
Canton	133	30	Smith	James	1	2			1	2	1		1				8		
Needham	148	39	Smith	James	1	1		1		1			1				5		
Wrentham	170	12	Smith	James	1	1	1		1			2		1			7		
Needham	148	45	Smith	Jason	3			1		1	1		1				7		
Medfield	89	30	Smith	Jeremiah			1			1			1				3		
Walpole	31	10	Smith	Jeremiah	1	2		1		1		2	1				8		
Stoughton	122	4	Smith	Jese	1	1	1	1					1	1			6		
Stoughton	122	5	Smith	Jese Junr		1							1				2		
Needham	148	21	Smith	Joel	1			1					1				3		
Dedham	139	46	Smith	John	2			1		1			1	1			6		
Medfield	89	25	Smith	John			1	1					4	1			7		
Sharon	36	1	Smith	John	1			1					1				3		
Walpole	31	8	Smith	John	3	2		1					1				7		
Medfield	89	26	Smith	John Jun				1					1				2		
Medfield	89	29	Smith	Jonathan	1	1			1		1	1		1			6		
Needham	148	26	Smith	Jonathan				1						1			2		
Needham	148	27	Smith	Jonathan Junr	2	3			1	1		1	1	1			10		
Roxbury	104	4	Smith	Joseph				1						1			2		
Stoughton	122	2	Smith	Joseph	2	1	2		1	1			1	1			9		
Medfield	89	23	Smith	Lebbens	1			1		2	1		1				6		
Canton	133	31	Smith	Lemuel	3			1		1		1					6		
Dedham	139	41	Smith	Lemuel		1		1		1			1	1			5		
Stoughton	122	7	Smith	Lemuel		2		1	1			2					6		
Weymouth	81	3	Smith	Lemuel	2	2		1		2	1		2				10	South Parish	
Walpole	31	12	Smith	Liffee	3		2	1		1		1	1				9		
Needham	148	23	Smith	Luther			1										1		
Walpole	31	2	Smith	Moses	2			1	1	1			1	1			8		
Dedham	139	42	Smith	Naham	2			1		1			1				5		
Dedham	139	39	Smith	Nathaniel		1			1	1	2		1				6		
Stoughton	122	8	Smith	Nathl	1	1	1	1		2			1	1			8		

Census table — Free White Males / Free White Females (FWM = Free White Males, FWF = Free White Females; age columns: under 10, 10 to 16, 16 to 26, 26 to 45, 45 and over)

TOWN	PG#	LN#	LAST NAME	FIRST NAME	FWM <10	FWM 10–16	FWM 16–26	FWM 26–45	FWM 45+	FWF <10	FWF 10–16	FWF 16–26	FWF 26–45	FWF 45+	TOTAL ALL OTHER	TOTAL SLAVES	TOTALS	DISTRICT/TOWNSHIP	NOTES
Franklin	163	29	Smith	Oliver N.	1		1	1		1		1					5		
Bellingham	159	10	Smith	Pelatiah	1		3		1	2		2					9		
Needham	148	36	Smith	Peletiah	1			1				2					4		
Walpole	31	11	Smith	Peter	2			1					1				4		
Stoughton	122	6	Smith	Philip				1				1					2		
Needham	148	43	Smith	Phinehas				1			1						2		
Medfield	89	27	Smith	Rachel				1			1		1				3		
Roxbury	105	16	Smith	Ralph	1	3	4	2	1	1	1	2		1	1		17		
Stoughton	122	20	Smith	Rebekah Wid									1				1		
Needham	148	41	Smith	Robert			1	1				1	1				4		
Walpole	31	16	Smith	Royal				1					1				2		
Dorchester	61	6	Smith	Saml		1		2			1		2				6		
Franklin	169	8	Smith	Samuel		1		1		2	1		1				6		
Walpole	31	3	Smith	Samuel				1	1				1				3		
Walpole	31	4	Smith	Samuel Jr	1			1		1			1				4		
Dedham	139	40	Smith	Sarah									1				1		
Milton	49	3	Smith	Seth	1			1					1				3		
Walpole	31	6	Smith	Seth			1	1		1		1					4		
Roxbury	102	24	Smith	Thaddeus	2			1		1			1				5		
Dedham	139	38	Smith	Thomas				1					1				2		
Roxbury	111	10	Smith	Thomas											2		2	2nd Parish	
Needham	148	42	Smith	Timothy	1	2			1			1	1				6		
Walpole	31	17	Smith	Timothy			1										1		
Medfield	89	31	Smith	Titus	2			1		2	1		1				7		
Dedham	139	24	Smith	William			1	1	1		1	1	2				7		
Needham	148	40	Smith	William			1	1					2				4		
Weymouth	81	5	Smith	William	1		2		1	1			1				6	South Parish	
Stoughton	122	9	Snow	Uriah			1	1					1				3		
Cohasset	153	50	So*	Elille	1	2		1			1		1				6		
Braintree	72	2	Soper	Edmund			1		2		2	1					6		
Cohasset	153	11	Souther	Joseph		1	1					1					3		
Cohasset	152	19	Souther	Joseph Jr	1		1	1		1	1		1				6		
Cohasset	152	23	Souther	Nathan			1				1						2		
Cohasset	152	26	Souther	Sarah	3					1		1					5		
Stoughton	122	12	Southworth	Consider	1		1				1						3		
Stoughton	122	10	Southworth	Jedidiah			1	1				1					3		
Stoughton	122	11	Southworth	Jedidiah Junr	2			1		1			1				5		
Sharon	36	7	Spaulding	David	1			1			1						3		
Dorchester	60	28	Spear	Aaron	3			1		1	2	1					8		
Quincy	43	2	Spear	Daniel		1		1				1	1				4		
Braintree	71	33	Spear	Deering	2			1				1	1				5		
Quincy	43	4	Spear	Elijah		1					1						2		
Canton	133	22	Spear	Eliza		1							1				2		
Dorchester	61	3	Spear	James	4			1					1				6		
Quincy	43	16	Spear	Jedh	2	1	1		1			1					6		
Quincy	43	8	Spear	Jno	1	1	2	1	2	1		2					10		
Dedham	139	25	Spear	John	2			1		2			1	1			7		
Randolph	126	28	Spear	John									1				1		
Randolph	126	25	Spear	Jonathan		2		1		1			1	1			6		
Randolph	126	26	Spear	Joseph	1	2		1		2	1		1	1			9		
Randolph	126	27	Spear	Joshua	2		1	1			1	1	1				7		
Dorchester	61	1	Spear	Lem Jr	1		1			1			1				4		
Dorchester	61	2	Spear	Leml				1					1				2		
Randolph	126	29	Spear	Mary Wid									1				1		
Randolph	126	24	Spear	Nathaniel	1	1	1	1		1	2		1				8		
Canton	133	34	Spear	Olive Wid.	2			1					1	1			5		
Quincy	43	9	Spear	Seth	2	1		3		4	1		1				12		
Stoughton	122	13	Spear	Simeon		2	1		1	1		1					6		
Quincy	43	3	Spear	Steph. Jr	2			1					1				4		
Quincy	43	10	Spear	Wm		1		1					1				3		
Bellingham	159	3	Spears	Benjamin		1		1		4			1				7		
Roxbury	103	9	Spooner	Sally	1					1			1				3		
Randolph	127	1	Spooner	William						1	1		1				3		
Wrentham	175	19	Sprague	Amos	1			1		2			1				5		
Dedham	139	27	Sprague	Esther Wid		2	2					1	1	1	1		8		
Dedham	139	28	Sprague	Rebeca Wid	1		2			1	1	2			1		8		
Roxbury	114	2	Spurr	Eliphalet		2	1		2		3	1					9	3rd Parish	
Dedham	140	33	Stacy	Persons				1									1		
Roxbury	112	7	Starr	Daniel				1		2			1				4	3rd Parish	
Dedham	144	36	Starr	Elizabeth		1		1		1	1	1	1				6	2nd Parish	
Dedham	139	31	Starr	Jonathan		1		1	2				2				6		
Needham	148	29	Steadman	Ebenezer	1	1		1	1	1			1				6		
Needham	148	25	Steadman	Joseph	1	1		1	1	1			1				6		
Foxborough	25	41	Stearns	Joshua	1	1		2		1	2		1				8		
Medfield	90	4	Stearns	Nathaniel	1		1	4					1	1			8		
Cohasset	154	11	Stephenson	Luther	1			1				1	1				4		
Cohasset	152	44	Stephenson	Luther Jun		1		1				1	1				4		
Cohasset	153	30	Stephenson	Martin			1			3			1				5		
Cohasset	152	28	Stephenson	Reuben	2	1	1	1		2			1				8		
Braintree	72	1	Stetson	Amos		1	3					1					5		
Quincy	43	6	Stetson	Amos				1									3		

TOWN	PG#	LN#	LAST NAME	FIRST NAME	FREE WHITE MALES					FREE WHITE FEMALES					TOTAL ALL OTHER	TOTAL SLAVES	TOTALS	DISTRICT/ TOWNSHIP	NOTES
					under 10	10 to 16	16 to 26	26 to 45	45 and over	under 10	10 to 16	16 to 26	26 to 45	45 and over					
Randolph	127	2	Stetson	Benja		1	1		1		1			1			5		
Randolph	127	4	Stetson	Gideon	1	1	3		1	1	1	1		1			10		
Canton	133	35	Stetson	Isaac				1		1			1				3		
Randolph	127	5	Stetson	Jonathan	1	1	2	1					1				6		
Randolph	127	6	Stetson	Peter			1						1				2		
Dorchester	60	26	Stetson	Thad	2			1	1				2				6		
Randolph	127	3	Stetson	William			1			1		1					3		
Needham	148	33	Stevens	Abijamin			1			1		1					3		
Needham	148	28	Stevens	Epheriam		1		3	1	1		2		1			9		
Needham	148	32	Stevens	Epheriam Junr		1		2		1		1	1				6		
Dedham	140	3	Stevens	Jane		1	1					1		1			4		
Randolph	127	9	Stevens	Wid										1			1		
Canton	133	36	Stickney	Susanna Wid.									2				2		
Roxbury	100	8	Stilling	Mary						3	1		1				5		
Milton	49	9	Stimpson	Josph	1			1		1				1			4		
Roxbury	113	20	Stimson	Charles			2						1				3	3rd Parish	
Roxbury	102	14	Stiner	John				1		1			1				3		
Weymouth	81	2	Stoddard	Hezekiah			1						1				2	South Parish	
Weymouth	81	4	Stoddard	Jesse	2		1					1	1				5	South Parish	
Canton	133	37	Stoddard	Mercy Wid.	1			1		2		1	1				6		
Cohasset	152	36	Stodder	James	1	1		1				2	1				6		
Cohasset	153	15	Stodder	Lydia									2				2		
Cohasset	154	2	Stodder	Matthew		1			1			3	1				6		
Canton	133	38	Stone	George	2			1		1		1					5		
Stoughton	122	19	Stone	James				1					1				2		
Quincy	43	15	Stone	Jno				1					1				2		
Roxbury	102	15	Stone	John			1			1			1				3		
Randolph	126	31	Stone	Timothy	2	1		1		1			1				6		
Cohasset	152	33	Stowel	Adam	2		1	2		3			1				9		
Dedham	139	45	Stowell	Fisher		1				1		1					3		
Dedham	139	34	Stowell	Isaac				1				1	1				3		
Dedham	139	35	Stowell	Jesse			3					1					4		
Dedham	139	37	Stowell	Joel	2		1				1	1					5		
Dedham	139	33	Stowell	Lemuel	1	2			1				1				5		
Dedham	139	36	Stowell	Timothy		1			1			1	1				4		
Dorchester	61	4	Straton	Jona		1						1					2		
Foxborough	26	2	Stratton	George	1	1	1	1				2	1				7		
Foxborough	25	40	Stratton	James		2		1		1	2	1		1			8		
Foxborough	26	11	Stratton	Joseph			1			3		1	1				6		
Foxborough	26	3	Stratton	Robert	1			1				1					3		
Randolph	127	8	Strong	Jonathan Revd	2	3		1		3		1	1				11		
Canton	133	39	Strowbridge	Samuel				1					1				2		
Canton	133	40	Strowbridge	Seth			1	1					1				3		
Walpole	31	14	Studson	Joshua	1		1	1					1				4		
Roxbury	112	9	Stutivant	Isaac			1		1	2			1				5	3rd Parish	
Milton	48	24	Sullivan	Jno	1	2	1	1		1		1					7		
Roxbury	115	11	Sullivan	John L.	1		3	1		1		1	1	1	3		12	3rd Parish	
Roxbury	99	3	Sumner	Clement	2	1	1		1	2	1	2		1			11		
Milton	49	5	Sumner	David		2			1	4		3	2				12		
Dedham	142	30	Sumner	Ebenezer		2			1	1			1				5	1st Parish	
Roxbury	106	7	Sumner	Edward	2	1	2	1	1	4	2	2	1				16		
Roxbury	104	15	Sumner	Elizabeth			1			1		2		1	2		7		
Milton	49	8	Sumner	Jabez	2			1		1			3				7		
Milton	48	25	Sumner	Jesse	2		2	1		1		1	1				8		
Foxborough	25	37	Sumner	John				1				1	1				3		
Foxborough	25	38	Sumner	John Jr	3	1		1					1				6		
Milton	49	10	Sumner	Lydia								1	1	1			3		
Dedham	142	31	Sumner	Margrett Wid		1				3	1		1				6	1st Parish	
Milton	49	6	Sumner	Mercy								1	1	1			3		
Dedham	142	29	Sumner	Nathaniel				1					1	1			3	1st Parish	
Dedham	142	32	Sumner	Nathaniel Junr	3	1		1		1	1	1	1				9	1st Parish	
Foxborough	25	42	Sumner	Roger	2			1		1			1				5		
Stoughton	122	14	Sumner	Roger			1	2	1	1	1		1				7		
Roxbury	99	7	Sumner	Samuel			4		1	4	1		1				11		
Milton	49	11	Sumner	Sarah			1					1		1			3		
Milton	49	7	Sumner	Seth		1		1				1		1			4		
Dedham	142	33	Sumner	William	2			1		2	1	1					7	1st Parish	
Foxborough	25	39	Sumner	William	2	1	1		1	2			1	1			9		
Dorchester	61	7	Sumner	Wm	2	3	5	3	2	2	2	2	1		1		23		
Cohasset	152	46	Sutton	John				1		5	1	1	1				9		
Stoughton	122	17	Swan	James	1	1			1	1			1				5		
Dedham	139	29	Swan	Joseph				1			1		1				3		
Dedham	139	23	Swan	Joseph Junr		1	1	1		2		1	1				7		
Stoughton	122	18	Swan	Luther	1			1		1			1				4		
Stoughton	122	15	Swan	Robert				1									1		
Stoughton	122	16	Swan	Robert Junr		1	2	1		1	1		1	1			8		
Needham	149	9	Swazey	Manuel	2			1					1				4		
Dorchester	60	29	Sweetland	Rebec.						1		4					5		
Milton	48	23	Swift	Jno		3	2		1		2		1		1		10		
Sharon	36	2	Swift	Job		2	2	2		1		1	2				10		
Dorchester	61	5	Swift	Nathl		1	1		1			2					5		
Milton	49	1	Swift	Saml	2	2			2	2		1		1			10		

TOWN	PG#	LN#	LAST NAME	FIRST NAME	FREE WHITE MALES					FREE WHITE FEMALES					TOTAL ALL OTHER	TOTAL SLAVES	TOTALS	DISTRICT/ TOWNSHIP	NOTES
					under 10	10 to 16	16 to 26	26 to 45	45 and over	under 10	10 to 16	16 to 26	26 to 45	45 and over					
Sharon	36	5	Swift	Samuel				1		2			1				4		
Roxbury	105	12	Symms	George	2	1		2			1		1				7		
Roxbury	107	26	Symms	Samuel			1			2		1					4		
Roxbury	104	25	Symms	Stephen	3		1			1	2		1				8		
Roxbury	107	20	Taber	Elnathan	2	1	1						1				5		
Sharon	36	14	Tabot	Josiah	2	1	1			2	1	1					8		
Milton	49	26	Tailor	Thom	1			1				1	1	1			5		
Milton	49	25	Tailor	Wm				4					1	1			6		
Dedham	142	38	Talbert	Ebenezer	1	1			1			1	1	1			6	1st Parish	
Dedham	142	37	Talbert	Enoch	2			1				1	1	1			6	1st Parish	
Dorchester	61	22	Talbot	Benj			1	1					1				3		
Canton	134	6	Talbot	David					1	1		1		1			4		
Milton	49	17	Talbot	George	1				1	3	1	1					8		
Dorchester	61	23	Talbot	Hannah									1	1			2		
Stoughton	122	24	Talbot	Isaac	1			1		1	1		1				5		
Stoughton	122	25	Talbot	Isaac Junr	3		1			1			1				6		
Stoughton	122	22	Talbot	Jabez		2		1					1				4		
Stoughton	122	23	Talbot	Richard			1			1		1					3		
Stoughton	122	21	Talbot	Samuel	1	2	1	1					1	1			7		
Roxbury	110	8	Talburt	Nathaniel		2		1		1			1				5	2nd Parish	
Canton	134	2	Tant	John	1		1	1		1			1				5		
Canton	134	3	Tant	John Jr	1			1		2		1					5		
Canton	134	5	Tant	Levi	1			1	1				1				4		
Canton	134	4	Tant	Samuel		1				1		1					3		
Braintree	73	1	Tant	Seth															Enumeration left blank
Braintree	72	38	Taylor	Benjm			1			3			1				5		
Wrentham	171	23	Taylor	Elizabeth								1	1	1			3		
Randolph	128	3	Temple	Samuel	1			1		1			1				4		
Franklin	169	27	Terry	John Junr			1			1	1	2					5		
Dedham	144	37	Thacher	Thomas Revd		1	1						1				4	2nd Parish	
Dorchester	62	13	Thatcher	Ceaser											2		2		
Braintree	72	17	Thayer	Abraham	3			1		2	1	1	1	1			10		
Roxbury	107	5	Thayer	Abraham	1			1		2			1				5		
Randolph	127	30	Thayer	Alexander	2			1		2			1				6		
Bellingham	159	27	Thayer	Alpheus	4	1		3			1		1				10		
Braintree	72	4	Thayer	Amos				1					1				2		
Roxbury	101	13	Thayer	Ann										2			2		
Dorchester	61	9	Thayer	Arodi				1				2	1				4		
Canton	134	9	Thayer	Asa	1		2					1					4		
Weymouth	81	25	Thayer	Barnabas	2	2		1		2	2		1				10	South Parish	
Dorchester	61	24	Thayer	Benj		1				1			1				3		
Randolph	127	25	Thayer	Benja				1						2			3		
Braintree	72	32	Thayer	Benjm	3	2		1				1	1				8		
Braintree	72	26	Thayer	Betty Wid.		1						2	2	1			6		
Milton	49	21	Thayer	Beza	2	1		1		3			1				8		
Braintree	72	19	Thayer	Caleb	2			1				2					5		
Stoughton	122	27	Thayer	Caleb			1		1		1		1				4		
Braintree	72	22	Thayer	Calvin	2	1		1					1				5		
Braintree	72	41	Thayer	Demetrius		1	1						1				3		
Bellingham	162	6	Thayer	Ebenezer	1			1					1				3		
Braintree	72	3	Thayer	Ebenz		2	5	1	1			1		1			11		
Bellingham	160	28	Thayer	Elias		1		1	1					1			4		
Bellingham	160	29	Thayer	Elias Junr		1		1				1					3		
Braintree	72	9	Thayer	Elijah	2		1	1		2	2	1					9		
Braintree	72	24	Thayer	Elijah				1					1				2		
Braintree	72	25	Thayer	Elijah 2d		1		1	1	1				1			4		
Randolph	127	31	Thayer	Ezra	3	2		1		1	1	1					9		
Quincy	43	17	Thayer	Gains	2	1		1		1		1					6		
Braintree	72	28	Thayer	Gideon				1						1			2		
Braintree	72	29	Thayer	Gideon Junr			1					1					2		
Braintree	72	18	Thayer	Isaac				1		3			1				5		
Randolph	127	12	Thayer	Jeremiah	2	1		1		1		1	1	1			8		
Braintree	72	27	Thayer	Job	1			1		1		1	1				5		
Braintree	72	31	Thayer	John				1				1		1			3		
Braintree	72	14	Thayer	Jonathan				1						2			3		
Randolph	127	23	Thayer	Jonathan		2		1		4		1	1				9		
Braintree	72	16	Thayer	Jonathan Junr	2	1	1	1	1	2		1	1				10		
Stoughton	122	26	Thayer	Joseph	3			1						1			5		
Braintree	72	12	Thayer	Josiah	1			1					1				3		
Braintree	72	33	Thayer	Levi	2	1	1			1		1	1	1			8		
Randolph	127	26	Thayer	Levi	2			1		1			1				5		
Randolph	127	32	Thayer	Levi Junr		1							1				2		
Bellingham	160	14	Thayer	Luther	2			1					1				4		
Randolph	127	18	Thayer	Luther	4		1	1		1			1				8		
Weymouth	81	17	Thayer	Luther	4			1						2			7	South Parish	
Randolph	127	15	Thayer	Meshech	2			1		1			1	1			6		
Randolph	127	20	Thayer	Micah				1						1			2		
Randolph	127	21	Thayer	Micah 2d	2			1		1		1		1			5		
Randolph	127	22	Thayer	Micah 3d			2			1			1				4		
Braintree	72	39	Thayer	Minott									2				2		
Medway East Parish	94	24	Thayer	Nahum			1			1		1					4		
Franklin	168	36	Thayer	Nathaniel	2	1	2		1	1		1	1	1			10		
Braintree	72	20	Thayer	Nathl			1		1	1		2	1	1			8		

130

TOWN	PG#	LN#	LAST NAME	FIRST NAME	FREE WHITE MALES under 10	10 to 16	16 to 26	26 to 45	45 and over	FREE WHITE FEMALES under 10	10 to 16	16 to 26	26 to 45	45 and over	TOTAL ALL OTHER	TOTAL SLAVES	TOTALS	DISTRICT/ TOWNSHIP	NOTES
Braintree	72	21	Thayer	Nathl 2d	3				1				1	1			6		
Braintree	72	15	Thayer	Nehem				1		1	1		1				4		
Randolph	127	14	Thayer	Noah	1				1		1			1			4		
Wrentham	174	30	Thayer	Noah			1					1		1			4		
Wrentham	174	29	Thayer	Obadiah A.		1	1	1		2			1				6		
Roxbury	112	29	Thayer	Obed		1	2		1	2		1					7	3rd Parish	
Weymouth	81	7	Thayer	Obediah				1			1		1				3	South Parish	
Randolph	127	11	Thayer	Paul	1				1	1	1	2	1				7		
Randolph	127	33	Thayer	Peter	1			1		2			1				5		
Randolph	127	34	Thayer	Peter				1									1		
Braintree	72	5	Thayer	Philip	2	1			1	1			1	1			7		
Bellingham	161	3	Thayer	Philo			1				1						2		
Randolph	127	24	Thayer	Phinehas			1			3	2	1					7		
Weymouth	81	24	Thayer	Randal	1		1					1					3	South Parish	
Braintree	72	8	Thayer	Richard	1		1	1	1			3		1			8		
Randolph	127	13	Thayer	Richard			1	1		3	2	1	1				9		
Weymouth	81	8	Thayer	Richard			1	1		3			1	1			7	South Parish	
Randolph	127	28	Thayer	Robert	3	2		1		1			1	1			9		
Randolph	127	16	Thayer	Rufus	1			2				1		1			5		
Braintree	72	13	Thayer	Saml W	2	1	1	1		2	1		1				9		
Randolph	127	17	Thayer	Samuel	1	1	1	1	1			2	1				8		
Randolph	127	10	Thayer	Shadrach	2	1						1					4		
Bellingham	160	15	Thayer	Silas	1	1	2		1		1		1				7		
Braintree	72	30	Thayer	Silvanus			1				1						2		
Randolph	127	29	Thayer	Simeon	1	1		1		1	1	1	1	1			8		
Braintree	72	36	Thayer	Solomon				1		2			1				4		
Braintree	72	6	Thayer	Solomon 2d	1		2	1		1	1		1				7		
Braintree	72	10	Thayer	Stephen		1	1	1		2	1	1	1				8		
Braintree	72	23	Thayer	Timothy	1	1		1		1			1				5		
Randolph	127	27	Thayer	Timothy			1			1		1					3		
Braintree	72	11	Thayer	Uriah	3		1		1	1	1	2	1				10		
Braintree	72	7	Thayer	William			1	1		5	2	1	1	1			12		
Dorchester	61	25	Thayer	Zach	2			1		3			1	1			8		
Braintree	72	42	Thayer	Zachariah				1					1				2		
Randolph	127	19	Thayer	Zacheus			1	1			2			1			5		
Braintree	72	34	Thayer	Zachl M.				2		1			1	1			5		
Weymouth	81	19	Thayer	Zenas	2			1		4	1		1				9	South Parish	
Roxbury	115	17	Thayer	Zephion	4			6	1		1		3				15	3rd Parish	
Medfield	90	5	Theboult	John				1					2				3		
Roxbury	102	13	Thomas	Caleb				1		2	1		1				5		
Walpole	31	18	Thomas	John		1		1		3		1					6		
Weymouth	81	12	Thomas	John	2			1		2			1				6	South Parish	
Braintree	72	37	Thomas	Nat. Robbins	1	1	7			1		2					12		
Medway West Parish	97	22	Thompson	Abigail									1				1		
Bellingham	160	12	Thompson	Amos	2			1		1		1	1				6		
Medway West Parish	97	21	Thompson	Ebenezer	1	1		1		1	2						6		
Walpole	31	19	Thompson	Elijah	1	1		1	1	1	1		1	1			8		
Wrentham	173	29	Thompson	Jason				1		1		2					4		
Medfield	90	6	Thompson	John	1			1		2			1				5		
Bellingham	158	16	Thompson	Joseph		2	3	1	1		1		1				9		
Milton	49	24	Thompson	Sam		2	2		1	2	1		1				9		
Canton	134	7	Thompson	Sarah Wid.								1	1				2		
Canton	134	8	Thompson	William			1			3		1					5		
Dedham	142	39	Thorpe	Eliphilet		1		1			1		1				4	1st Parish	
Wrentham	171	3	Thurber	Ozias	1			1		1		1					4		
Franklin	166	12	Thurston	Abijah		1	1		1	1	2		1				7		
Franklin	163	23	Thurston	Daniel	2	1			1		1		1				6		
Franklin	166	13	Thurston	Elizabeth								1	1				2		
Wrentham	178	6	Thurston	Samuel			1		1	1		1	1				5		
Milton	49	18	Tidd	Adam											4		4		
Foxborough	26	13	Tiffany	Isaac			1			1							2		
Foxborough	26	12	Tiffany	Joseph		1		1		1			1				4		
Canton	134	13	Tilden	Ezra	1		2		2		2	1		2			10		
Canton	134	12	Tilden	Josiah	1	1		1		3		1					7		
Canton	134	10	Tilden	Nathl				1					1				2		
Canton	134	11	Tilden	Nathl Junr			3	1		3	1		1				9		
Stoughton	122	28	Tilden	Sarah									1	2			3		
Medfield	90	7	Tilden	Stephen	1		1					2					4		
Dorchester	61	18	Tileston	Eben		1		1			1	1	1	1			6		
Dorchester	61	17	Tileston	Elisha					1			1	1				3		
Dorchester	62	6	Tileston	Euclid	3	1	2	1		1		1	1	1			11		
Dorchester	62	4	Tileston	Ezekiel	2	1			1	1		1	1				7		
Roxbury	102	9	Tileston	Nathaniel	2			2		1		1	1				7		
Dorchester	61	16	Tileston	Thom	1		1	1	3	1			1				8		
Dorchester	61	19	Tileston	Timo			2	1						1			4		
Wrentham	171	29	Tillingham	Allen	1		2	1		2		1			1		8		
Wrentham	179	20	Tilson	Nehemiah	1		1	1		2			1				6		
Weymouth	81	18	Tirrell	Benj	4			1		1			1				7	South Parish	
Weymouth	81	21	Tirrell	Jacob 2d	1			1		4			1				7	South Parish	
Weymouth	81	20	Tirrell	James 2d	2	1	2	1	1	1		1	1	1			11	South Parish	
Weymouth	81	11	Tirrell	John	2	2	1		1	2	1			1			10	South Parish	
Weymouth	81	9	Tirrell	Joseph		1	1	1						2			5	South Parish	
Weymouth	77	33	Tirrell	Levi				1		3		1					5	North Parish	

TOWN	PG#	LN#	LAST NAME	FIRST NAME	FREE WHITE MALES					FREE WHITE FEMALES					TOTAL ALL OTHER	TOTAL SLAVES	TOTALS	DISTRICT/ TOWNSHIP	NOTES
					under 10	10 to 16	16 to 26	26 to 45	45 and over	under 10	10 to 16	16 to 26	26 to 45	45 and over					
Weymouth	77	31	Tirrell	Noah				1	1					2			4	North Parish	
Weymouth	77	34	Tirrell	Noah Junr	2	2		1		3			1				9	North Parish	
Weymouth	81	13	Tirrell	Vinson		1	1	1		1	1		1	2			8	South Parish	
Dover	150	54	Tisdale	Billings			1		1			1	1				4		
Sharon	36	11	Tisdale	Edward			2	1				1	1				5		
Dover	150	55	Tisdale	Henry			1	2	1			2	1	1			8		
Walpole	31	22	Tisdale	James		1	1		1		1		1				5		
Roxbury	111	23	Titterton	Gabriel			1	1		1	2		1	2			8	2nd Parish	
Foxborough	26	14	Titus	Ruben		1		1						1			3		
Sharon	36	10	Toleman	John			1	1						1			3		
Brookline	114	29	Toleman	Jonas			1	1		1		1					4		
Dorchester	61	27	Tolman	Ann	1		2	1		1			1				6		
Dorchester	62	8	Tolman	Benj D	1			1		2			1				5		
Dorchester	61	11	Tolman	Ebenz			1	1	2			1		2			7		
Dorchester	61	14	Tolman	Ezckl	1		2	1						1			5		
Dorchester	62	9	Tolman	James	1		1	1		1	1	1					6		
Dorchester	61	13	Tolman	John	2	1	1					1		1			7		
Needham	148	48	Tolman	John		1						1		1			4		
Dorchester	61	12	Tolman	Jonas			1	1				2	1				5		
Dorchester	61	15	Tolman	Leml				1				1					2		
Dorchester	61	29	Tolman	Saml				1						1			2		
Stoughton	122	29	Tolman	Saml	2	1		1	1	2	1		1	3			12		
Dorchester	61	30	Tolman	Saml Jr	1			1		1		1					4		
Stoughton	122	30	Tolman	Thomas	2		1	1				1	1				6		
Sharon	36	12	Tolman	William	1	1	1		1		1		1				6		
Sharon	36	13	Tolman	Willm Jr	1		1					1					3		
Dorchester	62	1	Tolman	Wm	1			1		1	1		1				5		
Canton	134	14	Topliff	Abigail Wid.							1	1	1				3		
Dorchester	62	2	Topliff	Saml		1	2	1		1	1	1		1			8		
Dorchester	61	28	Topliff	Saml Jr			1			2	1	1					5		
Weymouth	77	38	Torrey	Benj				1	1					1			3	North Parish	
Weymouth	77	35	Torrey	Daniel				1				2		1			4	North Parish	
Weymouth	81	6	Torrey	David				1				2		1			4	South Parish	
Weymouth	77	36	Torrey	James		1											1	North Parish	
Weymouth	81	10	Torrey	James		1				1	2	2	1				8	South Parish	
Weymouth	81	22	Torrey	James Gershom	1		1						1				3	South Parish	
Weymouth	77	32	Torrey	Phillip	1			1				2		1	1		6	North Parish	
Weymouth	81	23	Torrey	Samuel	3	2		1				1	1	1			9	South Parish	
Weymouth	77	30	Torrey	Sarahl		1	1	1		1				1			5	North Parish	
Franklin	167	11	Torry	John				1				3	1				5		
Cohasset	152	31	Tower	Bethiah	2			1				1		1			5		
Randolph	127	37	Tower	Gideon	1		1	1				1		1			5		
Randolph	127	38	Tower	Gideon Junr	2	1	1		1	3	2	2	1				13		
Randolph	128	2	Tower	Isaac	1	1	1		1								4		
Braintree	72	35	Tower	James	2		2		1	3	2		2				12		
Braintree	72	40	Tower	John	1			1	1	1		1		1			6		
Cohasset	154	31	Tower	John				1						1			2		
Randolph	128	1	Tower	Joseph		1		1				1		1			4		
Cohasset	154	7	Tower	Levi	2	1	1	1		1	1	2	1				10		
Cohasset	154	1	Tower	Mary							1			1			2		
Dorchester	61	20	Townsend	David	2			2	1	1	1	2					9		
Dedham	140	2	Townsend	Horatio Esq	1			1	1	2		1	1	1	2		10		
Medfield	90	8	Townsend	Sarah				1					1				3		
Wrentham	175	29	Trask	Edward				1					1	1			3		
Quincy	43	21	Trask	Saml				1						1			2		
Roxbury	106	21	Trask	Samuel	3			1		2	1		1				8		
Dorchester	61	10	Travis	Joshua	2			1		2			1				6		
Franklin	169	24	Treddle	Syer											4		4		
Cohasset	152	38	Trent	John		1		1		3			1				6		
Dorchester	62	10	Trescott	Eben		2		1			1		1				5		
Dorchester	62	11	Trescott	Jona				1						1			2		
Dorchester	62	12	Trott	Luke		1		1		1			1	1	1		5		
Quincy	43	20	Trott	Thom	1		1			2	1		2				7		
Dorchester	62	7	Trow	Richard		3	1		2			2					8		
Weymouth	81	16	Trufant	David	1			1		2			2				6	South Parish	
Weymouth	81	14	Trufant	Jonathan	1	1		1	1					2			6	South Parish	
Weymouth	81	15	Trufant	Joshua			1										1	South Parish	
Roxbury	113	3	Trull	Jonathan	1	1		3		2	1		1				9	3rd Parish	
Dorchester	61	26	Tucker	Alh*	2		1	1					1				5		
Milton	49	28	Tucker	Amal	1		1	1		1			1				5		
Canton	134	16	Tucker	Benja		1	1	1				1		1			5		
Canton	134	18	Tucker	Daniel	2		2	1				1					6		
Milton	49	12	Tucker	David	1	1		1	1		1		1				5		
Milton	49	23	Tucker	Eben		1								1			3		
Wrentham	172	31	Tucker	Ebenezer	1			1	1					1			4		
Wrentham	172	32	Tucker	Ebenezer Junr		1		2				2					5		
Dorchester	62	3	Tucker	Elijah		2	1			1	1	1					6		
Milton	49	32	Tucker	George	1		1						1				3		
Milton	49	13	Tucker	Isaac		1		1	2	1			1				6		
Canton	134	15	Tucker	James		1		1		1	2		2				7		
Milton	49	31	Tucker	James	2	1		1		1		2					7		
Milton	49	27	Tucker	Jaret		1	1	1		1	1	1					6		
Milton	49	20	Tucker	Jereh				2					2	1			5		
Wrentham	176	14	Tucker	Jeremiah	1			1	1			1					4		

TOWN	PG#	LN#	LAST NAME	FIRST NAME	FREE WHITE MALES					FREE WHITE FEMALES					TOTAL ALL OTHER	TOTAL SLAVES	TOTALS	DISTRICT/ TOWNSHIP	NOTES
					under 10	10 to 16	16 to 26	26 to 45	45 and over	under 10	10 to 16	16 to 26	26 to 45	45 and over					
Canton	134	17	Tucker	John	1	2			1	2	1	1	1				9		
Canton	134	21	Tucker	Lemuel	1		1					1					3		
Milton	49	14	Tucker	Nathl	1	1	2	2		1	2	1					10		
Dorchester	62	5	Tucker	Phinehas			1			2	1	1					5		
Milton	49	19	Tucker	Saml	3	1	1		1	1	2		1				10		
Canton	134	19	Tucker	Samuel	2	2	1		1	1	1		1				9		
Canton	134	20	Tucker	Simeon	2			1	2	2		1	1				9		
Milton	49	29	Tucker	Tim		1		1	1			2	1				6		
Milton	49	30	Tucker	Tim Jr			1					1					2		
Weymouth	77	28	Tufts	Cotton		1		1	1	1	1	1	1				7		North Parish
Weymouth	77	29	Tufts	Cotton Junr		1	1	2		2		1	1				8		North Parish
Walpole	31	20	Turner	Abner				1		1			1				3		
Medway East Parish	94	23	Turner	Amos	2	3	1			2			1				9		
Milton	49	22	Turner	Benj	2		1					1					4		
Franklin	167	21	Turner	Calvin	2		1			1		1	1				6		
Medfield	90	9	Turner	Calvin	3		1			2		1					7		
Roxbury	106	3	Turner	Edward		2	1			3	1	1	1				9		
Dorchester	61	21	Turner	Elisha		1	1			1		1					4		
Milton	49	16	Turner	Elisha	2	1	1			2	1	1					8		
Medfield	90	10	Turner	George				1		1	1		1				4		
Dedham	142	41	Turner	Hezekiah	1			1		1	1		1				5		1st Parish
Wrentham	173	9	Turner	Isaiah	1		1	1		1	2		1				7		
Walpole	31	23	Turner	Jacob		2		1		4		1					8		
Weymouth	77	37	Turner	Jacob		1		1		1				1			4		North Parish
Dedham	140	1	Turner	James	1	1	1				1	1	1	1			73		
Cohasset	154	9	Turner	Job	1	1			1	1	2	1			1		8		
Dedham	142	40	Turner	Joseph				1			1						2		1st Parish
Walpole	31	24	Turner	Joseph				1									1		
Walpole	31	21	Turner	Nathan	1	1		1		1	2		1	1			8		
Braintree	73	31	Turner	Plato											1		1		
Wrentham	176	13	Turner	Samuel	2			1				1	3				8		
Randolph	127	35	Turner	Seth		1		1					1				3		
Randolph	127	36	Turner	Seth Junr	1		1	1		1	1	1					6		
Quincy	43	19	Turrell	Joseph		1		1				1	1				4		
Quincy	43	22	Turrell	Nathl	2		1			2		1					6		
Quincy	43	18	Turrell	Thom			2			1	1						4		
Milton	49	15	Turrill	Benj				1			1		1				3		
Bellingham	160	11	Twichell	Morris	1		1					1					3		
Medway West Parish	97	23	Twiss	Samuel		1	1			1		1					4		
Wrentham	178	21	Tyler	David				1		3		1					5		
Quincy	43	23	Underwood	Eben	2		1			1	1						5		
Dorchester	62	14	Underwood	Rufus			2			1		1					4		
Canton	134	22	Upham	Abijah				1						1			2		
Canton	134	23	Upham	Amos	1	2		1		2		1	1				8		
Canton	134	24	Upham	Jonathan				1		1		1					3		
Canton	134	25	Upham	Nathan			1			1		2					4		
Dorchester	62	19	Vanicar	Henry	2		1			3		1					7		
Dorchester	62	15	Vaughn	Jno				1						1			2		
Dorchester	62	16	Vaughn	Mary									1	1			2		
Braintree	73	5	Veazie	Benjm				1					2	1			4		
Braintree	73	8	Veazie	Joseph	3		1			2		1					7		
Braintree	73	7	Veazie	Leml Junr	1		1			2	1						5		
Braintree	73	6	Veazie	Lemuel		1	1		1	1		1					5		
Braintree	73	10	Veazie	Silas				1				1	1				3		
Quincy	43	25	Veesey	Elijah	2	2	1	1		2	1			2			11		
Quincy	43	24	Veesey	Metran			1							2			3		
Quincy	43	26	Veesey	Wm			1							1			2		
Wrentham	173	33	Vince	Moses		1	1			1	1		1				5		
Weymouth	81	35	Vining	Bela		1	1						1				3		South Parish
Weymouth	81	28	Vining	David		2		1		1	1	1	1				7		South Parish
Weymouth	81	32	Vining	Deboh Wid						1		1					2		South Parish
Weymouth	81	31	Vining	James	1		1				1						3		South Parish
Weymouth	81	29	Vining	Joseph	1			1				1					3		South Parish
Weymouth	81	30	Vining	Joseph Junr	1	1	1			2	1		1				7		South Parish
Weymouth	81	34	Vining	Saml Holbk	1		1			1		1					4		South Parish
Dorchester	62	17	Vinson	Benj	3			1		3		1	1				9		
Weymouth	81	26	Vinson	John		1		1						1			3		South Parish
Weymouth	81	27	Vinson	John Junr	1	2		1	1	3	1	2	1				12		South Parish
Weymouth	81	33	Vinson	Thomas			1					1					2		South Parish
Braintree	73	11	Vinton	Jemima Wid	1		1			1			1				4		
Braintree	73	3	Vinton	John		1		1				1	1				4		
Braintree	73	4	Vinton	John Junr	2		1			3	1	1					8		
Braintree	73	2	Vinton	Josiah	1		3	1		3	1	1					10		
Randolph	128	4	Vinton	Oliver	1		1			1		1					4		
Bellingham	161	22	Vorce	Amariah	3			2					1				6		
Milton	50	4	Vose	Alexa	2	1		1		1			1				6		
Milton	50	15	Vose	Benj		1	1		1		2			1	2		8		
Milton	50	1	Vose	Daniel		1		1		1	1		1		1		6		
Milton	50	10	Vose	Elijah	3	1		1		1	1	1	2				11		
Milton	50	7	Vose	Hannh									1				1		
Stoughton	122	31	Vose	Jeremiah	2	1	1		1		2	2		1			10		
Milton	50	13	Vose	Joseph			1	1			1	1	1		1		6		

TOWN	PG#	LN#	LAST NAME	FIRST NAME	M<10	M 10-16	M 16-26	M 26-45	M 45+	F<10	F 10-16	F 16-26	F 26-45	F 45+	TOTAL ALL OTHER	TOTAL SLAVES	TOTALS	DISTRICT/ TOWNSHIP	NOTES
Milton	50	2	Vose	Lewis	1			1					1				3		
Milton	50	9	Vose	Lydia	1		1			1			1	1			5		
Braintree	73	9	Vose	Mark	2		1	1		1	1		1				7		
Milton	50	8	Vose	Mary										1			1		
Milton	50	14	Vose	Moses	1			1			1		1				4		
Milton	50	11	Vose	Nathan		2		1		1	2	1	1				8		
Roxbury	111	22	Vose	Oliver		1		1	1				1	1			5	2nd Parish	
Milton	50	5	Vose	Saml				1					1				2		
Milton	50	6	Vose	Saml Jr			1			2		1	1				5		
Milton	50	12	Vose	Sarah										2			2		
Milton	50	3	Vose	Stephen				1					1				2		
Dorchester	62	18	Vose	William	3	1	1	1		2		1	1	2			12		
Milton	50	16	Vose	Wm		2		1		2			1				6		
Dedham	142	48	W*son	Joseph				1					1				2	1st Parish	
Weymouth	81	38	Wade	Amasa	1			1		2			1				5	South Parish	
Braintree	73	24	Wade	Lot	1			1		3			1				6		
Stoughton	122	34	Wadsworth	Abigail Wid							1			1			2		
Milton	50	21	Wadsworth	Benj	3			1		2		1	1				8		
Stoughton	122	33	Wadsworth	Benja		1		1					2				4		
Canton	134	29	Wadsworth	David	1	1		1		3			1				7		
Canton	134	30	Wadsworth	Elisha	3			1		1			1				6		
Stoughton	122	32	Wadsworth	George							2	3	1	1			8		
Milton	50	24	Wadsworth	Jno	1	1	2	2					1	1			8		
Milton	50	20	Wadsworth	Josh	1			1		2	1		1				6		
Milton	50	19	Wadsworth	Wm	1		2	1		1			1				6		
Roxbury	105	19	Wait	Benjamin		1	1			2		1					5		
Roxbury	105	20	Wait	Rebecca		1						3	2	1			7		
Roxbury	105	24	Wait	Samuel			1	3		1		2		1	2		10		
Dedham	140	25	Wakfield	George				1		1	1	1					4		
Wrentham	174	31	Walcott	Ebenezer	2	1	1	1		2			1				8		
Randolph	128	6	Wales	Atherton					1					1			2		
Randolph	128	10	Wales	Atherton Jun	2	1				1	1	1					7		
Braintree	73	15	Wales	Benjm	1	2		1		1		1	1	1			8		
Dorchester	62	20	Wales	Eben Esq.		2		1			1	3					7		
Dorchester	63	4	Wales	Eben Jun	2		1	1	1	2			2				9		
Randolph	128	5	Wales	Elisha		1	1	1		2	2	1		1			9		
Randolph	128	9	Wales	Ephraim		1	1	1		1	1						5		
Randolph	128	11	Wales	John		1	2			1		2					6		
Randolph	128	7	Wales	Jonathan	1			1					1				3		
Randolph	128	8	Wales	Jonathan Jun			1										1		
Stoughton	122	36	Wales	Joshua	1	2	3	1		1	1	2	1				12		
Braintree	73	14	Wales	Nathl		1	1	1		1		1	1				6		
Stoughton	122	37	Wales	Nathl	1			1		2				1			5		
Stoughton	122	35	Wales	Samuel		1	1	1		4		1	1				9		
Randolph	128	12	Wales	Silence Wid								2		1			3		
Dorchester	63	5	Wales	Stephen	1		1			2			1	1			7		
Roxbury	112	14	Wales	William	1		1			2			1	1			6	3rd Parish	
Needham	148	49	Walker	Azariah	4			2		1	1	1	1		1		12		
Medway East Parish	94	25	Walker	Comfort	2	1	1			2		1	1				8		
Dorchester	63	16	Walker	Spencer	1			1		7	2		1				12		
Dorchester	63	15	Walker	Wm	1	1	1	1		1			1				6		
Walpole	31	25	Wallet	Andrew	2	1		1	1		1	1		1			8		
Roxbury	114	1	Wally	Thomas		1	1			1		2	1				6	3rd Parish	
Wrentham	172	18	Walton	Amos		2			1			1		1			5		
Roxbury	101	14	Ward	John	1		1			1	1		1	1			7		
Milton	50	17	Ward	Joshua	1			1		3			2	1			8		
Roxbury	101	15	Ward	Samuel		1	1	1					1				4		
Wrentham	174	25	Ware	Abiel	1							2		1			4		
Franklin	166	3	Ware	Amariah	1		2	1			1		1	1			7		
Wrentham	174	3	Ware	Asa	2		1		1	2			1	1			8		
Wrentham	172	11	Ware	Benjamin		1		1	1				1	1			5		
Franklin	169	10	Ware	Billy	1			1					1	1			4		
Needham	148	50	Ware	Daniel	2	2				1		1	2				9		
Wrentham	178	26	Ware	Daniel	1	1		1		1			1				5		
Wrentham	172	12	Ware	David				1	2			1		1			5		
Franklin	169	6	Ware	Eli	1		3	1				1	1	3			10		
Wrentham	180	8	Ware	Elias	2	2	2	1		2		1	2				12		
Needham	149	4	Ware	Elijah				1		1	2		1				5		
Needham	149	3	Ware	Epherim		1	1	1			1		1				5		
Wrentham	179	33	Ware	Ezra		1	1		1		1	2					6		
Wrentham	178	14	Ware	Hezekiah		1							1				2		
Wrentham	176	2	Ware	Ichabod		1		1						2			4		
Franklin	164	31	Ware	Jabez				1						1			2		
Franklin	166	2	Ware	Jesse			1	1	1	1		1	1	1			7		
Wrentham	173	30	Ware	Joel		2		1		2	1		1				7		
Needham	149	5	Ware	Jonathan		1		1				1	1				4		
Medway West Parish	97	24	Ware	Joseph	3	1		1		1			1				7		
Needham	149	16	Ware	Joseph	1						1	1	1				5		
Wrentham	174	33	Ware	Joseph			1							1			2		
Wrentham	174	11	Ware	Josiah	1		1		1	1	1		1				6		
Needham	149	14	Ware	Luther			1			1	1		1				4		
Wrentham	181	7	Ware	Molly							1	2	1				4		

TOWN	PG#	LN#	LAST NAME	FIRST NAME	FREE WHITE MALES					FREE WHITE FEMALES					TOTAL ALL OTHER	TOTAL SLAVES	TOTALS	DISTRICT/ TOWNSHIP	NOTES
					under 10	10 to 16	16 to 26	26 to 45	45 and over	under 10	10 to 16	16 to 26	26 to 45	45 and over					
Wrentham	173	32	Ware	Nathan			2	1	1			2	1	1			8		
Needham	149	2	Ware	Nathaniel				1						1			2		
Wrentham	172	15	Ware	Nathaniel		2	3	1			1	2		4			13		
Needham	149	7	Ware	Nathaniel Junr	1			1		3			1				6		
Wrentham	173	15	Ware	Oliver		2			1	1	1			1			6		
Wrentham	182	3	Ware	Oliver 2d	1			1						2			4		
Wrentham	177	1	Ware	Paul	2		2	1		1			1	1			8		
Franklin	165	1	Ware	Phinehas		2	1		1	1			2	1			8		
Wrentham	174	12	Ware	Samuel	1	1	1		1	1		1		1			7		
Wrentham	174	26	Ware	Timothy			1						1				2		
Roxbury	99	1	Warner	Jonathan	1	1			1	2	1	2		1			9		
Foxborough	26	15	Warren	Ebenezer	1	1		1	1	2	1	4		1			12		
Roxbury	103	33	Warren	Samuel				1					1	1			3		
Cohasset	152	37	Warwick	Saban	2			1		2			1				6		
Weymouth	78	7	Waterman	David	2			1		3			1				7	North Parish	
Weymouth	78	5	Waterman	Hannah Wid				1			1	1		1			4	North Parish	
Stoughton	122	38	Waters	Asa	1	1		1		1			1				5		
Stoughton	122	39	Waters	Zebulon	1			1		1							3		
Needham	149	15	Watkins	David	1			1					1				3		
Roxbury	108	4	Watson	Nathan			4						1				5		
Dedham	140	8	Weatherbee	Benjamin	1	2		2					1	1			7		
Dedham	142	42	Weatherbee	Benjamin				1						1			2	1st Parish	
Dedham	140	29	Weatherbee	Comforth	1		2	1		2			1	1			8		
Dedham	142	43	Weatherbee	David	1	1		1					1				4	1st Parish	
Dedham	140	27	Weatherbee	Joseph			1	1		1	1		1	1			6		
Dedham	140	22	Webb	Daniel		1	1	1					1	1			5		
Roxbury	114	7	Webb	Ebenezer		1		2					1	1			5	3rd Parish	
Quincy	43	28	Webb	Jona			1	1		1	2	5		1			11		
Weymouth	78	4	Webb	Saml Junr		2		2		1		1		2			8	North Parish	
Weymouth	77	44	Webb	Thomas			1	2				1		3			7	North Parish	
Weymouth	78	9	Webb	Thomas		1	1	1		1	2	1	1	1			9	North Parish	
Quincy	43	31	Webster	Thom				1						1			2		
Dorchester	63	21	Welch	Wm	2			1		2			1				6		
Roxbury	106	31	Weld	Benjamin	1	1	4		1	2	1	1	1				12		
Roxbury	109	5	Weld	David	1	1	2	4	1		1	2		1			13	2nd Parish	
Roxbury	112	34	Weld	Ebenezer		3	2		2			2		1	1		11	3rd Parish	
Roxbury	112	28	Weld	Elijah	1	1			1				1	1			5	3rd Parish	
Roxbury	112	37	Weld	Jacob	1		6		1	2	1		2	1	1		14	3rd Parish	
Roxbury	112	31	Weld	John				1						1			2	3rd Parish	
Roxbury	113	2	Weld	Mary						1		1	1	1			4	3rd Parish	
Roxbury	112	35	Weld	Nathaniel		1			1					1			3	3rd Parish	
Roxbury	103	32	Weld	Samuel	1	2	1					1	1	1			7		
Roxbury	113	14	Weld	Sarah									1	1			2	3rd Parish	
Roxbury	112	36	Weld	Thomas		2	2		1	3	1	1	1		1		12	3rd Parish	
Roxbury	113	1	Weld	William Gordon	1	1		1					1				4	3rd Parish	
Braintree	73	27	Weld	Ezra	1			1		2			1	1			6		
Foxborough	26	24	Welman	Oliver	1			1			1		1	1			5		
Canton	134	41	Wentworth	Benjamin				1									1		
Canton	134	40	Wentworth	Ebenezer	2	1		1		2			1	1			8		
Canton	134	32	Wentworth	Jerusha Wid.	1			1					1	1			4		
Canton	134	38	Wentworth	John Jr	1	1	3	1		3	1		1				11		
Canton	134	33	Wentworth	Joseph	3				1	2			1				7		
Canton	134	31	Wentworth	Judith Wid.										1			1		
Dorchester	63	2	Wentworth	Moses	1			1						1			3		
Canton	134	36	Wentworth	Nathl	2			1		1			1				5		
Canton	134	37	Wentworth	Obed	1			1		1			1				4		
Canton	134	35	Wentworth	Oliver	1		1	1		1	1		1				6		
Canton	134	43	Wentworth	Paul				1					1	2			4		
Canton	134	42	Wentworth	Rachel						2			1				3		
Canton	134	34	Wentworth	Seth	1		1	1			1	1		1			6		
Canton	134	44	Wentworth	Simeon		1				1			1				3		
Sharon	36	22	Wentworth	Stephen				1									1		
Canton	134	39	Wentworth	Susanna Wid.						2			1	1			4		
Randolph	128	34	Wentworth	Theophilus	1			1		1			1				4		
Randolph	128	31	West	John		1							1				2		
Randolph	128	30	West	Thomas				1		1			1	1			4		
Weymouth	77	41	Weston	Deboh Wd			1				1	2		2			6	North Parish	
Roxbury	112	21	Wheeler	Deborah & Sarah	1						1	2	2				6	3rd Parish	
Canton	134	28	Wheeler	Hannah										1			1		
Medway East Parish	94	26	Wheeler	Lewis		1	1	1		2	1		1				7		
Canton	134	27	Wheeler	Samuel				1					1				2		
Canton	134	26	Wheeler	William					1					1			2		
Dorchester	63	14	Wheelock	Abel	5			1		1	1	1	1				10		
Medfield	90	11	Wheelock	Eleazer				1						1			2		
Medfield	90	12	Wheelock	Ephraim		1	2	1				1		1			6		
Medfield	90	13	Wheelock	Oliver				1					1				2		
Medfield	90	19	Wheelock	Seth			1	1		2	1						5		
Dedham	140	28	Wheelock	Timothy		1		1					1	1			4		
Cohasset	153	4	Wheelwright	Gershom	1	1	2		1	3	1	1	1				11		
Cohasset	153	5	Wheelwright	John				1						1			2		
Cohasset	153	21	Wheelwright	Micah					1				1				2		
Dedham	140	19	Wheeton	Jesse				1				1	1		3		6		
Wrentham	176	5	Whight	Edward		1	3		1			1	1	1			8		

TOWN	PG#	LN#	LAST NAME	FIRST NAME	FREE WHITE MALES under 10	10 to 16	16 to 26	26 to 45	45 and over	FREE WHITE FEMALES under 10	10 to 16	16 to 26	26 to 45	45 and over	TOTAL ALL OTHER	TOTAL SLAVES	TOTALS	DISTRICT/ TOWNSHIP	NOTES
Wrentham	176	6	Whight	William	1			1				1					3		
Medway West Parish	97	27	Whiston	Ezra			1	1					1				3		
Bellingham	162	17	Whitacer	William			1	1				1	1				4		
Sharon	36	21	Whitaker	Jonathan Revd	2		1	1				1	1				6		
Cohasset	153	20	Whitcomb	Israel		1		1		1			1	1			5		
Randolph	128	21	Whitcomb	Jacob		2	3	1		1		2		1			10		
Cohasset	153	14	Whitcomb	Job	1	1	1		1	1			1	1			7		
Randolph	128	23	Whitcomb	John				1			1		1				3		
Cohasset	153	19	Whitcomb	Joseph	1		1	1		1	2		1				8		
Cohasset	153	18	Whitcomb	Lott	1	1		1			1	2		1			7		
Randolph	128	24	Whitcomb	Moses	2			1		2	1		1				7		
Randolph	128	22	Whitcomb	Phebe		1	1			2	1		1				6		
Randolph	128	25	Whitcomb	Robert	2			1		1	1		1	1			7		
Roxbury	103	30	White	Aaron			4	1	1		1	3		1			11		
Weymouth	82	2	White	Aaron				1						1			2	South Parish	
Weymouth	78	1	White	Abiel	3	2	1	1		1	1	1	2	2			14	North Parish	
Dorchester	63	8	White	Abijah				2			1			2			5		
Braintree	73	12	White	Alexander	1	1	2	1		2			1				8		
Foxborough	26	23	White	Asa	1			1			1						3		
Weymouth	78	2	White	Asa		1		1		1			1				4	North Parish	
Weymouth	82	1	White	Asa			1		1				1				3	South Parish	
Randolph	128	17	White	Bailey		1		1		3	1		1				7		
Roxbury	102	4	White	Bartholomew			1		1	1		1					3		
Roxbury	114	13	White	Benjamin	1		2	1		1	2	2	2				11	3rd Parish	
Braintree	73	26	White	Benjm				1					1				2		
Weymouth	81	42	White	Benjm				1					1				2	South Parish	
Randolph	128	16	White	Caleb	3			1						1			5		
Randolph	128	14	White	Cornelius		1	3	2			1		1				8		
Weymouth	81	40	White	Daniel				1						1			2	South Parish	
Roxbury	113	15	White	David				1		2	1	1	1				6	3rd Parish	
Sharon	36	18	White	David	1	2	2	1			1	1		1			9		
Weymouth	81	43	White	David	1	1	1		1	2	1	1		1			9	South Parish	
Weymouth	82	3	White	David			2			1			1	1			5	South Parish	
Dedham	142	44	White	Ebenezer		1		1			1			1			4	1st Parish	
Braintree	73	13	White	Elihu	3			1		1		1	1	1			8		
Franklin	168	22	White	Elihu			1						1				2		
Medway West Parish	97	30	White	Elijah	3			1					1				5		
Wrentham	179	11	White	Eliphalet	1		1	1		1	1		1				6		
Milton	50	18	White	Elizabeth	3						1		1				5		
Dedham	142	45	White	George	1			1	1	1			1				5	1st Parish	
Weymouth	81	37	White	Hezekiah		1	1	1					1	1			5	South Parish	
Weymouth	77	40	White	Ja*	2		1						1				4	North Parish	
Dedham	144	40	White	Jacob	1			1				1					3	2nd Parish	
Dedham	142	47	White	James				1									1	1st Parish	
Roxbury	102	18	White	James			1	1	1			1					4		
Weymouth	81	41	White	James	3			1		1			1				7	South Parish	
Weymouth	82	4	White	Jeremiah	1		1						1				3	South Parish	
Milton	50	22	White	Jno	1		1					2					4		
Dorchester	63	11	White	Jno Jun	1			1		3			1				6		
Dorchester	63	12	White	John				1			1		2				4		
Weymouth	77	39	White	John	2		2			2	1	1	1				9	North Parish	
Franklin	168	23	White	Jonathan	1		1			1		1					4		
Weymouth	82	5	White	Jonathan	1	1		1		1		1	1				6	South Parish	
Randolph	128	13	White	Joseph			1	1			1	1	1				5		
Sharon	36	20	White	Joseph	2	1		1		1			1				6		
Randolph	128	19	White	Lot	1			1			1		1				4		
Weymouth	78	8	White	Lurania								1	1				2	North Parish	
Roxbury	110	31	White	Luther			1					1	1				3	2nd Parish	
Wrentham	178	24	White	Luther	2			1		1			1				5		
Dorchester	63	7	White	Mary		1	2							1			4		
Randolph	128	20	White	Micah	3	1		1		1	2		1				9		
Franklin	168	26	White	Nathan	1			1		2	1	1					6		
Weymouth	77	43	White	Nathl	2	4	1			2	1	1					11	North Parish	
Randolph	128	15	White	Rhoda Wid	2								1				3		
Roxbury	115	8	White	Samuel		1	1						1	1			3	3rd Parish	
Roxbury	113	21	White	Sarah							1		1				2	3rd Parish	
Weymouth	81	39	White	Silas		1		1		1			1				4	South Parish	
Foxborough	26	25	White	Simeon	2			1		1	1		1				6		
Randolph	128	18	White	Simeon			1			2		1					4		
Dedham	142	46	White	Thomas			1	1					1				3	1st Parish	
Quincy	43	29	White	Man.									2		4		6		
Dover	151	6	Whiting	Aaron	4	1	2	1		2			1				11		
Dedham	140	5	Whiting	Abner			2		1	2		1					6		
Franklin	163	17	Whiting	Asa		1		1			1	1	1				5		
Dedham	140	18	Whiting	Calvin	2	1	1	1		2		1	1	1			10		
Dedham	144	39	Whiting	Daniel Col				1									1	2nd Parish	
Wrentham	177	14	Whiting	David	2			1		2			1	1			7		
Roxbury	110	24	Whiting	Ebenezer		1		1	1		1	1	1			2	8	2nd Parish	
Dedham	140	24	Whiting	Edward		1		1					2				4		
Medway West Parish	97	29	Whiting	Elias	3			1	1	1		1					7		
Franklin	169	21	Whiting	Elizabeth									1				1		
Wrentham	175	21	Whiting	Elkanah	2	1		1	1		1		1				7		
Dover	151	7	Whiting	Ellis			1						1				2		
Dedham	140	11	Whiting	Hannah Wid		1				1	1	2		1			6		
Dedham	140	14	Whiting	Hezekiah	1			1		1		1	1				5		

TOWN	PG#	LN#	LAST NAME	FIRST NAME	M <10	M 10–16	M 16–26	M 26–45	M 45+	F <10	F 10–16	F 16–26	F 26–45	F 45+	TOTAL ALL OTHER	TOTAL SLAVES	TOTALS	DISTRICT/ TOWNSHIP	NOTES
Wrentham	175	23	Whiting	Jerusha	1	1	1			1	2	1	1				8		
Roxbury	105	17	Whiting	Joel	1		2	1			1	1	1				7		
Franklin	163	1	Whiting	John	2			2		1	1		2				8		
Wrentham	172	23	Whiting	John		1	1	2	2		1	2	2				11		
Wrentham	175	9	Whiting	John 3d	3		2	1		2			1				9		
Franklin	167	29	Whiting	Joseph					1			1		1			3		
Dedham	140	13	Whiting	Joseph & Paul	1			2		2			1	1			7		
Franklin	169	22	Whiting	Joseph 2nd	3	1	1	1		1			2				9		
Dedham	140	15	Whiting	Joseph Dr.			1	1			1		2				5		
Dedham	140	7	Whiting	Joshua		1	1			1	2	1					6		
Wrentham	172	19	Whiting	Lewis			2		1	1	1	1	1				7		
Wrentham	175	22	Whiting	Marjory		1						1					2		
Needham	149	1	Whiting	Mary Wid.		1				1	1		1				4		
Dedham	140	12	Whiting	Moses	1	1	2	1		1		1	1	1			9		
Dedham	144	38	Whiting	Nathaniel		2	1			2	1	3		1			11	2nd Parish	
Wrentham	175	20	Whiting	Otis	1	1	1	1		2	1		1				8		
Franklin	165	13	Whiting	Peter		1	1		1						1		4		
Dedham	140	10	Whiting	Rufus	1			1		2	2		1				7		
Dedham	140	6	Whiting	Samuel				1					1				2		
Roxbury	110	28	Whiting	Seth	1	1	1	1		1	1		1				7	2nd Parish	
Dedham	140	16	Whiting	Stephen		1		1					2				4		
Wrentham	180	6	Whiting	Thaddeus	4	2		1		1		1					9		
Medway West Parish	97	28	Whiting	Timothy	1			1		1			1				4		
Dedham	140	17	Whiting	Timothy & Solomon		1		2		1	1	1	1		1		9		
Dedham	140	9	Whiting	William		1	1		1				1	2			6		
Dover	151	3	Whiting	William		1	1	1	1			2		1			7		
Randolph	128	26	Whiting	William		1				1							2		
Bellingham	161	11	Whitley	William				1			1	1					3		
Weymouth	77	42	Whitman	Abiah		1	1						1	1			4	North Parish	
Roxbury	103	16	Whitman	Hannah									1				1		
Weymouth	78	3	Whitmark	Peter	1	1	1			1		2		1			7	North Parish	
Weymouth	78	6	Whitmark	Saml	2			1	1	2			1	1			8	North Parish	
Braintree	73	28	Whitmarsh	Saml					1	1			1				3		
Brookline	115	7	Whitney	Elijah		1	3	2		1		1			1		9		
Roxbury	105	30	Whitney	Elisha		1	5		1	1	1	1					10		
Roxbury	110	33	Whitney	Jacob				1					1				2	2nd Parish	
Medway East Parish	94	27	Whitney	Joshua		2		1			1		1				5		
Dorchester	63	17	Whitney	Moses	1	1	1			1		1					5		
Quincy	43	27	Whitney	Peter Rev.			1			1		1					3		
Sharon	36	23	Whittemore	Edward	2			1			1						4		
Roxbury	112	24	Whittemore	Jacob	4	1			2	2	1	2	1				13	3rd Parish	
Sharon	36	15	Whittemore	Joshua	2	1		1		2	1		1				8		
Roxbury	109	2	Whittemore	Michael	4		1	1		2		1					9	2nd Parish	
Roxbury	108	12	Whittemore	Nancy		2	2					1		1			6		
Canton	134	51	Whydon	Comfort	1			1	1	1		1		1			6		
Canton	134	52	Whydon	Nathaniel	1			1									2		
Randolph	128	27	Whyton	Samuel	2			1		1		1					5		
Medway West Parish	97	26	Wight	Aaron	3		1		1	1	3	3	1		1		14		
Bellingham	159	29	Wight	Abram		1		1		1			2	1			6		
Dover	150	56	Wight	Amos					1		1	1					3		
Medfield	90	18	Wight	Asa					1	2		1					4		
Dover	151	5	Wight	Caleb	1		1					1					3		
Dedham	140	20	Wight	Ebenezer Esq	1	3		1	1	1		1	1	1			11		
Bellingham	159	28	Wight	Eliab	2		2	1		1	2		1	1			10		
Dedham	140	4	Wight	Henry	1		2		1	1		1		1			7		
Medway West Parish	97	25	Wight	James					2				1				3		
Medfield	90	14	Wight	Jonathan		1		1		1		1	2		1		8		
Medfield	90	15	Wight	Jonathan Junr	3			1		1			2				7		
Dedham	140	21	Wight	Joseph	2		3	1			2		1				9		
Foxborough	26	26	Wight	Lemuel Jr	3			1		1		1					6		
Medfield	90	17	Wight	Moses	1	2			1	1	1	1	1				8		
Medfield	90	16	Wight	Nathan		1		1					1				3		
Wrentham	175	34	Wight	Thomas	2				1	1	1			1			6		
Foxborough	26	22	Wilbor	Elisha	1	1		1		1		1					5		
Braintree	73	17	Wild	Elijah	3			1	1	1			1				7		
Randolph	128	28	Wild	John	1	1			1	1	1		1	1			7		
Braintree	73	19	Wild	Jonathan			1	1		2	2		1				7		
Walpole	31	26	Wild	Jonathan	3	1		1	1	1	1		2		1		11		
Dorchester	63	24	Wild	Joseph			1	1		1	2	1					6		
Milton	50	23	Wild	Joseph					1			3		1			5		
Randolph	128	29	Wild	Joshua	2			1					1				4		
Braintree	73	22	Wild	Levi				1					1	1			3		
Braintree	73	20	Wild	Paul	1	2		1		3			1				8		
Braintree	73	25	Wild	Person	1		1	1		2			1	1			7		
Canton	134	45	Wild	Richard	1			1		2	1		1				6		
Braintree	73	18	Wild	Silas		1			1			1		1			4		
Braintree	73	21	Wild	Silas Junior	2	2				4			1	1			11		
Braintree	73	23	Wild	Thomas	3			1		1		1					6		
Braintree	73	16	Wild	William Junr	1	1	1	1			1	1					6		
Weymouth	77	45	Wilds	William	2	1	1			1		1	1				7	North Parish	
Roxbury	107	22	Willard	Simon	3	1	3			3		1	1	1			14		
Cohasset	153	49	Willcutt	Hannah										1			1		

TOWN	PG#	LN#	LAST NAME	FIRST NAME	FREE WHITE MALES					FREE WHITE FEMALES					TOTAL ALL OTHER	TOTAL SLAVES	TOTALS	DISTRICT/ TOWNSHIP	NOTES
					under 10	10 to 16	16 to 26	26 to 45	45 and over	under 10	10 to 16	16 to 26	26 to 45	45 and over					
Cohasset	153	1	Willcutt	Jesse					1			1		1			3		
Cohasset	154	21	Willcutt	Joel	2		2	1		2	1		1				9		
Cohasset	153	8	Willcutt	John	1			1	1	1			1				5		
Cohasset	153	48	Willcutt	John		1		1	1	1	1		1				6		
Cohasset	153	45	Willcutt	Thomas	2	1				2		2	1				10		
Franklin	167	25	Williams	Abigail	3							2	1				6		
Needham	149	8	Williams	Asa	1			1					1				3		
Dorchester	63	22	Williams	Caleb				1					1				2		
Dorchester	63	18	Williams	Eben			2	1						1			4		
Roxbury	104	3	Williams	Hannah		1		2			3	1	1		1		9		
Roxbury	103	17	Williams	Henry H.			1	1									2		
Roxbury	112	26	Williams	Isaac	1	1	1		1	1		2		1			8	3rd Parish	
Dorchester	63	9	Williams	Jno	4			1				2	1				8		
Dover	151	4	Williams	John			1						1				2		
Roxbury	106	8	Williams	John		1		1	1		1	1	1	1			7		
Roxbury	100	5	Williams	John D.	2	1	4		1		1	1		1			14		
Roxbury	105	23	Williams	John F.			1						1				2		
Roxbury	100	6	Williams	Joseph	1	1	1	2	2		1	2	2	2			14		
Medway East Parish	94	28	Williams	Levi	2			1					1				4		
Weymouth	81	36	Williams	Revd Simeon			2		1	1	1	1		1			8	South Parish	
Milton	50	25	Williams	Sam	2			1		2			1				6		
Roxbury	99	6	Williams	Stedman	2	1	3	1		1	1	1	1				11		
Roxbury	104	12	Williams	Stephen		1	4	1				2	1				9		
Roxbury	103	25	Williams	Stephen 3d	2	2	1	1		3	2		2				13		
Roxbury	112	27	Williams	Stephen Junr	1	1	1		1			1					5	3rd Parish	
Dorchester	63	23	Williams	Thom	2		1	1			1		1				6		
Roxbury	108	27	Williams	Thomas Doc	1	1	3	3	1				2	2	1		14		
Roxbury	106	29	Williams	Thomas Junr Esq	2		3	2			1	2	2		1		13		
Roxbury	112	23	Williams	William	3			1		1	1		1				7	3rd Parish	
Wrentham	171	27	Williams	Williams	1	2	3		1			1		1			9		
Milton	50	26	Williams	Zebh	1	1		1		2			2				7		
Foxborough	26	18	Willis	Job		1						1	1	2			5		
Sharon	36	16	Willis	Solomon				1				5	1				7		
Roxbury	111	5	Wilson	Aaron		1		1						1			3	2nd Parish	
Dorchester	63	13	Wilson	Abiathar	1			1	1				1				4		
Foxborough	26	17	Wilson	Daniel	1	1		1			1	2		1			7		
Roxbury	110	20	Wilson	Ephraim		2		1		2			1				6	2nd Parish	
Dover	151	1	Wilson	Epperaim		2		1					1				4		
Wrentham	173	7	Wilson	Jared	1	1	1			1			1				5		
Quincy	43	30	Wilson	Jno				1									1		
Dedham	140	23	Wilson	John	1	1	1	1			1		1				6		
Cohasset	155	4	Wilson	Lucy		1							1				2		
Needham	148	52	Wilson	Nathaniel	1			1					1				3		
Needham	149	6	Wilson	Nathaniel Junr		1	1			1		1					4		
Dover	151	2	Wilson	Samuel					1					2			3		
Dorchester	63	3	Wilson	Wm	3			1				1	1				6		
Roxbury	112	25	Winchester	Gulliver			4	2	1			4	1	1			13	3rd Parish	
Brookline	114	12	Winchester	Nathaniel	2	2	2		1	2	1	1					11		
Roxbury	114	8	Winship	Joseph			1						1	1	1		3	3rd Parish	
Foxborough	26	16	Winston	Shadrack	4	2		1				1	1				9		
Dorchester	63	25	Wiswell	Daniel	1	1		1		1	1		1				6		
Bellingham	158	5	Wiswell	David	4			1		1			1				7		
Dorchester	63	20	Wiswell	Ichabod	1		1				1	1		1			6		
Dorchester	63	10	Wiswell	Jno	1		2			1			1				5		
Dorchester	63	19	Wiswell	Jno		1	1	1				1		3			7		
Wrentham	172	21	Witherell	Abel		1		1				1		2			5		
Sharon	36	17	Witherton	William	1		1	1		2		2					7		
Dorchester	62	29	Withington	Danl	3	2	2	1		1	1		1				11		
Dorchester	62	22	Withington	Eb Jr	1	1	2		1			3		2			10		
Dorchester	63	1	Withington	Eben			1	1	1	1		1	1				5		
Canton	134	49	Withington	Edward				1					1				2		
Dorchester	62	26	Withington	Edwd	2		4	3	1	1		1	3	1			16		
Dorchester	62	28	Withington	Eliz									2				2		
Brookline	114	32	Withington	Enos	1			1					1				3		
Canton	134	46	Withington	Henry B.			1		1		1			1			4		
Dorchester	62	30	Withington	I.W.	2	1		1		1			1				6		
Dorchester	62	25	Withington	Jno	1			1				1					3		
Canton	134	48	Withington	John	2	1		1	1	1		1					7		
Dorchester	62	23	Withington	Lem		2		1				2	1				6		
Roxbury	100	7	Withington	Lewis	1			1					1	1			4		
Canton	134	47	Withington	Mather	1	1	1		1	1	1	1	1				8		
Dorchester	62	24	Withington	Noah		1		2					1				4		
Dorchester	62	31	Withington	Phil.			1	1				1	1				4		
Roxbury	103	5	Withington	Phinehas	2	1	3	1		2	5	1	1	1			17		
Dorchester	62	21	Withington	Saml		1	1	4	1	1		3	1				12		
Canton	134	50	Withington	Samuel	1			1					1				4		
Dorchester	62	27	Withington	Thom	1		1					1	1				4		
Foxborough	26	19	Wood	Bridget Wd			1		1		2	1					5		
Sharon	36	24	Wood	Jethro				1					1				2		
Sharon	36	19	Wood	Joseph	1	1		1	2		1		1				7		
Roxbury	109	4	Wood	Lemuel	1			1		1	1		1				5	2nd Parish	
Dorchester	63	6	Wood	Rebeckah	2							1					3		
Roxbury	113	11	Woodard	Abigail	3			1		1			1				6	3rd Parish	
Roxbury	99	4	Woodard	John Chever	1	3	1	1		1	1	1					10		
Roxbury	112	4	Woodard	Josiah	2	1		1		2	1		1	1			9	3rd Parish	

TOWN	PG#	LN#	LAST NAME	FIRST NAME	under 10	10 to 16	16 to 26	26 to 45	45 and over	under 10	10 to 16	16 to 26	26 to 45	45 and over	TOTAL ALL OTHER	TOTAL SLAVES	TOTALS	DISTRICT/ TOWNSHIP	NOTES
			HEADS OF HOUSEHOLD		FREE WHITE MALES					FREE WHITE FEMALES									
Needham	148	51	Woodcock	Samuel	2	2			1	2		2		1			10		
Roxbury	112	11	Woods	George	1				1			1		1			4	3rd Parish	
Randolph	128	32	Woods	Samuel				1					1	1			3		
Randolph	128	33	Woods	Samuel Junr				1		2			1				4		
Medfield	90	20	Woodward	Artemas			3	1		1	1	1	1				8		
Needham	148	53	Woodward	Asa			1	1		1			1				4		
Dedham	140	26	Woodward	Deborough			1	1			1	1		1			5		
Franklin	169	26	Woodward	Holland	3				1		1		1				6		
Franklin	164	28	Woodward	James	2	1		1		1	2		1				8		
Franklin	164	27	Woodward	Nathan	1			1			1		1	1			5		
Foxborough	26	27	Worse	Joel				4	1	1	1			1			8		
Roxbury	99	5	Worsley	Joseph	2	1	2	3		2		1	1				12		
Roxbury	107	17	Worts	Robert	1			1		2		1	1				6		
Foxborough	26	21	Wright	Jonathan				1						1			2		
Foxborough	26	20	Wright	Lemuel				1				1	1				3		
Medway East Parish	94	29	Wright	Luther Rev.			1				1						2		
Roxbury	104	2	Wyman	John	2		1	1		2		1	1	1			9		
Roxbury	103	3	Wyman	Thomas			1		1				1				3		
Roxbury	103	10	Wyman	Thomas Junr	3			1		2	1		1				8		
Roxbury	101	11	Wyman	William		1			2			1	2	1			7		
Roxbury	108	9	Young	James	1			1		1		1					4		
Milton	50	27	Young	Jno	1				1				1				3		
Roxbury	108	10	Zeigler	George	2	1	1	1		1		1	1	1			9		

Suffolk County

TOWN	PG#	LN#	LAST NAME	FIRST NAME	FREE WHITE MALES under 10	10 to 16	16 to 26	26 to 45	45 and over	FREE WHITE FEMALES under 10	10 to 16	16 to 26	26 to 45	45 and over	TOTAL ALL OTHER	TOTAL SLAVES	TOTALS	DISTRICT/ TOWNSHIP	NOTES
Hingham	137	1	Lincoln	Solomon		1		1		2			1				5		
Hingham	137	2	Davidson	John	1			1					1				3		
Hingham	137	3	Irving	Elijah			1					1					2		
Hingham	137	4	Lane	Isaac	1		2						1				4		
Hingham	137	5	Lincoln	Sarah		1							1				2		
Hingham	137	6	Lincoln	Seth		2	1		1	1	1	2		1			9		
Hingham	137	7	Kingsman	John	3			1		2			1	1			8		
Hingham	137	8	Newell	Joseph	1	1		1		2		1	1				7		
Hingham	137	9	Beal	Benjamin			3			1			1				5		
Hingham	137	10	Hobart	Shubael		1	1			3		1		1			7		
Hingham	137	11	Hobart	Leavitt	1	1		1		1			1				5		
Hingham	137	12	Hobart	Deborah								1	1				2		
Hingham	137	13	Hobart	Samuel		1	1		2			1		2			7		
Hingham	137	14	Thaxter	Joseph	1		1		2			2	1				7		
Hingham	137	15	Liste	Henry M	1		1					1			1		4		
Hingham	137	16	Butler	Rebecca		1					4		1				6		
Hingham	137	17	Hobart	Japeth				1					1				2		
Hingham	137	18	Lincoln	Ezekiel	3			1			1		1				6		
Hingham	137	19	Lincoln	Beza		1		1		2	1		2				7		
Hingham	137	20	Smith	Hobart	1			1		3	1		1				7		
Hingham	137	21	Dunbar	Laban	2		1						1				4		
Hingham	137	22	Wilder	Nathaniel	1			1	1	1			1				5		
Hingham	137	23	French	Reuben	1			1		2			1				5		
Hingham	137	24	*	*			1						1				2		Ink mark covers name
Hingham	137	25	Lincoln	Caleb	1	1			1	2	1		1				7		
Hingham	137	26	Humphrey	Noah			1		1			1		1			4		
Hingham	137	27	Stodder	Thomas			2		1	1	1			1			6		
Hingham	137	28	Humphrey	Noah Junr	1		1	1		1		1					5		
Hingham	137	29	Stodder	Jacob	1			1		1	1			1			5		
Hingham	137	30	Stodder	Nathaniel				1						2			3		
Hingham	137	31	Marsh	Stephen				1						1			2		
Hingham	137	32	Marsh	Stephen Junr	3	1		1		1			1				7		
Hingham	137	33	Marsh	Samuel	1			1		1			1				4		
Hingham	137	34	Todd	James	1	1			1	1		1		1			6		
Hingham	137	35	Todd	William			1			1		1					3		
Hingham	137	36	Lincoln	Charles	3			1		2			1				7		
Hingham	137	37	Lincoln	Stephen		1		1					2				4		
Hingham	137	38	Lincoln	Calvin	1			1		1			1				4		
Hingham	137	39	Beal	Joseph	1			1		1		1	1	1			6		
Hingham	137	40	Beal	Joseph Junr			2					1					3		
Hingham	137	41	Beal	Jacob				1			1		1				3		
Hingham	137	42	Beal	Rebecca										2			2		
Hingham	137	43	Beal	James				1					1				2		
Hingham	137	44	Beal	Laban	1			1		1			1				4		
Hingham	137	45	Hunt	Samuel			1			1			1				3		
Hingham	137	46	Lincoln	Israel				1					1				2		
Hingham	137	47	Lincoln	Barnabas	1		3		1	2	2	1		1			11		
Hingham	137	48	Lincoln	Jotham			2	1		2			1				6		
Hingham	137	49	Marsh	Lott	1			1		2	1		1				6		
Hingham	138	1	Beal	Israel				1	1				2	1			5		
Hingham	138	2	Stowel	Israel	2	1		1		1		2	1				8		
Hingham	138	3	Lincoln	Israel Junr				1		3	1		1				6		
Hingham	138	4	Marsh	John				1					1	1			3		
Hingham	138	5	Marsh	Thomas				1					1				2		
Hingham	138	6	Marsh	John Junr		1		1		3		1	1				7		
Hingham	138	7	Lincoln	Elijah	1			1		1			1	1			5		
Hingham	138	8	Le Britton	Edwd											5		5		
Hingham	138	9	Stodder	John Junr	1			1		1			1				4		
Hingham	138	10	Lincoln	Joseph	1	1		1		1		1	1				6		
Hingham	138	11	Hearsey	Gilbert Junr	1		2			1			1				5		
Hingham	138	12	Lincoln	Daniel	1	1		1		3	1		1				8		
Hingham	138	13	Stowel	Elizabeth									1				1		
Hingham	138	14	Shattuck	William		2			1	1	1		1				6		
Hingham	138	15	Stodder	Stephen	1	2		1		2	1	2	1	1			11		
Hingham	138	16	Waterman	Lydia		1							1	1			3		
Hingham	138	17	Danniels	John			1					1	1				3		
Hingham	138	18	Stowel	Adam		1		1		1			1				4		
Hingham	138	19	Lincoln	Joshua		1		1				1	1	1			5		
Hingham	138	20	Lincoln	George	2			1		1			1				5		
Hingham	138	21	Cain	Daniel			1	1		1	2			1			6		
Hingham	138	22	Cain	David				1				1	1				3		
Hingham	138	23	French	Theodore		1		1				1					3		
Hingham	139	1	Lincoln	Mathew			1	1				1	1				4		
Hingham	139	2	Lincoln	Noah				1					1				2		
Hingham	139	3	Lincoln	Welcome				1				1	1				3		
Hingham	139	4	Stowel	Joshua				1		1	1	1	2	1			6		
Hingham	139	5	Marble	James	2	1		1		1	2		1				8		
Hingham	139	6	Hearsey	Mary	1	1	1			1	1	1		1			7		
Hingham	139	7	Hearsey	Gilbert Junr				1			2	1		1			5		
Hingham	139	8	Hearsey	Jonathan	2			1					1				4		
Hingham	139	9	Hearsey	Ebed		1			1			1		1			4		
Hingham	139	10	Thaxter	Francis	1								1				3		
Hingham	139	11	Thaxter	Jonathan	1			1					1				3		
Hingham	139	12	Bates	Caleb		1	2						1				4		
Hingham	139	13	Thaxter	Quincy	1			1		3	1	1	1				8		
Hingham	139	14	Thaxter	John Esq				1			1			3	1		6		
Hingham	139	15	Loring	Thomas		2			1			3	1				7		
Hingham	139	16	Norton	Samuel		1	1					1		2			6		
Hingham	139	17	Lincoln	Enoch				2					1	1			4		
Hingham	139	18	Lincoln	Ezra		1		1			2		1				5		

TOWN	PG#	LN#	LAST NAME	FIRST NAME	FREE WHITE MALES					FREE WHITE FEMALES					TOTAL ALL OTHER	TOTAL SLAVES	TOTALS	DISTRICT/ TOWNSHIP	NOTES
					under 10	10 to 16	16 to 26	26 to 45	45 and over	under 10	10 to 16	16 to 26	26 to 45	45 and over					
Hingham	139	19	Lincoln	Jonathan		2			1	1		1		1			6		
Hingham	139	20	Thaxter	Daniel	1			1					1				3		
Hingham	139	21	Lincoln	Abner	2			1		3			1				7		
Hingham	139	22	Lincoln	Nathan		1		1				2	1	1			6		
Hingham	139	23	Southard	William	2			1			1	1	1				6		
Hingham	139	24	Lewis	Ebenezer				1						1			2		
Hingham	139	25	Gill	Thomas				1						1			2		
Hingham	139	26	Hearsey	Thomas		1	1	1	1		1	1		1			7		
Hingham	139	27	Lothrop	Ambrose			1						1				2		
Hingham	139	28	Blake	Joseph				1				1	1	1			4		
Hingham	139	29	Lord	Thomas		1		1		1			1				4		
Hingham	139	30	Cushing	Perez			1							1			2		
Hingham	139	31	Lincoln	Abel			1			1		1					3		
Hingham	139	32	Lincoln	Job	1			1					1	1			4		
Hingham	139	33	Andrews	Ephraim	1			1		1	1		1	1			6		
Hingham	139	34	Andrews	Thomas		1		1		1			3	1			7		
Hingham	139	35	Andrews	Joseph				1					1	1			3		
Hingham	139	36	Lincoln	David Junr	2	1	1	1		1			1				7		
Hingham	139	37	Leavitt	Jairus			1	1		1	1	1					5		
Hingham	139	38	Leavitt	Jairus	1			1				1	1				4		
Hingham	139	39	Beal	Jedediah			1	1						2			4		
Hingham	139	40	Bates	Asa	2			1					1				4		
Hingham	139	41	Price	Nathan Esqr		1	1	1		1	2	1	1		2		10		
Hingham	139	42	Loring	Lydia								1		1			2		
Hingham	139	43	Cobb	Elisha B			1					1					2		
Hingham	139	44	Barker	Deborah			1			1			1				3		
Hingham	139	45	Thaxter	Seth			1	1		2		1	1				6		
Hingham	139	46	Briton												2		2		No first name listed
Hingham	140	1	Gay	Jotham Esqr				1		1	1	3	2				8		
Hingham	140	2	Bassett	Joseph		1	1						1				4		
Hingham	140	3	Waters	Isaac		2		1	1	1	1	1	1				8		
Hingham	140	4	Souther	John	1	1	1		1	2	2	1	1				10		
Hingham	140	5	Sprague	Amos Jr			1			2		1					4		
Hingham	140	6	Barns	Ezekiel											2		2		
Hingham	140	7	Waters	Mehitable				1					2				3		
Hingham	140	8	Hammond	Joseph		1		1				1		1			4		
Hingham	140	9	Lincoln	David	1		1	1				1		1			5		
Hingham	140	10	Burrell	Leavitt	1			1		2			1				5		
Hingham	140	11	Mansfield	Job				1									1		
Hingham	140	12	Mansfield	Ruth									1	1			2		
Hingham	140	13	Mansfield	Mary									1				1		
Hingham	140	14	Stodder	Reuben Jr		1		1			1	1	1				5		
Hingham	140	15	Gardner	Isaac	1	1		1		2	1		1				7		
Hingham	140	16	McNeal	Sarah						3	1	1					5		
Hingham	140	17	Gardner	Mary	1					1		1		1			4		
Hingham	140	18	Hudson	William	1			1		1			1				4		
Hingham	140	19	Stodder	Othniel		1		1					1				3		
Hingham	140	20	Stodder	George			1					1					2		
Hingham	140	21	Hearsey	Laban	3	1	1	1					1	1			8		
Hingham	140	22	Barns	John			1	1			3		1				6		
Hingham	140	23	Barns	Ensign	2	1		1		2	1		1				8		
Hingham	140	24	Stodder	Daniel		1		1					1				3		
Hingham	140	25	French	Jonathan	1	1		1		1		2	1				7		
Hingham	140	26	Hearsey	Abijah Junr			1			1			1				3		
Hingham	140	27	Remington	Elisha	2	1		1		1			1				6		
Hingham	140	28	Lincoln	Nathaniel				1						1			2		
Hingham	140	29	Stowell	Noah	1			1		1		1	1				5		
Hingham	140	30	Lincoln	Mary	1	2						2	1				6		
Hingham	140	31	Lincoln	Levi Junr				1		2			2				5		
Hingham	140	32	Thaxter	Duncan	1			1		1			1				4		
Hingham	140	33	Hobart	Joanna								1		1			2		
Hingham	140	34	Manor	Nathaniel	2			1		2			1				6		
Hingham	140	35	Lowell	William		1			1		1	2		1			6		
Hingham	140	36	Hearsey	Noah	1			1		1		2		1			6		
Hingham	140	37	Hobart	Caleb	1		1	1				1		1			5		
Hingham	140	38	Gill	Caleb	1		1					1		1			4		
Hingham	140	39	Lincoln	Jedediah	1			1					1				3		
Hingham	140	40	Lincoln	Levi Junr		1		1					1				4		
Hingham	140	41	Lincoln	James				1			1	1	1				4		
Hingham	140	42	Gill	John			1	1			1	1	1				5		
Hingham	140	43	Gill	Nathaniel				1				1	1				3		
Hingham	140	44	Gill	Nathaniel Junr	1	1		1			2		2				7		
Hingham	140	45	Hobart	Else							1		1				2		
Hingham	140	46	Beal	John Junr				1						1			2		
Hingham	140	47	Thayer	Timothy	3	1		1				1	2				8		
Hingham	141	1	Jones	Solomon	1					2		2					6		
Hingham	141	2	Lane	Leavitt			1										1		
Hingham	141	3	Lane	Elisha				1					1				2		
Hingham	141	4	Kingsman	Thomas				1		1	1	1	1				5		
Hingham	141	5	Sprague	Josiah	3			1		1	1		1				7		
Hingham	141	6	Cushing	Isaac		1		1		1		1					4		
Hingham	141	7	Lewis	Elijah Junr	2	1		1		2			1				7		
Hingham	141	8	Cushing	Jacob			1	1				1		1			4		
Hingham	141	9	Gross	David			1			1			1	1			4		
Hingham	141	10	Dunbar	Benjamin Junr	1			1		3			1				6		
Hingham	141	11	Sprague	Jesse	1			1					1				3		
Hingham	141	12	Jones	Benjamin Junr			1			2		1					4		
Hingham	141	13	Stephenson	James			1			1			1				3		
Hingham	141	14	Leavitt	John	1	1							1				4		
Hingham	141	15	Loring	Joshua	1	2	1		1			1		1			7		

TOWN	PG#	LN#	LAST NAME	FIRST NAME	FREE WHITE MALES under 10	10 to 16	16 to 26	26 to 45	45 and over	FREE WHITE FEMALES under 10	10 to 16	16 to 26	26 to 45	45 and over	TOTAL ALL OTHER	TOTAL SLAVES	TOTALS	DISTRICT/ TOWNSHIP	NOTES
Hingham	141	16	Fearing	Thomas Capt		2	2		1	1		2		2			10		
Hingham	141	17	Hearsey	Ezekiel	2			1					1				4		
Hingham	141	18	Smith	Jonathan				1			1		1				3		
Hingham	141	19	Lasall	Jonathan				1				1	1				3		
Hingham	141	20	Fearing	Lydia	1						1		2				4		
Hingham	141	21	Sprague	Noah				1					1				2		
Hingham	141	22	Cushing	Mathew				1					1				2		
Hingham	141	23	Fearing	Shubael		2		2		1		1	1	1			8		
Hingham	141	24	Lewis	Thomas				1					1				2		
Hingham	141	25	Dunbar	Joshua	1		1					1					3		
Hingham	141	26	Bryant	Thomas	1			1		3		1					6		
Hingham	141	27	Nye	Henry	2		2					1					5		
Hingham	141	28	Stodder	Asahel	1	2	1	1		2		1					8		
Hingham	141	29	Stodder	Demrick	3		1			2	1		1				8		
Hingham	141	30	Hearsey	Rebecca						1		2					3		
Hingham	141	31	Hearsey	Susannah	2						1	1					4		
Hingham	141	32	Pittee	Nathaniel	1	1		1		2	1		1	1			8		
Hingham	141	33	Leavitt	Joshua Junr	2	1		1				1					5		
Hingham	141	34	Cushing	Elisha		3		1		1	1	1	1	1			9		
Hingham	141	35	Thaxter	Abigail									1	1			2		
Hingham	141	36	Lane	Rufus	1	1		1		2	1		1				7		
Hingham	141	37	Dawes	Eliza	1	1					1	1					4		
Hingham	141	38	Lovis	William	1			1		2							4		
Hingham	141	39	Hobart	Jeremiah			1			2		1					4		
Hingham	141	40	Prouty	Samuel	3		1			2		1	1				8		
Hingham	141	41	Lewis	Marsh			1					1					2		
Hingham	141	42	Lemmon	Phebe											1		1		
Hingham	141	43	French	George	2		1					1					4		
Hingham	141	44	Loring	Ruth	1					1	1		1				4		
Hingham	141	45	Loring	Elizabeth								1					1		
Hingham	142	1	Whitton	Ezra	1		2	1		1		2					7		
Hingham	142	2	Binney	Rebecca							1		1				2		
Hingham	142	3	Bailey	Loring		1		1					1				3		
Hingham	142	4	Ware	Henry Revd	3		1			3		2	2		1		12		
Hingham	142	5	Thaxter	Jacob		1		1			1		1				4		
Hingham	142	6	Stodder	Sarah							1		2				3		
Hingham	142	7	Cushing	Isaiah Esqr		1	1	1			1		1				5		
Hingham	142	8	Thaxter	Thomas Dr		1	1	1		1		1	1				6		
Hingham	142	9	Cushing	Benjamin Esqr		1		2		1			2				6		
Hingham	142	10	Hayden	Caroline						1		1					2		
Hingham	142	11	Cushing	William		1		1		1	1		1		2		7		
Hingham	142	12	Cushing	Elizabeth	1	1	1	1			1		2				7		
Hingham	142	13	Stodder	John				1					1				2		
Hingham	142	14	Dill	Lemuel		1		1		1	1		1				5		
Hingham	142	15	Loring	Rachel						1		2					3		
Hingham	142	16	Lane	Jonathan			1	2					2				5		
Hingham	142	17	Bangs	Ruth								1	2				3		
Hingham	142	18	Lincoln	Luther			1				1	1					3		
Hingham	142	19	Thaxter	Henry	1	1		1			1		1	1			6		
Hingham	142	20	Cushing	Benjamin			1			1	1						3		
Hingham	142	21	Loring	Peter		1		1		1		1					4		
Hingham	142	22	Thaxter	Thomas Junr			1			1	1	2					6		
Hingham	142	23	Thaxter	Benjamin				1					1				2		
Hingham	142	24	Barker	Susanah								2		2			4		
Hingham	142	25	Corthel	Robert	2			1		3			1				7		
Hingham	142	26	Hearsey	Peter	2	1	1	2		2	1	1	1				11		
Hingham	142	27	Hearsey	Abijah		2		1				1		1			5		
Hingham	142	28	Hearsey	Reuben	1		2	1		1	1		1				7		
Hingham	142	29	Beal	Elihu		2		1		1	1	1					6		
Hingham	142	30	Hearsey	Isaiah				1			1		1				3		
Hingham	142	31	Adams	Joseph	2			1		1			1	1			6		
Hingham	142	32	Fillmore	Spiller				1				1			1		3		
Hingham	142	33	Houses	Alms Work	1				7		1	2	12		1		24		
Hingham	142	34	Burr	Levi Junr	1		1	1		2	3		1				9		
Hingham	142	35	Mansfield	Joseph				2					1				3		
Hingham	142	36	Burr	Theophilus	3		1			1			1				6		
Hingham	142	37	Burr	Emme								1	1				2		
Hingham	142	38	Burr	David		1	2		1		1	1		1			7		
Hingham	142	39	Souther	Daniel	2	1		1	1	1	1	1	1				9		
Hingham	142	40	Leavitt	Joshua	1	1		1			1		1				5		
Hingham	142	41	Leavitt	Jeorum		1				2	1						4		
Hingham	142	42	Burr	Jonathan			1	1		1		1	1				5		
Hingham	142	43	Jones	Benjamin		1		1			1		1				4		
Hingham	142	44	Lovis	Joseph				1					1				2		
Hingham	142	45	Andrews	Benjamin	1	1		1		1		1	1				6		
Hingham	142	46	Jones	Thomas				1			2		1				4		
Hingham	143	1	Beal	Malcom	2		1		1	1	1		1				7		
Hingham	143	2	Beal	Joshua				1					1				2		
Hingham	143	3	Wilder	Thomas Junr		1		1		2	2	2					9		
Hingham	143	4	Stodder	Samuel	2	1		1		1	1		1				7		
Hingham	143	5	Stodder	Reuben				1									1		
Hingham	143	6	Barns	Canterbury	2						2		1	1			7		
Hingham	143	7	Barns	Benjamin Junr	1	2	1	1	1	2				1			9		
Hingham	143	8	Barns	Benjamin				1					1				2		
Hingham	143	9	Barns	George	1	1		1		1			1				5		
Hingham	143	10	Walker	John			1	1				1					3		
Hingham	143	11	Lincoln	Martin		1		1			1	1					4		
Hingham	143	12	Lowell	Samuel				1					1				2		
Hingham	143	13	Tower	Malachi	1	2	1	1	2		1		1	1			10		
Hingham	143	14	Lane	Hannah	1					1			1				3		

TOWN	PG#	LN#	LAST NAME	FIRST NAME	FREE WHITE MALES under 10	10 to 16	16 to 26	26 to 45	45 and over	FREE WHITE FEMALES under 10	10 to 16	16 to 26	26 to 45	45 and over	TOTAL ALL OTHER	TOTAL SLAVES	TOTALS	DISTRICT/TOWNSHIP	NOTES
Hingham	143	15	Hobart	Hawkes	1	2	2		1	2		1		1			10		
Hingham	143	16	Hobart	Lucretia	1					1		1		1			4		
Hingham	143	17	Wilder	Isaiah		1		1			2		1				5		
Hingham	143	18	Simmons	Allen	2	2		1		3			1	1			10		
Hingham	143	19	Howard	James	1		1	1					1				4		
Hingham	143	20	Lane	Josiah		1	1	1					1				4		
Hingham	143	21	Lane	Leavitt	2	1		1		3	1		1				9		
Hingham	143	22	Humphrey	Candis								1		6			7		
Hingham	143	23	Burrell	Benjamin	3			1		2			1	2			9		
Hingham	143	24	Stodder	Isaiah				1					1	1			3		
Hingham	143	25	Gardner	Stephen				1						1			2		
Hingham	143	26	Gardner	Stephen 2d	1	2	1		1			1		1			7		
Hingham	143	27	Gardner	Jeremiah		1			1			1		1			4		
Hingham	143	28	Whitton	Daniel Junr	1			1		1			1				4		
Hingham	143	29	Whitton	Charles			1			1		2					4		
Hingham	143	30	Whitton	Zechariah			1	1		1	2	1		1			7		
Hingham	143	31	Lowell	Enoch	2			1		3			1				7		
Hingham	143	32	Thayer	Randall		1			1					1			3		
Hingham	143	33	Whitton	Daniel			1		1	1	1			1			5		
Hingham	143	34	Whitton	Benjamin				1					2				3		
Hingham	143	35	Whitton	Benjamin Junr			1	1				1	1				4		
Hingham	143	36	Wilder	Isaac			1	1				1	1	1			5		
Hingham	143	37	Wilder	Bela			1						1				2		
Hingham	143	38	Dunbar	Daniel	2	1			1		1		1				6		
Hingham	143	39	Hearsey	Joshua				1		1	1	1		1			5		
Hingham	143	40	Hearsey	Joshua Junr	2		2	1		1			1				7		
Hingham	143	41	Stodder	Laban	1	3	2		1	4	1			1			13		
Hingham	143	42	Gardner	Stephen 3d	1		1			2		1					5		
Hingham	143	43	Dunbar	Robert	2			1		3			1				7		
Hingham	143	44	Farrow	Desire									1				1		
Hingham	143	45	Shoot	Prince											2		2		
Hingham	143	46	Carter												5		5		No first name listed
Hingham	144	1	Lasall	Samuel				1		1			2				4		
Hingham	144	2	Sprague	Bela			2	1					1	1			5		
Hingham	144	3	Cushing	George Russell			1	1				2	2				6		
Hingham	144	4	Cushing	Ebenezer				1					2				3		
Hingham	144	5	Cushing	Thomas	2	1		1		1			1				6		
Hingham	144	6	Cushing	Hosea	3			1					1				5		
Hingham	144	7	Cushing	Charles Whiting		2		1		2	1	1					7		
Hingham	144	8	Whitton	Solomon	1			1					2	2			6		
Hingham	144	9	Bryant	Barker			1					1					2		
Hingham	144	10	Corthel	Levi Junr	2			1		1			1				5		
Hingham	144	11	Cushing	Caleb	2	1		1		2			1				7		
Hingham	144	12	Cushing	Joseph			1		1			1		1			4		
Hingham	144	13	Cushing	Ebed	2			1		1			1				5		
Hingham	144	14	Stodder	Richard				1					1				2		
Hingham	144	15	Cushing	Stephen	1	1		1		1		1	2	1			7		
Hingham	144	16	Cushing	John	2	2	1			3			1	1			10		
Hingham	144	17	Cushing	Silence								2		1			3		
Hingham	144	18	Burr	Levu Junr	2	1		1		2			1				7		
Hingham	144	19	Beal	John		1	2		1			2		1			7		
Hingham	144	20	Stodder	Ichabod		1						1					2		
Hingham	144	21	Stodder	Enoch		2		1				2		1			6		
Hingham	144	22	Beal	Hannah									1	1			2		
Hingham	144	23	Stodder	Rebecca						1	2		1				4		
Hingham	144	24	Bream	Phillis											1		1		
Hingham	144	25	Tailor	Cato											2		2		
Hingham	145	1	Cushing	Ezekiel			1			2			1				4		
Hingham	145	2	Whiton	Elijah		1	1		1			1		1			5		
Hingham	145	3	Whiton	Moses		2	2		1			1		1			7		
Hingham	145	4	Hearsey	Israel		1		1				2		1			5		
Hingham	145	5	Hearsey	Israel Junr	1			1		1			1				4		
Hingham	145	6	Hearsey	Nathaniel	2			1				1					4		
Hingham	145	7	Lewis	Elijah				1				1		1			3		
Hingham	145	8	Wilder	Joseph		1		1		1	1	1					6		
Hingham	145	9	Fower	Isaiah		1		1					1				3		
Hingham	145	10	Fower	Isaiah Junr	3	1				1			1				6		
Hingham	145	11	Wilder	Edward Capt	2	1	1		1	5	3	2	1				16		
Hingham	145	12	Wilder	Hannah									1				1		
Hingham	145	13	Sprague	Jacob	1			1		1			1				4		
Hingham	145	14	Jacob	John Junr	1			1		2	1		1				6		
Hingham	145	15	Jacob	Daniel				1		2			1				4		
Hingham	145	16	Jacob	Peter	3			1		1			1				6		
Hingham	145	17	Cushing	Jonathan	2	1		1		2			1				7		
Hingham	145	18	Gardner	Robert				1					2				3		
Hingham	145	19	Cushing	Robert		1		1		3	2		1	1			9		
Hingham	145	20	Dunbar	Metzer	2	1	1		1	3	1		1				10		
Hingham	145	21	Cushing	Theophilus Esq	1	1	2		1	1			2		2		10		
Hingham	145	22	Loring	Job	2		2	1			1	2		1			9		
Hingham	145	23	Shute	Daniel Revd				1				1	2				4		
Hingham	145	24	Shute	Daniel Junr Doct	3	1	1	1		1	1	1	1				10		
Hingham	145	25	Cushing	Seth	2		1	1		1			1				6		
Hingham	145	26	Cushing	John			1	1				2	1				5		
Hingham	145	27	Whiton	Enoch			1			3			1				5		
Hingham	145	28	Cushing	Mary								1	1				2		
Hingham	145	29	Lewis	David			1			1			1				3		
Hingham	145	30	Jacob	John		1		1			1		1				4		
Hingham	145	31	Jacob	Jotham	1		1			1			1				4		
Hingham	145	32	Stowers	Mary									1				1		
Hingham	145	33	Hearsey	John	1	2		1		3	1			1			9		

TOWN	PG#	LN#	LAST NAME	FIRST NAME	FREE WHITE MALES					FREE WHITE FEMALES					TOTAL ALL OTHER	TOTAL SLAVES	TOTALS	DISTRICT/ TOWNSHIP	NOTES
					under 10	10 to 16	16 to 26	26 to 45	45 and over	under 10	10 to 16	16 to 26	26 to 45	45 and over					
Hingham	145	34	Dunbar	David	1			1				1					3		
Hingham	145	35	Whiton	Jacob					1								1		
Hingham	145	36	Gardner	Perez	1			1		2	1		1				6		
Hingham	145	37	Fower	Laban				1				1	1				3		
Hingham	145	38	Fower	Joshua				1						2			3		
Hingham	145	39	Sprague	Seth	1			1			1			1			4		
Hingham	145	40	Sprague	Rachel										2			2		
Hingham	145	41	Dunbar	Amos	1	1		1		1		1	1	2			8		
Hingham	145	42	Sprague	Alice								1	1	1			3		
Hingham	145	43	Fower	Bela				1					1				2		
Hingham	145	44	Hobart	Edmund	2		2		1	3	2		1				11		
Hingham	145	45	Whiton	Israel	2	1	1	1		1			1				7		
Hingham	145	46	Lewis	Ezra	2			1		2			1				6		
Hingham	146	1	Norton	Joshua				1									1		
Hingham	146	2	Campbell	Caleb		1		1						1			3		
Hingham	146	3	Wilder	Samuel				1						1			2		
Hingham	146	4	Wilder	Samuel Junr			1			3	1		1				6		
Hingham	146	5	Sprague	Reuben		1	2		1	1	1	3		1			10		
Hingham	146	6	Wilder	Daniel		2			1	3		2	1				9		
Hingham	146	7	Gardner	Samuel	2	2			1	3	1	1	1	1			12		
Hingham	146	8	Whiton	Josiah			1					1	1	1			4		
Hingham	146	9	Whiton	Sarah		1		1				2		1			5		
Hingham	146	10	Whiton	Enoch	1	1		1		3	1		2	1			10		
Hingham	146	11	Gardner	John					1								1		
Hingham	146	12	French	Nathaniel	2			1	1				1				5		
Hingham	146	13	Dill	Daniel	1			1		1			2				5		
Hingham	146	14	Gardner	Samuel Junr	2		1						1				4		
Hingham	146	15	Whiton	Amasa				1			1	2		2			6		
Hingham	146	16	Whiton	Davis			1	1		2	1		1				6		
Hingham	146	17	Dunbar	Enoch		1		1					1				3		
Hingham	146	18	Gardner	Solomon	2			1					2				5		
Hingham	146	19	Loring	Nat				1				1					2		
Hingham	146	20	Whiton	Elijah Junr	1			1					1				3		
Hingham	146	21	Whiton	Theophilus			1			1		1					3		
Hingham	146	22	Dunbar	Benjamin					1		1			1			3		
Hingham	146	23	Cushing	Nehemiah			1					1					2		
Hingham	146	24	Whiton	Elisha					1			1		1			3		
Hingham	146	25	Stodder	Isaiah Junr	3			1		1			1	1			7		
Hingham	146	26	Stodder	Caleb	2			1		2			1				6		
Hingham	146	27	Stowers	Elijah		1		1					1	1			4		
Hingham	146	28	Thomas	Benjamin	2		1			2			1	1			7		
Hingham	146	29	Leavitt	Samuel	3	1		1		1	1		1				8		
Hingham	146	30	Jones	Eunice								1	1	1			3		
Hingham	146	31	Burr	Thomas		1	1	1	1				2	1			7		
Hingham	146	32	Fearing	Margaret									3	1			4		
Hingham	146	33	Fearing	Hawkes	3	2	2		1		2	2	1				13		
Hingham	146	34	Sprague	Amos	1			1	1	2				1			6		
Hingham	146	35	Sprague	Moses			3		1			1		1			6		
Hingham	146	36	Sprague	Hannah			1						1	1			3		
Hingham	146	37	Sprague	David	1	1	1		1					1			5		
Hingham	146	38	Whiton	Stephen			1							1			3		
Hingham	146	39	Ripley	Nehemiah	1	2	1		1	2			1				8		
Hingham	146	40	Loring	Jonathan	2	1		1		1			1	1			7		
Hingham	146	41	Berry	Thomas				1					1				2		
Hingham	146	42	Jones	Thomas Junr				1				1		1			3		
Hingham	146	43	Lincoln	Ebenezer			1	1						1			3		
Hingham	146	44	Sprague	Peter			1					1					2		
Hingham	146	45	Leavitt	Elijah	1			1		2			1				5		
Hingham	146	46	Howard	Thomas	3	1		1			1			1			7		
Hingham	146	47	Leavitt	Jacob		2	2		1		1	2		1			9		
Hingham	146	48	Sprague	Jesse			2		1	1	1						5		
Hingham	146	49	Gilbert	Nathaniel	1				1			1	1				4		

145

TOWN	PG#	LN#	LAST NAME	FIRST NAME	FREE WHITE MALES under 10	10 to 16	16 to 26	26 to 45	45 and over	FREE WHITE FEMALES under 10	10 to 16	16 to 26	26 to 45	45 and over	TOTAL ALL OTHER	TOTAL SLAVES	TOTALS	DISTRICT/ TOWNSHIP	NOTES
Hull	147	1	Good	Robert	2	1		1	1	3			1	2			11		
Hull	147	2	Read	Samuel			1			1			1				3		
Hull	147	3	Dill	Dorothy	1					1		1	1				4		
Hull	147	4	Poor	Ebenezer	1			1		2			1				5		
Hull	147	5	Sprague	Elizabeth									1				1		
Hull	147	6	Tirrell	Gideon	1		1	1		3	2		1				9		
Hull	147	7	Mott	Stephen			1			1		1		1			4		
Hull	147	8	Dill	Esther	2	2	2			1			1				8		
Hull	147	9	Sasain	Charles	1		1		1		2	1	1				7		
Hull	147	10	Lowell	Samuel	1		1		1	1		1	1				6		
Hull	147	11	Loring	Samuel		1		1			1		1				4		
Hull	147	12	Loring	Daniel	1	1		1		2	1		1				7		
Hull	147	13	Soper	Samuel				1						1			2		
Hull	147	14	Jones	Thomas	1		1	1				1	1				5		
Hull	147	15	Gould	Elisha				1				1		1			3		
Hull	147	16	Souther	Judith		1						1		2	1		5		
Hull	147	17	Philips	Mary										1			1		
Hull	147	18	Newcomb	Oliver	2			1		1			1				5		
Hull	147	19	Greenleaf	Bethsheba									1				1		
Hull	147	20	Loring	John				1					1				2		
Hull	147	21	Greenleaf	Stephen				1									1		
Hull	147	22	Finer	Robert			1			1		1	1				4		
Hull	147	23	Rinner	Spencer	1			1		4	1		1				8		
Hull	147	24	Anderson	Ezekiel		2	1		1	2			1				7		
Hull	147	25	Hunt	Winnefred	1								1				2		
Hull	147	26	Lord	James												2	2		

TOWN	PG#	LN#	LAST NAME	FIRST NAME	FREE WHITE MALES under 10	10 to 16	16 to 26	26 to 45	45 and over	FREE WHITE FEMALES under 10	10 to 16	16 to 26	26 to 45	45 and over	TOTAL ALL OTHER	TOTAL SLAVES	TOTALS	DISTRICT/ TOWNSHIP	NOTES
Hingham	137	24	*	*			1							1			2		Ink mark covers name
Hingham	142	31	Adams	Joseph	2			1		1			1	1			6		
Hull	147	24	Anderson	Ezekiel		2	1		1	2			1				7		
Hingham	142	45	Andrews	Benjamin	1	1		1		1		1	1				6		
Hingham	139	33	Andrews	Ephraim	1			1		1	1		1	1			6		
Hingham	139	35	Andrews	Joseph				1					1	1			3		
Hingham	139	34	Andrews	Thomas		1		1		1			3	1			7		
Hingham	142	3	Bailey	Loring		1		1						1			3		
Hingham	142	17	Bangs	Ruth									1	2			3		
Hingham	139	44	Barker	Deborah			1			1			1				3		
Hingham	142	24	Barker	Susanah								2		2			4		
Hingham	143	8	Barns	Benjamin				1						1			2		
Hingham	143	7	Barns	Benjamin Junr	1	2	1	1	1	2				1			9		
Hingham	143	6	Barns	Canterbury	2			1			2		1	1			7		
Hingham	140	23	Barns	Ensign	2	1		1		2	1		1				8		
Hingham	140	6	Barns	Ezekiel											2		2		
Hingham	143	9	Barns	George	1	1		1		1			1				5		
Hingham	140	22	Barns	John			1	1				3		1			6		
Hingham	140	2	Bassett	Joseph		1	1		1					1			4		
Hingham	139	40	Bates	Asa	2			1					1				4		
Hingham	139	12	Bates	Caleb		1	2						1				4		
Hingham	137	9	Beal	Benjamin		3				1			1				5		
Hingham	142	29	Beal	Elihu		2		1		1	1	1					6		
Hingham	144	22	Beal	Hannah							1			1			2		
Hingham	138	1	Beal	Israel			1	1				2	1				5		
Hingham	137	41	Beal	Jacob				1		1			1				3		
Hingham	137	43	Beal	James				1					1				2		
Hingham	139	39	Beal	Jedediah			1	1					2				4		
Hingham	144	19	Beal	John		1	2		1			2		1			7		
Hingham	140	46	Beal	John Junr				1					1				2		
Hingham	137	39	Beal	Joseph	1			1		1		1	1	1			6		
Hingham	137	40	Beal	Joseph Junr		2					1						3		
Hingham	143	2	Beal	Joshua				1					1				2		
Hingham	137	44	Beal	Laban	1			1		1			1				4		
Hingham	143	1	Beal	Malcom	2		1		1	1	1		1				7		
Hingham	137	42	Beal	Rebecca									2				2		
Hingham	146	41	Berry	Thomas				1					1				2		
Hingham	142	2	Binney	Rebecca						1			1				2		
Hingham	139	28	Blake	Joseph				1			1	1	1				4		
Hingham	144	24	Bream	Phillis											1		1		
Hingham	139	46	Briton												2		2		No first name listed
Hingham	144	9	Bryant	Barker			1					1					2		
Hingham	141	26	Bryant	Thomas	1			1		3		1					6		
Hingham	142	38	Burr	David		1	2		1	1	1		1				7		
Hingham	142	37	Burr	Emme								1	1				2		
Hingham	142	42	Burr	Jonathan			1	1		1		1	1				5		
Hingham	144	18	Burr	Levu Junr	2	1		1		2			1				7		
Hingham	142	36	Burr	Theophilus	3			1		1			1				6		
Hingham	146	31	Burr	Thomas		1	1	1				2	1				7		
Hingham	142	34	Burr	Levi Junr	1		1	1		2	3		1				9		
Hingham	143	23	Burrell	Benjamin	3		1			2			1	2			9		
Hingham	140	10	Burrell	Leavitt	1			1		2			1				5		
Hingham	137	16	Butler	Rebecca		1						4		1			6		
Hingham	138	21	Cain	Daniel		1	1			1	2			1			6		
Hingham	138	22	Cain	David					1				1	1			3		
Hingham	146	2	Campbell	Caleb		1		1					1				3		
Hingham	143	46	Carter												5		5		No first name listed
Hingham	139	43	Cobb	Elisha B		1					1						2		
Hingham	144	10	Corthel	Levi Junr	2		1			1			1				5		
Hingham	142	25	Corthel	Robert	2			1		3			1				7		
Hingham	142	20	Cushing	Benjamin				1			1	1					3		
Hingham	142	9	Cushing	Benjamin Esqr		1		2		1			2				6		
Hingham	144	11	Cushing	Caleb	2	1		1		2			1				7		
Hingham	144	7	Cushing	Charles Whiting		2		1		2	1	1					7		
Hingham	144	13	Cushing	Ebed	2			1		1			1				5		
Hingham	144	4	Cushing	Ebenezer				1						2			3		
Hingham	141	34	Cushing	Elisha			3		1	1	1	1	1	1			9		
Hingham	142	12	Cushing	Elizabeth	1	1	1					1		1			7		
Hingham	145	1	Cushing	Ezekiel				1		2			1				4		
Hingham	144	3	Cushing	George Russell		1	1					2	2				6		
Hingham	144	6	Cushing	Hosea	3			1					1				5		
Hingham	141	6	Cushing	Isaac		1		1		1			1				4		
Hingham	142	7	Cushing	Isaiah Esqr		1	1	1				1		1			5		
Hingham	141	8	Cushing	Jacob		1	1					1	1				4		
Hingham	144	16	Cushing	John	2	2		1		3		1	1				10		
Hingham	145	26	Cushing	John			1	1				2	1				5		
Hingham	145	17	Cushing	Jonathan	2	1		1		2			1				7		
Hingham	144	12	Cushing	Joseph		1		1				1		1			4		
Hingham	145	28	Cushing	Mary								1	1				2		
Hingham	141	22	Cushing	Mathew				1					1				2		
Hingham	146	23	Cushing	Nehemiah		1						1					2		
Hingham	139	30	Cushing	Perez			1						1				2		
Hingham	145	19	Cushing	Robert		1		1		3	2		1	1			9		
Hingham	145	25	Cushing	Seth	2		1	1		1			1				6		
Hingham	144	17	Cushing	Silence								2		1			3		
Hingham	144	15	Cushing	Stephen	1	1			1		1		2	1			7		
Hingham	145	21	Cushing	Theophilus Esq	1	1	2		1			2		1	2		10		
Hingham	144	5	Cushing	Thomas	2	1		1		1			1				6		
Hingham	142	11	Cushing	William		1			1		1	1		1	2		7		
Hingham	138	17	Danniels	John			1				1		1				3		

TOWN	PG#	LN#	LAST NAME	FIRST NAME	FWM under 10	FWM 10 to 16	FWM 16 to 26	FWM 26 to 45	FWM 45 and over	FWF under 10	FWF 10 to 16	FWF 16 to 26	FWF 26 to 45	FWF 45 and over	TOTAL ALL OTHER	TOTAL SLAVES	TOTALS	DISTRICT/TOWNSHIP	NOTES
Hingham	137	2	Davidson	John	1			1						1			3		
Hingham	141	37	Dawes	Eliza	1	1							1	1			4		
Hingham	146	13	Dill	Daniel	1		1						2				5		
Hull	147	3	Dill	Dorothy	1					1		1	1				4		
Hull	147	8	Dill	Esther	2	2	2			1			1				8		
Hingham	142	14	Dill	Lemuel		1	1			1	1			1			5		
Hingham	145	41	Dunbar	Amos	1	1		1		1		1	1	2			8		
Hingham	146	22	Dunbar	Benjamin				1			1		1				3		
Hingham	141	10	Dunbar	Benjamin Junr	1			1		3			1				6		
Hingham	143	38	Dunbar	Daniel	2	1		1		1			1				6		
Hingham	145	34	Dunbar	David	1			1					1				3		
Hingham	146	17	Dunbar	Enoch		1		1					1				3		
Hingham	141	25	Dunbar	Joshua	1		1					1					3		
Hingham	137	21	Dunbar	Laban	2		1						1				4		
Hingham	145	20	Dunbar	Metzer	2	1	1	1		3	1		1				10		
Hingham	143	43	Dunbar	Robert	2		1			3			1				7		
Hingham	143	44	Farrow	Desire										1			1		
Hingham	146	33	Fearing	Hawkes	3	2	2	1		2	2	1					13		
Hingham	141	20	Fearing	Lydia	1							1		2			4		
Hingham	146	32	Fearing	Margaret									3	1			4		
Hingham	141	23	Fearing	Shubael			2	2		1		1	1	1			8		
Hingham	141	16	Fearing	Thomas Capt		2	2	1		1		2		2			10		
Hingham	142	32	Fillmore	Spiller				1					1		1		3		
Hull	147	22	Finer	Robert			1			1		1	1				4		
Hingham	145	43	Fower	Bela			1						1				2		
Hingham	145	9	Fower	Isaiah		1	1							1			3		
Hingham	145	10	Fower	Isaiah Junr	3	1	1						1				6		
Hingham	145	38	Fower	Joshua				1						2			3		
Hingham	145	37	Fower	Laban				1				1	1				3		
Hingham	141	43	French	George	2		1						1				4		
Hingham	140	25	French	Jonathan	1	1		1		1		1		1			7		
Hingham	146	12	French	Nathaniel	2		1	1					1				5		
Hingham	137	23	French	Reuben	1		1			2		1					5		
Hingham	138	23	French	Theodore		1		1				1					3		
Hingham	140	15	Gardner	Isaac	1		1	1		2	1		1				7		
Hingham	143	27	Gardner	Jeremiah		1		1			1		1	1			4		
Hingham	146	11	Gardner	John				1									1		
Hingham	140	17	Gardner	Mary	1					1	1		1				4		
Hingham	145	36	Gardner	Perez	1			1		2	1		1				6		
Hingham	145	18	Gardner	Robert				1						2			3		
Hingham	146	7	Gardner	Samuel	2	2		1		3	1	1	1	1			12		
Hingham	146	14	Gardner	Samuel Junr	2		1					1					4		
Hingham	146	18	Gardner	Solomon	2			1					2				5		
Hingham	143	25	Gardner	Stephen				1						1			2		
Hingham	143	26	Gardner	Stephen 2d	1	2	1						1	1			7		
Hingham	143	42	Gardner	Stephen 3d	1		1			2		1					5		
Hingham	140	1	Gay	Jotham Esgr			1			1	1	3	2				8		
Hingham	146	49	Gilbert	Nathaniel	1							1	1				4		
Hingham	140	38	Gill	Caleb	1		1					1	1				4		
Hingham	140	42	Gill	John		1		1		1	1		1				5		
Hingham	140	43	Gill	Nathaniel				1			1		1				3		
Hingham	140	44	Gill	Nathaniel Junr	1	1	1			2			2				7		
Hingham	139	25	Gill	Thomas				1						1			2		
Hull	147	1	Good	Robert	2	1		1	1	3		1	2				11		
Hull	147	15	Gould	Elisha				1			1		1				3		
Hull	147	19	Greenleaf	Bethsheba									1				1		
Hull	147	21	Greenleaf	Stephen				1									1		
Hingham	141	9	Gross	David			1			1		1	1				4		
Hingham	140	8	Hammond	Joseph		1		1			1		1				4		
Hingham	142	10	Hayden	Caroline							1	1					2		
Hingham	142	27	Hearsey	Abijah		2		1			1		1				5		
Hingham	140	26	Hearsey	Abijah Junr		1		1		1		1					3		
Hingham	139	9	Hearsey	Ebed		1						1		1			4		
Hingham	141	17	Hearsey	Ezekiel	2		1						1				4		
Hingham	138	11	Hearsey	Gilbert Junr	1		2			1			1				5		
Hingham	139	7	Hearsey	Gilbert Junr			1			2	1		1				5		
Hingham	142	30	Hearsey	Isaiah			1				1		1				3		
Hingham	145	4	Hearsey	Israel		1	1					2	1				5		
Hingham	145	5	Hearsey	Israel Junr	1		1			1			1				4		
Hingham	145	33	Hearsey	John	1	2		1		3	1		1				9		
Hingham	139	8	Hearsey	Jonathan	2		1						1				4		
Hingham	143	39	Hearsey	Joshua			1			1	1	1		1			5		
Hingham	143	40	Hearsey	Joshua Junr	2		2	1		1			1				7		
Hingham	140	21	Hearsey	Laban	3	1	1						1	1			8		
Hingham	139	6	Hearsey	Mary	1	1	1			1	1		1				7		
Hingham	145	6	Hearsey	Nathaniel	2		1					1					4		
Hingham	140	36	Hearsey	Noah	1				1	1		1		1			6		
Hingham	142	26	Hearsey	Peter	2	1	1	2		2	1	1	1				11		
Hingham	141	30	Hearsey	Rebecca						1			2				3		
Hingham	142	28	Hearsey	Reuben	1		2	1		1	1		1				7		
Hingham	141	31	Hearsey	Susannah	2							1					3		
Hingham	139	26	Hearsey	Thomas		1	1	1	1		1	1		1			7		
Hingham	140	37	Hobart	Caleb	1		1	1			1		1				5		
Hingham	137	12	Hobart	Deborah									1	1			2		
Hingham	145	44	Hobart	Edmund	2		2	1		3	2		1				11		
Hingham	140	45	Hobart	Else						1			1				2		
Hingham	143	15	Hobart	Hawkes	1	2	2	1		2		1		1			10		
Hingham	137	17	Hobart	Japeth				1						1			2		
Hingham	141	39	Hobart	Jeremiah			1			2			1				4		

148

			HEADS OF HOUSEHOLD		FREE WHITE MALES					FREE WHITE FEMALES					TOTAL ALL OTHER	TOTAL SLAVES	TOTALS	DISTRICT/ TOWNSHIP	NOTES
TOWN	PG#	LN#	LAST NAME	FIRST NAME	under 10	10 to 16	16 to 26	26 to 45	45 and over	under 10	10 to 16	16 to 26	26 to 45	45 and over					
Hingham	140	33	Hobart	Joanna						1			1				2		
Hingham	137	11	Hobart	Leavitt	1	1		1		1			1				5		
Hingham	143	16	Hobart	Lucretia	1					1		1		1			4		
Hingham	137	13	Hobart	Samuel		1	1		2			1		2			7		
Hingham	137	10	Hobart	Shubael			1	1		3		1		1			7		
Hingham	142	33	Houses	Alms Work					7		1	2	12		1		24		
Hingham	143	19	Howard	James	1		1	1					1				4		
Hingham	146	46	Howard	Thomas	3	1		1			1		1				7		
Hingham	140	18	Hudson	William	1		1			1		1					4		
Hingham	143	22	Humphrey	Candis								1		6			7		
Hingham	137	26	Humphrey	Noah		1		1				1		1			4		
Hingham	137	28	Humphrey	Noah Junr	1		1	1		1		1					5		
Hingham	137	45	Hunt	Samuel			1					1	1				3		
Hull	147	25	Hunt	Winnefred	1								1				2		
Hingham	137	3	Irving	Elijah			1					1					2		
Hingham	145	15	Jacob	Daniel			1			2			1				4		
Hingham	145	30	Jacob	John		1		1				1		1			4		
Hingham	145	14	Jacob	John Junr	1			1		2	1		1				6		
Hingham	145	31	Jacob	Jotham	1		1			1		1					4		
Hingham	145	16	Jacob	Peter	3			1		1			1				6		
Hingham	142	43	Jones	Benjamin		1		1				1	1				4		
Hingham	141	12	Jones	Benjamin Junr			1			2		1					4		
Hingham	146	30	Jones	Eunice								1	1	1			3		
Hingham	141	1	Jones	Solomon	1		1			2	2						6		
Hingham	142	46	Jones	Thomas				1		2			1				4		
Hull	147	14	Jones	Thomas	1		1	1				1	1				5		
Hingham	146	42	Jones	Thomas Junr				1				1		1			3		
Hingham	137	7	Kingsman	John	3			1		2			1	1			8		
Hingham	141	4	Kingsman	Thomas				1		1	1	1	1				5		
Hingham	141	3	Lane	Elisha				1						1			2		
Hingham	143	14	Lane	Hannah	1					1			1				3		
Hingham	137	4	Lane	Isaac	1		2					1					4		
Hingham	142	16	Lane	Jonathan			1	2					2				5		
Hingham	143	20	Lane	Josiah		1	1	1					1				4		
Hingham	141	2	Lane	Leavitt				1									1		
Hingham	143	21	Lane	Leavitt	2	1		1		3	1		1				9		
Hingham	141	36	Lane	Rufus	1	1		1		2	1		1				7		
Hingham	141	19	Lasall	Jonathan					1				1	1			3		
Hingham	144	1	Lasall	Samuel					1		1			2			4		
Hingham	138	8	Le Britton	Edwd											5		5		
Hingham	146	45	Leavitt	Elijah	1			1				1	1				4		
Hingham	146	47	Leavitt	Jacob		2	2	1			1	2		1			9		
Hingham	139	37	Leavitt	Jairus			1		1		1	1	1				5		
Hingham	139	38	Leavitt	Jairus	1				1		1	1					4		
Hingham	142	41	Leavitt	Jeorum			1			2		1					4		
Hingham	141	14	Leavitt	John	1	1		1				1					4		
Hingham	142	40	Leavitt	Joshua	1	1		1				1	1				5		
Hingham	141	33	Leavitt	Joshua Junr	2	1	1					1					5		
Hingham	146	29	Leavitt	Samuel	3	1		1		1	1	1					8		
Hingham	141	42	Lemmon	Phebe											1		1		
Hingham	145	29	Lewis	David			1			1			1				3		
Hingham	139	24	Lewis	Ebenezer				1						1			2		
Hingham	145	7	Lewis	Elijah				1				1		1			3		
Hingham	141	7	Lewis	Elijah Junr	2	1		1		2			1				7		
Hingham	145	46	Lewis	Ezra	2			1		2			1				6		
Hingham	141	41	Lewis	Marsh				1						1			2		
Hingham	141	24	Lewis	Thomas				1						1			2		
Hingham	139	31	Lincoln	Abel			1			1	1						3		
Hingham	139	21	Lincoln	Abner	2		1			3			1				7		
Hingham	137	47	Lincoln	Barnabas	1		3		1	2	2	1		1			11		
Hingham	137	19	Lincoln	Beza		1		1		2	1	2					7		
Hingham	137	25	Lincoln	Caleb	1	1		1		2	1	1					7		
Hingham	137	38	Lincoln	Calvin	1		1			1		1					4		
Hingham	137	36	Lincoln	Charles	3		1			2		1					7		
Hingham	138	12	Lincoln	Daniel	1	1		1		3	1	1					8		
Hingham	140	9	Lincoln	David	1		1	1				1		1			5		
Hingham	139	36	Lincoln	David Junr	2	1	1	1		1			1				7		
Hingham	146	43	Lincoln	Ebenezer			1	1						1			3		
Hingham	138	7	Lincoln	Elijah	1			1		1			1	1			5		
Hingham	139	17	Lincoln	Enoch				2					1	1			4		
Hingham	137	18	Lincoln	Ezekiel	3			1			1		1				6		
Hingham	139	18	Lincoln	Ezra		1	1				2		1				5		
Hingham	138	20	Lincoln	George	2		1			1			1				5		
Hingham	137	46	Lincoln	Israel				1					1				2		
Hingham	138	3	Lincoln	Israel Junr				1		3	1		1				6		
Hingham	140	41	Lincoln	James				1			1	1		1			4		
Hingham	140	39	Lincoln	Jedediah	1			1					1				3		
Hingham	139	32	Lincoln	Job	1			1					1	1			4		
Hingham	139	19	Lincoln	Jonathan		2		1		1		1		1			6		
Hingham	138	10	Lincoln	Joseph	1	1		1		1		1	1				6		
Hingham	138	19	Lincoln	Joshua			1	1				1	1	1			5		
Hingham	137	48	Lincoln	Jotham		2	1			2		1					6		
Hingham	140	31	Lincoln	Levi Junr			1			2			2				5		
Hingham	140	40	Lincoln	Levi Junr		1		1					1	1			4		
Hingham	142	18	Lincoln	Luther				1					1	1			3		
Hingham	143	11	Lincoln	Martin		1	1				1		1				4		
Hingham	140	30	Lincoln	Mary	1	2							2	1			6		
Hingham	139	1	Lincoln	Mathew			1	1					1	1			4		
Hingham	139	22	Lincoln	Nathan		1		1				1	2	1			6		

TOWN	PG#	LN#	LAST NAME	FIRST NAME	FREE WHITE MALES					FREE WHITE FEMALES					TOTAL ALL OTHER	TOTAL SLAVES	TOTALS	DISTRICT/ TOWNSHIP	NOTES
					under 10	10 to 16	16 to 26	26 to 45	45 and over	under 10	10 to 16	16 to 26	26 to 45	45 and over					
Hingham	140	28	Lincoln	Nathaniel				1						1			2		
Hingham	139	2	Lincoln	Noah				1						1			2		
Hingham	137	5	Lincoln	Sarah		1							1				2		
Hingham	137	6	Lincoln	Seth		2	1		1	1		1	2		1		9		
Hingham	137	1	Lincoln	Solomon		1		1		2				1			5		
Hingham	137	37	Lincoln	Stephen		1			1					2			4		
Hingham	139	3	Lincoln	Welcome				1					1	1			3		
Hingham	137	15	Liste	Henry M	1		1						1		1		4		
Hull	147	26	Lord	James												2	2		
Hingham	139	29	Lord	Thomas		1		1					1				4		
Hull	147	12	Loring	Daniel	1	1		1		2	1		1				7		
Hingham	141	45	Loring	Elizabeth										1			1		
Hingham	145	22	Loring	Job	2			2	1		1	2		1			9		
Hull	147	20	Loring	John				1						1			2		
Hingham	146	40	Loring	Jonathan	2	1		1		1			1	1			7		
Hingham	141	15	Loring	Joshua	1	2	1		1		1			1			7		
Hingham	139	42	Loring	Lydia								1	1				2		
Hingham	146	19	Loring	Nat				1					1				2		
Hingham	142	21	Loring	Peter		1		1				1		1			4		
Hingham	142	15	Loring	Rachel						1				2			3		
Hingham	141	44	Loring	Ruth	1							1	1	1			4		
Hull	147	11	Loring	Samuel		1		1			1		1				4		
Hingham	139	15	Loring	Thomas		2		1					3	1			7		
Hingham	139	27	Lothrop	Ambrose			1							1			2		
Hingham	142	44	Lovis	Joseph				1						1			2		
Hingham	141	38	Lovis	William	1			1		2							4		
Hingham	143	31	Lowell	Enoch	2			1		3			1				7		
Hingham	143	12	Lowell	Samuel				1						1			2		
Hull	147	10	Lowell	Samuel	1		1	1		1		1	1				6		
Hingham	140	35	Lowell	William		1		1		1	2			1			6		
Hingham	140	34	Manor	Nathaniel	2			1		2			1				6		
Hingham	140	11	Mansfield	Job				1									1		
Hingham	142	35	Mansfield	Joseph				2						1			3		
Hingham	140	13	Mansfield	Mary										1			1		
Hingham	140	12	Mansfield	Ruth									1	1			2		
Hingham	139	5	Marble	James	2	1		1		1	2			1			8		
Hingham	138	4	Marsh	John				1					1	1			3		
Hingham	138	6	Marsh	John Junr		1		1		3		1	1				7		
Hingham	137	49	Marsh	Lott	1			1		2	1		1				6		
Hingham	137	33	Marsh	Samuel	1			1		1				1			4		
Hingham	137	31	Marsh	Stephen				1						1			2		
Hingham	137	32	Marsh	Stephen Junr	3	1		1		1				1			7		
Hingham	138	5	Marsh	Thomas				1						1			2		
Hingham	140	16	McNeal	Sarah						3	1	1					5		
Hull	147	7	Mott	Stephen			1			1		1		1			4		
Hull	147	18	Newcomb	Oliver	2			1	1				1				5		
Hingham	137	8	Newell	Joseph	1	1		1		0		1	1				7		
Hingham	146	1	Norton	Joshua			1										1		
Hingham	139	16	Norton	Samuel		1	1	1				1		2			6		
Hingham	141	27	Nye	Henry	2		2					1					5		
Hull	147	17	Philips	Mary									1				1		
Hingham	141	32	Pittee	Nathaniel	1	1		1		2	1		1	1			8		
Hull	147	4	Poor	Ebenezer	1			1		2				1			5		
Hingham	139	41	Price	Nathan Esqr		1	1	1		2	1	1			2		10		
Hingham	141	40	Prouty	Samuel	3			1		2			1	1			8		
Hull	147	2	Read	Samuel			1			1			1				3		
Hingham	140	27	Remington	Elisha	2	1		1		1			1				6		
Hull	147	23	Rinner	Spencer	1		1			4	1		1				8		
Hingham	146	39	Ripley	Nehemiah	1	2	1	1		2			1				8		
Hull	147	9	Sasain	Charles	1		1	1		2	1	1					7		
Hingham	138	14	Shattuck	William		2		1	1	1			1				6		
Hingham	143	45	Shoot	Prince												2	2		
Hingham	145	24	Shute	Daniel Junr Doct	3	1	1	1		1		1	1	1			10		
Hingham	145	23	Shute	Daniel Revd				1				1	2				4		
Hingham	143	18	Simmons	Allen	2	2		1		3			1	1			10		
Hingham	137	20	Smith	Hobart	1		1		3	1		1					7		
Hingham	141	18	Smith	Jonathan				1				1		1			3		
Hull	147	13	Soper	Samuel				1						1			2		
Hingham	139	23	Southard	William	2			1			1	1					6		
Hingham	142	39	Souther	Daniel	2	1		1	1	1	1	1	1				9		
Hingham	140	4	Souther	John	1	1	1		1	2	2	1	1				10		
Hull	147	16	Souther	Judith		1						1		2	1		5		
Hingham	145	42	Sprague	Alice								1	1	1			3		
Hingham	146	34	Sprague	Amos	1		1		1	2				1			6		
Hingham	140	5	Sprague	Amos Jr		1				2		1					4		
Hingham	144	2	Sprague	Bela		2	1						1	1			5		
Hingham	146	37	Sprague	David	1	1	1	1						1			5		
Hull	147	5	Sprague	Elizabeth									1				1		
Hingham	146	36	Sprague	Hannah		1							1	1			3		
Hingham	145	13	Sprague	Jacob	1			1		1				1			4		
Hingham	141	11	Sprague	Jesse	1			1						1			3		
Hingham	146	48	Sprague	Jesse		2		1		1	1						5		
Hingham	141	5	Sprague	Josiah	3			1		1		1	1				7		
Hingham	146	35	Sprague	Moses			3	1				1		1			6		
Hingham	141	21	Sprague	Noah				1						1			2		
Hingham	146	44	Sprague	Peter		1						1					2		
Hingham	146	40	Sprague	Rachel										2			2		
Hingham	146	5	Sprague	Reuben		1	2	1		1		1	3	1			10		

TOWN	PG#	LN#	HEADS OF HOUSEHOLD		FREE WHITE MALES					FREE WHITE FEMALES					TOTAL ALL OTHER	TOTAL SLAVES	TOTALS	DISTRICT/ TOWNSHIP	NOTES
			LAST NAME	FIRST NAME	under 10	10 to 16	16 to 26	26 to 45	45 and over	under 10	10 to 16	16 to 26	26 to 45	45 and over					
Hingham	145	39	Sprague	Seth	1				1	1				1			4		
Hingham	141	13	Stephenson	James				1		1			1				3		
Hingham	141	28	Stodder	Asahel	1	2	1	1		2			1				8		
Hingham	146	26	Stodder	Caleb	2			1		2			1				6		
Hingham	140	24	Stodder	Daniel			1		1					1			3		
Hingham	141	29	Stodder	Demrick	3			1		2	1		1				8		
Hingham	144	21	Stodder	Enoch			2		1			2		1			6		
Hingham	140	20	Stodder	George			1					1					2		
Hingham	144	20	Stodder	Ichabod			1					1					2		
Hingham	143	24	Stodder	Isaiah					1				1	1			3		
Hingham	146	25	Stodder	Isaiah Junr	3			1		1			1	1			7		
Hingham	137	29	Stodder	Jacob	1			1		1	1			1			5		
Hingham	142	13	Stodder	John				1					1				2		
Hingham	138	9	Stodder	John Junr	1			1		1			1				4		
Hingham	143	41	Stodder	Laban	1	3	2		1	4	1			1			13		
Hingham	137	30	Stodder	Nathaniel				1					2				3		
Hingham	140	19	Stodder	Othniel		1		1					1				3		
Hingham	144	23	Stodder	Rebecca						1	2		1				4		
Hingham	143	5	Stodder	Reuben				1									1		
Hingham	140	14	Stodder	Reuben Jr		1		1			1	1	1				5		
Hingham	144	14	Stodder	Richard				1		1				1			2		
Hingham	143	4	Stodder	Samuel	2	1		1		1	1		1				7		
Hingham	142	6	Stodder	Sarah									1	2			3		
Hingham	138	15	Stodder	Stephen	1	2		1		2	1	2	1	1			11		
Hingham	137	27	Stodder	Thomas			2		1	1	1			1			6		
Hingham	138	18	Stowel	Adam			1		1	1				1			4		
Hingham	138	13	Stowel	Elizabeth										1			1		
Hingham	138	2	Stowel	Israel	2	1			1	1		2	1				8		
Hingham	139	4	Stowel	Joshua				1	1	1	1	2		1			6		
Hingham	140	29	Stowell	Noah	1			1		1		1		1			5		
Hingham	146	27	Stowers	Elijah		1		1					1	1			4		
Hingham	145	32	Stowers	Mary										1			1		
Hingham	144	25	Tailor	Cato											2		2		
Hingham	141	35	Thaxter	Abigail									1	1			2		
Hingham	142	23	Thaxter	Benjamin				1					1				2		
Hingham	139	20	Thaxter	Daniel	1			1					1				3		
Hingham	140	32	Thaxter	Duncan	1			1		1			1				4		
Hingham	139	10	Thaxter	Francis	1			1					1				3		
Hingham	142	19	Thaxter	Henry	1	1		1			1		1	1			6		
Hingham	142	5	Thaxter	Jacob		1		1				1		1			4		
Hingham	139	14	Thaxter	John Esq				1			1		3		1		6		
Hingham	139	11	Thaxter	Jonathan	1			1						1			3		
Hingham	137	14	Thaxter	Joseph	1		1	2				2	1				7		
Hingham	139	13	Thaxter	Quincy	1			1		3	1	1	1				8		
Hingham	139	45	Thaxter	Seth			1	1		2	1		1				6		
Hingham	142	8	Thaxter	Thomas Dr		1	1		1		1		1	1			6		
Hingham	142	22	Thaxter	Thomas Junr				1		1	1	2	1				6		
Hingham	143	32	Thayer	Randall		1		1						1			3		
Hingham	140	47	Thayer	Timothy	3	1		1					1	2			8		
Hingham	146	28	Thomas	Benjamin	2		1			2			1	1			7		
Hull	147	6	Tirrell	Gideon	1		1	1		3	2		1				9		
Hingham	137	34	Todd	James	1	1			1	1		1		1			6		
Hingham	137	35	Todd	William			1			1		1					3		
Hingham	143	13	Tower	Malachi	1	2	1	1	2		1		1	1			10		
Hingham	143	10	Walker	John			1	1					1				3		
Hingham	142	4	Ware	Henry Revd	3			1		3		2	2		1		12		
Hingham	138	16	Waterman	Lydia		1							1	1			3		
Hingham	140	3	Waters	Isaac		2	1	1		1	1	1	1				8		
Hingham	140	7	Waters	Mehitable				1						2			3		
Hingham	146	15	Whiton	Amasa				1			1	2		2			6		
Hingham	146	16	Whiton	Davis			1	1		2	1		1				6		
Hingham	145	2	Whiton	Elijah		1	1	1				1		1			5		
Hingham	146	20	Whiton	Elijah Junr	1			1					1				3		
Hingham	146	24	Whiton	Elisha				1				1		1			3		
Hingham	145	27	Whiton	Enoch				1		3			1				5		
Hingham	146	10	Whiton	Enoch	1	1		1		3	1		2	1			10		
Hingham	145	45	Whiton	Israel	2	1	1	1		1			1				7		
Hingham	145	35	Whiton	Jacob				1									1		
Hingham	146	8	Whiton	Josiah			1						1	1			3		
Hingham	145	3	Whiton	Moses		2	2	1				1		1			7		
Hingham	146	9	Whiton	Sarah		1		1				2		1			5		
Hingham	146	38	Whiton	Stephen			1	1						1			3		
Hingham	146	21	Whiton	Theophilus			1			1		1					3		
Hingham	143	34	Whitton	Benjamin				1						2			3		
Hingham	143	35	Whitton	Benjamin Junr			1	1					1	1			4		
Hingham	143	29	Whitton	Charles			1			1		2					4		
Hingham	143	33	Whitton	Daniel			1	1			1	1		1			5		
Hingham	143	28	Whitton	Daniel Junr	1			1		1			1				4		
Hingham	142	1	Whitton	Ezra	1		2	1		1		2					7		
Hingham	144	8	Whitton	Solomon	1			1					2	2			6		
Hingham	143	30	Whitton	Zechariah			1	1		1	2	1		1			7		
Hingham	143	37	Wilder	Bela			1							1			2		
Hingham	146	6	Wilder	Daniel		2		1		3		2	1				9		
Hingham	145	11	Wilder	Edward Capt	2	1	1		1	5	3	2	1				16		
Hingham	145	12	Wilder	Hannah										1			1		
Hingham	143	36	Wilder	Isaac			1		1			1	1	1			5		
Hingham	143	17	Wilder	Isaiah		1	1				2	1					5		
Hingham	145	8	Wilder	Joseph		1			1	1	1	1	1				6		
Hingham	137	22	Wilder	Nathaniel	1			1	1	1				1			5		
Hingham	146	3	Wilder	Samuel					1					1			2		

TOWN	PG#	LN#	HEADS OF HOUSEHOLD		FREE WHITE MALES					FREE WHITE FEMALES					TOTAL ALL OTHER	TOTAL SLAVES	TOTALS	DISTRICT/ TOWNSHIP	NOTES
			LAST NAME	FIRST NAME	under 10	10 to 16	16 to 26	26 to 45	45 and over	under 10	10 to 16	16 to 26	26 to 45	45 and over					
Hingham	146	4	Wilder	Samuel Junr				1		3	1		1				6		
Hingham	143	3	Wilder	Thomas Junr		1		1		2	2	2		1			9		

NOTES

www.ingramcontent.com/pod-product-compliance
Lightning Source LLC
Chambersburg PA
CBHW080251290526
45790CB00005B/1776